Turkey Reframed

Turkey Reframed

Constituting Neoliberal Hegemony

Edited by İsmet Akça,
Ahmet Bekmen and Barış Alp Özden

PLUTO **PRESS**

First published 2014 by Pluto Press
345 Archway Road, London N6 5AA
www.plutobooks.com

British Library Cataloguing in Publication Data

A catalogue record for this book is available from the British Library

ISBN 978 0 7453 3385 4 Hardback
ISBN 978 0 7453 3384 7 Paperback
ISBN 978 1 8496 4979 7 PDF eBook
ISBN 978 1 8496 4981 0 Kindle eBook
ISBN 978 1 8496 4980 3 EPUB eBook

Library of Congress Cataloging in Publication Data applied for

10 9 8 7 6 5 4 3 2 1

Typeset from disk by Swales & Willis

Contents

Introduction

İsmet Akça, Ahmet Bekmen and Barış Alp Özden

'Looking at parties in Britain, which party do you think is similar to the AKP?'
  'We describe ourselves as conservative when it comes to family values.
  When it comes to the economy, we are liberal.
  And when it comes to income and poverty, we are socialist.'

This response was given by Mehmet Şimşek, the Minister of Finance of the Justice and Development Party (Adalet ve Kalkınma Partisi – AKP) government, while speaking as a guest at the Liberal Democrat Party's 'Friends of Turkey' group in 2011. The reporting newspaper added that the audience all laughed at this answer. Beyond doubt, Şimşek's statement indicates the self-confident position of a political party that has been governing Turkey for more than ten years, with an increased share of votes in every election, and that is generally considered to be the party most likely to govern for the foreseeable future. As Şimşek's comments illustrate, such a strong position allows party officials to make hegemonic claims about almost every issue affecting Turkey: the AKP represents both the left and the right. This self-confidence is not restricted just to party officials. Recently, an AKP-inclined pop-singer, a media vulture, went to Caracas to join the funeral march for Hugo Chavez and attacked 'the so-called leftists of Turkey' for their non-participation. Although right-wing politics, with almost all of its variations, has been the dominant and governing side in Turkish politics, as a result of the ongoing AKP era, it has become a respectable and positive, rather than reactionary, political identity, perhaps for the first time in its history. This edited volume is about understanding this reconfiguration of Turkish politics that British Lib-Dems reflexively laughed at.

The first decade of the 2000s, which was marked both by the major economic crisis of 2001 and by the coming to power of the ex-Islamist cadres organised under the AKP, has been a period of radical change in Turkish society and politics. The AKP era represents the reconsolidation of the neoliberal hegemony after the devastating effects of the 2001 crisis in particular and the 30-year painful constitution of the neoliberal hegemony in general. The main claim of this volume is that the AKP era, with all its peculiarities, should be contextualised within this general process of neoliberal hegemony constitution. Therefore, rather than discuss the hegemony of a political party, we discuss hegemony in its class terms, which has been put into effect and consolidated through the practices of a political party, namely the AKP. For us, the AKP matters in this context.

Throughout the 2000s, one symptom of this hegemonic struggle has been that the demarcations among political actors in Turkey have been radically rearranged, whether in line with or contrary to the call of the hegemonic actor(s). While moderate Islamists, conservatives and liberals have easily situated themselves on the side of the AKP, some circles of the left have also given credit to the process the AKP implemented by considering it as democratisation, since it managed to make the military step back politically. In fact, this odd realignment has its intellectual and political roots in Turkey's recent history. One relatively new viewpoint on Turkey, which emerged after the 1980 military coup and gained popularity among intellectuals of both left and right during the 1990s, conceives of the peculiar character of Turkey's democratisation process as a struggle against the tutelage of bureaucratic elites, especially the Turkish military. This 'dissident but hegemonic'[1] analysis of socio-political power relations in Turkey argues that the main axes of political conflict have been dichotomies such as state–society, centre–periphery, and bureaucracy–bourgeoisie. Whereas the first element in each dichotomy represents repressive and authoritarian tendencies in Turkish politics, the second is considered either as the ensemble of democratic forces or as the fundamentals on which genuine democratisation can be based. Thus, to some extent, this was the Turkish counterpart of the 'state-civil society debate' that took place in the 1980s and 1990s among Western and Eastern European intellectual and political circles (see Keane 1988). Similarly, it implies a changed focus of political enquiry and action. Thanks to the political clashes of the 2000s, basically between the blocs represented by the AKP and the high ranks of the civil-military bureaucracy, this particular viewpoint started to resonate with the policies of the AKP and has become a kind of political epistemology for Turkey. It is shared by people from widely different political backgrounds, whether liberals, liberal leftists, Islamists or conservatives.

By explaining the recurrent militarisation of political power relations in Turkey with regard to the will of the state actors, this analytical framework employed a state-centric theoretical approach. As Yalman comments, the post-1980 period has witnessed the rise of a state-centric (in analytical terms) but anti-statist (in normative terms) discourse, which has become hegemonic in academic and public milieus (Yalman 2002). Conventionally known as the 'strong state tradition' (Heper 1985), this approach to the state is based on a series of arguments about Ottoman-Turkish history, produced by scholars from diverse theoretical and political traditions. These arguments centre around a peculiar historical continuity incarnated in a 'strong state-weak society tradition' in Ottoman-Turkish history, the claim about the weakness of the bourgeoisie and its dependence on the state, the presentation of the cleavage between the bourgeoisie and the civilian and military bureaucratic elites as the main dynamic of power relations and social change, the everlasting dominance of a patrimonial state–society relationship in which the highly independent state is not respon-sible to the social forces of the allegedly non-autonomous market economy.[2]

This hegemonic narrative is replete with many theoretical and historical-empirical problems. While a comprehensive exposure of these problems goes beyond the limits of this essay, it is beneficial to draw attention to certain points. First, the state is depicted as outside and above society, as an entity in itself. According to this approach, the state elite – who are solely concerned with increasing their economic and/or political interests – exert power over the rest of society and are able to exert this power in defiance of all other societal actors, including the dominant classes. Second, when considered within this hegemonic framework, socio-political power relations are reduced to conflicts among the elites, and the social, and especially the class-based, nature of politics is largely ignored. Third, neither the institutional architecture of the state nor the practices of the state elites are assumed to be constructed by specifically class-based socio-political relations of dominance. The militarist-nationalist institutionalisation of the state and the political sphere takes place at the expense of its capitalist institutionalisation, and the class-based nature of the state and the political sphere is covered up to the extent that the connections between these are ignored. Fourth, the authoritarian nature of the state and the political sphere in Turkey is explained solely through the nationalist and militarist crystallisation of the state and the power of the state elites (and especially the military elites and their military patronage). In this way, the connections between capitalist socio-political relations and the capitalist crystallisation of the state are rendered invisible.[3]

In contrast to this approach, contributors to this volume suggest that neither the classical *Kemalist/secularist* stance, which cannot go beyond merely problematising the AKP's Islamic background and alleged secret agendas, nor the intellectual/political positions derived from the above-mentioned approach, which define the AKP as *the* actor or the trigger of the democratisation process, offers a satisfactory explanation of recent developments in Turkey. As the most determined and determining neoliberal actor in Turkey, the AKP has maintained the 'free economy-strong state' line of the New Right. That is, its main project has been to constitute and consolidate a type of society based on neoliberal and conservative premises. Thus, its so-called democratisation project is rather a project of replacing military tutelage with a neoliberal authoritarian regime. Following this third line of argument this edited volume aims to reconsider the AKP period as a new attempt to overcome the obstacles against building a neoliberal hegemony in Turkey that began in the 1980s, by building a specific type of neoliberal hegemony that mixes various Islamic and conservative motives with neoliberal policies and ideology. This argument's premise is that the real historical and social meanings of AKP policies can be best revealed by analysing them in terms of the conflicts and dilemmas of this process.

In line with the criticisms outlined above, the theoretical framework suggested here is based on the strategic-relational approach that concentrates on the power struggles between socio-political actors, and which is not structuralist-functionalist or instrumentalist with regards to relations among the state, politics and classes.[4] According to this approach, there is an ontologically intrinsic relationship between the state, politics and classes as long as an economic understanding of capitalism and class relations is not in question; that is, capitalist class relations cannot take place without the state and politics. Through such a perspective, which denies essentialist dualisms such as state-bourgeoisie, state-market or state-economy, both social classes and the hegemony of the bourgeoisie can only be constituted with and within the state. The state, which is neither an instrument that can be simply manipulated by a class (or a class fraction) nor a subject by itself with universal rationality and absolute autonomy, is first and foremost the institutional form taken by a social relationship (a sphere where power relations are intensified) and the integrity of the institutions where power relations are engraved (the institutional materiality of the state) (Poulantzas 2000: 49–120). Contrary to the state-centric approach, the onto-logical priority here lies in the practices of actors rather than institutions, so the institutional architecture of the state is constructed through the practices within socio-political power relations. The institutional architecture formed by these power struggles then exerts limiting or strengthening effects over social and political groups in a specific temporal-spatial context through a 'strategic selec-tivity' mechanism (see Jessop 2002: 40).

Following the conceptualisation of Jessop, the socio-political power relations in question can be systematically analysed through the analyses of 'hegemonic projects' and the processes of forming 'strategies of accumulation' that are part of these. Hegemonic projects are thus considered as national-popular pro-grammes of action geared towards securing the unity of the power bloc (e.g. of the dominant classes and class fractions) on the one hand, while producing and acquiring the consent and support of the subaltern classes through economic redistribution mechanisms and ideological-political practices on the other. A capitalist hegemonic project needs to encompass a strategy of capital accumu-lation that defines a specific growth model, which is expected to unite distinct capital fractions under the hegemony of a specific fraction. The dominant capital fraction can establish its economic hegemony to the extent that it can sacrifice its short-term economic-corporative goals. Otherwise, it ends up tending towards economic domination. On the other hand, hegemony, in the general sense, is the organisation of different class-based and class-related (but not necessarily class-conscious) societal powers under the political, intellectual and moral leadership of one class (or fraction). Since the modern capitalist state and political sphere construes itself in reference to the dominance not of a class, but rather of a national-popular entity, such leadership is always established through a hegemonic project that aspires to a representation of this entity, though in an incomplete way. In this context, hegemonic projects constitute the way in which political class dominance is established in capitalist societies (Jessop 1990a: 196–220). They encompass social and political problems that are not directly class-related in order to be successful (see Jessop 1990a: 208; Laclau 1977: 162). Therefore, such an approach enables us to analyse the articulation of problems based on class, identity, gender etc., without reducing any one of them to one of the others.

Hegemonic projects are construed through processes that are organised in different social spheres and at different levels, with the participation of distinct social and political actors. Following Gramsci, who problematises dual opposi-tions, such as state–civil society or oppression–consent, hegemony, as the con-struction of a contingent unity among the economic, political, cultural and ideological phases of capitalist relations of production, is produced within each of the spheres of civil society, political society and the state. However, it can also be argued that the political society plane, which operates via the political parties that are candidates for political power, has exceptional importance in the construction of particular hegemonic projects. These are projects that are to be built in reference to the national-popular entity and that will also cater to actors that are encumbered by non-class based social problems, as well as to the different social classes. The political actors that undertake a hegemonic project are both limited by the social actors organised at different levels, and also seek to convince these sectors of society to participate in the specific hegemonic project by conceding some of their interests. The construction of the hegemonic project is perpetual and not limited by structural boundaries within a given framework of time and place, but rather is replete with open-ended struggles whose outcomes are uncertain.

★ ★ ★

The essays collected in this volume span a broad array of questions and issues, including the peculiarities of the Turkish political economy in transition to neoliberalism, the role of political, religious, ethnic and gender related issues in shaping political actors, and the cultural and ideological elements involved in the conformation of the dominant discourse and alliance. However, the chapters also share some commonalities that unite researchers of diverse backgrounds and interests. First, there is a general sense expressed in the essays that a proper understanding of the reconsolidation of neoliberal hegemony under the AKP's leadership requires an historical analysis of the social and political struggles that have put their stamp on the political sociology of Turkey during the last three decades. Unlike liberal assessments, which tend to portray this transformation in terms of the rational choices of individual actors, the essays in this collection recover the rich history of social and political conflicts and struggles inherent in the successive attempts at hegemonic projects. In addition, there is the shared understanding that the promises of consolidated neoliberal power, and of the AKP administration as the expression of a successful convergence of neoliberal governance with authoritarian and populist politics, are at best shallow and prone to challenges from both subordinated groups and systemic crises. Finally, there is a shared attention to a multidisciplinary and empirical approach, rather than limiting analyses to the structures and strictures of particular theoretical models.

Part I explores the political dynamics and actors of the post-1980 period with regard to their roles in making and challenging neoliberal hegemony. Against the dominant narratives of political change in Turkey, according to which the culmination of ideas, desires, morality and religious beliefs, as well as of the economic power of the peripheral forces of society against the state elites, account for the rise of their 'authentic' political representatives to power, contributions to this volume draw attention to the plurality of political actors and the significance of class analysis in order to come to terms with this change.

The volume starts with two chapters studying inter-class and intra-class relations and transformations of the state form in successive periods after 1980 to reveal the complex dynamics behind the rise of the AKP as the main political actor implementing radical economic and political changes in Turkey in the last decade. İsmet Akça's chapter analyses the political sociology of post-1980 Turkey through a theoretical framework that focuses on socio-political power relations in the course of manufacturing hegemonic projects. Akça suggests that the various attempts at hegemonic unity during the 1980s and 1990s were doomed to failure due to their exclusionary nature, and led to a rise in political authoritarianism and further militarisation of the political scene. In contrast, the AKP managed to overcome the political hegemony crisis by manufacturing unity between the dominant classes and class fractions, obtaining the active or passive consent of subordinated classes, and articulating the non-class issues of politics to its project. The chapter concludes by indicating existing and potential fissures and antinomies of the AKP's neoliberal, conservative, and authoritarian populist hegemonic project. The class analysis of Turkey's neoliberal transformation is strengthened by Ahmet Bekmen's lengthy account of the evolution of relations between the bourgeoisie and the state post-1980. Bekmen first focuses on how state power was restructured by the neoliberal mentality of government, before relating this restructuring to capital accumulation. After giving a short account of the pre-AKP period, Bekmen analyses the AKP era mainly in terms of intra-capital tensions to understand the role of the AKP in this context.

A common, if not dominant, interpretation of the AKP's rise to power sees it as a victory against Kemalist nationalism. Güven Gürkan Öztan's chapter innovatively uses the distinction between official and unofficial nationalisms to demonstrate the persistence of nationalism as a political ideology that defines the contours of legitimacy in Turkish politics. Gürkan shows that the struggle for hegemony between different Turkish nationalisms was definitively settled in the 2000s when the AKP managed to establish its own version of 'acceptable nationalism' as part of its populist conservative ideology, blending nationalist symbols and religious motifs with a neoliberal discourse of productivity and wealth creation. Gürkan argues that the success of this neoliberal nationalism can be explained through the reconfiguration of middle-class values and identity after the 2001 crisis. The significant role of ideological and discursive shifts in Turkish politics during the last decade is also underlined by Mehmet Sinan Birdal who explores the changing foreign policy discourse in parallel with Turkey's assertive and ambitious goal of becoming a global power. Far from being a revisionist strategy, Birdal suggests, 'the Davutoğlu Doctrine' serves to legitimise the AKP's rule and policies in domestic politics, and has become a central component of the party's populism.

The intricate relationships between neoliberalism, populism and nationalism in the AKP's ideology can also be traced in its Kurdish policy. İrfan Aktan's chapter analyses the distinctive traits of the AKP's policies and discourses regarding the Kurdish question compared to previous governments, and shows the multiplicity of strategies the party manipulates in order to politically control the active elements of Kurdish society. Aktan's analysis is particularly original in its focus on the internal political and social dynamics of the Kurdish movement in order to get a better sense of the AKP's strategic attempts at incorporating sections of the Kurdish social base, whose support it is competing for with the Kurdish movement.

Uraz Aydın's chapter explores the transformation of the media in Turkey in terms of changing property relations, professional practices and the media's ideological role. Since the early 1980s, the structure of the media industry has significantly changed in Turkey in the direction of more competition and concentration, which has radically transformed the production of knowledge and cultural legitimation. Aydın analyses in detail the role the media has played in infusing market values into every aspect of social life, and also records the rising prominence of the Islamic-conservative media to show how this medium has become instrumental in manufacturing consent for the AKP's increasingly authoritarian policies.

This part of the volume closes with Erbatur Çavuşoğlu and Julia Strutz's study of land and urban development policies. Any observer of Turkey's political sociology and political economy in the last decade can recognise the rapid and unprecedented transformation of Turkey's urban landscape and its implications for national and local politics. Çavuşoğlu and Struz provide an examination of the reproduction of space through state-led urban transformation projects to explain how Islamic neoliberalism reconciled with developmentalism has used the construction sector to form a national-popular project while adopting the corporatist tradition of the country to deny the separate interests and demands of the urban lower classes.

The essays in Part II bring new research and new perspectives to bear on the questions of the transformation of the social problems and movements that have conditioned both the success and failure of hegemonic projects throughout the last thirty years in Turkey. In the opening chapter, Barış Alp Özden seeks to identify the processes and strategies that have enabled the neoliberalism project to become hegemonic in Turkey by focusing on the implications of the social welfare transformation for changing state–society relations. Özden shows that the neoliberal populist strategy pursued in the last decade has proved very capable of accomplishing deep-seated market oriented reforms in a number of critical policy areas, such as labour markets and health care, while still managing to address the material aspirations of the most destitute. This analysis of the welfare regime change in Turkey is followed by Ece Öztan's exploration of the breakings and reconciliations in gender regimes through policies and discourses on sexuality, family and caring relations. By way of focusing on policies of marriage, abortion and assisted reproduction techniques, and discourses based on heteronormative familism, pronatalism and women's voluntarism, this chapter examines the gender politics of the neoliberal-authoritarian hegemony project based on notions of 'difference' and 'protectionism'.

The following two chapters address the reformation of the working class and the question of the decades-long weakening and near disappearance of the labour movement in Turkey. The situation for labour unions in Turkey has become very precarious for various reasons, some of which are discussed in Doğan's contribution to this volume. Doğan particularly stresses the precarisa-tion of the labour force and the conservatism of trade unions, which has prevented them from adopting organisational strategies targeting the working population at large, while also recording the sporadic but ephemeral signs of revitalisation of working-class movements. The fragmentation of the working class is also analysed in Serkan Öngel's case study of metal workers in Gebze district, one of the most important industrial centres in Turkey, located on the periphery of İstanbul. The article traces the impacts of social fragmentation that has transformed the daily life practices, workplace culture and identity, and the organisational and political inclinations of Gebze's working class.

The transformation of working-class culture and identity is also the subject of Ali Ekber Doğan and Yasin Durak's chapter, which addresses the often neglected issues of the rise of the conservative Islamist bourgeoisie in the newly industrialising provincial cities of Turkey and the impact of new conservative forms of socialisation on class relations in these cities. The article reveals the key role of the socio-spatial practices of Islamist municipal administrations and local labour control regimes in justifying neoliberalism to the working classes in the rapidly industrialising provincial cities of Konya and Kayseri.

The last chapter of the book is devoted to a discussion of the shift in the epicentre of political opposition to the government's implementation of neoliberal policies. In this chapter, Erdem Yörük argues that the Kurdish war and the internal displacement of the Kurds during the 1990s totally changed the ethnic composition of the working class in Turkey by simultaneously proletari-anising the Kurds and Kurdicising the proletariat. This process, Yörük seeks to show, enhanced the radicalisation of the Kurdish movement which became the main force resisting the constitution of neoliberal hegemony in Turkey.

The main argument of this book, to repeat, is that the present political and social transformations in Turkey need to be situated in the larger context of the construction of a neoliberal hegemony that has had a painful and up-and-down history of almost thirty years. After the AKP's latest striking victory (with 50 per cent of the total votes) in the general elections of June 2011, many observers came to the conclusion that this history of turbulence and conflict had reached a point of relative stabilisation. Beyond doubt, the main task of the existing AKP government will be to replace the existing constitution put into effect by the 1980 military coup leaders with a new one in order to inscribe the new balance of forces into the institutional materiality of the state. However, hegemony is never absolute and complete and is hence always open to contestation. The contributions to this edited volume offer important clues in that sense too. Many of the chapters are also helpful in understanding the origins of the recent popular uprising commonly known as the Taksim, Gezi resistance, which is more deeply analysed in the postscript.

The analysis of this new era, in terms of both the success of neoliberal hegemony, its antinomies and the contestations to it, should still be based on the analysis of the old one. That is, in terms of Hegel's metaphor, the AKP's success represents the moment for the owl of Minerva to spread its wings over the last thirty years of Turkey. This edited volume is intended to contribute to this task.

★ ★ ★

We would like to thank the Department of Scientific Research Projects of İstanbul University and the Coordination of Scientific Research Projects of Yıldız Technical University for their financial support to our project.

For the proofreading and editing of the whole text, we are grateful to Jerry Spring. We also thank Erkal Ünal, Sultan Şahin and Aslıgül Berktay for their translation of some of the chapters into English.

And we are thankful to the staff of the Pluto Press, for their encouragement and patience.

NOTES

1   It is dissident to the extent that 'its statism is justified by its stridently anti-state call for an intellectual realignment in which the acceptance of market liberalism would be at the heart of a new public consensus. And it would be hegemonic to the extent that its conceptual categories, as Max Weber put it, would have a meaning in the minds of individual persons, partly as something actually existing, partly as something with normative authority so that they have a powerful, often decisive, causal influence on the course of their actions' (Yalman 2002: 23).

2   In order to give a sense of the richness of the theoretical frameworks, one can cite those working from within the different currents of modernisation theory, such as Heper (1985, 1992); Kazancıgil (1981), Sunar (1974) and Mardin (1969, 1973, 1992); from within critical institutionalism, such as Buğra (1994a; 1994b) and Öniş (1998); from within a left Weberian approach, such as İnsel (1996) and İnsel and Aktar (1985–87); and from within Marxian theory, such as Keyder (1987).

3   For a more elaborated and critical discussion of this statist hegemony in Turkish historiography, see Akça (2006: 161–213), and also Yalman (2002) and Dinler (2003). The state-centric mode of the conceptualisation of the state is not specific to Turkish historiography. Even though one does not always find direct references to those state-centric theorists, prominent studies on the Ottoman-Turkish state nevertheless fit in well with the same problematic: analysing the state as an entity clearly differentiated from the society and as an autonomous subject capable of taking measures in pursuit of its own, quite distinctive interests. In the words of Jessop (2001: 4), the state-centred theorists argue that 'the state is a force in its own right', 'state activities and impact are easily explained in terms of its own distinctive properties as an administrative or repressive organ', and they emphasise 'state managers' ability to exercise power independently of (and even in the face of resistance from) non-state forces.' For some prominent works from within this theoretical approach, see Evans et al. (1985), Migdal (1988) and Stepan (1988). For critical evaluations of this theoretical approach, see Jessop (2001), Cammack (1989) and Mitchell (1991).

4   With regards to this ontological position, see especially Sayer (1987), Ollman (1993), Poulantzas (2000) and Jessop (1990, 2002, 2008).

PART I

Politics of Hegemony

Hegemonic Projects in Post-1980 Turkey and the Changing Forms of Authoritarianism

İsmet Akça

The post-1980 period has witnessed the rise of a state-centric analytical approach in both academic and public milieus in explaining the socio-political power relations and form of the state in Turkey, which has become 'hegemonic but dissident' (Yalman 2002). In this line of analysis, the authoritarian nature of the state and the political sphere in Turkey is explained solely by the exclusive power of the state elites over other social actors, including dominant classes and social groups. As a result, class-based socio-political power relations and the capitalist crystallisation of the state are rendered invisible and ignored in explaining the authoritarian restructuring of the political sphere and the state. The political horison has likewise been limited to a democratisation discourse understood simply as the implementation of formal-legal reforms and civilianisation vis-à-vis the military tutelage regime (Akça 2010a).

This chapter draws upon criticisms of such hegemonic state-centric analyses to analyse the socio-political power relations and changing forms of authoritarianism in the post-1980 period through the problematic of hegemony, i.e. through the formation of 'hegemonic projects' and 'accumulation strategies', as outlined in the introduction of this volume. Although hegemonic projects are manufactured in civil society, political society and the state with the participation of distinct social and political actors, in this chapter I will specifically focus on the level of political society, in which the political parties have exceptional importance in the formation of hegemonic projects in a process of interaction with different social classes and groups. The authoritarianism of the post-1980 period is thus analysed within such a political sociological framework. As Gramsci long ago underlined, 'the 'normal' exercise of hegemony on the now classical terrain of the parliamentary regime is characterised by the combination of force and consent, which balance each other reciprocally, without force predominating excessively over consent' (Gramsci 1999: 80). Or, as Mark Neocleous puts it, 'the question of hegemony is not about coercion *or* consent, but about coercion *and* consent' (Neocleous 1996: 42). In that sense, this chapter aims to analyse attempts to form capitalist hegemonic projects and to explore the dynamic relationship between consent and coercion within those processes by dividing post–1980 Turkey into four sub-periods.

The first is the coup d'état of 12 September 1980 and the subsequent military regime. This period can be read through the installation of neoliberal capitalism via militarism, the re-structuring of class-based power relations, and the construction of an authoritarian state form. The second period is the Motherland Party (ANAP) period, which was characterised by a failed attempt at hegemony in the framework of New Right politics. The 1990s, the third sub-period, was marked by a crisis of political hegemony and the dominance of the Neoliberal National Security State. The most recent period, since 2002, has seen the successful implementation of the hegemonic project of the ruling Justice and Development Party (AKP) through neoliberal, conservative and authoritarian populism.

Neoliberal Militarism and Authoritarian Statism

Even though the military coup of 12 September 1980 should not be over-emphasised as a factor that explains everything related to the political sociology of our day, it did constitute an important breaking point in the formation of contemporary Turkey. The military intervention was both a consequence of, and a response to, an organic crisis that itself combined crises of capital accumulation and hegemony that had been gradually deepening from the second half of the 1970s onwards. The 1970s were marked by a global accumulation crisis that was manifested in Turkey as the crisis of the inward-oriented accumulation strategy based on import substituting industrialisation policies. The accumulation crisis was organically related to the declining profit rates and its symptomatic manifestation was the lack of foreign currency (Barkey 1990; Keyder 1987; Boratav 1987). After 1977, all fractions of the bourgeoisie agreed to contextualise the crisis in terms of class struggle, specifically by complaining about high wage levels, trade union rights, collective bargaining, and the other rights of the working class (Ozan 2012). The working-class organisations responded by radicalising their struggle in order to resist such attacks. 'The number of strikes and days lost to strikes increased rapidly, from an average of 65 strikes and just under one million days between 1973 and 1976 to 190 strikes and 3.7 million days between 1977 and 1980' (Keyder 1987: 192). In short, the second half of the 1970s was a period of protracted and heightened class struggle. By 1978, by putting aside intra-class cleavages for the time being in order to focus on the task of disciplining the working class, fractions of the bourgeoisie came to the conclusion that the adoption of IMF-guided neoliberal austerity measures was inevitable. The economic decisions of 24 January 1980 anticipated both the stability measures and structural adjustment policies guided by the International Monetary Fund (IMF) and World Bank (WB) (Sönmez 1980, 1984). However, the minority government of the centre-right Justice Party (AP) did not have the necessary political power to apply them. Instead, it was the military regime that was able to implement them.

The military intervention was not the inevitable result of the accumulation crisis yet the latter was part of, and a negative factor in, the crisis of hegemony. The political scene was marked by a crisis of representation, which was itself a symptom of the crisis of hegemony. On the one hand, the left populist strategy of the centre-left Republican People's Party (CHP), which was unable to win enough votes to form a single-party government, was unable to get the consent of the Turkish bourgeoisie or the more radical fractions of the working class (Ataay 2006). On the other hand, the authoritarian populist strategy of the centre-right AP won the support of important sections of the bourgeoisie but lost, to an important extent, its capacity to get the consent of the dominated classes. In the second half of the 1970s, the AP moved closer to radical right parties (both Islamist and nationalist), formed coalition governments with those parties, and consistently called for an authoritarianisation under the parliamentary regime by arguing for the necessity of 're-establishing the state authority' (Cizre-Sakallıoğlu 1993; Demirel 2004). Outside parliamentary politics, the revolutionary leftist politics emerged to become more popularised in the 1970s. However, it too was incapable of developing a counter-hegemonic project due to its engagement in an escalating armed anti-fascist struggle, which isolated radical leftists from ordinary citizens, and also because of the ideological and political crisis which was reflected in the dramatic fragmentation of the socialist and communist left (Aydınoğlu 2007; Salah 1984). The political crisis was deepened further by the violent response to the rise of the revolutionary left and working-class movements by the security actors of the state and the fascist movement in Turkey. Thus, because parliamentary politics could not develop a hegemonic project to establish the unity of the dominant classes and gain the consent of the dominated classes, it was unable to deal with Turkey's multifaceted crisis.

As a result, all the fractions of the bourgeoisie, together with their political and military representatives, who considered that their survival was at stake, engaged in an open class struggle through authoritarian strategies, first under the civilian regime, then under the military regime (Sönmez 1984). In fact, the 12 September process had already started in 1978. The militarisation of the political sphere had been increasing during the 1970s as the political struggle of the working class and revolutionary left movements became radicalised. From the end of 1978, the major cities were already governed by martial law administration with the military assuming the role of policing everyday life, and using extensive coercion and violence in order to discipline both the radical left political movements and the working class (Üsküll 1997). The National Security Council closely monitored and intervened in the parliamentary political process (Çelik 2008). As Simon Clarke (1992: 148) notes, 'a crisis in the state form arises when the working-class challenge to the power of the capital extends to a challenge to the constitutional authority of the state'. By 1980, this was the perception of the Turkish bourgeoisie and the military. It was the political dimension of the protracted class struggle of the 1970s that reflected itself as a crisis of state. In the military officers' language, this corresponded to a threat to the survival of the state, to state security issues, according to which 'the constitutional order and the security of life and *property* was under challenge'.[1]

A clear illustration of the organic relation between the class struggle and the military intervention came from Halit Narin, the then head of the most radical organisation of the Turkish bourgeoisie, namely the Turkish Confederation of Employer Associations (TİSK). Just before the military intervention, he commented that 'production will not increase unless the DGMs [State Security Courts] are founded' and then, just after the military intervention, referring to the workers, added, 'Up until now you laughed, now it is our turn' (Ozan 2012).

Hector Schamis' (1991) arguments concerning the Latin American military interventions in the 1970s (Chile and Uruguay in 1973, Argentina in 1976) also apply to Turkey in 1980. That is, these military interventions were qualitatively different from previous bureaucratic authoritarian interventions and military regimes since they totally broke with the previous hegemonic project and accumulation strategy to engage in a total restructuring. 'Their policies display a striking similarity to the neoconservative projects of some advanced industrial countries. Issues such as "ungovernability", "crisis of the state" and "demand overload" (Schamis 1991: 202) were on their agenda. Their practice was not a deepening of ISI through the political and economic exclusion of popular masses, as was the case with bureaucratic authoritarianism. Rather, they restructured the economy, society and politics through 'a combination of market economics and repressive tactics' (Schamis 1991: 207). Since the social and political struggle of the working class was seen as responsible for the organic crisis in question, the main concern of the military regime was 'putting an end to class-based politics' (Yalman 2002: 38). This was also the main prerequisite of the transition to the new accumulation strategy, materialised in the decisions of 24 January 1980. The military regime also implemented the neoliberal stabilisation and structural adjustment policies required by the IMF and WB (Sönmez 1984).

Ending class-based politics no doubt meant the disciplining of the working-class movement, the radical left and the democratic social opposition in order to solidify the political power of the bourgeoisie. In this context, the violence and coercion against these societal powers constituted a strategy of discipline in the short run. Under the military regime, more than 650,000 people were detained; police files were opened on about 1,680,000 people; there were 210,000 political trials, in which 7,000 people faced the death penalty; 50 of 517 death penalties were executed; 300 people died in prisons for allegedly unspecified reasons; 171 people died from torture; 1,680,000 people were classified in police files, 388,000 people were deprived of their right to a passport; 30,000 people were fired from the civil service; 14,000 people lost their citizenship; 39 tonnes of published material were destroyed; and 23,677 associations were closed down (Öngider 2005; Mavioğlu 2004).

The long-term strategy of the military regime included restructuring the institutional architecture of the state, narrowing the political sphere for dominated social classes and groups, limiting the possibilities of political democracy, and the securitisation of the political to inscribe and establish a new balance of forces between classes. In fact, such changes were not specific to countries such as Turkey, nor they can be explained solely by the autonomous political power of the military. This transformation, which can be conceptualised through Poulantzas' concept of 'authoritarian statism', reflected rather a structural tendency of neoliberal capitalism. Poulantzas first used the concept of 'authoritarian statism' in 1978 in order to describe the new 'normal form of state' under construction in the face of the crisis of capitalism. Authoritarian statism is characterised by:

> intensified state control over every sphere of social life *combined with* radical decline of the institutions of political democracy and with draconian and multiform curtailment of so-called 'formal' liberties', the transfer of power from the legislative to the executive and to the limited and upper levels of public administration, the extensive use of decree laws, the decline of law and the elimination of the formal separation of powers, crisis of political representation reflected in the decline of political parties and their statisation by losing their social-class ties. (Poulantzas 2000: 203–204, see also 217–247)

The Turkish military regime institutionalised such a state form through the 1982 constitution and all the main laws it enacted. Among the 669 laws enacted under the military regime were laws on political parties, elections, trade unions, collective bargaining and strikes, the senior judicial system (Constitutional Court, Court of Appeal, High Council of Judges and Prosecutors), State Security Courts, martial law and the state of emergency. The new juridico-political structure produced by the military regime thus narrowed the boundaries of the political sphere and political participation to a great extent. It favoured a metaphysical, sacred state positioned against the individual and society. All basic and political rights and freedoms were undermined by legal terms open to arbitrary interpretation, such as 'the survival of the state', 'national security', 'public order' and 'public morality'. The executive was especially strengthened over the legislative in the name of the creation of a state-strong government-strong administration that could not be touched by societal powers. The decision-making mechanisms within the executive were centralised even more through the prime minister, in institutions directly connected to the prime ministry or in institutions such as the National Security Council (MGK). Governmental decrees were frequently used in order to bypass the legislative in favour of the executive. The capacity of political parties to establish organic relations with trade unions and organised social classes and groups was severely undermined. Their scope of activity was severely contracted and their closure was made easier. The universities were put under strict state control by establishing the Council of Higher Education (YÖK) (Parla 1993, 1995; Tanör 2002).

Organised labour was excluded from the political decision-making process and disciplined economically. Labour union activities were first suspended then severely restricted through the new legislation on trade unions, collective bargaining and strikes (Doğan 2005 and in this volume). Another strategy was the depoliticisation of class identities and discrediting the trade union movement through the discourse of authoritarian individualism, 'by appealing to virtuous virtues of individuals' (Yalman 2002: 41). The military regime differentiated good workers, who were industrious, patriotic and did not define themselves by class identity, from bad workers, who were ideological and oriented towards class struggle. As the leader of the 1980 coup makers, General Kenan Evren, put it:

> Industrial peace was disturbed with strikes and similar action slowing down production so that the economy, already suffering from bottlenecks, worsened further because of ideologically inspired strikes . . . All rights of the industrious and patriotic Turkish worker will be safeguarded within the framework of current economic conditions. However, the activities of certain labour bosses who exploit the innocent Turkish worker and resort to all kinds of pressures and tricks to use them in the direction of their own ideological views and personal interests instead of trying to protect workers' rights will never be permitted. All sorts of measures will be taken for all employers to help improve labour peace without deviating from legal rules. (General Secretariat of the National Security Council 1982: 27, 231–232)

The peculiarity of this subsequent authoritarian state form in countries in which the transition to neoliberal capitalism was realised by a military regime is the central role of the military. In Turkey's constitution, the military bureaucracy was defined as the third organ of the executive, along with the government and the state president. The MGK, which was founded by the 1961 constitution after the military coup of 27 May 1960, was reinforced by the 1980 constitution to become more influential in the political sphere. The number of military members increased and the members are cited one by one, while the power of sanction of MGK decisions was strengthened, the military members' dominance was increased, and its power to enforce decisions was also enhanced. In addition, the content of the 'national security' concept became so widely defined that all issues pertaining to the political, economic, social and cultural spheres, and both internal and external threats, could be categorised as 'national security issues', hence under the authority of military power. The MGK has become an institution collecting data, analysing issues, defining principally the political orientation, and controlling and following up the implementation of policies in all these areas. That is, the MGK and its general secretariat have been given new powers that make it a shadow government. 'A double-headed political system' both at the executive and juridical levels was created, with the military enjoying prerogatives at political, juridical and economic levels (Cizre-Sakallıoğlu 1997; Çelik 2008; Bayramoğlu 2004).

The critical point to emphasise here is that this new authoritarian state form was not solely or even primarily the result of the autonomous political power of the Turkish military, as suggested in the hegemonic state-centred paradigm (Akça 2010a). Rather, it was a combined result of neoliberalism and militarism. The securitisation of politics was part of the 'invalidation of democracy, which lies at the centre of the 'politics of neoliberalism' (Munck 2005). As for the technocratisation of economics and politics, which is the other main strategy of 'the invalidation of democracy', that was institutionalised by the New Right policies of subsequent civil governments.

The 1980s: The New Right's Failed Attempt at Hegemony

The transition to an electoral regime took place in November 1983, when the newly founded ANAP got 45 per cent of the votes in the general election from which previous political parties and many of their prominent figures were banned. The ANAP and its leader, Turgut Özal, followed an almost typically New Right political line, though with some Turkish peculiarities. While the ANAP was able to form a single-party government between 1983 and 1991, its percentage of the vote fell continuously, to 36.3 per cent in 1987, 24 per cent in 1991, and just 21.8 per cent in the local elections of 1989.

New Right policies, which articulate neoliberalism, conservatism and authoritarianism, may be best characterised as the politics of 'the free economy and the strong state', according to which 'to preserve a free society and a free economy the authority of the state has to be restored' (Gamble 1988: 28). Thus, the New Right adopts an anti-statist position that rejects the democratic, welfare state in favour of the market, individualism, civil society, family, and religious and national bonds. Paradoxically, however, 'the state is to be simultaneously rolled back and rolled forward. Non-interventionist and decentralised in some areas, the state is to be highly interventionist and centralised in others . . . more interested in restoring social and political authority throughout society' (Gamble 1988: 28–29). In this sense, the ANAP followed a perfect New Right political line, while also strengthening it with some typical Turkish right-wing populist themes. The latter has always depicted the power bloc in Turkey as composed of the state elites as opposed to the bourgeoisie, the conservative silent majority which in Turkey is included among the dominated classes such as workers and peasants.[2]

The ANAP's hegemonic project was formed by the articulation of three main pillars, just like its counterparts in many different countries: neoliberalism, conservatism and authoritarianism (Özkazanç 1996, 2007: 15–112). To start with neoliberalism, the ANAP deepened neoliberal economic and social policies, the transition to which had already been realised by the military regime. The ANAP promoted an export-oriented accumulation strategy that was mainly dependent on the reduction of labour costs by politically and economically disciplining the working class (Boratav 2011). The ANAP government also used various incentivising policies, such as tax rebates and preferential loans and credits in order to encourage an export-growth strategy. However, this resulted in a new form of rent-seeking for the Turkish bourgeoisie rather than putting an end to rent-seeking as supporters of the neoliberal market would expect (see Bekmen in this volume). Neoliberalism is not simply related to economic and social policies but also has to do with a new governmental rationality with its construction of a new order of reality. Thus, in Turkey, not only the market economy but also a market society lay at the centre of the Turkish New Right's hegemonic efforts. Market fetishism was manufactured by presenting the market as the antidote to all socio-economic problems, as the magic instrument of the New Right (Yalman 2009). The New Right's critique of the democratic, welfare state form was echoed in countries like Turkey in the form of criticising the populist-developmentalist state. Hence, the dismantling of this state form, which had already been started by the military regime, was of primary importance for the ANAP too. The ANAP government centralised economic decision-making in the hands of Prime Minister Özal, in the institutions directly under his control, and in a very limited number of technocrats closely connected with Özal (see Bekmen in this volume). By its technocratisation of the economy and centralisation of economic decision-making, the ANAP completed the establishment of the 'authoritarian statist' form of state.

Conservatism was the second pillar of the ANAP's New Right politics, although the military regime had already added an Islamic element to its ideological discourse through its adoption of the Turkish-Islamic synthesis as a strategy for disciplining the social and political movements of the working class and manufacturing national harmony between classes. As for the ANAP, it, in a sense, socialised the Turkish-Islamic synthesis. As a political party bringing together liberal, nationalist and religious-conservative political elites under one roof, the ANAP revitalised the Turkish centre-right's strategy of conservative modernisation. This allowed it to succeed in 'manufacturing consent on the part of the masses regarding the promise that it could be possible for them to benefit from the material gains of modernisation while preserving their identity' (Taşkın 2008: 54–55). This strategy has both identity politics and class dimensions. Regarding identity, through its political discourse emphasising the importance of nation, religion and family (Bora 2005), by reinforcing the religious apparatuses of the state, and in its organic connections with various religious communities, the ANAP's conservative modernisation strategy was able to appeal to the sensitivities of the Sunni Muslim-Turkish identity and integrate those identity groups into its hegemonic project. This also perfectly conformed with the New Right's anti-statist rhetoric to the extent that this strategy could present itself as an antidote to the Turkish state's authoritarian secularism and modernisation from above although, in practice, the ANAP never abandoned the use of state power to implement its identity policies. Regarding class, by articulating its conservatism with neoliberalism, the ANAP was also able to present the market as an opportunity for social mobility of those groups.

The ANAP's third pillar was authoritarianism. Its use of law and order rhetoric, its preservation of the judicial-political framework constructed by the military regime, and its New Right anti-political technocratic policies provided clear evidence of its authoritarianism. The ANAP both centralised decision-making processes pertaining to economic and social issues and ideologically constructed such issues as technical matters which only experts, not the people, could discuss, reason about, and participate in decision-making. During its eight years in power, rather than dismantling the authoritarian statist form constructed by the preceding military regime, the ANAP continued and extended it by its technocratisation of politics and reinstitutionalisation of the state's authoritarian architecture. The government's discourse of law and order, defense of bans on previous political parties and elites and on trade union activities, the continuation of martial law in some cities until 1987 were some of the continuities with the military regime in order to prevent the repoliticisation of the society (Tanör 2002). In addition, even though the ANAP tried to present itself as being opposed to the military as part of its rhetorical anti-statism, it did not implement any substantive civilianisation reforms apart from some minor, symbolic efforts, such as Özal's casual dress while inspecting military troops or his nomination of a Chief of Staff against the military's own preference, although this was a first in Turkish history. The most the ANAP was able to achieve was the establishment of a kind of division of labour: while the civilian government took responsibility for economic and social policies, the military controlled issues pertaining to political democratisation (Heper and Evin 1988). Such a division of labour assisted the ANAP's power discourse since it could present the military, the state, rather than the government, as being responsible for the ongoing authoritarianism.

One of the main characteristics of the ANAP's New Right policies, which also differentiated it from the classical right-wing populism, is that it was based on a 'two-nation hegemonic project'. According to Jessop, 'one-nation hegemonic projects' are expansive hegemonic strategies geared towards achieving the support of the whole population through material and symbolic rewards, while 'two-nation hegemonic projects' aim for a more limited hegemony that gains only the support of strategically important sectors of the population while passing the costs of the project onto other sectors (the second nation) (Jessop 1990a: 211). In one way or another, a one-nation project has the goal of integrating the subaltern and disadvantaged members of society within its project. Two-nation projects, on the other hand, see no harm in getting rid of the ballast with the understanding that not everybody can or need stay on board. According to Jessop, 'two nation projects require containment and even repression of the "other nation" at the same time as they involve selective access and concessions for the more favoured "nation"' (1990a: 211–212). The ANAP, despite its rhetorical references concerning the unity of the nation and the unification of all tendencies, also represented a break from the classic centre-right populism through its New Right political approach, which turned towards a two-nation strategy.

Economically, politically and culturally, the ANAP's two-nation hegemonic project was exclusionary and repressive. Economically, the ANAP's first nation was able to include the different fractions of the bourgeoisie and secular and religious-conservative urban middle classes. Its export-oriented industrialisation strategy, trade liberalisation, post-1989 financial liberalisation, IMF guided economic stabilisation measures, and the disciplining of the working class were all welcomed by the big bourgeoisie which was organised in industry, commerce, and finance at the same time thanks to its use of holding company structures. Even though the big bourgeoisie made some criticisms of the ANAP's tendency to build clientelistic and informal relations with various capital groups, and demanded a more formal and institutionalised relationship, it nevertheless enjoyed the benefits of these informal relations too. As to the small- and medium-scale bourgeoisie, even though they were critical of financial liberalisation, they also benefited from the ANAP's anti-labour policies since low industrial wages were an essential element in the export-oriented strategy that these sections of the bourgeoisie depended on for their capital accumulation strategy (Boratav 1995: 76–80). Yet, despite common interests, intra-class cleavages in the bourgeoisie deepened, especially after financial liberalisation in 1989.

The other important component of the ANAP's social base was the secular and conservative parts of the urban middle classes. Parallel to the flourishing of sectors such as banking, export and import, advertising, media and various services, new occupational layers mainly composed of managerial and professional white-collar workers emerged relatively quickly. This brought about a process of differentiation among the broader range of Turkey's middle classes. Whereas these new managerial figures were easily integrated into the premises of the market economy through new career opportunities and consumption patterns, some of the more traditional segments of the middle class, such as teachers, lost ground, in terms of both living standards and status. Although the cultural-cum-religious diversities that would culminate in a fierce political struggle after the second half of the 1990s persisted within these layers, the consolidation of a social stratification that gradually isolated the prosperous from newly impoverished segments of the middle classes became one of the Turkish New Right's achievements. The ANAP tried to gain the consent of the disadvantaged middle class through various political tactics including, for example, the foundation of the Mass Housing and Public Participation Board (MHPPB), which merged two different funds within the same board. This reflected the ANAP government's tactical pattern of extending property ownership through both privatisation and mass state-subsidised housing in order to create popular capitalism. Although one of the announced aims of MHPPB was to transfer some of the income from privatisation revenues into mass housing projects that were supposed to solve the lower classes' housing problems, a survey conducted in 1993 in four cities (İstanbul, Ankara, İzmir and Gaziantep) concluded that the policies of the board actually benefitted the middle rather than lower classes (Şenyapılı 1996: 10).

Although the ANAP's two-nation strategy was able to manufacture an urban and market-oriented social base, the second nation of its hegemonic project remained very wide, including workers, peasants, civil servants, the new urban and rural poor, trade unions, leftists, Kurds and Alevis. These societal sectors, excluded from the ANAP's neoliberal market fetishism and Muslim-Turkish conservative identity politics, were the main social components of a second nation that posed a threat to the wealth and security of the first nation (Tünay 1993; Taşkın 2006). These groups' dissatisfaction manifested itself in both electoral results and organised working-class activity, such as the spring protests that began in 1989, and the strike by Zonguldak mine workers in 1990–91. For these groups, the social consequences of neoliberal accumulation strategies were increased poverty and unemployment, declining real wages, deteriorating terms of trade for the agricultural sector and reduced social security spending (see Boratav 2011; Sönmez 2009).

Finally, the ANAP's hegemonic project also contained some contradictions in its identity policies. On the one hand, the ANAP's conservatism, based on a Turkish-Sunni Muslim identity, successfully gained the consent of a specific section of the medium-scale, export-oriented bourgeoisie and urban middle class, who defined themselves by their religious identity. On the other hand, it was also exclusive since it was based on the controlled mobilisation of Sunni Islam and ethnic Turkish identity. This particularly alienated Alevis, Kurds and occasionally urban secularists. In addition, by the beginning of the 1990s, the market- and consumption-based cultural orientation triggered during the ANAP period was alienating the party's religious conservative social base (Taşkın

2006). Thus, as a result of the highly exclusivist nature of its two-nation hegemonic project, the Turkish New Right's first attempt to develop an expansive
hegemony in both the social and political spheres was unsuccessful (Tünay 1993;
Yalman 2002; Özkazanç 2007).

The 1990s: The Crisis of Political Hegemony and the
Neoliberal National Security State

The 1990s was marked by a protracted crisis of political hegemony and the
domination of the military over the political sphere in the form of a neoliberal
national security state. The causes of this crisis were twofold: neoliberal economic
and social policies, and the militarisation and securitisation of questions of
identity politics, such as the Kurdish question and the rise of political Islam. The
resulting political vacuum, which was itself partially produced by the military
through its securitisation of politics, was in turn filled by the military.

Crisis of Political Hegemony

The 1991 general election results signalled both the demise of the ANAP's New
Right strategy and the rise to power of a coalition between the centre-right True
Path Party (DYP) and the centre-left Social Democratic Populist Party (SHP).
In the course of the electoral campaign, these two parties had promised new
redistributive policies, political democratisation via a new constitution, and a
political solution to the Kurdish question. That is, they addressed the concerns of
various sections of the ANAP's second nation. However, in the aftermath of the
1994 financial crisis and the militarisation of the Kurdish question, the initiatives
of the already fragile DYP-SHP coalition faded away rapidly (Saybaşılı 1995).

Looking at the general elections of the 1990s (1991, 1995 and 1999), one
observes that the highest percentage of votes for the winning parties ranged
between just 21.3 and 27 per cent. The political scene was marked by the
fragmentation of centre-right and centre-left (two parties competing with each
other in each political position) and also the rise of Islamist (Welfare Party, RP)
and radical nationalist (Nationalist Movement Party, MHP) parliamentary
parties. Consequently, the governments formed after these elections were weak
coalitions, although this situation was not the reason but rather the symptom of
Turkey's political hegemonic crisis (see Ataay 2002: 199–215). The picture meant
that none of the existing political parties was able to manufacture a successful
hegemonic project that would unify the dominant classes and class fractions, get
the active or passive consent of the dominated classes and of the social groups
suffering from authoritarian laicist, nationalist, statist identity politics.

The hegemonic crisis of the 1990s had both class and identity politics dimensions. The class dimension directly related to the ravages of neoliberal
accumulation strategies, which were exacerbated in the 1990s because of several
severe economic crises in 1994, 1999, 2000 and, most devastatingly, 2001. Two
capital accumulation strategies dominated this period. The first was financial
accumulation, whereby the economy became dependent on, and therefore

fragile because of, uncontrolled financial inflows and outflows. The second was an export-oriented strategy based on decreasing labour costs. The economic cost of these accumulation strategies and the resulting economic crises were paid by Turkey's workers, urban poor, lower middle classes, fixed income receivers, peasants, small businesses, shopkeepers and craftsmen (Yeldan 2001a; Boratav 2011). To the extent that successive coalition governments failed to challenge and/or change these accumulation strategies, which were also forced on them by standard IMF stand-by agreements, they could not get the consent of the dominated classes.

As to the identity politics dimension of the political hegemony crisis, on which I will elaborate below, at the beginning of the 1990s, the military opted for a new strategy that totally militarised the Kurdish question and destroyed all hopes of a political solution. Similarly, in response to the Islamist RP's rise to power as a partner in the coalition government that formed after the 1995 elections, the military intervened once again in 1997, through the National Security Council decisions of 28 February. Neither centre-right nor leftist parties opposed the military's moves to militarise and securitise these issues, and even became active supporters of them. However, their failure to de-securitise and politicise identity questions only deepened their own crises of hegemony. Losing both their popular appeal and ties with Turkey's excluded social classes and cultural identity groups, these centre-right and centre-left political parties could not differentiate their power discourse and strategy from those of the state elites of the national security state. As a result, they failed to win substantial electoral support to achieve their own hegemony. This crisis of hegemony was then translated into a political instrument by the military for the further securitisation and militarisation of the political sphere. The resulting neoliberal national security state, at the centre of which stood the military, dominated the political sphere throughout the 1990s (Öngen 2002; Bozarslan 2001; Özcan 2006).

Militarisation of the Kurdish Question: War-Making Is State-Making

It is conventionally acknowledged that war-making has historically been closely related to state-making, with important impacts on the form of the state (see Tilly 1990; Mann 1993). Since 1984, Turkey has also experienced an officially undeclared 'internal war' in its east and southeast regions that has been a decisive factor in the consolidation of the national security state and the domination of the military over the political sphere.

This military conflict between the PKK (Partiya Karkaren Kurdistan, Kurdistan Workers' Party) and the Turkish military began in 1984. It has been reported that between 1984 and 1998 more than 35,000 people were killed, most of whom were civilians. Some 1,179 villages and 6,153 settlements were destroyed, and almost 1 million people were internally displaced (Human Rights Watch 2002). In 1987, emergency rule (OHAL) had already been introduced in the eight provinces of the southeast region, to which five new provinces were added in the following years. The emergency rule vested the provincial governors with extraordinary coercive powers, which increased the domination of the security forces, especially the military, over the daily administration of the region (Üskül 2003).

By 1990, the perception of threat among military officers had already changed. According to both high ranking military officers and civilian security bureaucrats, the PKK had already become a second authority, a rival state-like organisation in the region, claiming to fulfil the functions of the judiciary, taxation, compulsory conscription and so on (Kışlalı 1996; Cemal 2003). As a result, the Chief of Staff of the period, General Doğan Güreş, stated the change in threat priority in 1993: 'As far as strategic concepts are concerned, I have changed the priorities of the Turkish armed forces vis-à-vis possible threats. From now on, the internal threat is the first priority for the Turkish Army' (quoted in Özdağ 2007). This perception represented a threshold in the militarisation of the Kurdish question in that the state started to be reorganised to operate as a war machine, using formal and legal, and informal and illegal, structures.

The first three years of the 1990s were marked by a reorganisation of the military forces. New special commando forces were established within both the army and the police forces. The material infrastructural power of the army was strengthened by new military equipment purchases such as combat helicopters and infrared combat glasses. The army began to change from a division-based structure to a corps-brigade-battalion structure to increase rapid response and mobilisation (Balta Paker 2010). In 1993, at the Emergency Situation Coordination Committee meeting, the area control concept was accepted and it was further decided that, as the main method of area control, villages suspected of supporting the PKK or vulnerable to PKK attacks would be evacuated. Villagers' willingness to join local paramilitaries, known as temporary village guards, which had originally had a purely military function, soon became a criterion for differentiating friend from foe (Balta Paker and Akça 2013). JİTEM (Jandarma İstihbarat ve Terörle Mücadele, Gendarmerie Intelligence and Counterterrorism), despite not even being officially recognised in the 1990s, was founded to run the state's illegal operations in the name of fighting terrorism (Kılıç 2010). Village evacuations, human rights violations and unidentified killings became a normal part of everyday life especially in the periphery predominantly inhabited by Kurds. Meanwhile, legal Kurdish political parties were repeatedly banned (Jacoby 2005).

The changing strategies of the state's internal war-making not only pertained to a strictly military restructuring but also had effects on state-making at the macro-political and ideological levels. For example, the fact that the country was declared to be at war was used as one of the main reasons for deepening the National Security State structure during the 1990s. All social and political questions were securitised and the politico-ideological terrain colonised by the radicalisation of an exclusivist ethnic Turkish nationalism based on anti-Kurdish sentiments (Balta Paker 2010; Yeğen 2006). Following Michael Mann's distinction, Tim Jacoby argues that, whereas 'in the thirteen predominantly Kurdish provinces of the south-east of the country' autocratic militarism dominated, in the areas of the country not administered by emergency rule, semi-authoritarian incorporation was dominant. Autocratic militarism is characterised by 'the repression of all forms of dissent', and relies on the deployment of both regular security forces and paramilitary formations. Semi-authoritarian incorporation includes both incorporative and exclusionary strategies. That is, it combines 'limited representation to members of both 'in' and 'out' groups within the framework of 'limited electoral democracies' with the use of selective repression and coercion in response to fears of worker radicalism, and ethnic or religious politics (Jacoby 2005).

The Rise of Political Islam and the Further Securitisation of Politics

The vacuum that emerged in the crisis of political hegemony provided the route through which political Islam emerged in the 1990s. The RP, which had replaced the National Outlook (*Milli Görüş*) movement that had represented Turkish political Islamism since 1970 and gained 11.8 and 8.6 per cent of the votes in the 1973 and 1977 general elections respectively, achieved important electoral successes in the 1990s. First, in the municipal elections of 1994 it got 23 per cent of the vote on the national level, and won in several major cities such as İstanbul and Ankara. Then, in the 1995 general elections, by winning 21.4 per cent of the vote, it emerged as the leading party to form a coalition government with the centre-right DYP in June 1996, although this only lasted one year. The RP's rise was the outcome of the crisis of political hegemony and provided an alternative response to this crisis forged in terms of identity politics. During the 1990s, in a period when class-based politics was repressed, identity politics was expressed in both intra- and inter-class-based social unrest.

The RP's political Islamism articulated ideological elements such as a culturalist and moralist critique of Westernism, monopolist capitalism and Kemalism as its so-called local representative. The RP's ideal of a 'just economic order' (*Adil Düzen*), corresponded to a 'utopian picture of an egalitarian petit-bourgeois society composed of individual entrepreneurs' and a pro-market position; its religious communitarianism was based on the project of multiple legal-orders as a remedy for multi-culturalism and a substitute for democracy; it also incorporated anti-Americanism and anti-Europeanism (Gülalp 1999a, 1999b; Şen 1995). In this way, the RP's political Islamism succeeded in repre-senting both some of the winners and losers of neoliberal global capitalism in Turkey through its discourse based on the justice of an Islamic social and political order set against the power bloc of Turkey, which was allegedly composed of a Westernised, culturally estranged, secularist and state-monopolist bureaucracy, the big bourgeoisie and urban middle classes.

Through such a hegemonic project, the RP formed a multi-class political movement, bringing together small- and medium-scale bourgeoisie, and primarily the provincial pious capitalist class organised under the Association of Independent Industrialists and Businessmen (MÜSİAD), the peripheral segment of the working class, and Turkey's upwardly mobile, religious-conservative professional middle classes (Gülalp 2001; Öniş 1997). This project drew on three sources of support. First, Turkey's political Islamists had always been well-organised among small, independent businesses, which were in conflict with the urban-based big bour-geoisie. However, under the changed conditions of export-oriented industrialisation and flexible forms of employment and accumulation, these fractions of the bourgeoisie had gained a new importance to become a newly emerging, dynamic section of industrial capital. This does not mean that this entire fraction of the bourgeoisie was Islamist, but rather that the bourgeoisie that Turkish Islamism relied on came from this fraction of the bourgeoisie. The anti-monopolist, anti-rent seeking, anti-statist elements of the RP's 'Just Economic Order' discourse particularly responded to the criticisms and aspirations of this fraction of the bourgeoisie, who were very critical of the mainly İstanbul-based major capital groups (holding companies) organised under the Turkish Industry and Business Association (TÜSİAD). The latter fraction of the bourgeoisie had long been integrated within global neoliberal capitalism, profiting from the financial accumulation model due to their control of financial capital and their historically developed preferential access to state resources and protection. The challenging move by this fraction of the capitalist class has become apparent in its ambitions to profit from the privatisation process, in its favouring an alternative form of integration with the world capitalist economy using the discourse of 'Islam Common Market' rather than the integration with European Union project, in its attempt to enter into the sectors, such as finance and automotive, previously controlled by big holding companies, in its opposition to the IMF-backed financial accumulation model, which favoured a small number of big capital groups with the capability of controlling the money capital at the expense of small- and medium-scale real sector capital groups. In brief, this new fraction of capital started to be a threat to the big capital of which the military capital was a part. Even the ex-chairman of the Union of Chambers and Commodity Exchanges of Turkey (TOBB) was complaining about their exclusion from the foreign trips of the previous government which favoured MÜSİAD (Buğra 1998; Öniş and Türem 2001; Uğur and Alkan 2000; Doğan 2010b). The RP's second source of support was the newly emerging segment of the pious professional middle classes, composed of university students and the intelligentsia, which possessed cultural capital and desired upward mobility, yet were blocked because of their Islamic identity. Finally, the 'Just Economic Order' appealed to those most unorganised, informal and peripheral fractions of the working class in urban areas who were 'unable to find secure employment and engaged in marginal activities' (Gülalp 2001: 445). The RP was able to fill the vacuum created by a historical conjuncture in which left-wing political parties had lost their connections with the urban poor.

Regarding identity politics, the RP was able to appeal to Sunni-Muslim religiously-conservative voters by politicising their sense of cultural exclusion with its promises to integrate them into economic, cultural and political spheres. In addition, the RP also won support from among the Kurdish electorate by opposing the nationalist-statist-militarist political line of other parties, while aiming to overcome ethnic cleavages through a sense of Muslim brotherhood.

The RP's rise to power, and some of its governmental practices, such as its symbolic and practical attempts at increasing Islamic visibility in the public sphere, its organic relationship with MÜSİAD members, its attempts to develop international economic and political cooperation with Islamically-oriented Middle Eastern states, its economic and political voicing of international Islamic alternatives in the face of the hegemony of the USA and the EU (Özcan 1998), all caused the reaction of important social groups in Turkey. The RP's ideological and political approach to the hegemonic project of political Islam was far from fulfiling the needs of a hegemonic project for the most globalised fractions of the Turkish bourgeoisie, the organised fractions of the working class, the urban and secular middle classes and the political and military elites, who all felt threatened by a Turkish Islamist project. The RP's rise to governmental power challenged both economic-corporative and political-ideological interests and the orientations of these sections of the population. Domestically, it was this social base that the military intervention of 1997 was able to draw on; internationally, the USA supported the intervention while the EU failed to voice any significant reaction to it.

Emboldened by this support, the military intervened through the MGK decisions of 28 February 1997, criticising what it claimed were the RP-led government's 'anti-secular' policies. These decisions declared *irtica*, or Islamic fundamentalism, to be the main threat to the foundations of the Turkish republic (along with Kurdish separatism), and urged the government to take pro-secular policy measures against anti-secular activities (*Radikal,* 31 March 1997). The so-called 28 February process aimed at eradicating the power of political Islam in the political, educational, economic-financial, media and public spheres, and redesigning Turkish politics in line with the ideologies of Turkey's centre parties (Bayramoğlu 2001: 282). Soon after the MGK decisions, TOBB, TİSK, the Confederation of Turkish Trade Unions (Türk-İş), DİSK, and the Confederation of Tradesmen and Handicrafts (TESK) formed an initiative called the 'Five Civilian Initiative', which actively campaigned against the RP-led government. This cleavage based on identity politics, which has its own dynamics, also overlapped with a separate intra-class cleavage. This explains why, for instance, TÜSİAD, which had started to develop a more liberal democratic orientation under the hegemonic project of European Union membership, did not hesitate to support the military's intervention and the subsequent policies designed to discipline so-called Islamist capital. In January 1996, TÜSİAD added to its internal regulations that it was committed to secularism (Cizre and Çınar 2003).

Subsequent pressures from the military pushed the RP-DYP coalition government to resign in May 1997. Shortly after that, in January 1998, the Constitutional Court decided to close RP for anti-secular activities, and banned its key policy makers from politics. Meanwhile, another court case was opened against MÜSİAD for anti-secular activities. The Chief of Staff even released a list of companies that it claimed represented the 'Islamic bourgeoisie', asking for them to be boycotted (Cizre and Çınar 2003; Bayramoğlu 2001). To fight the rise of political Islam, the military elites also suggested further Westernisation and integration into the world economy, which they believed would make a political Islamist project impossible (*Hürriyet,* 4 November 1997). The military's policy preferences, such as entering the EU, accelerating privatisation integration with the world economy were openly stated in the military's then secret Document of National Security Policy, updated in 1997. Notably, the military's 28 February decisions represented a complete reversal of its promotion of the Turkish-Islamic synthesis following the 1980 coup, when it assumed that religious discourse could play a moral and ideological role in consolidating Turkish society in the face of neoliberal capitalism (Atacan 2005; Cizre and Çınar 2003).

During the 28 February process, the military not only constructed new institutional devices but also adopted a new strategy. A unit called the Western Study Group (Batı Çalışma Grubu) was instituted in the general staff headquarters and a new organ called the Prime Ministerial Crisis Management Center (Başbakanlık Kris Yönetim Merkezi) was founded in January 1998. Meanwhile, the general staff headquarters became very active in addition to its role in the MGK. The military's new strategy led it to act like a political party constructing its own social support base and actively manufacturing consent for its actions. 'It has appealed directly to the organised groups of the modernised urban-secular sectors' (Cizre and Çınar 2003: 322). In a sense, the military discovered 'civil society', or to put it more accurately, civil society was militarised to a previously unseen extent. For example, the military began holding briefings with representatives of universities, media, business organisations and the bar association, becoming thoroughly entrenched in politics through both formal and informal mechanisms. However, by further exacerbating the statisation and securitisation of Turkish politics, this only deepened the political hegemony crisis (Cizre and Çınar 2003; Bayramoğlu 2001).

The military intervention of 28 February 1997 arose from the struggle between two different hegemonic projects defended by two social blocs based on crosscutting class alliances and mobilised by the ideological language of identity politics. On the one side was the social bloc formed by the İstanbul-based big bourgeoisie, which is totally integrated with global capitalism and its Western power centres, some sections of organised labour (DİSK and Türk-İş), and the urban middle classes. The military was the political actor actively engaged in manufacturing the consent of this social bloc. On the other side was the social bloc composed of the newly emerging conservative Anatolian bourgeoisie, the unorganised working classes in post-Fordist production, the section of labour organised by Hak-İş, the union most closely affiliated with political Islam, and the conservative new middle classes. This bloc was represented politically by the RP, which proposed a new way to integrate into the global capitalist economy through cooperation with Middle Eastern Muslim countries.

Although the military intervention disciplined Islamic parties and business organisations in the short-term, it actually deepened the existing political hegemonic crisis since the statisation and securitisation of politics encouraged political parties to decouple from dominated social classes and identity groups. After the closure of the RP, its successor, the Virtue Party (Fazilet Partisi, FP), was also closed by the Constitutional Court in June 2001. The triple coalition government that formed after the 1999 elections was not only unable to transcend this hegemonic crisis, but its continuation of neoliberal economic policies also caused the worst economic crisis in the country's history in 2001. An opposition faction within FP then opted to establish a new party, the AKP. The latter claimed to be a totally new party, whose political position it defined as 'conservative democrat', claiming to break with the political Islamists' '*Milli Görüş*' past.

The AKP and Its Hegemonic Project: Neoliberal, Conservative, Authoritarian Populism

The 2001 economic crisis was the biggest in Turkish history. Together with the accompanying political crisis and resulting instability, it led to a deeper organic crisis in which almost all political parties became completely discredited in the eyes of the electorate, who held them responsible for the disastrous turn of events. The AKP, which entered the political scene in 2002, just as this organic crisis unfolded, revitalised the neoliberal hegemony by 'the absorption of Islamism into secular neoliberalism more or less successfully at all levels of the hegemonic formation' (Tuğal 2009: 51). The AKP won the 3 November 2002 elections with 34 per cent of the vote and 65 per cent of the seats in Parliament,[3] which enabled it to form the first non-coalition government since 1991. The AKP then consolidated its hegemonic power by winning the 22 July 2007 elections with 46.6 per cent of the votes and 62 per cent of the seats in Parliament. In its most recent election victory on 12 June 2011, it won 49.9 per cent of the votes and 62 per cent of the seats. The AKP's political and electoral performance is exceptional, not only in the post-1980 neoliberal period but also in all Turkish history. The following section analyses the AKP's hegemonic project and political strategy in terms of neoliberal-conservative-authoritarian populism.

Understanding the AKP's Hegemonic Project

A successful hegemonic project, including its accumulation strategy, should create unity among fractions of the bourgeoisie, while manufacturing the consent of the dominated classes and articulating to its hegemonic class project other socio-political issues not immediately emanating from class relations. The AKP has succeeded in all these points. It moved to fill the vacuum left by the collapsing centre-right by reinventing a Turkish centre-right-type populist strategy under the rubric of 'conservative democracy', though in a totally different historical setting. The AKP's hegemonic project articulated the following elements:[4]

- IMF (International Monetary Fund) and WB (World Bank) oriented neoliberal economic policies, especially the realisation of second wave structural reforms;
- redistribution policies based on neoliberal social policy programmes;
- supposedly reformist political policies regarding democratisation understood as a struggle on behalf of an assumed national will against bureaucratic-military tutelage;
- conservative modernisation instead of political Islamism, i.e. normalisation of religious conservatism in political, economic, cultural and daily spheres, and the integration of Turkey's Sunni-Muslim political, economic and cultural elites;
- foreign policies based on a neo-Ottomanist imperial strategy in the Middle East within the framework of US neo-imperialism.

The AKP's hegemonic project successfully united the dominant class fractions, gained the consent of the dominated classes, and appealed to important identity groups who had previously felt excluded. To start with the dominant class fractions, the AKP gained the support of the İstanbul-based big bourgeoisie, the small- and medium-scale bourgeoisie, especially the Muslim-conservative sections of the latter, urban Muslim-conservatives, and also some from the upwardly-mobile secular middle class. These various fractions of the bourgeoisie were united by the AKP's neoliberal economic policies, based on financial capital inflows and its financial accumulation strategy, privatisation, the reduction of real wages, especially in manufacturing, and the legalisation and extensive use of subcontracting. Even though the AKP's financial accumulation strategy disadvantaged the export-oriented, small- and medium-scale industrial bourgeoisie, it was able to compensate for this with other policies that systematically reduced labour costs. While MÜSİAD, with organic ties to the AKP, unsurprisingly supported the government, TOBB, a business organisation representing those apparently disadvantaged sections of the bourgeoisie, also gave its support. TÜSİAD, the business organisation representing the big bourgeoisie, which had struggled against political Islamism and the newly emerging MÜSİAD-based bourgeoisie during the 1990s, welcomed the strong AKP government for implementing the second wave neoliberal economic policies and structural reforms of the WB (Ataay and Kalfa 2009). While this does not mean that intra-class contradictions and struggles totally disappeared at the economic-corporate and/or political-hegemonic levels, it does indicate how the AKP successfully articulated different intra-class interests to an important extent (see Bekmen, and Doğan and Durak in this volume, Sönmez 2009).

Regarding the dominated classes, which were economically and politically excluded by neoliberal policies, the AKP was particularly successful in gaining the consent of the most unorganised and informal sections of the working class, the rural poor, and housewives by introducing a neoliberal social policy regime. In this, the government was following global concern over governing poverty through the new programmes and strategies developed by the WB since the end of 1990s. This new neoliberal social policy regime included neoliberal poverty reduction and social assistance programmes, workfare programmes, social security reforms that included those hitherto excluded from the formal system, and the extensive use of religious charity organisations. A new model of social policies was implemented in various forms: social aid, the Green Card, conditional cash transfers, free distribution of school books, and the subsistence aid given by both the Social Aid and Solidarity Fund of the Prime Ministry and foundations connected to it at the centre, as well as through local government (Özden in this volume; Yıldırım 2009; Buğra 2007; Buğra and Keyder 2006; Buğra and Adar 2008). Despite the fact that the AKP implemented neoliberal policies at the expense of labour and oppressed organised labour, neoliberal social policies allowed the AKP to manufacture the consent of the urban and rural poor, newly formed due to neoliberal economic policies. These measures, intended to make poverty sustainable rather than eradicating it, undermined the idea of an active, organised and democratic citizenship, yet were still able to gain the passive consent of the dominated classes (Yıldırım 2009).

The AKP was also able to articulate issues related to identity politics as part of its hegemonic project, especially to get the consent of religiously-conservative Turks and Kurds. Its stance of conservative modernisation promised the so-called 'silent Muslim majority' the opportunity 'to benefit from the material gains of modernisation while preserving their identity' (Taşkın 2008: 54–55). However, it should be noted that the AKP's interpretation of cultural conservatism was more marked by the vestiges of political Islamism than its centre-right predecessors (Yıldız 2008). For example, it integrated into every sphere of public life Turkey's religiously conservative economic, political and cultural elites, who had previously felt excluded by their identity. Regarding important questions of identity politics, such as Islam's relation to secularism and the Kurdish question, the AKP promised political democratisation, understood as the dismantling of the statist-nationalist authoritarian policies of previous governments.

The articulating element of this hegemonic project has been populism (Yıldırım 2009; Akça 2011; Dinçşahin 2012). I use this much debated concept as a specific mode of politics. As Laclau (2005a: xi) notes, 'populism is, quite simply, a way of constructing the political'. Specifically, populism is a mode of politics that constructs the main axis of political conflict as lying between a power bloc composed of elites and a popular-national bloc. As a political strategy, it divides society into two major antagonistic camps and claims to represent and fulfil both the material and non-material aspirations of the popular-national bloc economically, politically and culturally. 'Dominant class populisms' are also marked by 'an economic project that utilises widespread redistributive or clientelistic methods', 'a top-down process of political mobilisation that . . . bypasses institutionalised forms of mediation', 'personalistic and paternalistic leadership', 'a heterogeneous, multi-class political coalition', and 'an amorphous or eclectic ideology' (Roberts 1995: 88). Or, as Stavrakakis puts it, populism involves 'the construction of a symbolic antagonism between 'the people' and 'the elite' through the notion of unfulfiled demands and an anti-institutional attitude in the discourse of politicians subsequent to a crisis' (Stavrakakis 2005: 243). Two remarks should be made about this core definition. Firstly, different types of populist politics (for example right-wing or left-wing populisms) manufacture the power bloc and the popular-national bloc with different social content since they appeal to different social classes and social groups (Laclau 1977). Secondly, populism can be either democratic or authoritarian depending on whether it opens the political sphere to oppressed social classes and social groups and whether it politically empowers or weakens those groups (Hall 1980, 1985).

The AKP, which claims to have broken with its political Islamist roots in previous parties, regenerated Turkish centre-right populism (Sunar 2004; Mert 2007) to make it consonant with the totally new setting of neoliberal capitalism (Yıldırım 2009). In a very similar vein to Turkish centre-right populism, the AKP has also constructed the axis of political conflict as lying between *the power bloc* composed of the Kemalist state elites and their civilian ties that excluded the 'nation' (expressed as *millet*, a Turkish word which has strong religious connotations) politically, economically, and culturally. It is argued that the bureaucratic elites identified with a top-down Westernist, secularist modernist position dominated over *the national bloc* composed of both the dominant and the dominated classes whose common point is to constitute the excluded 'silent Sunni-Muslim majority'. Hence, the AKP's neoliberal-conservative populism addressed the material and non-material aspirations of the masses by manufacturing a political antagonism between 'the silent Muslim majority and a disproportionally active and influential Westernist minority' (Taşkın 2008: 55). This power bloc and the tutelary regime it constructed are said to be institutionalised in the following state apparatuses: The military, the president, the high judiciary organs (such as Constitutional Court, the Supreme Court of Appeal, Council of State, High Council of Judges and Public Prosecutors [HSYK]), and the Higher Education Council (YÖK). Turkish right-wing populist rhetoric fits also with the neoliberal anti-statist political and ideological discourse, which depicts the state as the main obstacle for economic development, free market functioning, and business activities. The following quotation from Recep Tayyip Erdoğan speaks for itself:

> Do you know what the real problem in Turkey is? Bureaucratic oligarchy. We, as the executive, want to do something. Do you think that we have the easiness that the private sector enjoys. Believe me, we do not have this easiness. We said we would govern according to the merchant mentality. We still think the same. (*Yeni Şafak*, 19 June 2004)

This supposedly anti-statist rhetoric, emanating from the articulation of Turkish right-wing populism and neoliberalism, depicts democratisation as a struggle against the bureaucratic power bloc and the so-called tutelary regime. In the following sections of this chapter, I will discuss whether the AKP's move against the tutelary regime has brought about democratisation or has been substituted by a new authoritarian state form.

Have EU Candidacy and Civilianisation Brought About Democratisation?

There is no doubt that the AKP, which claimed to have abandoned Turkish political Islamism, namely the National Outlook Movement ('Milli Görüş Gömleğini 28 Şubat'ta Çıkarttık', *Akşam*, 14 August 2003), has integrated a discourse on democracy and human rights into its party programme and political discourse. The party's self-identification as 'conservative democrat' is also a sign while, recently, the party started to present itself as the advocate and architect of 'advanced democracy' in Turkey: 'AK Party defines advanced democracy as an institutionalised and free democracy in which an individual's indispensable, non-transferrable, immune rights and freedoms can be fulfiled and protected against all kinds of the authority of the state. Advanced democracy is one in which the will of the citizen has a direct impact on state institutions not only through elections but also through decisions and controls exercised by citizens in every aspect of public life' (AK Parti 2012: 9).

Two factors have determined the AKP's discourse and practices concerning democratisation: its neoliberal-conservative populist power strategy and EU membership requirements. Let's start with the second stimulus, namely the EU project. In the post-1999 period, Turkey's accession to the EU has become the main political issue of domestic politics. The majority of different sections of the population, from the ex-Islamist to Kurdish political movements, from almost all fractions of the bourgeoisie to a significant part of organised labour, and unorganised popular sections, saw EU candidacy as the magical device that would solve Turkey's economic, social, political and cultural problems. In that sense, EU membership was constructed by conservative, liberal and left-liberal circles as a perfect hegemonic apparatus. The AKP's pro-EU stance (Usul 2008; Doğan 2005) has had two effects. First, it has functioned as a hegemonic apparatus to get the consent of the dominated classes and other repressed social groups. Secondly, it has served to consolidate the AKP's political power vis-à-vis the military and secular establishment.

The AKP's democratisation reforms have been limited to some constitutional and legal changes through reform packages required for EU membership, especially between 2002 and 2005, which was a period of 'Euro-enthusiasm' (Usul 2008). Those reforms covered the following areas: abolition of the death penalty, accepting the constitutional supremacy of international law over domestic law, the abolition of State Security Courts, reinforcing constitutional equality between sexes, some minor changes in the Penal Code and Anti-Terror Law and, most importantly, several reforms concerning civil–military relations that curbed the autonomous political power of the military (see below). Although some EU reforms have been important (see Hale and Özbudun 2010: 55–67), most have had no real impact on making state–society relations more democratic.

The EU reform process slowed down in the aftermath of the rejection of the proposed EU constitution in France and the Netherlands in 2005, which was interpreted by Turkish public opinion and the government as signalling resistance to Turkey's membership. The post-2006 period, and especially after 2007, was marked by a new wave of authoritarianism. In particular, government legislation has been in the direction of reversing its earlier reforms in some of the most critical EU reform areas, such as the Anti-Terror Law, freedom of expression and State Security Courts (see below). Overall, the AKP 'lacks a practical democratisation agenda independent from EU membership requirements' (Çınar 2008: 122).

The core of EU-stimulated reform packages has concerned civilianisation by curbing the 'autonomous political power of the military' (Cizre 2008b). This brings us to the first factor, namely that a neoliberal–conservative populist power strategy determined the AKP's understanding of democracy. This has been based on the idea of representing 'the national will' against the state elite's tutelage, against the *status quo* materialised in the apparatuses of the tutelary regime. It therefore includes the minimum of democracy: the formation of political power through electoral process. This understanding of democracy has been one of the main stimuli behind the AKP's political reformism, since the secular state establishment has had strong suspicions about, if not belief in, the party's alleged hidden Islamic intentions. In other words, the AKP's political Islamist legacy has paradoxically forced it to engage in a more reformist stance than its right-wing predecessors. Hence, the AKP has mainly defined democratisation as 'the normalisation of the Turkish political system' (Akdoğan 2006: 52).

The AKP's claim to political reformism in dismantling the tutelary regime has been most clearly evidenced in its struggle against the military and its civilianisation reforms (Akça and Balta Paker 2013; Cizre 2008b). The AKP did not have the opportunity granted to its centre-right predecessors, which the military regarded as more or less legitimate political actors, to develop relatively stable relations and alliances with the military. Instead, hardliners within the military have perceived the AKP government as the successor to the political Islamist movement, seeing it as a threat to the secular foundations of the Turkish Republic. As a result, the AKP, despite its willingness, has been unable to develop good relations with the military, choosing instead to carry out legal and institutional reforms to limit the military's political role, both as a requirement of the EU accession process and also to consolidate its own political power. Two other main reasons also pushed the AKP to introduce civilianisation reforms. The first is that the AKP's struggle against the core actor of the tutelary regime, namely the military, has helped its neoliberal-conservative populist strategy. The second is that its neo-Ottomanist desire to become an imperial power in the Middle East could not be realised so long as the military remained politically autonomous from the government.

Hence, between 2002 and 2005, the AKP engaged in a 'war of position' against the military, to use Gramsci's term, especially by using Turkey's EU candidacy for leverage. This legitimated its curbs on the power of the MGK and the Secretariat General. For example, the Seventh EU Harmonisation Package, passed on 7 August 2003, made significant amendments to the composition, role and functions of both the MGK and the Secretariat General. The MGK, previously the main institution of military influence, was transformed from being an executive decision-making board into an advisory board. Moreover, the internal composition of the MGK was radically altered: the majority of members were now to be civilians, while its post of secretariat, which had always been held by a high-ranking general, could now be a civilian appointed by the president from a list of candidates selected by the prime minister. Even more importantly, the frequency of MGK meetings was decreased to once every two months instead of monthly. This amendment indirectly but effectively decreased the MGK's importance in domestic policy making. Moreover, through amendments to the Law on the Establishment of and Broadcasting by Radio and Television Corporations, Wireless Communication, and the Protection of Minors from Harmful Publications, the MGK's prior authority to nominate one member to each relevant board was ended. Besides the amendment to the structure and responsibilities of the MGK, parliament annulled the provision in the Law on Higher Education that allowed the General Staff to select one member of the Higher Education Council (Akça and Balta Paker 2013: 80). During this period, in order to weaken the AKP government, the military elites took several actions, ranging from coup attempts to the promotion of anti-AKP public campaigns. Although there were signs that the AKP's leaders were aware of these attempted coups against their government back in 2003 and 2004, given its relatively narrow electoral base at that time and its inability to penetrate state institutions, the AKP did not feel strong enough to wage a war of manoeuvre, so did not struggle against these attempts. In the event, the military's attempts to unseat the government failed anyway because they had a narrow social base and hardly any international support. However, the AKP government's rather passive stance paved the way for a counter attack by the military in the following period, marked by the slowing down of EU reforms and the remilitarisation of the Kurdish question (Akça and Balta Paker 2013: 81–82).

The AKP had tried to forge relatively close relations with the military by taking an anti-Kurdish movement stance, for instance by making amendments to the Anti-Terror Law. However, this tactic collapsed during the presidential candidacy debate in spring 2007 when the AKP proposed the Minister of Foreign Affairs, Abdullah Gül, as its presidential candidate. The military opposed his candidacy because Gül's wife wears a headscarf, with the Turkish General Staff publishing a memorandum on its website, later called the 'e-memorandum', on 27 April 2007 warning of the danger to secularism. In addition, when parliament voted for Gül, the Constitutional Court also tried to block his candidacy at the behest of the opposition CHP by reaching a totally arbitrary decision concerning the minimum number of parliamentary deputies required for the vote for the presidential candidate to be valid. However, the government easily circumvented this obstacle by calling early general elections in July 2007, which led both to a greater share of the vote and parliamentary seats, and Gül's taking the presidency. On March 2008, the opposition to the AKP struck back when the chief prosecutor opened a case to close the AKP (Akça and Balta Paker 2013: 83–84).

These events pushed the AKP to shift its strategy towards open struggle against the military. Already, between 2002 and 2007, the AKP government had been able to penetrate – albeit to a limited extent – the judiciary and begin to exert more extensive influence over the police. During the new period, however, its increasing control over the police and judiciary would become crucial as the government launched an offensive against the military based on allegations of military-inspired plots to overthrow the government. On 20 October 2008, following the uncovering of an arms dump and associated documents in an İstanbul house, the *Ergenekon* trial began. The trial led to waves of arrests of academics, politicians, journalists, lawyers, businessmen and high-ranking serving and retired military officials. Among the charges levelled in the indictment are 'membership of an armed terrorist group, aiding and abetting an armed terrorist organisation, attempting to destroy the government of the Republic of Turkey or to block it from performing its duties, inciting people to rebel against the Republic of Turkey, being in possession of explosives, using them, and inciting others to commit these crimes, acquiring secret documents on national security' (Park 2008). In February 2010, further arrests led to a trial called '*Balyoz*' (Sledgehammer), named after an alleged 2003 plot to foment chaos and destabilise the government in order to justify a military coup. Recently, the court imposed jail sentences of around 20 years for many high ranking officers, including former chiefs of the air, navy and land forces. Most recently, in the Supreme Military Council meetings of August 2010 and 2011, the AKP government vetoed proposed promotions of several high-ranking generals due to their alleged connections to coup plotters (Akça and Balta Paker 2013: 86).

By 2013, we can say that the AKP has won its political battle against the military, and there is no doubt that this civilianisation has been an important step towards democratisation. However, such civilianisation by itself is a necessary but not sufficient condition for democratisation, and in Turkey it has not brought about democratisation for two reasons. Firstly, civilianisation remains incomplete because there are still functions that should be under the competence of the civilian authorities but have not yet achieved this, such as the military budget, internal security and intelligence gathering. In addition, the subject areas of NSC meetings are still too broad, while the military retains an important role in internal security through specific institutions, the chief of general staff still has authority and prerogatives in areas other than strictly external security issues, parliamentary control over the military does not work effectively, and the military's economic power remains untouched (Akay 2009; Akça 2010b). More importantly, there is convincing evidence that the credibility of the *Ergenekon* and *Balyoz* trials has been undermined because the revanchist political concerns of the government took precedence over legal procedures and obligations. This has led even those sections of the public that have consistently supported civilianisation to express unease and question the legality and impartiality of the trial process. The second weakness of current civilianisation is that the AKP government, having begun the process, did not go further to establish a democratic state form but instead manufactured a civilian authoritarian state form.

Conquering the State, Preserving the Authoritarian State Form

One of the main criteria of democratisation is that the state form changes so as to reduce the limits imposed on the political sphere, which necessitates a change in the state form. However, the anti-statist rhetoric and practice of the AKP's neoliberal-conservative populism was trapped within its critique of the Kemalist state elites' control of the state apparatuses rather than the state form *per se*. Thus, the party's populist rhetoric claims that 'the reconquering of the political, cultural and economic echelons is a just and legitimate act in renewing their authenticity or in returning them to the long-excluded genuine sons of the Millet [nation]' (Taşkın 2008: 55). Hence, the AKP's claim to unite the nation with its own state was limited to having the state conquered by the supposedly genuine representatives of the Sunni Muslim and Turk *millet*. Having defeated the military on the political battleground, the AKP then attempted to gain control of the other apparatuses of the so-called tutelary regime, including the presidency and YÖK after the presidential elections. However, harder work was needed to gain control of the high judicial organs. This was achieved through the constitutional amendments concerning the Constitutional Court and High Council of Judges and Public Prosecutors, passed in the 12 September 2010 referendum, which opened the way for the executive (both the government and the presidency) to exert control over these juridical apparatuses and ensure their takeover by pro-AKP cadres (Akça 2010c; Atikcan and Öğe 2012: 9).

Thus, the AKP's main concern was conquering the state apparatuses by a new neoliberal-conservative elite group rather than reforming the authoritarian state form. In this sense, the AKP's understanding of democracy fails to include a structural democratic transformation of the relationship between state and society, politics and society, and between various groups in society (Çınar 2008: 122). Many critical analyses of neoliberalism have long emphasised that the real practice of the politics of neoliberalism has been the invalidation of democracy and the de-politicisation of politics (Munck 2005; Bonefeld 2006). In particular, the technocratisation of economic and social policy issues, the policing of dissident voices through securitisation and penalisation have contracted the political sphere. The structural tendency of neoliberalism has been towards an authoritarian state form that the dominated classes cannot penetrate. As under-lined above, through its civilianisation reforms, the AKP certainly dismantled the military-centred Neoliberal National Security State. Unfortunately, however, it substituted it with a police and judiciary-centred security state form. Although the AKP government has always claimed to be establishing a balance between security and freedoms, it gives priority to the former as the precondition for democracy with its rights and freedoms. In other words, security has been at the centre of the AKP's political and governing rationality. However, as Neocleous remarks, such seemingly liberal claims about the need to balance security and liberty have always severely restricted freedoms, and provided 'illiberal justifi-cations for a range of extreme and dangerous security measures' (Neocleous 2008: 12). This has been the case for the AKP period in Turkey too.

A new state form has emerged under the AKP period, at the centre of which now stand the police and the judiciary in place of the military. This new authoritarian state form has been constructed through a series of legal changes, particularly after 2005. In 2005, the new Penal Code redefined terror crimes in a way that included many legitimate political and social protest acts, while special courts for serious crimes (Özel Yetkili Mahkemeler) replaced the old State Security Courts. A very broad range of crimes have been included within the competence of exceptional trial processes. For example, changes in the Anti-Terror Law of 2006 defined 50 crimes that were previously listed under the Penal Code as terror crimes if 'they are committed as acts of a terrorist organisation'. These legal changes give extraordinary discretionary power to specially authorised prose-cutors. With these changes, a penal system has emerged that creates a huge state of exception. The latter allows the police and the judiciary to work with specific reference to the idea of an 'enemy' as if they are at war (İnancı 2011). Terrorism is the key to this state of exception in that it is not the act itself but the person acting that is punished. Thus, Penal Code article 220/6 defines a terrorist as follows: 'even if a person is not a member of a terrorist organisation, if he acts in the name or in favour of the terrorist organisation, he will be treated as a terrorist'. Similarly, the definitions of terror and terrorist in the Anti-Terror Law are so broadly defined that a very broad range of issues, actors and acts may be deliberately and arbitrarily treated as involving terror or terrorists (Göktaş 2012).

This new form of state of exception makes a distinction between the 'acceptable' citizen and the terrorist, with the latter deemed to fall within the scope of an exceptional legal order. Besides socialists and Kurds, who have always been defined as 'internal enemies', now the Kemalist elites (civil and military bureaucrats, journalists, academic scholars etc.) are also treated as enemies of the state. The key point here is that the decision about who will be seen as citizen or terrorist is now directly taken by the 'sovereign', to use Agamben's term (Agamben 1998). In Turkey, this sovereign is currently the AKP government, the police and judiciary, who are, to an important extent, under the control of either the party or the allied Fethullah Gülen community (Ertekin 2011; Özsu and

Ertekin 2013; Şık 2011, 2012). Political crimes have been replaced by the term terror and terrorist so that, on the one hand, it links itself to a 'political' activity, hence making politics appear to be something bad, while on the other hand, it delegitimises various political acts as if they were violent (Ertekin 2012).

There is no doubt that, after 12 September 1980, the military regime and the subsequent Neoliberal National Security State of the 1990s used the judiciary to implement the political decisions of the militarist-authoritarian state's elites against the social and political opposition (especially, Kurdish, Islamist and radical leftist movements, but also the labour and student movements) and as an obstacle to democratic politics. Indeed, during the first AKP government's early years, the judiciary continued to play the same role against the AKP itself (Hale and Özbudun 2010: 74–75). However, especially during the second half of the AKP period, the judiciary has become a direct actor rather than a mere implementer. In this new neoliberal penal state, politics has become 'judicialised' once again, with so-called 'political crimes' criminalised as terrorist acts and, most importantly, to cite Agamben (1998) again, the political sphere has been dominated by 'the criminalisation of the political adversary'. That is, the whole range of social and political opposition to the AKP, be it Kemalist-nationalist, socialist left or Kurdish, is constructed as part of terrorist organisations and activities against the state, which the AKP now identifies with itself. Many trials were opened by the special serious crimes courts, known variously as *Ergenekon, OdaTV, Devrimci Karargah and KCK* (Kurdistan Communities Union). The lack of a separate judicial police force has also resulted in an increase in the discretionary power of the police forces, allowing the latter to dominate the prosecutors rather than vice versa. Consequently, police reports are reproduced almost identically in prosecutors' indictments, which are also based on clearly political analyses and evaluations (İnanıcı 2012). This juridico-political structure has severely damaged freedoms of the press, speech, assembly and association in Turkey.

The police forces, too, have been at the centre of this new authoritarian state form through the function of social control. The neoliberal restructuring of the Turkish police force in line with global developments has created a new state apparatus appropriate for policing the poor and dissidents (Berksoy 2010, 2012). This represents a transition from 'a post- to a pre-crime society', in which 'the pre-crime logic of security aims at forestalling risks and preventing that which has not yet occurred and may never do so' (Zedner 2007: 262). As the strategic plan for 2009–2013 of the Turkish police forces states: 'The aim is to increase the capacity to dissuade those with the intention to commit a crime' (Berksoy 2012: 82). The idea of proactive policing introduced by the neoliberal security paradigm, aims to survey, control and passify the potential criminal rather than find and punish the actual criminal (Gönen 2012). Analysis of the professional socialisation of police officers shows that their professional education defines social protest as the irrational, emotional, savage and destructive, instinct-oriented acts of the masses, who should be treated as the enemy as if in a war (Uysal 2012). This justifies the use of force to repress any collective protest. Differentiating the so-called terrorist from the citizen is now the responsibility of the new sovereigns, namely the government, the judiciary, and the police. As the terrorist is seen as 'bare life' in Agamben's (1998) sense, the use of force and punishment becomes the main governing rationality for policing dissident and oppositional forces.

Repressing the Social and Political Opposition

On the one hand, democracy is about 'juridically formalised conditions', including popular sovereignty based on free elections, 'legal freedoms of speech, conscience, assembly, association and the press, backed by the rights under the law and freedom from arrest without trial' (Eley 2007: 182). In Turkey, these conditions have been undermined by the police and judiciary-centred neoliberal security state constructed and endorsed by the AKP in which an anti-democratic parliamentarian regime currently dominates. On the other hand, as historical experience shows, democracy and democratisation are also, even mainly, about the expansion of democratic capacities to all social classes and groups through their own autonomous collective actions, through social and economic conflicts and struggles, through popular mobilisations of unusual intensity and scale (Eley 2007: 184, 200). The AKP's neoliberal-conservative populism has failed here too in that, when confronted with collective and popular protests, it has opted for repressive measures.

This situation is the combined result of neoliberalism and the Turkish right-wing populism's monolithic view of the national will. The policies of neoliberalism are based on the contraction of the political sphere and the exclusion of the dominated social classes and groups when they act through their own autonomous will and organisations. Neoliberal populism has manufactured consent for neoliberal capitalism by gaining the passive consent of the masses without actively mobilising them. As Weyland (2001: 16) notes, neoliberal populism is 'less institutionalised', 'adopts a more anti-organisational stance, reaches followers in the private sphere, and depends on the confidential responses of individual citizens, not on collective manifestations by the people in the public sphere'. Like Turkish right-wing populism, the AKP's neoliberal-conservative populism is based on a chain of equivalence between democracy, the will of the nation, the will of the electoral majority, the will of the party in government and the will of the AKP's leader. According to the political rationality of this chain of equivalence, any other voices other than that of the party in power, its leader and its supporters are deemed as not part of the national will and hence not worthy of democratic consideration. The result has been a very monolithic understanding of the national will and a majoritarian understanding of democracy. Even those scholars who are not radically critical of the AKP, such as M. Hakan Yavuz, have noted the problem of its identification of the 'moral majority' with Sunni-Hanafi Muslims:

> While the AKP believes that it represents the values of 'the nation', it has not still developed a political discourse recognising and protecting the differences that were silenced in its abstracted view of the nation . . . what the party understands from 'the nation' is restricted to the Hanafi-Turkish element and the 'demands' introduced by the party are also limited to those of the Hanafi-Turks. (Yavuz 2004)

In fact, the AKP's 'conservative democrat' approach does recognise differences at the level of society but denies the power relations between them by claiming their harmonious unity' (Çınar 2008: 122; AK Parti 2012: 5). Thus, according to Erdoğan, 'the biggest damage one can cause to this country is to bring our differences to the political level', which helps explain why the AKP 'reproduces Kemalism's distaste for "politicisation"', while rejecting the state's tutelage over the political class' (Çınar 2008: 122). Unlike the previous authoritarian state and ideology, which denied the existence of social differences, the AKP accepts their existence (for instance, ethnic and religious identities) but not their presence at the political level, since it sees itself as the only legitimate representative of the national will. This results in 'single actor pathology' whereby the AKP sees and presents itself as the only actor of democratisation and provider of democratic solutions to the ossified problems of the country.

At each critical juncture, the AKP's populist political strategy has represented legitimate political adversaries as inner enemies, imposing a folk devil image that suppresses the potential of the nation. For instance, during the referendum campaign on constitutional amendments in 2010, the 'coalition of evil' included opposition political parties, the media, PKK, and so on. As Erdoğan saw it:

> CHP opposes the constitutional amendments. MHP does as well. So does the BDP. Some media institutions are opposed to these amendments. The gangs, which hope to benefit from darkness, oppose them. The elite, who rely on the status quo, oppose a 'yes' vote, as does the terrorist organisation [PKK]. What could be more evident? CHP, MHP, BDP, YARSAV [the Union of Judges and Prosecutors], and the terrorist organisation all came together against the people who say 'yes'. Can Turkey benefit from such a coalition? This is the question. These groups can never agree on any issue in Turkey. They run away from democracy and freedom. However, they agreed to oppose the amendments that will enlarge the people's horizons. This is a coalition of evil. (*Hürriyet*, 1 August 2010, quoted in Dinçşahin 2012: 638)

Another example comes from the presidential election crisis of 2007. In response to mass protests against Abdullah Gül's candidacy, Erdoğan stressed the primacy of the electoral majority, presenting Gül as the candidate of the *millet* rather than the tutelary elite bloc: 'The Assembly will have the final say, and the decision of our Assembly will be the decision of our nation' (quoted in Dinçşahin 2012: 630), referring to the heart of the nation (*Sine-i millet*). Drawing on the Democrat Party's right wing populist discourse of the 1950s, Erdoğan stated, 'We first started the process of "enough, the nation has the last word"; now we say "enough, the nation will make the decision"' (quoted in Dinçşahin 2012: 634). This time, Erdoğan constructed a power bloc that included the Constitutional Court, the military, the current president, the Council of Higher Education, CHP and NGOs organising the republican rallies as the enemies of the 'millet' (Dinçşahin 2012: 632).

The AKP's authoritarian populism clearly reveals itself in its distaste for the organised opposition groups, without limiting itself to expected movements like the working class, women or environmentalists, but in some cases even targeting bourgeois organisations that do not comply with the AKP's views. For instance, again during the referendum campaign in 2010, the government put enormous pressure on such NGOs to express their support for the amendments. For instance, TÜSİAD, the association of the big bourgeoisie in Turkey, had some reservations about the changes concerning the judiciary. Erdoğan's reaction was that 'those who remain neutral today, on an issue related to the national benefit, will be neutralised tomorrow' (*Radikal*, 18 August 2010).

There is no doubt that one of the main targets of this authoritarian populism has been the labour movement. On the one hand, the AKP seems to adopt the politics of toleration in order to regulate or repress dissent, thereby leading to the de-politicisation or passivity of the working class. This politics of tolerance is motivated by the idea of order and peaceful coexistence and by the disassociation of subjects from their political struggle. Thus, the AKP's politics of toleration is a means to produce a docile working-class subject, aimed at subsuming labour under the category of the poor through a policy of public philanthropy by transferring funds to the poor through increased public expenditure (Eğilmez 2012: 3–4, 8). However, dissident voices among the working class, which cannot be governed through such policies of toleration and neoliberal social policies, are repressed. For instance, the May Day struggles of 2007, 2008 and 2013 over reclaiming İstanbul's Taksim square as a historical and symbolic place is a case in point. In every year, the attempts by the working class to gather were harshly repressed by the police, with Erdoğan's statements making clear the AKP's approach to the working class: 'The end of the world comes when the tail leads the head' (*Ayakların baş olduğu yerde kıyamet kopar*) (*Radikal*, 22 April 2008). The AKP attempted to prevent the politicisation of labour through the May Day protests by turning the day into an official holiday for labour and solidarity in 2009, before revoking the 33-year-old ban on Taksim square May Day meetings in 2010. Currently, however, a recently started urban restructuring project in Taksim is being used to justify a permanent ban on collective protests in Taksim square.

A final example may be given concerning agricultural producers. In June 2006, nut producers protested about the government's unresponsive attitude when market prices fell below cost prices, particularly the stance of the then Minister of Finance, Kemal Unakıtan, whose son was a nut trader. Around 100,000 producers occupied a main highway for eight hours in a spontaneous and non-radical protest in support of their demands. Erdoğan's reaction was to claim, 'this is an act in order to vilify the government and many illegal organisations participated in this protest . . . Once again, as it was the case in Diyarbakır, women and children were put on the road. They held the traffic up. Nobody has the right to aggrieve the citizens for 8–9 hours' (*Hürriyet*, 2 August 2006).

The same repressive politics can be observed concerning identity politics. It should be underlined once again that, unlike the classical Turkish nationalist-statist approach, which denies the existence of cultural identity differences, the AKP has accepted their existence at a societal level while denying their autonomous politicisation in any way that it cannot control as the self-appointed sole representative of the nation. Thus, under the AKP, Sunni-Hanefi Muslims, especially the political and cultural elites, have become integrated into the political, economic and cultural echelons, but autonomous civil society organ-isations are not welcomed. Sunni-Hanefi middle-class elites participate in the decision-making processes through GONGOs (government-oriented non-governmental organisations) rather than relatively autonomous NGOs. As to other cultural identity groups such as Alevis and the Roma, the AKP also followed policies of recognition, launching a series of reform initiatives (*açılım paketleri*) with workshops that influenced governance strategy having a central role. However, the AKP did not allow autonomous organisations of these identity groups to represent them, preferring instead to co-opt pro-AKP organisations. Like the Ottoman *millet* system, the AKP's policies of recognition are based on a hierarchical and asymmetric relationship between the dominant Sunni-Hanefi-Turkish Muslims and other identity groups (see Yalçınkaya 2009).

There is no doubt that the Kurdish question lies at the heart of any democ-ratisation debate in Turkey. It is not possible here to present a detailed analysis of the development of this question under AKP rule (see Çandar 2009; Yavuz and Özcan 2006; Musluk 2010). Having both internal and external political aspects, trapped in power politics complicated by tactics, strategies and conjunctural moments, the Kurdish question during the AKP era has changed dynamically. Certainly, the AKP's political attitudes have been different from those of previous governments that based their policies on a politics of denial. Instead, the AKP has adopted the politics of recognition by accepting the existence of the Kurdish question, though without accepting the politicisation of this issue. Thus, once again, the AKP's acceptance of societal differences is undermined by its rejection of their politicisation in the name of Turkey's national unity and indivisibility (AK Parti 2012: 5, 24). The AKP's policy on the Kurdish question has been consistently based on a dual strategy that differentiates between the 'good Kurd' and the 'bad Kurd'. Good Kurds were seen as citizens and part of the AKP's *millet* to the extent that they shared Sunni-Muslim identity. In other words, the AKP promoted religious identity through concrete policies to strengthen religious identity at the expense of Kurdish ethnic identity as a tool to depoliticise the ethno-political question. In addition, for the good Kurds, the AKP has promoted various legal reforms, especially within the context of EU membership and the Kurdish opening, which the AKP later renamed the *Milli Birlik ve Kardeşlik Projesi* (National Unity and Brotherhood Project). However, such reforms fell a long way short of meeting the demands of the Kurdish social and political movement.

Meanwhile, the AKP has attempted to eliminate the bad Kurds, which includes not only the armed branch of the Kurdish movement, i.e. PKK, but also all the politicised elements of the Kurdish movement from legal political parties to trade unionists. In other words, the 'pathology of the single actor' is manifested here too. As in the other issues discussed above, due to its monolithic and majoritarian understanding of the national will, the AKP labels any other political actor concerning the Kurdish question as dividing the national will. Two main policies resulted from this approach that determined the AKP's political attitude towards the bad Kurds. The first one was its use of classical nationalist rhetoric and its support of lynching attempts. For example, following protests by Kurdish people against the prime minister during his visit to Diyarbakır in November 2008, Erdoğan's reaction was: 'We said one nation, one state, one motherland. Those who oppose to this may go anywhere they want' (*Radikal*, 3 November 2008). Concerning attempted lynchings of Kurds by Turks in many cities, the prime minister supported them as the legitimate reaction of citizens against terrorists. For instance, following one such incident on 6 April 2005, just after the Kurdish spring festival of Newroz, Prime Minister Recep Tayyip Erdoğan declared that 'the sensitivity of the people is very important. When their national sensitivity is touched upon, the reaction to this will be different. Please, nobody should abuse this' (*Milliyet,* 8 April 2005). Similarly, after the 2006 Newroz protests, in which the police harshly intervened, Erdoğan said: 'even if they are children or women, whoever they be, our security forces will make the necessary intervention'. The AKP's second main policy has been the trials of KCK activists and cadres of the Kurdish social and political movement. The AKP was aiming to eliminate the Kurdish political movement before entering any peace negotiations. The so-called KCK trials started in April 2009, just after the local elections in which the Kurdish political movement defeated the AKP in Kurdish cities. By the beginning of 2013, around 8,000 activists of the Kurdish movement, among them politicians, elected mayors, trade unionists, journalists, NGO managers and activists, and academicians were in jail on remand, and their trials still continue. The current so-called peace negotiations and initiatives by the AKP government are run to a great extent non-publicly, still aiming to by-pass the Kurdish political movement. Thus, as with other issues, it seems that the AKP's neoliberal-conservative populism has failed to expand the political sphere in the context of Kurdish question too. Rather, it has tried to depoliticise the issue and eliminate any actors who wish to politicise it. In short, an anti-political political stand has appeared regarding identity politics.

Conclusion

After almost two decades of crisis of political hegemony under neoliberal capitalism, the AKP could manufacture an expanded hegemony on the basis of neoliberal, conservative and authoritarian populism. It revitalised the neoliberal hegemony by articulating religious conservatism and neoliberalism, and could win succeeding elections with increasing electoral and popular support. However, hegemony is never absolute and complete but always incomplete and partially fixed, hence open to contestation. As Geoff Eley and Keith Nield (1980: 269) note:

> hegemony is not a fixed and immutable *condition* . . . but is an institutionally negotiable *process* in which the social and political forces of contest, breakdown and transformation are constantly in play . . . [Hegemony is] a *process* of class relations in which concrete and determinate struggles for cultural, economic and political power or jurisdiction represent the decisive terrain of specific historical analysis.

This is also valid for the AKP's expanded hegemony. There are several explicit or implicit fissures regarding the AKP's hegemonic project. To start with, even though the AKP's economic performance has been successful in terms of economic growth and expansion in the context of 'regulatory and social neo-liberalism', Turkish economy has its own structural weaknesses such as large current account deficits and high dependency on external short-term capital flows (Öniş 2012). Hence, a global crisis of capitalism or a less favourable global economic environment would have important negative effects on Turkey's economic performance. This may, on the one hand, break the unity of the dominant classes and trigger the intra-class cleavages such as those between the big versus medium- and small-scale bourgeoisie, between those capital groups with a more openly Islamic conservative identity and more organic relations with the AKP and urban-based, more secular, capital groups. On the other hand, a severe economic crisis may trigger an important increase in unemployment and would also have negative effects on the redistributive capacity of the AKP's neoliberal populism, which would mean a loss of hegemonic capacity for dominated classes. Such an economic crisis may also negatively affect important parts of urban middle classes, some of which would face unemployment, proletarianisation, and loss of consumption capacity. The world economic crisis in 2008 produced almost all of these effects, as a result of which the only elections in which AKP lost votes have been the local elections in spring 2009. In addition, such a moment of crisis may mobilise different fractions of the working class and lower middle class which are already affected by the ravages of neoliberal policies such as informal, unsecure, flexible conditions of work, commodification of public services and urban areas.

The second important fissure may result from the combination of authoritarianism and conservatism in the AKP. The AKP's neoliberal and conservative populism is authoritarian rather than democratic. As Gamble characterises such an approach: 'It is populist because it draws upon popular discontent with many aspects' of the preceding state form 'to win support for a radical right programme. It is authoritarian because in the implementation of its programme it further increases the central power of the state and weakens opposition to it' (Gamble 1988: 183). After the referendum for constitutional changes in September 2010 and the electoral victory in June 2011, AKP, which totally controlled the state apparatuses, intensified the authoritarian policies which had already come to the front after the 2007 general elections. The AKP's authoritarian populism does not accept any social, political and even individual opposition or critic as legitimate. It rather blames them as being not part of the national will, being an attack to the national will, if not terrorist acts. In addition, the AKP's majoritarian understanding of the national will and its capacity to control the state apparatus have pushed the party to be more daring in transforming the daily life in its own mirror image, in line with religious conservatism through such policies as the restrictive regulation on the sale and consumption of alcoholic beverages, anti-abortion regulations, promotion of childbirth and the injection of courses of religion into the educational system. Such conservative and authoritarian policies have already started to estrange urban, secular, more liberal-oriented population groups over whom the AKP could establish its hegemony before. Especially, urban lower (but also upper) middle classes, who feel themselves culturally, economically and politically excluded because of conservative and authoritarian policies, form an important point of fissure concerning the AKP's hegemony.

Last but not least, the fate of the Kurdish question forms one of the most important points of fissure for the AKP's hegemonic project since the Kurdish movement, with its social, political, and armed branches, is the most organised and powerful oppositional actor of the country. In addition, the fate of the Kurdish question is also very critical for the AKP's ambitious neo-Ottomanist imperial strategy in the Middle East within the framework of US neo-imperialism. To the extent that the AKP continues to develop policies within the framework of single actor pathology by bypassing and eliminating the Kurdish movement, this may trigger re-militarisation of the Kurdish question, which will hence affect the balance of forces to an important extent.

NOTES

1 For a source in English to follow the military's perception, see General Secretariat of the National Security Council (1982).

2 For a more detailed definition of Turkish right-wing populism, see below in the section on the AKP.

3 CHP came second, winning 20 per cent of the votes. Since no other political party crossed the 10 per cent national threshold required to gain a seat in the Parliament, the AKP took a disproportionate *two-thirds* of the seats.

4 For inspiring and useful sources to understand the AKP's hegemonic project see Yıldırım (2009), Tuğal (2009), Cizre (2008a), Dinçşahin (2012), Şen (2010), Taşkın (2008), Öniş (2012), Uzgel and Duru (2009), Ataay and Kalfa (2009), Sümer and Yaşlı (2010) and Doğan (2010).

CHAPTER TWO

State and Capital in Turkey During the Neoliberal Era

Ahmet Bekmen

The well-known Trilateral Commission Report of 1975 starts with the following question: 'Is political democracy, as it is exists today, a viable form of government for the industrialised countries of Europe, North America and Asia?' (Crozier, Huntington and Watanuki 1975: 2). In response to this rhetorical question, the report suggested calling the crisis in these societies a state of 'ungovernability.' Against left-wing explanations based on various conceptualisations, such as 'the fiscal crisis', 'the legitimacy crisis' or 'structural inequality', the conservative attack has redefined the issue by reducing it to the conflict between the capacities of democratic governments and the increasing demands of democratic societies. This was a strategic response since it implicitly proposed a new political agenda with the aim of cutting existing forms of relationship between political 'supply and demand'. Hence, what underlies this approach is a class struggle between the political claims of labour and capital with regard to their different strategies of reproduction (Offe 1984).

This political agenda required a new framework to reconfigure both relations between labour and capital and intra-capital relations; and it was the state itself that was supposed to intervene to make this possible, specifically through restructuring its own internal architecture (Jayasuriya 2001a). Poulantzas conceptualised the earliest stage of this transformation as the constitution of 'authoritarian statism', arguing that authoritarian statism implied 'intensified state control over every sphere of socio-economic life; combined with radical decline of the institutions of political democracy; and with draconian and multiform curtailment of so-called 'formal' liberties, whose reality is being discovered now that they are going overboard' (Poulantzas 2000: 203–204). However, it is a particular type of authoritarianism that functions completely differently from the well-known practices of fascism, military dictatorship and bureaucratic authoritarianism. Rather than direct repression, though it may be employed from time to time as in the case of Turkey, authoritarian statism is inclined towards a gradual transformation that has critical effects on the functioning of the liberal democracy by incapacitating political parties, the parliament, the judiciary and some sections of the bureaucracy, and empowering the technocratic-minded elite within the executive branch (Panitch 1994, 1996; Cammack 1998; also see Brown 2003). By transferring the effective usage of state power to the technocratic and administrative domains of government, this rearrangement of the liberal state has rendered the formal procedures of liberal democracy pointless. Thus, contrary to the liberal claims that the neoliberal turn represents the *retreat* of the state, a Poulantzasian conceptualisation of the neoliberal transformation considers it more as a *reshuffling* of the powers employed by various apparatuses of the state.

This chapter explores the peculiar response of state and capital to 'ungovernability' in Turkey that emerged during the 1970s. Although different from the experiences of the Western world in terms of the decisive role of the military regime during the transition period, the neoliberal transformation in Turkey also generated the basics of authoritarian statism. Therefore, this chapter explores the neoliberal attempt to overcome the particular ungovernability of Turkey, by focusing specifically on the shifting relations between state and capital and on the parallel transformation of state power, particularly during the 1980s, 1990s and the era of the Justice and Development Party (AKP) as sub-periods with their own specific features. In contrast to approaches that attribute an autonomous personality to the state, either by overemphasising and theorising the 'unpredictable actions of the patrimonial state' (Buğra 1994a), or by regretting the lack of 'state autonomy' (Öniş 1998), it sticks to a Poulantzasian foundation, which argues that the state is nothing but the condensation of power relations among the classes (Poulantzas 2000: 49–120).

This chapter is based on the assumption that the almost 30-year history of developing a neoliberal hegemony in Turkey reached a state of relative stabilisation during the successive governments of the AKP. This was constituted by building relative unities in two domains of hegemony: providing a wider base of consent among the subordinate classes; and unifying different sections of capital under the premises of a 'sustainable' capital accumulation strategy (Jessop 1990a: 196–220). Regarding the first domain, though undermined partly by the recent urban uprisings (see the postscript in this volume); by successfully articulating its ideological and political tactics, the AKP has gained a popular base among the subordinate classes like that enjoyed by its equivalents in Hungary and Russia.

As for the second domain, one should admit that, in the peculiar Turkish context, 'things are a little bit difficult.' In the theoretical framework of Poulantzas, unity among capital fractions, called the 'power bloc', is constituted on the political level by the political representative or representatives of capital, depending on the conjuncture. It is not a relationship between 'equals', and thus involves contradictions in itself. As Poulantzas puts it,

> (i) the power bloc constitutes a contradictory unity of politically dominant classes and fractions under the protection of the hegemonic fraction; (ii) the class struggle, the rivalry between the interests of these social forces, is constantly present, since these interests retain their specific character of antagonism. (Poulantzas 1978: 239)

Therefore, for the political representative, governing the contradictions among the capital fractions is a constant struggle, but one that must be conducted to ensure the continuity of the hegemonic framework. When the AKP came to power in 2002, it represented more than an ordinary change of governing party. In Turkey, the Islamist political tradition emerged out of power struggles among capital fractions in the 1960s to represent small- and medium-scale capital groups. The AKP eventually became the political representative of this fraction, especially of those that have vigorously grown since the 1990s. Therefore, the AKP's rise to power meant the rise of the claim of this capital fraction on existing power relations. However, integrating them into the power bloc under the hegemony of major capital groups required skillful tactics, both economically and politically. It required tactical economic arrangements since there were, and are, some contradictions between the needs and interests of the capital groups politically represented by the AKP and the hegemonic framework established after the 2001 economic crisis under the hegemony of the large capital. It required political tactics since the integration of the social forces represented by the AKP, into the existing relations of power, required a radical shift with regard to the balances of power within the state, as demonstrated after 2007 by various inner-state clashes, mainly between the civil and military bureaucracy and the AKP. In other words, as 'the ruling classes find their historical unification in the state' (Gramsci 1999: 52), the AKP's mission was to render this unification possible. However, in the political and economic context of Turkey, it was a highly complicated task that necessitated overcoming accumulated and inter-penetrated problems of more than thirty years.

Towards 1980

It would not be an exaggeration to claim that Turkey's modern history was 'reloaded' in the 1960s. Although industrialisation certainly did not start in this era, it deepened thanks to the Import Substitution Industrialisation (ISI) strategy implemented after the 1960 military coup (Keyder 1987: 141–165; Göker 2004). Hence, industrial capital and labour both became more and more effective social-cum-political actors. Similarly, although the dynamics of a modern class society also certainly did not emerge during this era, it became increasingly functional and observable. Parallel to the state's ISI strategy, industrial capital, especially the İstanbul-based conglomerates, while also incorporating large landowners, Anatolian-based middle-scaled enterprises and import merchants, gained prominence to become the central figure of the emerging power bloc. In a country where the ratio of savings remained low, which made investments dependent on public resources and mediation, bureaucratic and political centres of distribution gained crucial importance. Such a configuration easily turns tensions between capital groups and fractions into a political issue, which was exactly what happened in Turkey in the second half of the 1960s. Specifically, the Anatolian-based small- and medium-scale enterprises, by claiming that mostly the large-scale industrialists were benefiting from the incentive measures, built up opposition within the officially recognised leading organisation of capital, namely the Union of Chambers and Commodity Exchanges of Turkey (TOBB). Since TOBB was a crucial power base kept under control by the governing

Justice Party (AP), this opposition immediately became political. Necmettin Erbakan, having been elected TOBB Chairman, but then urged by AP to resign, founded a new party from whose Islamist political line the AKP would later emerge in the 2000s. Meanwhile, İstanbul-based conglomerates separated themselves institutionally from TOBB by founding the Turkish Industry and Business Association (TÜSİAD). As a result of this process, the lines demarcating capital fractions became much clearer.

Towards the end of the 1970s, it became widely accepted that Turkey had reached a state of 'ungovernability'. Due to the combined effects of both the global economic crisis, triggered by the petroleum crisis of 1974, and the internal contradictions of the ISI strategy, Turkey's external debt steadily rose to a level that culminated in a classic debt crisis during the late 1970s and early 1980s. Besides, thanks to the militancy of an increasingly politicised working-class movement and the rise of the revolutionary left, the economic crisis extended into the social and political spheres. Towards the end of the 1970s, the capital bloc, under the leadership of the İstanbul-based conglomerates, now represented by TÜSİAD, had already come to the conclusion that a rupture in terms of both economic and political order was obligatory. A radical strategy to overcome the state of ungovernability was formulated, which would articulate three main patterns of transformation into a consistent hegemonic project: the authoritarian reconstitution of the social and political spheres so as to free both from the dynamics of class struggle; transition to a new strategy of capital accumulation; and restructuring the state power. However, there was no political actor available to reform the system accordingly and simultaneously reproduce consent among the oppressed; that is, to rebuild the hegemony in a new framework. Thus, the crisis turned into a crisis of political representation on the part of the capital bloc (Ozan 2012).

Given this lack, the required radical transformation started through the successive interventions of two different non-political actors, the first one being the institutions of emerging global capitalism. In 1980, with an inflation rate of 107 per cent and an unbearable foreign debt burden, Turkey was forced into accepting the loan conditions of the IMF and the World Bank. Through the performance criteria of the IMF in the stand-by programme of 1980 and the Structural Adjustment Loans implemented with the decisive participation of the World Bank, Turkey's structural adjustment process was almost completely determined by the policies of these international institutions. The loans were conditional on various measures that constituted the core of the adjustment process, such as implementing incentives in order to increase exports on labour-intensive sectors like the textile, garment and food industries, rather than durable consumer goods; liberalising the import regime; favouring private investment at the expense of public investment; rationalising public investment; decreasing agricultural subsidies; reforming the State Economic Enterprises and decreasing resource transfers to these Enterprises; reforming the tax system and reforming the state's personnel regime by introducing a contractual personnel system. However, in order to cope with the high rate of inflation, the short-term policy was to reduce domestic demand by restraining wages while removing controls on prices, interest rates and exchange rates. Thus, it was a neoliberal restructuring plan *par excellence*. On 24 January 1980, this plan, starting with a currency devaluation of 32 per cent, was implemented according to a plan prepared by the then Prime Ministry Undersecretary, Turgut Özal, and accepted generally as a milestone in the transition to neoliberalism in Turkey (Sönmez 1980).

However, the issue of 'the political actor' was still unresolved since none of the existing political parties had the capacity to put into practice the policies proposed by the IMF and World Bank. At this point, there was the second non-political intervention when the military took power in a coup on 12 September 1980. While the 1960 military coup had made the transition to the ISI strategy possible, the 1980 coup secured the conditions for the transition to neoliberalism by crushing both the working-class movement and the political organisations of the revolutionary left. During the military regime, 600,000 people were taken into custody, 200,000 people were prosecuted and thousands were tortured. The constitution dictated by the military regime was approved in 1982 through a referendum conducted in a strictly controlled environment.

The 1980s: The Era of Neoliberal Centralism

The 1982 Constitution, by strictly restricting the political sphere through the restructuring of political and social institutions, and by significantly strengthening executive power as a 'strong state and authoritarian administration' has delineated the limits of politics in Turkey for more than three decades. However, the designers of the constitution failed to predict that another power centre of authoritarian democracy, the neoliberal technocracy, would gradually become dominant within the new framework established by the constitution itself. With the unexpected victory of Turgut Özal and his then newly founded party, the Motherland Party (ANAP), in the first election after the coup in 1983, the neoliberal agenda found its needed political actor. Özal, who considered himself a technician rather than a politician, played a decisive role in the neoliberal transformation. The most striking feature of the Özal era was the further strengthening of the Prime Ministry, surrounded by an inner cabinet group, composed of Özal's 'old team' from the bureaucracy, and some new bureaucrats responsible for economy, mostly young economists working at the IMF, the World Bank, and various American universities. Working with this team, Özal increasingly bypassed parliament, the traditional bureaucracy and even his own cabinet and party, by relying on this highly effective central power within the body of the state. This narrow circle of economic governance was provided with extraordinary powers, not only at the expense of legislative and judicial power, but also other components of executive power. The main underlying reason was to eliminate or bypass all procedural and institutional hindrances that might slow down the neoliberal reform process (Aksoy 1995; Bekmen 2003).

Neoliberal centralisation involved restructuring the state from above, realised through *ad hoc* mechanisms (Sönmez, Ü. 2011a), such as governmental decrees and extra-budgetary funds, and by new institutions, such as the Undersecretariat of Foreign Trade and Treasury. Governmental decrees issued formally by the cabinet, after having been prepared by Özal's close circle of inner-cabinet comrades and bureaucrats, became the most practical administrative tool to bypass parliamentary procedures. In fact, Özal's government was not the first to do this: beginning in the mid-1970s and accelerating after the 1980 coup, governance by decrees had become a common policy in Turkey, and between 1976 and 1993, 426 governmental decrees were promulgated. This frequent use of decrees was significant in the neoliberal restructuring of the state apparatus since almost all aimed at reconstituting public institutions, reorganising administrative procedures and changing laws regarding civil servants. In this regard, the formation of the Undersecretariat of Foreign Trade and Treasury, affiliated to the Prime Ministry, was definitely the most critical bureaucratic alteration in this top-down restructuring (see Batur 1998). The main priority of this new institution was to eliminate barriers to the government's neoliberal economic growth project, especially the Ministry of Finance with its authority to audit the fiscal domains of the administration. Due to his experience as a bureaucrat in the 1960s and 1970s, Özal viewed this ministry as an obstacle to rapid economic growth because of its strict commitment to the idea of '*hazine menfaati*' (the benefits of the Treasury). Through the new Undersecretariat, the government institutionally divided two key aspects of the state's fiscal power: while the Ministry of Finance remained responsible for collecting public revenues, the Undersecretariat took over authority to organise public expenditure. Thus, the centralised neoliberal core took a crucial opportunity to gain autonomy from the existing control mechanisms within the state apparatus, in this case the Ministry of Finance. After dispersing the ministry's previously unified authority over the budget, Özal's managerial team also intervened in the structure of the budget, thereby minimising the authority of the traditional bureaucratic centre. This was achieved through the development of an extra-budgetary fund system, which essentially meant creating a parallel budget directly under the control of the government. The revenues collected by its funds were exempted from normal administrative and judicial control mechanisms, such as those of the Parliament or the High Court of Account. In other words, by this system the government gained the right to transfer public revenues directly into funds functioning outside the legal and administrative boundaries of the budget. By the end of this decade, the ratio of fund system revenues to the revenues of the consolidated budget had reached 57 per cent. What is more, 75 per cent of the total fund resources fell under the direct control of the Prime Ministry (Oyan and Aydın 1987).

Thus, two authoritarian centres of power, namely the military rulers and the neoliberal managerial bureaucracy, became the basis on which the neoliberal economic growth strategy relied. Primarily, it was an export-led growth strategy based on the political-cum-economic repression of labour. Following the 1980 coup, the military government prohibited collective bargaining until 1984. Although the more moderate union, TÜRK-İŞ (Confederation of Turkish Trade Unions), was allowed to survive after the coup, albeit under rigid control, all activities of the more militant union, DİSK (Confederation of Progressive Trade Unions of Turkey), were suspended until it was reinstated in 1992. Under these anti-labour conditions, Turkish capitalists were being rapidly incorporated into global capitalism through the liberalisation of the commodity trade, while the transition to financial liberalisation was realised at a controlled pace. Through low-value-added sectors such as textile and garment, Turkey's manufacturers became integrated into global production chains as sub-contractors. Both the political repression and the increasing level of sweatshop-style working conditions prompted by this integration resulted in a further weakening of the labour movement. Although it seemed as if it was coming to life again at the end of 1980s, it would never be able to reclaim its effective and militant position of the pre-1980 period (see Doğan's contribution to this volume).

In addition to the anti-labour policies of this era, capitalists of various scales also benefited from neoliberal policies of 'non-statist protectionism' introduced by the managerial bureaucracy. The neoliberal growth strategy was based on supporting the export-oriented segments of capital through various types of export incentives, such as tax rebates and preferential loans and credits. In this regard, 1980 was not a rupture but a change in terms of the mechanism of rent-seeking. By eliminating bureaucratic control mechanisms over the rent distribution process and constituting its own institutions and mediations, the neoliberal government, specifically the managerial team, became itself the centre of rent-creation and distribution.[1] The above-mentioned Undersecretariat of Foreign Trade and Treasury, with its extra-ordinary powers, both *de facto* and *de jure*, became the centre of this policy. Major industrialists quite easily oriented themselves to the policies of neoliberal centralism. In particular, those con-glomerates that included 'Foreign Trade Companies' in their organisational structures, whose legal basis was established during the first year of the structural adjustment programme in 1980, benefited greatly from export incentives (Öniş 1998: 217–238). Large capital groups like *Koç* and *Sabancı*, having experienced a decrease in profits in the late 1970s, made a rapid recovery to become the leading beneficiaries of the new era (Sönmez 1992).

In this period, Turkey's exports rose from \$2.9 billion in 1980 to \$12.9 billion in 1989, while its foreign trade volume almost doubled. However, an investment boom did not accompany this quantitative development since these increases resulted from the overuse of industrial capacity that had remained unutilised during the pre-1980 era. Besides, against expectations, neither the older TÜSİAD conglomerates nor the new generation of entrepreneurs of the Özal era invested in the medium- or high-value-added sectors that would result in an industrial upgrade. Instead, they preferred to exploit the cheap labour of low-value-added sectors and make use of export incentives, which also led to a wave of fictitious exports. The export sector was based on labour and resource intensive goods up to a level of 70 per cent, whereas it remained almost totally import-dependent in diversified and high-technology goods. Thus, the 1980s became a period for the consolidation of Turkey's position as a country specialised in labour and resource intensive consumer and intermediate goods (Köse and Öncü 2000: 84). Meanwhile, although public investment was cut according to the recipes of the neoliberal development strategy, a new capital faction that was supposed to invest in competitive sectors did not appear as predicted. On the contrary, after export incentives were cut due to both the IMF pressure and the implementation of the GATTS regulations, the interest of

Turkey's capital groups turned more heavily towards sectors such as construction, tourism and land speculation.

Thus, Turkey's large-scale capital groups adjusted themselves to the new export-led growth strategy by adopting a more conservative position, instead of a positive and aggressive one that would have increased their global competitiveness. This conservative stand was driven by the need for foreign funding and credit, which has always been a determining factor for the Turkish economy because of the permanently low ratio of both public and private savings in Turkey. Therefore, Turkish capital groups have always had to find foreign funding and credit in order to sustain and develop their business. Towards the end of the 1970s, at a time of rising economic crisis, TÜSİAD became fully convinced that the flow of the foreign funds was bound to the reorientation of the capital accumulation strategy. This conservative position of the private sector was also shared by the economic bureaucracy, one of whose main concerns has always been to keep the country's creditworthiness high in order to sustain budgetary deficits (Yalman 2009: 280). This mutually shared agenda of both capital and the state took on a new shape in the 1990s that paved the way for a particular form of financialisation of the economy.[2]

The 1990s: The Loss of the Vision . . . ?

Despite some elements of unorthodoxy, such as the slow pace of privatisation (Öniş 1998: 183–196), Turkey's 'actually existing neoliberalism' of the 1980s fits into the context of the then current neoliberal agenda. In terms of the anti-labourism and neoliberal centralisation of state power, the Özal government engaged in real shock therapy, as did its counterparts elsewhere (see Gamble 1994; Petras and Vieux 1994; Munck 1997; Fernandez and Mommen 1996; Weyland 1996; Teichman 1997; Williams 2002). However, the same cannot be claimed for the 1990s. Due both to the reconfiguration of the political sphere and the peculiar financialisation of its economy, Turkey's articulation to the new course of the neoliberal agenda that emerged in 1990s was delayed by about a decade. According to Peck and Tickell's classic definition, the transition from the 1980s to the 1990s represented a shift from a negative agenda 'preoccupied with active destruction and discreditation of Keynesian-welfarist and social-collectivist institutions (broadly defined)' to a constitutive one 'focused on the purposeful construction and consolidation of neoliberalised state forms, modes of governance, and regulatory relations' (2002: 384). Throughout the 1990s, Turkey stayed out of this updating.

Economic liberals, in praising the Özal era, call the 1990s 'the lost decade', accusing the then dominant political figures of lacking Özal's vision. However, they simply ignore the fact that Özal's technocratic rule was accompanied by the military regime, and after the relative retreat of this regime in 1987, administering neoliberalism in Turkey was not a matter of vision anymore. In addition to the political turmoil that prevailed throughout the 1990s, the successive economic crises of 1994, 2000 and 2001, with the last two being particularly devastating, crushed the already weak social base of consent for the existing system instituted by Özal. All in all, it would not be an exaggeration to state that the 1990s represent Turkey's second hegemonic crisis, following that of the 1970s.

The transformation of the political sphere turned the 1990s into a catastrophe for those of a moderate neoliberal viewpoint. There were two main dynamics that brought about the unstable conditions for a neoliberal agenda. First, after the political bans following the 1980 coup were lifted as a result of the 1987 referendum, the number of political parties of both the centre-right and centre-left proliferated. Due to the rise of popular opposition and the parallel pro-liferation of political actors, parliamentary politics became relevant again. Second, centrifugal political forces, such as the Kurdish movement and the political Islam, complicated the political sphere throughout the 1990s. In response, national security, in its widest sense, became the priority. Whereas the first dynamic meant that weak, unstable and relatively short-lived coalition governments became the norm for the 1990s, the second one created new opportunities for the security apparatuses of the state to constantly intervene in politics, varying from legal ones, such as the military, to illegal and 'deep' paramilitary forces. On the whole then, the 1990s were an era of dispersal and fragmentation in terms of the use of state power and, consequently, years of a retreat by the managerial bureaucracy.

In fact, this political fragmentation was grounded in the failure of the first wave of the Turkish New Right to establish a wider social base for a stable political hegemony. Towards the end of the 1980s, it became obvious that the accumulation strategy based on the economic and political repression of the working class was no longer sustainable. 'The Spring Actions' of 1989, the first wave of mass actions led by trade unions after the 1980 military coup, were evidence of wider social unease. At the same time, the accumulation strategy was also failing to satisfy big capital 'politically', although its economic satisfaction was unquestionable. That is, although the 1980s allowed the large businesses represented by TÜSİAD to recover, their tensions with the government had been steadily rising due to Özal's ambition to create a new generation of busi-nessmen around him. In this sense, a political figure such as Özal, who enjoyed the almost personal power to control public incentives, represented both an opportunity and a threat for business. Although almost all capital groups benefited individually from these public incentives, gradually, Özal's discri-minatory attitudes and the clientelist relations he set up individually with almost all capital groups became more and more against the general interest of big business. Consequently, some prominent groups in TÜSİAD began to support the new political alternative of the centre-right, DYP (The True Path Party), led by a pre-1980 leader, Süleyman Demirel. In 1991, these two separate pressures, from below and above, respectively labour and business, brought about a new coalition government constituted by DYP and the Social Democratic Populist Party (SHP), ending the so-called Özal vision.

As a matter of fact, from 1988 onwards, negative signals had also been coming from the economy. Beside the social pressures of wage earners, exports and economic growth were both declining. A wage rise of 142 per cent for public workers and an increase in agricultural subvention purchases were two signs of the transition to a neo-populist era within the neoliberal framework (see Boratav, Yeldan and Köse 2000). Increasing domestic purchasing capacity had also prompted production for the domestic market rather than exports, which caused a decrease in export revenues. These double effects, the increase in domestic expenditure and the decrease in revenues, resulted in a public deficit problem that became the central economic issue for the 1990s. Although Özal could have compensated for the deficit through broadening the tax base to include the wealthy classes, he preferred removing all obstacles to the financialisation of the Turkish economy. Foreign exchange controls on capital outflows were removed, and both current accounts and capital accounts were completely liberalised. As a result, the dynamics of hot money flows and associated financial actors increasingly dominated the economy in a vicious circle: procurement of hot money inflows through the combined policy of an overvalued Turkish Lira and high interest rates; ensuring continuous inflows by progressively increasing interest rates, meaning increasingly expensive borrowing; further increasing of the deficit due to overburdening of debt. Thus, a policy introduced to overcome the public deficit resulting from the 'new populism' of the early 1990s turned out to be the main reason for the continued deficit throughout the 1990s (see Cizre-Sakallıoğlu and Yeldan 2000; Balkan and Yeldan 1998).

In fact, contrary to liberal claims that it was the populist distribution policies of the 1990s that caused the economic breakdown at the end of the decade, there was a wide array of business beneficiaries who enjoyed the yields of financialisation throughout the 1990s. At the centre of the 1990s' strategy of non-statist protectionism was the mechanism of resorting to domestic public debt to overcome both the budgetary deficit and external debt. However, in fact, the distinction between 'domestic' and 'external' was somewhat ambiguous. By taking advantage of Turkey's poorly regulated banking system, commercial banks started to buy large amounts of government bonds with high interest rates by borrowing from abroad at lower interest rates. Almost all the commercial banks enjoyed such arbitrage profits throughout the 1990s, and lending expensively to the public by borrowing cheap credits from abroad became the main method of capital accumulation for almost all capital groups. Consequently, by the end of the decade, it was not foreign but domestic debt that predominated within the total public debt: 'while interest payments on domestic debt absorbed less than 20 per cent of tax revenues at the end of the 1980s, this proportion rose steadily throughout the 1990s, exceeding 75 per cent at the end of the decade' (Akyüz and Boratav 2003: 1551–1552). In the 1980s, the main mechanism that business groups had used for exploiting public resources was foreign trade companies; in the 1990s it was commercial banks. Almost every large conglomerate of TÜSİAD, which already dominated the private financial sector, managed to make a killing by founding its own commercial bank. The political environment of the 1990s was helpful in this regard as political assets, based on clientelist relations that were easily established with the partners of the era's unstable and weak coalition governments, helped in obtaining banking licences.

Correspondingly, in the 1990s, the level of manufacturing investment gradually decreased, while phases of economic growth on the eve of the economic crises of both 1994 and 2000/2001 were not due to production and exports, but mainly domestic consumption, and were accompanied by inflation of 90 per cent, and large high foreign trade and budget deficits. Although the above-mentioned mechanisms of financialisation increased the profitability of capital, the production of the surplus value constantly dropped. In fact, the sudden stops and reversals of hot money flow were just triggers for the economic crises Turkey underwent throughout the 1990s. As Oğuz puts it, 'as the productive capacity could not endure the debt burden, all the flows could be reversed at any time. Whatever the triggering factor in each case, this was the structural cause of all the crises in 1994, 1998, 2000 and 2001' (Oğuz 2009: 7; also see Ercan 2003).

When the wave of the globally-experienced economic crisis that first emerged in the Far East and South Eastern Asia in 1997 before hitting Russia in 1998, arrived in Turkey, as a country suffering from unsustainable levels of debt and inflation, it was forced to turn to the IMF again. The 1998 stand-by agreement was so strict that it is correct to define the period of 1998–2008 as the era of the 'different governments and one policy' (Bağımsız Sosyal Bilimciler 2007). However, rather than protecting Turkey from the economic crisis in the making, IMF engagement paved the way for it (see Akyüz and Boratav 2003; Yeldan 2006). First, in November 2000 and then February 2001, Turkey suffered two successive economic crises, with the second being particularly devastating (Aybar and Lapavitsas 2001). By destabilising the coalition government, the catastrophic months of crisis imposed further engagement with the IMF and a new wave of structural adjustments that would transform the scene radically.

The reform process was launched with the recruitment of World Bank expert Kemal Derviş as Minister of Economy. His programme of institutional transition, called the 'Transition to the Strong Economy', was mainly based on Central Bank independence; the integration of independent regulatory institutions into the system, the most important being the Banking Regulation and Supervision Agency; and the re-regulation of public financing and debt management. Independent institutions founded in order to regulate sectors such as tele-communications, energy, and above all banking became the most significant instruments of the second wave of neoliberal regulatory reform in Turkey (Sönmez, Ü. 2011b). Through these institutions, strategically significant sectors were regulated in compliance with global rules and procedures. That is, these institutions were inserted into the regulatory environment of the Turkish state as the local connection points of global regulatory neoliberalism (Jayasuriya 2005; Lee and McBride 2007). Among them, the Banking Regulation and Supervision Agency (BDDK) was the most crucial one. This institution was designed as the institutional basis for the internalisation of the state's financial apparatuses, with 'the important task of analysing and implementing the Basel II accords intended to bring Turkish risk management and capital adequacy standards in line with international norms' (Marois 2011: 181). On the other hand, the independence of the Central Bank meant that the choice of macro-economic approach, based on achieving price stability, was freed from politics to gain a technocratic institutional form (Akçay 2009). Besides, new laws addressing public financing imposed several international standards for public spending on the *modus operandi* of the Turkish state.

The chief characteristic of the reform process was to link Turkey to the main premises of economic constitutionalism[3] by imposing neoliberal discipline[4] on both the institutional and fiscal designs of the state apparatus. In this regard, it should not be forgotten that the 2001 reforms, in the guise of de-centralisation, brought about a particular form of centralisation that is considerably different from that of 1980s. First, by founding new institutions, such as BDDK, the 2001 reforms created powerfully equipped domestic hubs of ultra-centralist regulatory mechanisms, which function on a global level without any interference by domestic actors and politics. Though the policy domains under re-regulation were public in nature, they were pulled out of the debate, depoliticised and bound to the operating rules of global capital. Second, for the sake of global capital flows, the financial apparatuses of the state were further consolidated to keep them solid and isolated. Thus, in Turkey, the 2001 reforms also brought about 'the increasing centralisation of domestic financial authority around the Treasury, and the massive build-up of foreign reserves to ward off foreign capital fears' (Marois 2012: 2). In short, this was a particular form of centralisation, which tended to found powerful institutions of regulation and management centralised around the international standards of neoliberal capitalism (see Scheurman 2008: 29–47; Jayasuriya 2001b).

All the amendments concerning the reform process were put into effect in an extremely technocratic way, sometimes in defiance of the members of the formal government. The relevant laws were enacted without even a proper parliamentary or inner-cabinet debate, let alone any wider societal debate, under Kemal Derviş's motto of '15 laws within 15 days'. The question of the political actor remained irrelevant, at least till the coming elections in 2002, which eliminated from politics almost all those parties that had shared in governing during the economic crisis.[5] In other words, the political sphere that was wiped out by the military coup in 1980, was reshuffled at the beginning of the 2000s, but this time as a consequence of an 'economic coup', so to speak. However, the 2002 election also opened a new era for Turkey in which the existing balances of power were destroyed by a new political actor, namely the AKP.

The AKP Era: *The Prince* Between the Fractions of Capital

A recent report, the Turkish Industrial Strategy Document 2011–2014, prepared by the Ministry of Industry and Trade in conjunction with the representatives of the business, gives the following assessment of Turkey's situation:

> Despite its rapid growth after the crisis in 2001, the Turkish economy falls short of expectations with respect to global competitiveness. According to 2009 data of the World Economic Forum, Turkey ranks 61st among 133 countries on the competitiveness index. Turkey must make improvements in its weakest areas to be able to move upwards on this list. Therefore, first measures to be taken should be in improvements within the labour market, higher education and vocational training, financial markets, health-

care and elementary education, macroeconomic situation and physical infrastructure.

Particularly with the integration of China and India into the global economy, it no longer seems possible for Turkey to be able to rely upon cheap labour to get ahead in the competitiveness. Increasing Turkish competitiveness requires the creation of an efficiently functioning market mechanism, an attractive investment environment and institutionalisation. Companies have to be able to sustain themselves through a highly skilled workforce. Furthermore, revisions must be made to ensure that infrastructure industries can provide qualified and low-priced inputs. (Ministry of Industry and Trade 2010: 12)

The report argues that Turkey's strategic target should be 'becoming the production base of Eurasia in medium and high-tech products'. As this quotation shows, aware of the country's existing quality and structural shortcomings, the new capitalist coalition led politically by the AKP will push for the further deepening of neoliberalisation, especially by inscribing its dynamics further in the social reproduction of labour. This section aims to deal with the nature of this capitalist coalition and the AKP's political role in consolidating it.

As a matter of fact, especially in the second half of the 1990s, almost everyone became aware that a capital accumulation mode based on financial speculation was no longer sustainable. However, to quote a statement used widely during the 2008 crisis, 'as long as the music was playing, they kept on dancing'. After the music stopped in the 2000 crisis before turning into a funeral march in 2001, the puzzling question concerned which social and political forces would support the new economic framework and manage to transform it into a consensus. As it turned out, the dynamics underlying the development of a power base for the new consensus had already been in evidence throughout the 1990s. As the board chairman of *Eczacıbaşı*, one of the biggest capital groups in Turkey, put it:

A while ago, people thought that 'every dog barks in his own yard'. Within the limits of this understanding, having a place in Turkey is enough. After this wave, just a brand and market share in Turkey will not suffice. The rules of the game are changing. If you cannot produce something marketable in Tokyo or New York, it means that you are losing the game. (quoted in Ercan 2009: 49)

Similar sentiments were expressed in 2008 by the board chairman of Sanko, one of the prominent Anatolian-based holdings:

Now, you would say (that I am a textile businessman and what have I got to do with the electricity sector) because everybody sees the issue this way. We are the fifth generation in textile and the first in electricity. For years, dams have been constructed and we just looked at them, but now we become shrewd. Let everybody understand this. (quoted in Ercan 2009: 13)

Such views indicate that the İstanbul-based large capital groups had reached a level of vigour stimulating them to seek markets abroad, and that some sections of the Anatolian bourgeoisie, which had grown steadily throughout the 1990s by articulating to global production chains as sub-contractors, had consolidated their position among capital groups in Turkey.

In this regard, the Custom Union Agreement with European Union (EU) that took effect at the end of 1995 motivated Turkish capital groups to build on their manufacturing base in order to take the advantage of free access to the European market. As of the 2000s, the share of traditional exports like textiles and garments has declined, while the share of medium-technology products, such as motor vehicles, basic metals, and machinery and equipment, has increased to reach 40 per cent of exports. This profound transformation was accompanied by a differentiation among capital groups, particularly after the mid-1990s. Gülten-Karakaş suggests categorising the actors of this differentiation by referring to them as capital fractions of dynamic *versus* primitive accumulation models (Gülten-Karakaş 2008, 2009). Whereas primitives relied completely or heavily on rents derived from banking activities in the 1990s, dynamic groups, while not ignoring the rentier benefits of the banking system, opted for a gradual shift towards reconfiguring their investments by focusing on sustainable and strategic sectors, international markets and partnerships with transnational capital groups. Hence, regulative intervention in 2001 was also about restructuring and disciplining the accumulation patterns of capital groups. Primitives were eliminated after their banks were confiscated by the state. Between 1997 and 2003, 22 banks were confiscated by the relevant state agency – the Savings Deposit Insurance Fund – and then, through merges and acquisitions, they were passed onto the dynamic capital groups and foreign banks. Thus, the economic crisis played its traditional role again by prompting further centralisation of capital thanks to the mediation of the state.

Based on this further centralisation of capital and the new regulatory framework established to consolidate it, post-2001 crisis economic policy was characterised by the following premises:[6]

- tight fiscal policy determined by the IMF with a primary surplus rate of 6.5 per cent in order to reduce public debt;
- anti-inflationary policy conducted by both the government and the independent Central Bank entrusted with the exclusive task of ensuring price stability;
- high interest rates to ensure the inflow of foreign funds; and
- an export-led growth strategy based on private sector initiative to take advantage of existing global conditions providing abundant and relatively cheap foreign funding and credits.

TÜSİAD has been the main supporter of this new 'consensus' established during and after the regulatory reform process. Meanwhile, they gained a strong ally as well. Through constituting partnerships and joint ventures with local capital groups and direct investments that reached a record level in mid-2000, foreign capital, represented by YASED (International Investors Association), took a prominent place within the new configuration of the capital bloc. Despite a slowdown after 2007, due to the next emerging global crisis, foreign direct investments increased rapidly in the mid-2000s, by 65 per cent in 2004, 260 per cent in 2005 and 101 per cent in 2006. This rapid and intriguing increase was closely connected with the the AKP's strong commitment to overcome the unorthodox aspect of Turkish neoliberalism, namely its extremely slow process of privatisation: $35 billion, out of the total privatisation income between 1986 and 2011 of $43 billion, has been acquired during the AKP's period in office, with foreign direct investment constituting 36 per cent of this total income. The prominence of foreign capital increased especially in the banking sector, with global financial capital groups, such as Citibank, HSBC and BNP Paribas, becoming active and important actors in the Turkish banking sector when it was restructured after the crisis. As of 2011, foreign capital share in the sector was 22 per cent, disregarding stock-exchange value, and 41 per cent including stock-exchange value.

Overall, it can be stated that, since the 2001 crisis, the hegemony of financial capital has been consolidated. First of all, the above-mentioned 'cleaning process' left the TÜSİAD bourgeoisie and foreign capital together dominating financial power in Turkey. Besides a considerable share within their total net profit, this domination also provided large capital groups with great power to control the economy. Moreover, thanks to the reconstruction of the banking sector after the 2001 crisis, through the independent Banking Regulation and Supervision Agency, this power is strictly linked to the global regulatory system of finance. Thus, the 2001 regulations enabled Turkey's tight integration into finance-led global capitalism, and this state of integration has beyond doubt been the key factor in overcoming the ambiguities of the 20-year-long attempt to constitute a neoliberal hegemony in Turkey. A solid hegemony should, though, go beyond the needs of the hegemonic capital fraction to first articulate the needs and demands of other capital fractions into the new strategy of capital accumulation, and second to incorporate at least a considerable level of popular consent into the hegemonic project. However, none of the political actors reigning in the 1990s enjoyed a sufficiently high level of political credit to undertake this difficult task. Instead, and in contrast to the case of 1980, the issue of the missing political actor was overcome through the rise of a new political power from the ashes of the Islamist movement.

A Peculiar Formation: Islamic Capital

The AKP, founded officially in 2001 after the split within the ranks of Erbakan's National View Movement, came to power just one year later, in 2002, with 34 per cent of votes in the general elections. None of the political parties of the previous parliament managed to pass the electoral threshold to re-enter parliament, and for the first time since 1960, the parliament comprised only two parties, the AKP and the Republican People's Party (CHP), with a considerable majority for the governing AKP. By then, new economic regulations had mostly been already implemented and, in this 'cleansed' arena, the AKP has been an eager follower of the economic programme introduced after the 2001 financial crisis. However, the AKP's role in constituting the neoliberal hegemony is not restricted to such a submissive role. Rather, the AKP should be viewed both as the outcome and the prompter of this 'passive revolution' (Tuğal 2009) that resulted in the incorporation of the Islamic-conservative masses into the wider neoliberal social project. As a governing party, in addition to its political and ideological advantages and skills, it succeeded in producing and consolidating social consent through various social policies (see Özden in this volume), which is precisely what makes the AKP the most valuable political actor for sustaining neoliberalism.

However, the main social actor of the passive revolution process has been Islamic capital groups. The AKP's coming to power represents their integration into the power bloc, which illustrates the pattern of neoliberal hegemony in Turkey in a very specific way. Defining itself as the 'authentic bourgeoisie' of Turkey, this capital fraction is organised under different business associations, such as MÜSİAD (The Independent Industrialists and Businessmen Association), TUSKON (Confederation of Businessmen and Industrialists of Turkey) and ASKON (Anatolian Lions Businessmen's Association), with MÜSİAD being the leading one (Buğra and Savaşkan 2012; see also Doğan and Durak in this volume). These Islamic business organisations represent enterprises varying in terms of scale, from İstanbul- and Anatolian-based large holdings to small- and medium-scale manufacturing firms still developing in the Organised Industrial Districts, mostly in Anatolia. Within this wide range, Sönmez (2010b) identifies two specific sections which have been growing much more aggressively. The first is manufacturing firms, who have made progress as sub-contractors to multinational manufacturing chains, by offering cheap and informal labour throughout the 1990s in Anatolia, while attaching increasing importance to technological investment and becoming more competitive in international markets. The second group of trading and construction firms have capitalised on their close relations with the AKP cadres, especially at the municipal level, to be favoured by public tenders. Besides, the flagships of Turkish Islamic capital, which have close relations with the higher ranks of the AKP or, in some cases, directly with Prime Minister Erdoğan, such as the Çalık Group, have already grown beyond MÜSİAD and become TÜSİAD members instead. Thus, the differentiation among Islamic capitalists, traceable back to the 1990s, should not be underestimated. In fact, it even reached the point where some MÜSİAD members declared that it was time for an institutional split between the large and small businesses.

However, though the wide inclusiveness of the concept of Islamic capital renders its usage ambiguous and problematic, it can still be suggestive and useful regarding three points. First, the emergence and development of this capital fraction, since its beginning in the 1960s, has always proceeded in parallel with the emergence and development of Islamist politics in Turkey. As with the birth of Islamist politics under Erbakan's National View Movement during clashes between Anatolian-based small- and medium-scale capital groups and the İstanbul-based industrialists, the AKP's split from the National View tradition as a neoliberal-conservative party was closely related to the articulation of dynamic Islamic capital groups with the global capitalism during the 1990s (see Öniş

2006b, 2006c). Thus, thanks to the rise of Islamist politics since the 1990s and the AKP coming to power in the 2000s, Islamic capital has managed to create a 'pertinent effect'[7] beyond its economic scale. Secondly, the religious–cum–social networks organising business relations among Islamic enterprises should be taken into consideration because membership of the same Islamic sect may help entrepreneurs overcome business problems that they would otherwise have to solve through market mechanisms. Thirdly, and most significantly, this capital fraction, which still largely comprises small- and medium-scale enterprises, particularly those that lost their access to financial resources due to the post-2001 crisis regulations in the banking sector, has particular interests and needs concerning macro-economic policies. Consequently, while TÜSİAD, with the advantage of dominating financial power, has firmly pushed for policies of fiscal discipline, small- and medium-scale enterprises, have constantly complained about shortage of credit, and appealed for more expansionary monetary policies, which would allow them to benefit from public credit, incentives and tenders. Thus, it should be emphasised that representatives of Islamic capital do not oppose policies of financial stability because of their religious or cultural beliefs. Rather, they do so because these policies have been unfavourable to their economic interests. Evidence of this is that these enterprises are not all Islamic, with the more 'secular' ones organising themselves under a relatively new organisation, TÜRKONFED (Turkish Enterprise and Business Confederation). This secular wing also suffers from the same problems as the Islamic enterprises, mainly shortcomings and difficulties with access to credit, to the extent that tension has recently emerged between them and their 'big partner', TÜSİAD. However, considering the fact that TÜRKONFED is considerably controlled by TÜSİAD and that TOBB, the primary umbrella organisation for medium-scale enterprises, turned out to be a battleground where the representatives of the Islamic-oriented enterprises became gradually influential, one can say that economic interests of the small- and medium-scale enterprises, in today's Turkey, are mostly represented by the Islamic business organisations. Thus, what is specific to Turkey is the *partial* overlapping of the more classical segregation between large *versus* medium-scale capital with a cultural–cum–political segre-gation, *specifically at the level of representation.* As stated above, Islamic capital owes this 'pertinent effect' to its organic ties with the governing Islamist-conservative political movement.

The 'unification of the ruling classes in the state' (Gramsci 1999: 52), or the consolidation of the power bloc as a 'unity of politically dominant classes and fractions under the protection of the hegemonic fraction' (Poulantzas 1978: 239), has been the most critical and complicated issue during the AKP era. In this regard, what is unique about the AKP's situation is its mediating position between the needs and orientations of different capital fractions. That is, on the one hand, the strategic orientation of large capital to upgrade its manufacturing base gradually by building on the macro-economic conditions based on the premises of financial stability. The historical anxiety of big business in Turkey, namely their fears about the continuity of the inflow of external credit and funding, underlies this orientation. Their business is bound to this inflow, and the continuous inflow of foreign financial resources is in turn tied to the financial stability of the country. Therefore, 'sound' macro-economic policies that tend to protect conditions of financial stability have become essential for TÜSİAD, that is, for the hegemonic capital fraction. On the other hand, small- and medium-scale capital groups, deprived of the financial sources they urgently need, tend to push for more expansionist policies, mostly to the detriment of financial stability. Therefore, the AKP, as the most dedicated political follower of the hegemonic consensus established after the 2001 crisis in Turkey, is pulled in two directions: to fulfil the requirements of financial stability demanded by large capitalists on the one hand, while trying to perform its role as a political actor organically tied to Islamic capital of satisfying the needs of this fraction by tactical manoeuvring on the other.

Limits, Tactics and Untouchables of the AKP

Balancing the conflicting needs of various capital fractions is an issue that requires more than the skills of a political actor, though the AKP's skillfulness is beyond doubt. First of all, it is directly related to the limits of and access to resources. In this regard, as stated above, one should remember that, due to the low ratio of savings, investments in Turkey still largely depend on foreign savings and global liquidity. Thus, sustainable growth is strictly bound to the availability of these financial resources. Fluctuations in the growth rate have always been the direct result of fluctuations in foreign financial resources. Due to this enduring dependency, the continuation of foreign financing is still the key issue when doing business in Turkey, especially for TÜSİAD's large-scale enterprises. The power of the prominent members of TÜSİAD within the financial sector arises from the intermediary role of their banks between foreign funds and domestic entrepreneurs. That is exactly why ensuring the stability of the macro-economic framework needed for funding inflows has been the main issue for TÜSİAD. However, for small- and medium-scale enterprises, this macro-economic framework, based mainly on fiscal discipline, has had several negative side effects. First, it means further tightening of already tight financing possibilities because of retrenchments imposed on state-based credit that could otherwise be a lifesaver for them. Second, it also reduces business opportunities due to reduced public expenditure on projects such as infrastructural investment.

Taking all these factors into consideration, from 2002, when it first came to power, until 2008, when the most recent global economic crisis commenced, the AKP has been remarkably fortunate because of the abundance of liquidity globally. Besides providing relatively cheap credit to business, this financial abundance has also been the structural cause of the enormous rise in foreign direct investment. Thus, the AKP, in its first term, managed to overcome tensions between components of the power bloc by both maintaining and deepening macro-economic discipline and satisfying the needs of small- and medium-scale business, especially its close circle. Investment increased due to the abundance of foreign credit. Besides, thanks to their clientelist relations at both municipal and national level, Islamic capital groups have been able to win a satisfactory share of privatisations and public tenders. They also have been the main beneficiaries of the AKP's policies on the flexibilisation of the labour market, since their competitiveness mainly depends on the exploitation of cheap and informal labour.

However, the main parametre s of these happy days changed rapidly after the global crisis commenced in 2008. Due to the collapse in Western European markets, exports declined, external finance dried up, and employment and domestic demand dropped sharply. Although the gradually increasing ratio of exports to Middle Eastern and other Islamic countries[8] compensated somewhat for the loss derived from the collapse of European markets, the export performance of the pre-crisis period has not yet been reached. Hence, Turkey's internal market has again become the main engine of economic growth, though it has actually shrunk drastically due to the draining of foreign funding and credit after the crisis.

In the economic circumstances of the global crisis, the underlying tensions among the capital fractions became visible, in some cases even within the AKP cabinet. Verifying Poulantzas's point that 'the State is not a monolithic bloc but a strategic battlefield' (Poulantzas 2000: 152), quarrels concerning the renewal of the ten-year stand-by agreement with the IMF, made in 2008, became critically importance in this regard, signalling a clear split among different representatives of capital. Whereas TÜSİAD insisted on renewing because of its distrust that the AKP would continue to impose fiscal discipline, most representatives of small- and medium-scale business, especially Islamic capital organisations, were against renewing the agreement in order to focus on economic growth rather than fiscal discipline. Two conditionalities proposed by the IMF were critical: first, the IMF pushed for the computerisation of tax administration; second, it demanded cuts in municipal expenditure. Both of these conditions were detrimental to the interests of small- and medium-scale businesses, especially Islamic capital groups, since they had been the main beneficiaries both of the 'flexible' tax collection system administered by politically-oriented state agencies and of municipal expenditure thanks to their close relations with the AKP-controlled municipalities. At the end of a long and sometimes harsh process of quarrels and vacillation, even sometimes among the administrative agencies of the economy, the AKP decided not to sign the new agreement because it would have mainly harmed the interests of those capital groups to which it is organically connected.[9] The effects of these intra-capital tensions within the cabinet have continued to be felt since through controversies over the independent Central Bank's policies. Whereas the Deputy Prime Minister Ali Babacan, as the main supporter of disciplinary neoliberalism in the cabinet, defended Central Bank policies aiming to maintain financial stability, Zafer Çağlayan, the Minister of Economy and a former president of TOBB, criticised Central Bank policies by claiming that they were hindering economic growth.

In some cases, this conflict within the power bloc intertwined with more direct religious-cultural codes as well, such as the debates over education reform. One of the most questionable results of the partial military intervention in 1997, which primarily targeted Islamist politics and its roots within civil society, including Islamic business groups, was the decision to increase the length of the compulsory education to eight years. This was a way of targeting the *İmam Hatip* religiously oriented high schools, which have always been of crucial importance for Islamic circles. In 2012, the AKP put education reform on its agenda by proposing to increase the length of compulsory education to twelve years divided into three four-year periods. In effect, the aim of this new reform was to reverse the 1997 military intervention's regulation regarding *İmam Hatip* high schools so, unsurprisingly, this dimension became the main axis of debate among the wider public. In addition, because this issue was also significant for different capital fractions, it created another conflict between TÜSİAD and MÜSİAD. TÜSİAD claimed that the AKP's bill would result in drop-outs, particularly for school-aged girls, and emphasised the need for well-qualified human resources, doubtless for the benefit of big business. On the other hand, MÜSİAD supported the bill since it allowed students to continue in vocational high schools after the first four years, while the middle-grade staff and skilled labour that would graduate from these vocational high schools were precisely what MÜSİAD members needed. Besides the revanchist attitude against the survival of the 1997 military intervention, the issue also concerned reshaping the labour market and the AKP cut the Gordian knot again in the way its organic allies desired.

The AKP also succeeded in paralysing TÜSİAD politically by using various tactics. As one of the civil supporters of the process leading up to the 1997 military intervention, TÜSİAD remained suspect for the AKP, so the party's leading figures, notably Erdoğan, have always denounced any opposition from TÜSİAD, especially if it was political in character. In this sense, the AKP has insistently pressured TÜSİAD to stay out of all political issues and focus on its own business, although this harsh attitude towards big business has also been accompanied by carrot and stick tactics. On the one hand, the AKP government did not hesitate to impose probably the highest tax fine in the Republic's history on the biggest media group, *Doğan* Group, in order to punish its negative attitude towards the government and to reorganise the media sphere (see Aydın in this volume). On the other hand, it rewarded another TÜSİAD member, *Doğuş* Group, with large-scale construction tenders as soon as its media sub-group had been cleaned of all oppositional figures.

Based on these cases, is it possible to claim that the AKP is becoming more and more the representative of the interests of Islamic capital groups at the expense of big business? Considering the fact that it has never hesitated to favour these groups openly, both in the privatisation and municipal tenders, there is no reason to question the steadiness of the relationship between the AKP and Islamic capital groups. Nevertheless, the AKP's general strategy towards capital should be regarded as continuing the traditional line of the Turkish centre-right. Just as Özal had attempted to create new capital groups close to him, and preferred to have one-to-one contacts with TÜSİAD members, the AKP, too, has tried to support its favoured Islamic capital groups while paralysing TÜSİAD as a corporate representative. Although the AKP and Islamic capital groups are related much more organically than Özal and his follower-entrepreneurs, this cannot obscure the fact that the AKP era has brought about a deepening in neoliberal discipline and the consolidation of large capital's hegemony; just as the hegemony of large capital was reconstructed during the Özal era.

Therefore, analysis should focus on the structural reorientation of the relationship between state and capital, rather than the tactical behaviour of the government. The reform process continuing under the title of 'Improving the Investment Climate in Turkey' could, and should, be taken into consideration in this regard. Begun by the previous government, this reform process is based on two main institutions: the Investment Advisory Council and the Coordination Council for the Improvement of Investment Environment (YOİKK). The Advisory Council consists of various groups: multinational corporations, such as Citigroup, BNP Baripas, Daimler Chrysler, Ford, Unicredit and Unilever; relevant state agencies; national business institutions, such as TÜSİAD, TOBB, YASED, TİM (Turkish Exporters' Assembly); and representatives of global institutions, such as the IMF, World Bank and the European Investment Bank. The Coordination Council, YOİKK, whose responsibility is to draft laws concerning the investment environment based on the proposals of the Advisory Council, consists of representatives of TÜSİAD, YASED, TOBB, TİM and the relevant state agencies. YOİKK works through technical committees, which draft various enacted laws, such as the Labor Law, the Law on Protection of the Topographies of Integrated Circuits, the Turkish Employment Agency Law, the Land Acquisition and Site Development Law, the Law on Social Insurance for Workers, the Law on the Recruitment of Expatriates, the Law on Social Insurance for the Self-Employed and Artisans, the Law on Inflation Accounting, the Law on the Protection of Intellectual and Industrial Property Rights, the Mining Law, the Law on the Establishment of the Investment Support and Promotion Agency of Turkey, the Corporate Income Tax Law, the Law on Withholding Taxes on Capital Gains, the Law on Fighting Smuggling, the Turkish Patent Institute Law, the Trademark Law Agreement and the Foreign Direct Investment Law (European Union Twinning Project for Turkey 2006: 63). In short, YOİKK functions as a quasi-parliament with regard to almost all issues intersecting in some way with business (see Özdek 2011). In other words, new domains of the state have emerged, freed from political intervention, where the representatives of capital directly involve themselves in making laws in order to manage *the common affairs of the whole bourgeoisie*'.

The Post-Crisis Tendency: Recentralisation

The underlying idea of the 2001 reforms was to establish a regulatory environment that would secure the critical domains of capital accumulation by linking them to the rules and regulations of global capitalism. Thus, alongside the premises of fiscal discipline, independent regulatory institutions were regarded as the basis of the new hegemonic consensus. In point of fact, in its first term, most of the AKP policies were shaped by the IMF in terms of the economy, and by the EU in terms of politics. These engagements provided the AKP with both a wider support base than its original voter base and also leverage against the power of the military. Most importantly, however, it provided an international anchor that encouraged foreign capital to invest in Turkey, resulting in foreign capital flows reaching an all-time high since, beside its EU anchor, the AKP generally remained loyal both to IMF conditions and the regulatory structure established after the 2001 crisis. In particular, it 'enhanced TCMB [the Central Bank] independence . . . by bringing its structures and duties closer to international standards and, most significantly, by legislating price stability and inflation-targeting as TCMB imperatives' (Marois 2011: 181). The AKP even increased discipline over public spending and debt, most importantly regarding off-budget expenditure, by enacting laws such as the Public Financing and Debt Management Law in 2002 and the Public Financial Management and Control Law in 2003. Thus, in its first term, the AKP's rule was acclaimed by a variety of political actors, ranging from liberal-leftists and liberals to conservatives and moderate Islamists, as well as the international actors of global capitalism.

However, the AKP's attitude towards the institutions and administrative features of regulated neoliberalism turned out to be ambiguous in character, especially after the termination of the IMF agreement. Whereas, on the one hand, the governing mentality of neoliberalism became further embedded into the functioning of the state apparatus, on the other hand, the tendency of recentralising economic management around the executive power became prominent again. More than the end of IMF tutelage in 2008, this recent tendency should be related to two historically overlapping causes. First, beyond doubt, the global economic crisis of 2008 was the leading motive for the AKP, as for other governments, to reconsolidate its executive power over economic management. As the Deputy Prime Minister Babacan emphasised, the AKP responded to the new conditions of global economic crisis by switching from automatic pilot to manual mode. In the depressed conditions, prominent AKP figures, including Erdoğan, did not hesitate to question the independence of the Central Bank. However, what is unique to Turkey was the overlapping of this economic motive with a political one. In 2007, with the *Ergenekon* trials, the AKP and its allies initiated a process that would have culminated in the serious weakening of Kemalist ranks within Turkey's civil and military bureaucracy. In addition to the economic crisis, this harsh political process increased the recentralisation of state power. Parallel to, though actually also as a means of continuing, the clash within the state, the AKP and its allies, the most important being the *Gülen* movement, launched a rapid and determined process to fill the bureaucracy with their own advocates. This ongoing process has spread into almost all state institutions, including those responsible for economic management, at the expense of liberal expectations for the rationalisation and managerialisation of the bureaucratic apparatus. In short, the AKP replied to both crises, the global economic crisis and the domestic state crisis, by centralising state power under its own control.

The clearest indication of this recentralisation tendency has been the more frequent employment of the same *ad hoc* mechanisms that had been of crucial importance for the Özal administration in the 1980s, with governmental decrees and omnibus bills[10] becoming the AKP's default legislative mechanisms in its second term. They have mostly been employed, as they were in the 1980s, to speed up or to by-pass the normal administrative and/or judicial processes. The biggest governmental operation conducted through the use of governmental decree was the foundation of new ministries through merging or altering older ones in 2011, just before the general elections. In this way, the AKP transformed the entire structure of the governmental body without any parliamentary debate. Another case is a recently enacted law concerning the specific obstacle faced during privatisation of public enterprises. Although the judicial resistance to privatisation, which slowed the process during the 1980s and 1990s, has been almost completely broken, the AKP still uses all necessary administrative mechanisms to prevent any unexpected delays and obstacles. A recent example concerns an article added to an omnibus bill at the last minute that authorises the Council of Ministers to invalidate judicial decisions calling a halt to already completed privatisations. Thus, the AKP decisively takes steps to recentralise the power around its executive power at the expense of the parliament and the judiciary.

In contrast, regarding recentralisation of economic management, the AKP has remained a tactician rather than a hard-liner. This current tactical recentralisation tendency has been revealed most obviously by the AKP's attitude towards the independent regulatory agencies. In this regard, Ali Babacan, the Deputy Prime Minister, made the AKP's position clear: 'It is time for the independent agencies to redelegate their authority.' Based on this clear position, the AKP issued a decree in 2011 authorising line ministries to inspect the activities of the independent agencies associated with them. This attempt to usurp control was widely criticised as an example of the AKP's trying to dominate state power, ironically even by those circles who had been opposed to the foundation of the same independent regulatory institutions in 2001. However, a closer analysis reveals the AKP's tactical view much more clearly because not every independent agency has been treated in the same way. Recent research based on the Gilardi Index, designed to measure the level of independence of such agencies, has shown that, whereas agencies considered of lesser significance, such as the Sugar Agency and the Tobacco and Alcohol Market Regulatory Agency, are almost completely controlled by the relevant ministries, others in charge of critical sectors of the economy have been treated more carefully: 'Amongst sectoral agencies, the Banking Regulation and Supervision Agency seems to have the highest level of *de facto* independence with 0.87, while the same figure is 0.58 for the Information Technology and Communications Authority and 0.54 for the Energy Markets Regulatory Agency' (Ozel 2012: 124–125). This indicates that the AKP has made tactical rather than normative choices when intervening in these agencies. Notwithstanding its clearly observable general tendency to consolidate executive power over the decentralised neoliberal bureaucracy, the AKP has preferred to take cautious steps with regard to sectors and issues, such as regulation of the banking sector and fiscal policy, considered by TÜSİAD and representatives of global capital as highly important for the effective functioning of the neoliberal economic framework.

Nevertheless, the AKP has also tended to consolidate its executive power within this framework, as clearly revealed by disputes over the Law of Fiscal Rule. The Fiscal Rule, as a regulation aiming to discipline deficit-biased national economies by legislating long-term limits on budgetary aggregates with regard to debts, deficits and expenditures, has become the subject of disagreement within the AKP. The Fiscal Rule Law was prepared by the Deputy Prime Minister Ali Babacan, to regain the trust of the financial markets after the termination of the IMF agreement in 2008. However, some ministries, such as the Ministry of Transport and the Ministry of Public Works, whose operations depend on the broader use of public spending, and who thus would suffer from the implementation of the Fiscal Rule, tried to loosen the conditions determined by the Law. Although the Law was approved by the sub-commissions of the Parliament and was supposed to be enacted by the parliamentary council, Erdoğan, at the last moment, withdrew the draft law, claiming that it would be pointless to create an internal IMF just as Turkey had freed itself from the real one. Instead, the government decided to establish fiscal discipline through the construction of medium-term fiscal plans, which revealed the AKP's tendency to regulate fiscal discipline through its own executive power.

What is beyond doubt, however, is that the case of the Fiscal Rule Law demonstrates that the AKP was not retreating from the premises of fiscal discipline. In addition to the upcoming elections of 2011, the particular reason for this initiative was to secure room for manoeuvre on behalf of the spending ministries and municipalities, whose operations had been of crucial importance for capital groups, especially those closest to the AKP. In this sense, like the Özal governments of the 1980s, the AKP has tried to foster those sectors, such as construction, that can ensure the continuity of capital accumulation, at least under the general conditions of global economic crisis. Moreover, just as Özal tried to do by founding a new state apparatus under his own control, namely the Mass Housing and Public Participation Board, so has the AKP dealt with this issue by creating new arrangements of centralisation. As this chapter is being written, almost everywhere in Turkey, urban transformation projects are in progress. İstanbul in particular has been turned into a giant construction site under the pretext of preparing for a possible future earthquake. Alongside the recently founded Ministry of Environment and Urbanism, the Housing Development Administration (TOKİ), established during the Özal era, has been revitalised as a leading institutional actor. TOKİ, since its foundation, has reported directly to the Prime Ministry due to its strategic significance, although there has always been a ministry responsible for public works and settlement (see Çavuşoğlu and Strutz in this volume). Currently, it 'builds public housing jointly with private contractors on public land, to which it has free access. It has been given powers to develop plans on lands over which it has control. It can develop urban regeneration projects in cooperation with local governments and has the authority to evaluate and price the land that is to be purchased. TOKİ is also given a free hand in its financial transactions, and is exempt from the procurement rules which usually apply to public entities' (Atiyas 2012: 76). Considering that construction has always been one of the sectors in Turkey in which both the large- and medium-scale capital groups have traditionally invested heavily, this powerful institutional framework that enables a highly-centralised decision making process for the distribution of urban rent clearly indicates the AKP's determination to side-step all possible bureaucratic or judicial hindrances. In this sense, centralisation has gone hand in hand with marketisation: the more public services are left to market forces, the more passionate the government becomes for founding centralised and technocratic-minded institutions, such as TOKİ, to control these domains of capital accumulation. Beyond doubt, creating clear and strong connections between public services, marketisation and technocratic administration is a strategy that the AKP has employed most successfully.

Overall, it is possible to conclude that the AKP has remained loyal to the general rules of the neoliberal consensus established after the 2001 crisis in Turkey, but has pushed to take the law into its own hands as much as possible during the global economic crisis. Thus, in order to be able to contextualise this current tendency of centralisation, one should also go beyond the domestic context of the government, which has been considered above at length, and pay attention to the global agenda of neoliberalism. In this regard, the shifting and the constant concerns of neoliberal administration should also be taken into consideration in two ways. First, the populist politician, seen from the 1990s regulationist viewpoint as the leitmotiv of developing countries, is no longer the dominant or decisive figure. Though populism does still matter politically and ideologically; economically, they either adapt themselves to the premises of neoliberalism or surround themselves with a neoliberal-minded management team. In this sense, contrary to regulationist concerns, administrative recentralisation does not necessarily mean a return to populism. Second, the main neoliberal concern is, and has always been, the isolation of economic management from the concerns of the wider society and its continuation in a technocratic way, that is depoliticisation (see Burnham 2000). This generic character does always produce a particular kind of centralism; and, in fact, the history of neoliberalism is the history of different types of centralisation because the institutional and procedural design of this continuation is a matter of conjuncture. One should not forget that the neoliberal mentality of a government is revealed by its centralising character, even to the extent of suspending the liberal democracy, as in the recent cases of Greece and Italy (see Gill 2011). Therefore, in conclusion, the centralisation of power in Turkey around the executive branch controlled by the AKP should be understood as a particular case of this general tendency within neoliberalism.

★ ★ ★

As stated right at the beginning of this chapter, the critical task of the AKP has been to consolidate the unification of the power bloc, and this has required both economic and political arrangements to be implemented. Despite a relatively good economic performance immediately after the first negative impact of the global economic crisis, it cannot be claimed that Turkish capitalism has overcome, or even started to overcome, its main structural problem. That is, although Turkey has drawn the global attention of investors with its recently high rates of growth, during the AKP era as a whole, between 2000 and 2011, the investment ratio has remained low, at an average rate of about 19 per cent of GDP, compared to an average of 27.5 per cent in emerging and developing economies (Eken and Schadler 2012: 36). In fact, as one researcher has noted, 'investment rates and domestic credit to the private sector have been disappointingly low. In this respect, 2001 does not represent a structural break. In particular, gross fixed capital formation, domestic credit to the private sector and domestic savings rates did actually fall since 2001' (Öniş 2009: 424). In other words, economic growth is still determined by the availability of foreign funds and, when they dried up thanks to the global economic crisis, growth rates dropped dramatically. Therefore, as stated above, the growth rate of the economy has always been fluctuant in character: according to the official statistics, it was − 4.8 per cent in 2009, 9.2 per cent in 2010, 8.8 per cent in 2011 and 2.2 per cent in 2012. Meanwhile, Turkey's current account deficit has become another issue to be dealt by economic management. The export-led strategy implemented during the AKP era has become the main reason for this increasing deficit, since it has been increasingly dependent on imports. Ironically enough, the Custom Union Agreement with EU, considered as providing the basis for industrial upgrading after the mid-1990s by liberal economists, has instead triggered an import boom in Turkey. By lowering tariff rates between Turkey and third party countries to the level between them and the EU, the agreement caused a rise in imports from countries such as China, whose competitiveness, based on cheap labour, domestic Turkish producers have found hard to counter-balance. In short, the AKP's export-led growth strategy has only brought about 'impoverishing growth' (Sönmez 2010a).

The political domain has also become more complicated. Beginning with the 2010 referendum over the constitutional amendments, the issue of a new constitution has become the main focus for almost all political and social actors in Turkey. Having capitalised on its use of state power, the AKP and its allies are now trying to consolidate existing power relations by engraving them into the structure of the state through a new constitution. Therefore, the issue at stake with regard to the new constitution is to reorganise the balances of power among the executive, legislative and judicial branches. Due to tensions both within the AKP and among its wider allies, it seems that this phase of centralising power will be more complicated. Whereas Erdoğan, as the strongest political figure in Turkey, and his close circle have been insisting on developing a presidential system, other prominent AKP figures and some of the wider allies seem to be critical of such a power configuration. In addition, the AKP's proposals to the parliamentary preparatory commission responsible for drafting the new constitution have already clearly revealed that the AKP will push for greater executive power, especially at the expense of the judiciary. Although it has already enjoyed greater use of state power than is allowed in an ordinary typical liberal-democratic state, the AKP, as the Islamic-conservative heir of the populist Turkish centre-right, still demands more, as its leader, Erdoğan, has made clear:

> Since the system is not established properly, the bureaucratic oligarchy unexpectedly takes a stand against you. Unexpectedly, you come up against the judiciary . . . Those looking from outside make assumptions and say, 'you have 326 deputies, that's the excuse as always'. But you know there is the thing called balance of powers; it stands against you as an obstacle. (*Milliyet*, 17 December 2012)

Whether or not a presidential or semi-presidential system, or, as Erdoğan himself once called it, 'a Turkish-style presidential system', will result from this internal negotiation-cum-struggle, it is already possible to claim that the new constitution will create a more powerful executive branch. Years ago, in the early

1970s, *Aydınlar Ocağı* (the Intellectuals Association), the then intellectual reference point for all right-wing political circles, regardless of their different stances, presented its understanding of democracy:

> The democracy of the future will be authoritarian democracy. The principles of authoritarian democracy began to become apparent due to ongoing process in the world. These principles can be taken as this trio: order-elections-authority. In authoritarian democracy, the social order is protected and regarded as superior. Elections are the main method and political power is determined by elections. Authority will be absolute and complete. Those who vote will provide those who are elected with the necessary authority and this authority will be used without any pity for anybody. (Aydınlar Ocağı 1973: 268)

This populist and authoritarian idea, which has inspired almost all Turkish right-wing political cadres, has continued from the 1970s to the 2010s, though transformed by merging with the technocratic rationality of neoliberalism, till appearing in Erdoğan's speech quoted above. It is beyond doubt that Erdoğan and his close circle are inclined to use this idea to consolidate authoritarian statism *a la Turque*.

As Machiavelli, the master of *real politique*, put it centuries ago, the fate of *the Prince* will be determined by the combination of *fortuna* and *virtu*.

NOTES

1 'In this context it should be noted that, in most Third World countries, the bourgeoisie itself is a creation of the state and this historical phenomenon has created cultural, sociological and economic traits that do not disappear with changes in the policy model. The very process of rent-seeking emanates from the bourgeoisie, not from the state *per se*, and this is a well-known, everyday characteristic of the Turkish scene, which only academic liberals ignore' (Boratav, Türel and Yeldan 1994: 65).

2 For a more detailed analysis of the economic transition to neoliberalism in Turkey see Yalman (2009) and Yeldan (2001a). For a more general analysis of the neoliberal period see Mütevellioğlu and Sönmez (2009).

3 'Economic constitutionalism refers to the attempt to treat the market as a constitutional order with its own rules, procedures, and institutions, operating to protect the market order from political interference. The increasing juridical role of the World Trade Organization, the shift towards independent central banks, and above all, the tough conditional agreements imposed by international financial institutions are factors that have moved towards economic constitutionalism. Economic constitutionalism demands the construction of a specific kind of state organisation and structure: a regulatory state, the purpose of which is to regulate and provide "economic order" within the global market' (Jayasuriya 2005: 18).

4 'Thus the state is also subjected to market disciplines. Indeed, public policy has been redefined in such a way that governments seek to prove their *credibility*, and the *consistency* of their policies according to the degree to which they inspire the *confidence* of investors. In this way, new political and constitutional initiatives in the sphere of money and finance are linked to the imposition of macroeconomic and micro-

economic discipline in ways that are intended to underpin the power of capital in the state and civil society' (Gill 2000: 4).

5 The only exception was the radical-right wing party MHP (Nationalist Movement Party), which was not able to enter parliament again until the next election in 2007.

6 For a more detailed economic analysis of the AKP era see Bağımsız Sosyal Bilimciler (2007, 2008, 2009).

7 'How can a criterion be defined which will lead us to decipher the existence of a class, or of a fraction, as a social force in a determinate formation . . . It can be said that this presence exists when the relation to the relations of production, the place in the process of production is reflected on the other levels by pertinent effects. These "pertinent effects" can be located in political and ideological structures as well as in social, political and ideological class relations' (Poulantzas 1978: 78–79).

8 Prior to the global crisis, the share of European buyers of Turkish exports was about 65 per cent. Due to sharp declines in aggregate demand with the economic crisis in Europe, this rate decreased to 56 per cent in 2010. North American countries too were important for Turkish exports, accounting for a 12 per cent share in 2000. However, their share declined to about 4 per cent in 2010. Instead, the share of Near and Middle Eastern countries climbed to 20 per cent in 2010 from 9.5 per cent in 2002, while the 13 per cent share of countries of the Organization of Islamic Conference increased to 29 per cent in the same period (Kaya, Y. 2011).

9 However, as the following section of the chapter explains, what was at stake was much more essential. This decision reflected the AKP's new tendency of 're-empowering the executive centre', which would become much clearer during the following years. That is, it signified not just a break but the reorientation of the AKP's main tendency in the context of global crisis.

10 Omnibus bills, known in Turkey as 'bag laws', are legislative bills that provide for a number of miscellaneous enactments or appropriations.

CHAPTER THREE

The Struggle for Hegemony Between Turkish Nationalisms in the Neoliberal Era

Güven Gürkan Öztan

In Turkey, nationalism is an ideology which has penetrated a whole array of different ideologies and political attitudes, ranging from Islamism to conservatism, and even to some fractions of the left. While its boundaries are quite ambiguous, its capacity to influence or determine politics is strong and inclusive. Through the intricate relationship nationalism has with other ideologies, it often transforms and diversifies itself, and the same can also certainly be said, to a large extent, about the effect that contact with nationalism has on other political attitudes and ideologies. Given this, rather than invoking a single nationalism, a much more pertinent analytical point of departure is to consider multiple nationalisms. Within this framework, I think that Thomas Hylland Eriksen's distinction between *formal* nationalism and *informal* nationalism (Eriksen 1993) is an ideal categorisation to start with. In the same spirit, Umut Özkırımlı distinguishes official nationalism and unofficial nationalism (Özkırımlı 2002: 708). Official nationalism is, roughly, a process imposed from above, with much bureaucratic or institutional structuring and practice behind it. As such, it is part of an official ideology whose ultimate aim is to create a homogenous, conflict-free and obedient society. It is, however, impossible for the cornered template of the official nationalism to be exactly or completely incorporated into society because the complicated nature of the social structure in terms of class and culture, and the inner dynamism of politics, form points of resistance and change some of the arguments suggested by official nationalism. At this stage, according to Özkırımlı, unofficial nationalisms step in to form 'alternatives' compatible with the standard grammar of nationalist ideology, yet differing from official nationalism. They are more sentimental, vivid, reactionary, and closely related to the everyday. On some occasions, unoffical nationalisms reconcile or overlap with official nationalism while, on some others, they compete with it. In the end, however, there is a symbiotic relationship between them, based on their interdependency (Özkırımlı 2002: 708–709). What this means is that, in order to understand the 'big picture' concerning nationalism, it is necessary not only to decode the interaction between official nationalism and unofficial nationalism, but also to scrutinise their class and cultural bases.

The aim of this article is therefore to discuss, without ignoring the differentiation between official nationalism(s) and unoffical nationalism(s), the changes experienced in Turkey throughout the 1980s, when neoliberalism gradually fortified itself, and the class bases all those changes rested upon. In order to shed light upon what has been experienced since the 1980s, I will first discuss the legacy of the residual nationalism(s); second, I will list the developments that hold Turkish nationalisms within a common terrain, and finally I shall attempt to present a periodisation of these changes. Within this framework, I will argue that, after 1980, a struggle for hegemony took place between Kemalist nationalism(s), Turkish-Islamic synthesis nationalism and neoliberal nationalism, which was settled definitely when the Justice and Development Party (AKP) came to power on its own in 2002. I will assert that, within this new configuration, where different versions of Kemalist nationalism (especially *ulusalcı*[1] or left-wing Kemalism and White Turk/elitist nationalism) and Turkish-Islamic synthesis nationalism have made an alliance, the politics of the neoliberal climate influencing the composition (and fragmentation) of the middle class come into play.

Discovering the Residue of Nationalisms

In Turkey, nationalism has a more deep-rooted history than Kemalism; yet, as the official ideology of the newly established Republic, Kemalism deployed nationalism at the centre of its political imaginary and left it without an opponent by rendering it official. Kemalist nationalism, which has become the official nationalism, has an identity that is essentially of a pronounced secularist and positivist character. At the same time, it contains ethnicist elements within it and, due to the fact that it gained momentum in the 1930s, its definition of 'acceptable' citizenship also includes ethno-religious references (see Yıldız 2001). Kemalist nationalism originated and thrived in the hands of the Republic's founding middle class. This middle class, which devoted itself to the nation-state and to the republic they identified with the nation-state, has a common mentality that especially saw modernisation and secularisation as a whole. They attempted to spread the basic principles of Kemalist nationalism through society by means of the state, although it also gradually gained strength in the centres of big cities as the lifestyle of the founding middle class. In consequence, this middle class, whose members were mostly urban and literate, by adopting Kemalist nationalism as the official nationalism, rose to a relatively dominant position politically and economically. It is also possible to talk about a Pan-Turkist and racist unoffical nationalism within this single party era (see Landau 1995; Atabay 2005). Pan-Turkist nationalism, whose adherents engaged in a direct political struggle, not with the official nationalism, but with the government and President İsmet İnönü in particular, gained notable strength and diversified immediately before and during the Second World War. However, partly for conjunctural reasons (for example, the military defeat of Germany), it could not attain an hegemonic position. Even so, ethnicist nationalism and racist tendencies would continue to exist in the long term.

In conformity with the *zeitgeist*, official nationalism was restored in the Cold War era, with anti-communism in all its inclusiveness being made a central part of the official nationalism. The unofficial nationalisms of the Cold War era, on the other hand, were more multifarious than they had been in the preceding single party period and, after 1960, they started to be represented in political parties and organisations. In the years following the coup of 27 May 1960, two nationalisms emerged. The first was a left-Kemalist nationalism, which placed strong emphasis on anti-imperialism and developed a cult of the founding leadership. The second was a Turkish-Islamic nationalism, which manifested itself within the Nationalist Action Party (MHP). The MHP cadres, who used their para-military power to perform acts of violence under the slogan of anti-communism in the 1970s, developed an understanding of nationalism in which Islam is perceived as the essential component of Turkishness, in contradistinction to the religion-free stance of official nationalism with its distanced approach to religion. Owing to this character, it became popular in both the provinces and cities, especially within the provincial lower middle classes (Can 2002: 663). Intellectual right wing foundations, such as the *Aydınlar Ocağı* (House of Intellectuals), participated in the process by producing new interpretations of the Turkish-Islamic synthesis. Meanwhile, the *ulusalcı* left or left-wing Kemalists preserved the basic characteristics of the founding middle class and their progressivist concerns. On account of their class positions, they felt themselves closer to the civil-military bureaucratic elite in their own political projections. Therefore, they produced a discourse which was modernist-secularist on the one hand, and anti-imperialist – favouring full independence – on the other. Even though it was disguised by the political polarisation of the 1960s and 1970s, *ulusalcı* leftist tendencies and Turkish-Islamic nationalists actually advocated similar arguments in a series of matters, such as their Social Darwinist pre-suppositions, authoritarian and militarist tendencies and xenophobic expressions. Nevertheless, their political symbols and point of references, and the social strata which they appealed to were so different that it took a long time to see the parallels between them.

When the coup of 12 September 1980 descended on the political life in Turkey like a nightmare, it brought about some partial changes in the positions of the competing nationalisms. After 12 September, one aspect of the official nationalism promoted by the coup leaders became the cult of Mustafa Kemal Atatürk and the continually repeated emphasis on Atatürk nationalism. The other aspect was the indoctrination of society with the Turk-Islam synthesis. Conservative-nationalist organisations guided those cadres who wanted to use Islam as a 'unifying element', though only to a degree that did not directly conflict with the basic principles of the Republic. The effect was that official nationalism was now largely a nationalism of the Turk-Islam synthesis. The following years would bear witness to a fierce struggle between the official nationalism and its alternatives. In the remaining part of this chapter, I shall offer a categorisation of the composition of Turkish nationalisms since the 1980s in terms of official nationalism and unofficial nationalism. In this regard, I will analyse the post-1980 era in three periods: 1980s: Turkish Nationalisms and Neo-Ottomanism in the Shadow of 12 September; 1990s: The Crisis of the Official

Nationalism; 2000s: The Hegemony of Neoliberal Nationalism and Efforts at Repairing Official Nationalism.

Turkish Nationalisms and Neo-Ottomanism in the Shadow of 12 September

As briefly mentioned above, in the first years following the coup of 12 September 1980, official nationalism gained a dual character by rebuilding itself on the bases of Kemalism and Turkish-Islamic synthesis at the same time. Meanwhile, the MHP line was staggering due to the confusions experienced even by its high-rank cadres. The *ülkücü* (idealist)[2] cadres who had carried out armed attacks before the coup in the name of the struggle against communism were sure that they were performing this organised violence for the sake of protecting the state. However, when the actors of the 12 September coup began to arrest and judge not only leftist but also some *ülkücü* cadres, they were dumbfounded, asking themselves how the 'state' could imprison or even execute its own 'true children'? After this trauma, and especially in the prisons, MHP members and street organisations began to rely more on Islamist arguments and strategies (Can 2002: 678). A significant proportion of the MHP's membership later split from the *ülkücü* movement under the leadership of Muhsin Yazıcıoglu to establish the Great Union Party (BBP), whose ideology included motifs of *ummah* (Arıkan 2008: 53–69). Meanwhile, another significant group of *ülkücü*s, who had figured in MHP cadres before 1980 but managed to avoid incurring the wrath of the coup regime, preferred to continue politics within the newly founded Motherland Party (ANAP), following the return to democratic politics in 1983.[3]

Under the leadership of Turgut Özal, the ANAP, with its general attitude of reducing politics to a technique of administration, gave priority to a rapid transition to a market economy along the lines begun by the 12 September coup leaders. In this period, when dreams of a 'Great Turkey' and 'joining the first league' were popular, there were also some social developments that would radically influence politics in the following years. Specifically, the rise of the capitalists as a result of the dissolution experienced in the provinces, and the rapid migration toward cities were striking factors. Educatedness, which had been the most important characteristic of the founding middle class, was now no longer as appealing as it had been before, unless it was crowned with entrepreneurship. The desire to rise in the market economy through entrepreneurial spirit, and a concern for stability, became key to the composition of the new middle class (Ünüvar 2010: 21). In this atmosphere, a tendency emerged to soften the official nationalism with liberal elements along a 'developmentalist' axis. However, with few exceptions, this tendency refrained from dealing with the taboos of the official nationalism, confining itself to criticising Kemalist elitism (see Alkan 1991: 57–62; Türköne 1991: 63–67). It was not until the 2000s that matters relating to the early republican period, which had been declared by official nationalism as almost taboo, could be discussed by the political powers, and even then only for pragmatic purposes.

Within the framework of this article, the period of Turgut Özal's presidency (1989–1993) is an issue with respect to discussions over neo-Ottomanism. Özal's presidency was a time when the tendency to create 'opportunities' for Turkey gained momentum in the context of the changing dynamics after 1991, particularly the dissolution of the USSR. Beginning from the end of 1980s, for the sake of establishing a 'great' and 'strong' Turkey, Turgut Özal and the intellectual circle around him[4] made neo-Ottomanism a reference point in parallel to a strategy of both responding to rising domestic demands to express suppressed identities and pursuing an 'active' politics to create a sphere of influence in foreign affairs. Neo-Ottomanism, ultimately the product of the effort to reconstruct the Ottoman past as a model to solve the problems of Turkey in the 1980s, envisaged the combination of traditional Ottoman pluralism with the contemporary liberal multiculturalism (Çolak 2006: 126). It is well known that Özal himself made an analogy between the 'Ottoman model' and American multiculturalism, which he deemed a success. As such, even though it cannot be denied that the neo-Ottomanism of the Özal period contained an Islamic kernel, it is also apparent that this argument corresponded to an intellectual framework which was, roughly speaking, at peace with the West and contained liberal elements within itself. As Yılmaz Çolak puts it: 'The imperial neo-Ottomanist vision conceived of the Ottoman cultural identity not as an anti-Western value, but as part of the globalising Western world' (Çolak 2006: 135). After Özal's death in 1993, the idea of neo-Ottomanism with a liberal slant lost its popularity. However, the political Islamist Welfare Party (RP) and the Islamist intellectuals surrounding it set about continuing the idea of neo-Ottomanism by situating it within a more religious framework. Subsequent discussions among the Muslim intelligentsia about Islamic multiple law, and an increase in anti-Western discourse in response to the Russian-Chechen conflict and Serb nationalism in the Bosnian War, determined the characteristics of the RP's neo-Ottomanism. Both the RP municipalities, which increased their effectiveness and influence, especially after the 1994 local elections,[5] and Islamist authors tried to keep alive the collective memory of the Ottoman past through rituals and symbols. Meanwhile, the supporters of Kemalist nationalism(s) spent the rest of the 1990s largely searching for alternatives to this popularisation of the Ottoman Empire.

The 1990s: The Crisis of the Official Nationalism

The 1990s was a time of crisis and floundering for the offical nationalism and its adherents. The Cold War had ended, but it was not as yet possible to break the narrow patterns of the bipolar world-order in state policies and activist politics. Moreover, the official nationalism was also shaken by a series of multi-dimensional developments at both global and local levels, with no satisfactory answers to this turmoil being evident. Two factors immediately draw one's attention: externally, the transformatory pressure exerted by globalisation on the concept of political sovereignty; internally, two fundamental cases that threw the official ideology into crisis, namely, the popular rise of political Islam and the sharpening Kurdish question. During the 1990s, the assassination of journalists and academics noted for their Kemalism, and the Sivas Madımak massacre in July of 1993,[6] created a serious fear amongst the secular intelligentsia about the future of the regime. In addition, the strengthening of the RP with its increased share of the vote in the 1994 local elections unsettled the secular-republican middle class – especially the *ulusalcı* left – who had forged a tight bond between secularism and nationalism. The same uneasiness was also felt by groups advocating the Turkish-Islamic synthesis, who identified themselves largely with the 'state' and the 'regime', especially the MHP after 1991. Accordingly, the MHP swiftly moved towards a nationalist line with a pronounced emphasis on secularism, in order to distance itself from the Islamist opposition and attitudes identified with reaction. It would later be proven that this orientation was, as it were, officially registered after the 28 February 1997 intervention, through which the secular regime was 'restored' by means of military threat.[7] Following these developments, the MHP obtained more votes in Turkey's western provinces, where the urban middle class was predominant, in the 1999 elections.

In the 1990s, nationalist actors and analysts discussing this process could not recognise the crisis of the official nationalism. This was partly because the official nationalism had largely lost its capacity to find answers acceptable to the masses, which had therefore made popular nationalism more attractive. Nationalist symbols, exhibited to provide ideological sustenance and contribute to a nationalist performance, were weak doctrinally, but their potential for massification was much stronger. This newly rampant nationalism was not only stimulated by the 'threat of Islamist reaction', but also by the 'low intensity war' being waged against the Kurdish separatist PKK. In particular, mass participation in the funerals of soldiers killed by the PKK was a leading way for popular Turkish nationalism to manifest itself, but soon national football matches and even concerts became nationalist forums. Within this framework of popular nationalism, there was also increased production and display of republican-Kemalist images in reaction to the rise of political Islam and Kurdish demands. The resulting plethora of Atatürk photographs, appropriately tailored for all professions, all sorts of Atatürk badges, objects inscribed with the national flag's star and crescent and Republican celebrations transformed into pop concerts[8] can no doubt be seen as part of Kemalist civil society's efforts to reform the crisis-ridden official nationalism. In this way, commodities that symbolised the 'state' and the 'regime' became part of the collective Kemalist identity, social relations and private sphere. Within the material-instrumental background of the 1990s, several material changes enlarged the sphere of influence of popular nationalism, particularly changes in the uses of mass media.

As briefly discussed above, the nationalist political atmosphere of the late 1990s reached its climax with the post-modern 28 February 1997 intervention, and the capture of the PKK leader Öcalan. During this process, the MHP not only embraced the 'state thesis', on the Kurdish question and the appropriate reaction to it, but was also able to convert nationalist reactions into votes. Two other factors that allowed the MHP to increase its votes in the 1999 elections so much that it became a partner in the resulting coalition government, were the social and political unrest of the 1990s and the transformation undergone by the party itself (see Bora and Can 2004). Regarding the latter, the MHP of the late 1990s became sympathetic towards privatisation, adopted conservative motifs, but also emphasised its adherence to the secular regime. That is, it came close to giving the impression of being a classic centre-right party. However, this new image of the MHP, and its sudden rise, was not sustainable for very long. As a partner in government, the MHP was unable to keep its pre-election promises to those factions which had enabled it to enlarge its nationalist base. Symbolically, the most striking of these promises was to ensure the execution of Öcalan and solve the 'headscarf problem'. To make matters worse, the party was then shattered by rumours of corruption and, following the 2001 economic crisis and subsequent elections, failed, like its former government partners, even to pass the 10 per cent electoral threshold to enter the next parliament (see Bora and Can 2004: 474–505; Arıkan 2008: 81–83). The MHP's sharp decline was also caused by the rapid, and remarkably successful rise of a new party, the Young Party (GP) which won support in the 2002 elections from the crisis-ridden lower middle classes to get 7.5 per cent of the overall vote. The MHP, eliminated from the parliament together with its other government partners, was only able to return to parliamentary politics at the 2007 elections, thanks mainly to the votes it secured from the western Aegean and Marmara regions, where there was intense opposition to the rising AKP.

The 2000s: The Hegemony of Neoliberal Nationalism and Efforts at Repairing Official Nationalism

The Flirtation Between Kemalist Nationalism(s) and Turkish-Islamic Synthesis Nationalism

In the 2000s, there was a transition from the crisis of the official nationalism to a new period in which neoliberal nationalism became dominant in the struggle for hegemony, and a new idea of official nationalism was formulated. It can even be argued that, at the close of the first decade of the 2000s, the neoliberal nationalism developed by the AKP and its intellectual supporters gradually became the official nationalism. Analysing this transformation, and the economic and political developments behind it, is necessary also to understand the other 'unofficial nationalisms' of this time, working closely with banal fascism. The 2001 economic crisis profoundly affected the class composition and political balances of Turkey. The secular-urban lower-middle and upper-middle classes, who had previously felt economically secure, were now faced with unemployment and unstability, which hardened their political attitudes. And in 2002 the Islamist AKP came to power alone, signifying the beginning of a new political era in which Kemalist nationalisms retreated to a more reactionary-defensive position. At this stage, it is important to distinguish the twin unofficial faces of Kemalist nationalism: 'White Turk' nationalism, and *ulusalcı* left.

'White Turk' nationalism is an urban-secular(ist)-modernist attitude that sublimates Western middle-upper class values and lifestyles as the ideal of Western civilisation, interpreting the constitutive ideology of the Republic as a large step towards this goal, and reading politics through a perspective that can be considered to be elitist. 'White Turk' nationalism, which easily articulates with racist and sexist discourses, popularised by journalist-writers, forms a discriminatory, derogatory, and often even sexist discourse through this emphasis on lifestyle. It primarily targets Kurds, actors identified with political Islam and religious people.

In contrast, the *ulusalcı* left similarly adhere to 'White Turk' nationalism in terms of their conceptualisation of the enemy, but differ from it regarding their autarchical, third-worldist, anti-imperialist emphases. The *ulusalcı* left tends to see globalisation wholly as an imperial project, considering nationalism as if it were an integral part of anti-imperialism. Thus, every anti-imperialist is a nationalist to some degree; and, in this sense, they consider that Atatürk was both a nationalist and a leftist.

Thus, to varying degrees, the *ulusalcı* left considers Kurds and Islamists (and also some other 'others') as the enemy, as well as the Turkish-Islamic synthesis nationalists. With the AKP's coming to power in 2002, a belief arose that these enemies were obtaining political support from both 'inside' and 'outside' Turkey. On this point, different versions of Kemalist nationalism, 'White Turk' nationalism, *ulusalcı* left and Turkish-Islamic synthesis nationalism converged. The rise of conspiratory theories as mythical narratives and the pathological states of mind accompanying them, functioned as a glue that bonded these otherwise divergent nationalisms. A nationalist blueprint was established, in which the integration process with the European Union (EU) was identified as disintegration, the USA was regarded as a global actor handing over Turkey to Islamists in pursuit of its own interests, and the Kurdish question was completely connected to the 'new imperialism' (see Topçu 2001: 186–189; Fırat 2002a: 88–94; Doğan 2002: 108–114; Özden 2002: 126–129). Within this axis, a clear tendency emerged for nationalists to refer to sacred values and for secularist-*ulusalcı* factions to organisationally act together.

Departing from the assumption that the nation-state was under threat, the *Kızıl Elma* (Red Apple) idea,[9] which prescribed the unification of the Kuvayı Milliye (national forces), called for a second war of independence by intentionally using a militarist discourse. The 'Red Apple Coalition' in popular discourse referred to an attempt to bring together nationalists on both sides of the political axis. A coalition, amalgamated from left and right elements since the end of the 1990s, aimed to gather left-wing Kemalists and Turkish-Islamic synthesists against the 'common enemies' such as Islamists, Kurds, the EU etc. Thus, the discourse of the coalition included Euro-scepticism, anti-minority stance and xenophobia. By correlating current issues so strongly with the survival of the regime, it became evident in their eyes that the distinction between left and right was 'artificial' (Yaşlı 2006: 81). This coalition, in which Kemalist nationalists and Turkish-Islamic synthesis nationalist organisations stood side by side, did not last long organisationally. Even though it is not possible today to see such a coalition, it is obvious that a state of convergence between these factions at a grassroots level has continued. Among the factors behind this, one can include those postulates of nationalism that agree with the shared principles of the founding regime and the political anxieties created by being in opposition and feeling one's back to the wall in the face of power. As well as the discourse of a 'second national struggle' among Kemalist and Turkish-Islamic synthesis nationalists, there was also a wide circulation of texts and images about the War of Independence, Atatürk and 'national sacrifices'. Leftist Kemalist factions, in particular, frequently argued that Atatürk and the War of Independence had served as examples for the Third World, and that the 'new war' against imperialism would spark the same reaction (see Öztaş 2002: 148–164). In this way, the Third World became a political project corresponding to the nationalism of the *ulusalcı* left, rather than a simple geographic location or positioning (see, for example, Fırat 2002b: 22).

As mentioned above, there was not only a struggle for hegemony at the ideological level, there were also collective acts of violence in the streets. The ethnic tensions and acts of lynching that began to occur more often after the mid-1990s, continued incessantly in the 2000s directly stemmed from fascistic tendencies.[10] These acts of lynching, which first targeted any Kurds directly or indirectly associated with the PKK, later took on a wider scope. These acts, presented to the public as a 'national reflex', or the ordinary spontaneous reactions of 'folks who love their country', and approved of or tolerated by official authorities, were often in fact organised, planned and programme attacks (see Bora 2008). Since 2002, so long as they did not question the legitimacy of the ruling AKP, these lynching campaigns have not been perceived as a serious problem by the government. As such, this situation demonstrates the boundaries that neoliberal nationalism has tried to entrench in society.

Neoliberal Nationalism Under the AKP

When the economic crises and corruption allegations reached a peak, both the centre right and left collapsed. The AKP, the outright victor of the elections of 3 November 2002, became the precursor of a neoliberal political transformation that would also have distinctive conservative motifs. The AKP's founders had grown up in the National Vision movement and, realising after the 28 February 1997 intervention that it was necessary to move towards a 'new' politics at peace with the Western world and consonant with liberal values, they found support from a wide circle of people, partly thanks to the effect of the political conjuncture. In a largely similar fashion to the Motherland Party, the AKP also pursued a strategy of including the different tendencies of the Turkish right within itself.

According to Hakan Yavuz, there are two basic factors behind the AKP's rapid rise after splitting off from the traditional political line under the leadership of Necmettin Erbakan, who had taken an explicit Islamist stand as the RP leader (Yavuz 2010: 7).[11] The first of these factors is the new bourgeoisie, whose roots can be traced back to Turgut Özal's neoliberal economic policy, but who attained their essential challenging power (despite the 28 February post-modern intervention) in the early 2000s. It is notable that the Independent Industrialists and Businessmen Association (MÜSİAD), the club of conservative entrepreneurs and bosses, increased its share of economic activity by urbanising and expanding its base, and entering new sectors. Economically liberal, politically conservative businessmen, who continued their contact with Anatolian cities and towns, moved closer to the 'reformist' wing that emerged from the National Vision movement. In addition, conservative and religious small shopkeepers and merchants joined the group supporting the AKP leader, Recep Tayyip Erdoğan, hoping that this party would bring 'stability' after the 2001 crisis.

The other factor cited by Yavuz was the 'new intellectual circle outside state control'. This intelligentsia, who were waging a war of influence with the traditional elites, was at loggerheads with Kemalism and leftist politics, (which it generally identified with Kemalism). This tendency to identify all leftist or socialist currents with the authoritarian-progressive *ulusalcı* left, led them to join in efforts to delegitimise the opposition to AKP power (see, for instance, Türköne 2001: 37–58). In fact, the same tactic was also often used in order to delegitimise the social and political opposition of Kurdish people, to the extent that many authors supportive of the AKP even asserted that the whole Kurdish political movement was under the tutelage of the PKK. This circle's intimate relations with neoliberal thought, their perceptions of political liberalism and economic liberalism as a whole, and their tendency to consider Turkish political history and current political positionings through a neoliberal perspective were all at work in the AKP's establishment of its own ideological hegemony.

Below, I will focus on the relationship between the ideological hegemony that formed around the AKP and official nationalism, to argue that neoliberal nationalism has been gradually made the official nationalism. As Erdoğan's dominance over the party and its base is well known, I shall frequently refer to his own statements. However, it is first necessary to clarify one point. That is, we should not forget that nationalists with stronger Islamist tendencies and nationalists emphasising Turkishness coexist within the AKP. While it is certain that who has the upper hand in the party varies from time to time, depending upon conjunctural developments, it is also obvious that neither current objects to the neoliberal economic order and its socio-political presuppositions. How then can one describe neoliberal nationalism, whose most conspicuous discursive examples we see in the words of the AKP leader, Erdoğan?

The AKP's 'Acceptable Nationalism' and Its Adversary

The neoliberal nationalism gaining strength under the AKP is essentially a sort of nationalism which is at peace with the market economy and its actors, blending nationalist symbols and a discourse of 'advanced democracy',[12] while trying to soften systemic tensions through populist-conservative or religious motifs. In addition, it is largely the product of the effort to construct a 'new' and 'acceptable' nationalism by way of condemning the sins of the founding official nationalism. Different political authors and thinkers who had suffocated under the pressure of various forms of official nationalism have pointed out the symptoms and residues of the nation-state process as the original source of Turkey's long-standing problems in its progress towards democratisation, but their voices were always suppressed. Because the AKP paid attention to these criticisms, thanks both to the neoliberal conjuncture and the Islamist opposition out of which it came, liberal and democratic circles developed sympathetic views about the AKP for a considerable amount of time. The reforms that the AKP government initiated in its early years, thanks to its positive and audacious approach to the EU integration process, and its uncommon determination to prevent the Turkish Armed Forces from intervening in politics, were also influential in the emergence of this sympathy. The AKP, which the urban and secular middle and upper classes viewed with suspicion, particularly refrained in its first period in power from presenting a public profile conflicting with the republican 'regime' and its symbols. Instead, on every possible occasion, Erdoğan and other party members underscored their commitment to democracy and the constitution in order to pre-empt possible criticisms (for instance, see *Türkiye Bülteni* 2003: 9–13). Whereas discussions about the official nationalism were generally avoided during this first period, in case they might turn into a discussion of a 'regime' problem by way of Kemalism, the same cannot be said for the second and third periods. This is because the AKP's spokespersons and circles close to the party, who had solidified their political success with successive election victories, began to construct their own 'acceptable nationalism', largely through criticising the Kemalism and official nationalism of the single-party period. The rigid secular attitudes and ethnicist emphases of the nationalism of the early republican period, tightly bound to the leadership cult of Atatürk, were ruthlessly attacked from a liberal-conservative viewpoint. As such, the reproduction of rituals of the official nationalism were gradually opened up for discussion. Not surprisingly, this also included problematising the relationship between Kemalism, the official nationalism and the military, particularly by condemning Kemalist nationalism, which critics accused of paving the way for the series of military interventions since 27 May 1960. Importantly, thanks to these criticisms, government opponents who described the 27 May 1960 coup as 'emancipatory' and drew inspiration from it for forming a new 'progressive alliance' could be politically discredited at a time when some people were drawing an analogy between the Democrat Party of the 1950s and the AKP.

The AKP government's vociferous criticisms of the authoritarian policies implemented during the Republican People's Party's (CHP) single-party period were an explicit message addressed to this party and its allies. The CHP offered only a shallow opposition through its constitutive official ideology and the polarisations created during the 2007 Presidency elections, in company with the 'republic meetings' that it helped organise.[13] The MHP, on the other hand, was at times accused of racism, and at other times, of defaming the AKP through the martyr funerals.[14] The *ülkücü* youth had already been active in the martyr funerals of the 1990s, but in 2000s they began to use this in order to criticise the Kurdish policy of the AKP, which led to an increase in accusations of exploiting the funerals for political gain. However, contrary to what was believed, these developments did not mean that the AKP and the milieu close to the party came to terms politically with the nationalist ideology. Rather, they directed their assaults against the founding official nationalism, which was outdated and trapped into inured rituals, and the unacceptable nationalism of the AKP's political opponents. Erdoğan's speech at the party's group meeting in November 2010, during the second period of the AKP government, provides a dramatic example of this attitude. In his speech, which contains a description of his party's version of nationalism and of the power bloc in general, Erdoğan stated:

Nationalism is not racism. Nationalism is by no means shouting slogans, chanting with various symbols, imposing intolerance as an ideology. Nationalism is gathering around certain ideals, certain values, uniting around a vision of the future, becoming a single heart for the sake of the tranquility and peace of all humanity. A common consciousness of history and culture holds people together, carrying them into the future as a nation. Nationalism is valuable as long as it can form this spirit, strengthen this emotional climate . . . Nationalism is not racism at all. For the main elements constituting a nation are not the blood ties, genetic codes, but history, culture, common ideals and common values. It is the utmost injustice and indignity, not only to this nation, but to this country as well, to discriminate between two martyrs, who fought for the same piece of land, for the same flag, for the same ideals and values, resting now in peace side by side, on the basis of their ethnicity, their language, their origin or their sect. We are a nation gathered under the meta-identity of the Turkish Republic, gathered around the same flag, the same national anthem, the same ideals and values. We have always perceived nationalism like this. (*Milliyet*, 9 November 2010)

Beginning from the 2007 election process, Erdoğan and other AKP members gained a series of positions in the competition among nationalisms by keenly describing nationalism as a 'unifying element' and using 'national symbols'. That is, the AKP responded to their opponents' nationalist discourse with their own 'acceptable nationalism'. This was presented as an extrovert, assertive, self-assured 'acceptable nationalism', formulated as compassion for, commitment to, and 'love of service' towards the nation. Thus, it was positioned as the opposite of introverted, reactionary, pessimistic nationalism. Certainly, the populist elements and symbols of the nationalist discourse all lay within this positioning. Commemorations reproduced in collective memory for the sake of nationalist purposes, heroic statements made on such occasions, visits to the cemeteries of the martyrs, and messages celebrating national and religious festivals, all fell within the national symbolism used by the AKP. The party also adorned public billboards with the celebratory message, 'Let Me Give My Life For Your Star and Crescent' for the 2007 religious holiday of the feast of sacrifice. Thus, Erdoğan broadcast messages of brotherhood through martyrdom, and the Turkish flag and pictures of Atatürk were often used at party demonstrations and in the *Türkiye Bülteni* (Bulletin of Turkey), which is the official media organ of the party. Almost every picture of the Prime Minister included the Turkish flag. This scene was also frequently repeated during the heatedly debated 'democratic opening' process. In response to criticisms, party spokespeople invariably reacted with the slogan of 'one flag, one state, one nation'. One should bear in mind that the 'democratic opening' itself was presented by the ruling party as a project of 'national unity and brotherhood'. From the AKP's perspective, the cement of this 'national unity and brotherhood' was Islam. Erdoğan's speech at the party's group meeting on 11 August 2009, which was also included in a pamphlet to explain the project to the public, is another example, with its references to slogans of the democratic opening, such as 'Do not let mothers cry':

No matter why her mother has lost her son . . . if the mother in Yozgat and the mother in Hakkâri say the same prayers in their sons' graveyards, if they pray the Yasin and the al-Fatihah for their son, if the community turn towards Mecca, then it means here [in the war between the Turkish Armed Forces and the PKK,] there is a very serious mistake. (*Milliyet*, 12 August 2009)

It is clear from this that the actors of the AKP, primarily Prime Minister Erdoğan and the intelligentsia close to the party, situate 'acceptable nationalism' within an 'executive' framework, just like Turgut Özal did, and tend to measure the country's 'real nationalist performance' according to the extent of its capacity to articulate with capitalist economy. We already know that the discourse of development, which had been transformed into a matter of 'survival' and 'pride' during the whole Cold War era by the Turkish right, is very strong. In other words, the developmental project of the Turkish right almost always went hand in hand with nationalism until, with Özal, it was articulated into neoliberalism. After the painful 1990s, the AKP found an environment in which it could reform the discourse by particularly emphasising such criteria as economic stability and domestic production, presented as the most valuable successes of the party.[15] Later on, steps taken towards establishing a domestic arms industry, which had been one of the key aims of the nationalist-militarist vision in Turkey for a long time, were treated as a 'national success'. The AKP Minister Veysel Eroğlu's words exemplify this defence of 'real nationalism':

To be a nationalist is to launch the 'Göktürk' [Skyturk] satellite into space. To be a nationalist is to produce 'ATAK' helicopters. To be a nationalist is to produce drones, which we call 'ANKA' as it resembles the Phoenix. It is to produce tanks, rifles, a series of guns, and even the motor factories of F-35s. We are even producing our submarines. We are exporting armoured vehicles to the world. Last year, we had 1 billion dollar exports in this sector.[16]

Since 2002, this emphasis on production and stability has continued to be the most important part of the AKP's political propaganda, and its definition of 'acceptable nationalism' has been equated with 'servicing the nation with love', this being the manifestation of the populist discourse. It is not just a coincidence that Erdoğan highlights on every possible occasion that the AKP are 'love-struck' with the nation.[17] It can also be easily argued that another aspect of the AKP's discourse, of 'being a servant to the nation' is a product of the party's effort to distinguish itself from traditional elitist politics and from the official ideology, seen as part of this politics (and Erdoğan himself has described such politics as 'being a master to the nation').

Nationalist Motifs of the the AKP's Neo-Ottomanism

Today, we see that the AKP reproduces official nationalism by regulating and modulating it according to neoliberal requirements, rather than keeping a distance from it. As mentioned above, the AKP's neo-Ottoman political vision, with its imperial references and roots that can be traced back to Özal's period, is an integral part of its neoliberal nationalism. Its main reference point is neither Central Asia, the so-called motherland of Turks, nor the 'spirit of 1923' because those imagined golden ages of Kemalist and Turkish-Islamic synthesis nationalisms have largely become dysfunctional. What is instead emphasised by the AKP spokespeople, and the intelligentsia sympathetic to it, is a justice- and power-oriented 'civilisation project', envisaged through a renowned Ottoman past. Domestically, this project signifies the possibility for different cultures and values to co-exist within Turkey. Internationally, for states that emerged out of the Ottoman empire, it is the harbinger of a unique model that consolidates a liberal economy and democracy. The AKP's neo-Ottomanism is thus more in accordance with the liberal model of Turgut Özal and his circle than with that of the AKP's predecessor, the RP, particularly in its refusal to categorically reject the West.

Domestically, the AKP government and the intelligentsia close to it have tried to render neo-Ottomanism most 'functional' in terms of the Kurdish question. The AKP government proposed a new multicultural definition of Turkish citizenship by revising a model inspired by the Ottoman Empire. So long as Islam is the common denominator, it strives to present Turkish citizenship as an 'inclusive' and 'appealing' meta-identity. This is the essence of the 'democratic opening' project, in which the Kurdish reality is described as folkloric wealth, and reform plans have been prepared in parallel with this. However, there is another side to this, which is the 'sharp sword' of the Ottoman Empire, that is, the power of the state. According to the historiographical approach of the Turkish right, an essential part of the mystification of the Ottoman past is its view of the state as 'mighty'. That 'might', not only described but also emulated, reserves the right to use physical power as an alternative to persuasion. On this point, the AKP has followed an authoritarian-militarist course against those Kurdish politicians who were not satisfied with the AKP's proposed line, perceiving the 'democratic opening' as insufficient. It is necessary to consider moves to discredit Kurdish politicians, military operations held in reserve, and operations against KCK (Union of Kurdistan Communities), alleged to be the urban organisation of the PKK, within this context.

Within the AKP's active foreign policy of *Pax-Ottomana*, there lies the promise that Turkey will protect the peace of people in the region, as did its predecessor, the Ottoman Empire. In line with the way Ahmet Davutoğlu, previously the Chief Advisor to the Prime Minister and then Minister of Foreign Affairs as of 1 May 2009, interprets international relations and Turkey's position, the ruling party tries to gain international legitimacy and power through this perspective. In particular, the AKP's Middle East policy is an ideal example where one can observe moves to achieve this goal. In this case, the AKP constructs another 'story of peculiarity', where Turkey is situated in the centre, and a nationalist narrative based on this story. Erdoğan has made various statements that resemble in many aspects those of Özal (see Özal 1992), in which he attributes a historical mission to Turkey, as can be seen from the following example:

Turkey is a country rising above a very rich cultural legacy with its great civilisational experience going back tens of thousands of years . . . We are a nation that has reigned over three continents, laying down works of art and traces wherever we went. Today, in these three continents, there are fraternal, friendly people who have the same origin as us. Besides, we are country with a central location, linking the West to the East, the North to the South, and Europe, Asia and Africa to each other, not only geographically, but also culturally and historically . . . In this panorama, no matter whether it is willing or not, Turkey has a role, a responsibility, a mission. (*Türkiye Bülteni* 2009: 13–14)

Conclusion

The neoliberal alliance grouping under the power of the AKP realised that the thoroughly archaic official nationalism and the associated unofficial Kemalist nationalisms were failing to satisfy the needs of Turkey's rising middle class and address changing balances in global capital flows. Therefore, they saw the AKP's rise as an opportunity in the country's transition to a modern liberal democracy. Setting to work with rapid reforms, the AKP ultimately established its power, but then adopted an increasingly authoritarian policy, internalising the 'state's reflexes' and delegitimising all its opponents. One of the clearest proofs of this has been the AKP's response to the Kurdish question because it horisontally cuts across those movements housing different Turkish nationalisms. Particularly in its third period in power, the AKP transformed its promises of a 'democratic opening', and waves of arrests and military operations, into a natural entity with two faces. Through various channels, it legitimised its strategy of suppresssing and illegalising the Kurdish opposition in the name of 'Great Turkey'. At the same time, Prime Minister Erdoğan and the AKP abandoned their enthusiastic and assertive approach to the EU integration process, reducing EU reforms to technical adaptations and sometimes turned into a typical centre-right party, resorting to an anti-Western populist discourse. In a series of matters (such as opening the border with Armenia and political relations with Israel), which had direct implications for internal politics, they displayed a nationalist approach.

Despite these failings of the AKP government, it is hard to say that the parliamentary opposition in Turkey is any better in terms of democracy and fundamental freedoms. Today, the various forms of Kemalist nationalism have substantially lost the struggle for hegemony. In particular, the reactionary and defensive politics pursued by the CHP in the first decade of the 2000s, and its general tendency to protect and favour Kemalist nationalisms, have eroded its potential to offer a viable political alternative. The MHP, the main actor in Turkish-Islamic synthesis nationalism, was drawn towards the official secularist line from the 1990s onwards, but then began to lose its dominance over those electoral constituencies from whom it traditionally secured its support in the competition between nationalisms. Instead, in these constituencies, it was the AKP, promising stability and growth, that rapidly gained strength. On the other hand, the MHP did increase its votes in major cities, especially on the coasts. As for those regions experiencing intensive Kurdish migration due to state policies of the 1990s in Kurdish regions,[18] it may be argued that the MHP can continue to increase its votes as long as the reactions of the 'native' population towards the newcomers take an ethnicist-nationalist form. The swing of the MHP and the CHP toward this secular-*ulusalcı* base is undoubtedly a factor in this increase. In some regions, it seems that the CHP carries the MHP, and in others vice versa. Nevertheless, it is very likely that the tension between the two parties will rise if the CHP shifts to a more moderate line on the Kurdish question. At the moment, the current political configuration supports fascistic-nationalist movements on the one hand, and an authoritarian identity of state power, on the other. Under these circumstances, the aim of subjecting the political centre to democratic transformation has itself been transformed into the consolidation of the centre through 'acceptable' nationalism.

NOTES

1 *Ulusalcı* is synonymous with *milliyetçi*, both of which literally mean nationalist. However, Kemalists have tended to use 'pure Turkish' *ulusalcı*, adopted as a result of the language reform, thus using their own version of the term nationalist.

2 *Ülkücü* literally means the person who has a nationalist mission. But as this 'ideal' belongs to the ultra-nationalist-fascist movement in Turkey, and the terms itself has obtained a specific connotation, I will refer to it in its Turkish form.

3 ANAP is a center right party established in Ankara on 20 May 1983. Under the chairman of Turgut Özal, the party came to power alone with 45.1 per cent of the votes in the 1983 elections.

4 This intellectual circle can be very roughly described as *Türkiye Günlüğü Dergisi*, to which figures like Mustafa Çalık, Cengiz Çandar, Yahya Sezai Tezel and Ahmet Turan Alkan contributed. For some other exemplary works where one can see neo-Ottomanist tendencies, see Çandar (1992: 31–34), Çalık (1992: 57–60).

5 In the 1994 local elections, the RP achieved great success, winning a significant number of metropolitan municipalities, including Ankara and İstanbul, and getting 19 per cent of the votes in the distribution according to provinces.

6 Thirty-three authors, thinkers and poets, an important number of whom were *Alevis*, came to Sivas in order to participate in a festival organised by the Pir Sultan Abdal Association, but they all deplorably lost their lives when the Madımak hotel was set on fire by an radical Islamist mob.

7 The 28 February process, which also became known as the 'post-modern coup', takes its name from the date (28 February) when the National Security Council (MGK) was convened. The Council took a number of decisions, such as eight years of compulsory primary education, in this session and gave notice to the Welfare-Path government (the coalition between the Welfare Party and the True Path Party) to implement them. Following the MGK decisions, the Chief Prosecutor of the Supreme Court opened a case for closing down the political Islamist RP, at which point, the RP Prime Minister, Necmettin Erbakan, resigned from his post, on 18 June 1997.

8 Republican festivals are the most important day for national rituals and official nationalism. However, the interest shown in official celebrations had decreased for understandable reasons. The idea to repopularise the republican festivals first came to the fore with the 1994 local elections, when the RP first started to rise, with the 75th anniversary celebrations. See Özyürek (2008).

9 *Kızıl Elma* (the Red Apple), in the Turkish mythology, symbolises the aims and the ideals of the Turkish state.

10 In her article analysing the lynching events, Zeynep Gambetti (2007: 30) points out the possible intersections between class and ethnicity. I agree with this possibility but I am also particularly interested in how this issue manifests itself.

11 In his own political line, Necmettin Erbakan was both a party leader and a religious leader. Always holding to the traditional strategy of organisation, Erbakan followed a severe anti-Western discourse throughout his political life. The AKP's founders, on the other hand, promised they would highlight a series of principles such as team work, common mind, and internal party democracy during the establishment of the party. See Çınar (2005: 109).

12 The AKP's 'advanced democracy' discourse is, at bottom, the reregulation of the realm of authority of the civil-military bureaucracy, which is thought to have restricted the 'people's will'.

13 Republic meetings were activities organised by Kemalist non-governmental institutions in major cities like İstanbul, Ankara, and İzmir in April and May before the 2007 Presidency elections.

14 For instance, even though he did not directly mention the MHP, Erdoğan did in fact address it through the following words: 'One cannot be a nationalist, playing upon the blood and funeral of the martyrs. We just say, cut this out. For Allah's sake, can you come forward and say "We came to power and did this, did that"? Can you say this? What did they do, ask them, I wonder what they would say. What is there to tell anyway, what kind of services are there which they can point to? What road did they construct, how many hospitals, how many schools did they build, to which village did they bring water?' *Türkiye Bülteni* (2008: 49).

15 For instance, speaking at the politics academy organised by the Osmaniye provincial organisation of the party, Erdoğan said, 'Nationalism happens if one loves his country and all this happens if you do something. You can be a nationalist if you raise Turkey to the level of being the 17th largest economy in the world. You can be a nationalist if you raise her to the level of being the 6th largest economy in Europe. You can be a nationalist if you make her a global, strong actor in its own region and in the world. You can be a nationalist if your country determines its own agenda, rather than its agenda being determined by others.' *Türkiye Bülteni* (2008: 26, 27).

16 For Minister Eroğlu's statements, see http://www.akparti.org.tr/site/haberler/milliyetcilik-atak-helikopterini-yapmaktir/8410 (accessed 14 February 2012).

17 There are many similar examples. Erdoğan has frequently likened the bond between his party and the nation to the famous love affair between Ferhat and Şirin. See *Türkiye Bülteni* (2008: 39).

18 Correlated with the Turkish army's strategy of territorial domination, many Kurds were subjected to forced migration as a result of village evacuations, especially between 1992 and 1994, in those regions where there was a fierce combat against the PKK. The displaced population faced long-term unjust treatment wherever they went (homelessness, exclusion, poverty, sickness, etc.). For a detailed analysis of this issue, see Ayata and Yükseker (2005: 5–42); Bozarslan (2001: 45–54). No doubt, this experience helps explain the emergence of new social traumas and unrests, one aspect of which has stirred up violence and discrimination (for example, the ethnicisation of crime in cities).

CHAPTER FOUR

The Davutoğlu Doctrine: The Populist Construction of the Strategic Subject

Mehmet Sinan Birdal

The transformation of Turkish politics since 2002 under Justice and Development Party (AKP) rule has been accompanied by an assertive and ambitious foreign policy discourse. For the leaders of the party and the pundits around them, this discourse indicated a reassertion of a strategic vision that had been suppressed since the fall of the Ottoman Empire and the foundation of the Republic. Following the populist discourse in domestic politics, the new foreign policy discourse was articulated as part of the 'normalisation' of Turkish politics and identity. This article argues that the AKP's foreign policy discourse serves two functions: to justify Turkey's strategic goal of rising to the status of a regional great power; and to legitimise the AKP's rule and policies in domestic politics.

I follow Ted Hopf's argument that 'states understand themselves through domestic others' and 'state identities are constructed at home as well as through interstate interaction' (Hopf 2002: 10). In other words, the foreign policy executives of a state define self-identity and self-interests in international politics in an analogous fashion to their definitions of self and other in domestic politics. Hopf uses a social cognitive approach, which provides 'an account of how a state's own domestic identities constitute a social cognitive structure that makes threats and opportunities, enemies and allies, intelligible, thinkable, and possible' (Hopf 2002: 16). In his empirical studies, Hopf maps Russian identity construction with regard to three kinds of others: historical, internal and external. The relation of the Russian self to each of these identities is embedded in a discourse of modernity as a metanarrative (2002: 154). This model provides an important insight for explaining the construction of the AKP's foreign policy discourse as an articulation of its neoliberal populism in domestic politics.

Explaining the consequences of the AKP's foreign policy discourse for Turkish foreign policy and for regional politics lies beyond the scope of this paper. Although such an endeavour would prove very fruitful for the theoretical debates in international relations and foreign policy analysis, the purpose of this chapter is mainly to analyse the predominant foreign policy discourse in Turkey in order to reveal its ideological content. The uncritical reception of many of the AKP's theses by scholars as well as pundits makes it imperative to situate the emergence of its foreign discourse in a historical and political context. Analyses of current Turkish foreign policy and strategy take the AKP's (and the larger liberal/conservative) discursive distinction between the Kemalist and the Neo-Ottoman (or Imperial) legacy as a given historical fact (Mufti 2009; Taşpınar 2008). In this article, however, I want to suggest not only that both of these categories are historically and socially constructed, but also that they have more in common than appears to be the case at first sight.

The rise of the AKP to power in Turkey in 2002 brought a puzzle to the fore: the old, Westernised elite, long regarded by the West as a valuable ally, seemed to be supporting an authoritarian regime, while the newly rising Muslim elite seemed to be at the vanguard of democratisation, and initiating reforms to integrate with the EU. The battle between secularist Kemalists and moderate Islamists has become a *leitmotiv* of any analysis of Turkish society since then. However, there is something terribly restricting in this portrayal for both the current political and scholarly imagination. Politically, by calling on one to choose sides, it colonises the political imagination to the extent that alternatives to this political cleavage are deemed impossible. As the Turkish Prime Minister Erdoğan puts it: 'Those who don't choose sides will be eliminated'.[1] This colonisation of political imagination also leads to the etiolation of scholarly imagination. Operating as 'discursive orthopedics' (Foucault 1990: 29), this duality restricts scholarly imagination through an uncritical reception of a popular discourse about Turkey, mostly circulating in the mass media.

Rejecting the idea of treating the Kemalist-Islamist divide as given, I approach these identities as 'particular modes by which human beings become subjects' (Smart 1989: 107) which are products of a certain historical episode with particular effects on Turkish society. From this viewpoint, Kemalism and Islamism appear as two sides of the same coin: a discourse about the difference of Turkey and its relation to modernity as a permanently deferred moment of the arrival of modernity. Both Kemalism and the AKP's liberal/conservative discourse follow the logic of subaltern nationalism identified by Partha Chatterjee, who distinguishes between the problematic and the thematic features of an ideology. The problematic involves the identification of historical possibilities or the practical programme of an ideology, which is justified by the latter's claims of validity, while the thematic is an epistemological and ethical system warranting practical inferences. Chatterjee argues that subaltern nationalism changes the problematic, but maintains the thematic aspect of nationalism. In other words, subaltern nationalism reasons within the same epistemological and ethical universe of colonial nationalism, despite the former's political opposition to the latter (Chatterjee 1999: 38). Prior to challenging colonialism, subaltern nationalism first constitutes its own sovereign sphere by dividing the social world into a material and a spiritual domain. In the material domain of economy, statecraft, science and technology, subaltern nationalism acknowledges Western superiority and warrants the imitation of Western institutions. However, in the spiritual domain of culture, religion and family, anti-colonialism asserts its superiority over Western culture (Chatterjee 1999: 52). Both the first wave of Islamism in the 19th and 20th century and Kemalism in the early 20th century resorted to this bifurcated discourse (Kurzman 2002: 3–27). Starting with the *Tanzimat* period, and continuing throughout the 19th and early 20th century, an excessively Westernised degenerate type, often portrayed as effeminate, emerged as the *leitmotiv* of the Ottoman and Turkish social imaginary (Mardin 1974; Moran 2009).

Both Kemalism and the AKP's liberal/conservative populism resort to the idea of a nation 'as a solid community moving steadily down (or up) history' (Anderson 1991: 26). Hence, they both employ the paradigmatic nationalist 'metaphor of the nation as journey, as something that is ever in the making but never quite reached' (Krishna 1999: 17). Sankaran Krishna refers to this process as the 'logic of deference', which 'secures the legitimacy of the postcolonial state by centring its historical role in the pursuit of certain desired futures' (1999: 17). Thus, 'the state literally buys time for itself as it deflects the adverse judgment of civil society "for the time being"' (1999: 18). Krishna points out that the logic of deference operates differently in subaltern and western nation-states: 'In the latter, the endless deferment is on the question of extending the idea of community to a global space . . . In the space called the postcolony, the endless deferment is on the question of achieving national unity itself . . . Thus, the "moment of arrival" [Here the author refers to Chatterjee 1999, MSB] as a nation is deferred endlessly in the postcolony' (1999: 18–19). Chatterjee defines the moment of arrival as an 'ideological unity of nationalist thought it seeks to actualise in the unified life of the state', going on to assert that 'nationalist thought at its moment of arrival is passive revolution uttering its own life-history' (Chatterjee 1999: 51).

In the Turkish context, both Kemalism (Savran 2010: 54–123) and the AKP's rule (Tuğal 2009) can be conceived of as transitory moments of arrival and passive revolutions, entailing 'a molecular transformation of the state, neutralising opponents, converting sections of the former ruling classes into allies in a partially recognised system of government, undertaking economic reforms on a limited scale so as to appropriate the support of the popular masses but keeping them out of any direct participation in the process of governance' (Chatterjee 1999: 45). Whether the AKP rule can be identified as a passive revolution or not has become the focus of recent debate (Morton 2012; Tuğal 2012). What matters for the purposes of this paper is that both regimes – the Kemalist and the AKP populist – facilitated the rearticulation of social and political relations, making them more compatible with the capitalist world economy. In this context, both regimes construct identity and difference within the framework of a global capitalist modernity.

By locating Turkish difference within a universal modernity, the AKP's hegemonic liberal/conservative discourse has much in common with its supposed arch-nemesis Kemalism than its proponents are ready to admit. The liberal/conservative discourse combines two narratives: an over-generalising tendency that regards the rising conservative movement in Turkey as a recurring social phenomenon following the Western model of modernisation; and a particularistic tendency that treats the phenomenon as uniquely 'Turkish', as a consequence of Turkish or Oriental political culture. The first narrative rests on the argument that, like the Calvinists of early modern Europe, the rise of the Muslim bourgeoisie is a symptom of free markets that will lead to democratisation and regional peace and stability as an unintended consequence (İnsel 2003; Knaus 2005; Nasr 2009; Keyman and Koyuncu Lorasdağı 2010; Laçiner 2011). The second narrative, in contrast, conceptualises contemporary conservatism as a peripheral movement rising against the political centre, thereby democratising Turkish political culture. Despite this apparent contradiction between universalising and particularising tendencies, both narratives operate together to explain how and why Turkey's different historical trajectory will finally converge with the trajectory of the West: namely, through a market economy and liberal democracy. However, this mode of explanation has two shortcomings. On the one hand, two vastly different historical trajectories are considered in terms of 'Western experience' providing the universal mechanisms for democratisation and creating a global measure against which non-Western trajectories can be measured. On the other hand, Turkish political culture is treated as a monolithic and given thing, remaining intact through centuries. The 'state tradition' and religion (in some versions geography) makes Turkey a unique case in which conservatives are the real engines of social change and democracy, while the so-called revolutionaries are in fact conservatives: in Turkey, the left is right and the right is left (Küçükömer 2009). I argue that this liberal/conservative explanation reiterates the Orientalist discourse about politics in the Middle East: 'History, politics, and economics do not matter. Islam is Islam, the Orient is the Orient, please take all your ideas about a left and a right wing, revolutions, and change back to Disneyland' (Said 1995: 107). Thus, a discourse combining a generalising narrative of modernisation and globalisation with a particularising narrative of nationalism is built on a syntax that is common to both Kemalism and the AKP's populism. The AKP's populism employs the rhetorical devices of subaltern nationalism to consolidate the party's rule in Turkey. As Hopf suggests, the foreign policy discourse of the AKP reflects the main contours of its domestic political discourse.

Neoliberal Populism

Since the early 2000s, the AKP has become the dominant actor in Turkish politics by articulating a neoliberal populist discourse. Previously, from the post-war years on, some form of Keynesian economic and social policy dominated Turkey's political landscape, with Turkish politics being shaped according to its position as a peripheral economy, largely dependent on agriculture and applying an import-substitution strategy to support an assembly industry. Mainstream political parties on both centre right and centre left responded to the imperatives of the growth policy prevailing internationally at the time, as well as to the political contingencies of a vertically and horizontally mobile society. These parties had to strike a balance to appeal both to urban and rural constituencies.[2] In this context, the populist policies accompanying both centre left and centre right discourses meant agricultural subsidies and salary increases for employees in the public sector.

However, such postwar populism became increasingly unviable as an export-oriented growth strategy and neoliberal practices, again following the predominant international dogma, came to be viewed as common sense in post-1980

Turkish politics. In the 1980s, while centre-right populism employed an anti-statist neoliberal discourse to justify privatisation and deregulation, neoliberal policies led to the centralisation and concentration of resources in the hands of the Prime Minister to an unprecedented degree. Technocratic populism was also a predominant political discourse during the 1990s (Cizre-Sakallıoğlu and Yeldan 2000). In this regard, the AKP's success lies in its execution of neoliberal reforms while using populist rhetoric as a legitimating discourse. In this political discourse, the anti-statist narrative of neoliberalism, which has been consolidated as the dominant ideology since the 1980s, simultaneously serves as a rhetorical device to 'interpellate' a democratic populist subject. Like other populist movements, the AKP rose to power in the context of an economic, social and political crisis. Panizza identifies a number of circumstances in which populist strategies might emerge: first, a breakdown of social order and loss of confidence in the political system due to economic crises, civil wars, ethnic conflicts or natural disasters; second, distrust of existing political parties and political traditions due to corruption, malpractice and a self-serving political elite; third, economic, social and cultural changes due to urbanisation, economic modernisation, demographic changes in the balance between social classes and between regional and ethnic groups, and globalisation; fourth, the emergence of forms of political representation outside traditional political institutions (Panizza 2005: 11–13). Almost all of these circumstances were present in the Turkish political landscape after the 2001 economic crisis.

In this context, populist actors successfully build a movement around a variety of unfulfilled demands against the establishment. As a mode of identification, populism rests on the notion of the sovereignty of the people and the conflict between the powerful and the powerless (Panizza 2005: 4). Claiming to represent the wise yet silent majority, populist discourses constitute a political subject based on two central concepts: the heartland and the people (Taggart 2000; Laclau 2007). These discourses identify technocratic and degenerate elites, powerful minorities, organised interest groups, and complex political institutions and processes as the enemies of the people. According to Ernesto Laclau, populist discourses make use of several rhetorical devices through which the part represents the totality, or the partial represents the universal. Thus, the populist political subject representing the people becomes hegemonic.[3] Since the people as a universal is an impossible object, hegemonic identity is an empty signifier. In Laclau's words, the particularity of the populist subject embodies an 'unachievable fullness' (Laclau 2007: 71). Emptiness, however, does not mean being abstract. On the contrary, the empty signifier allows the hegemonic discourse to appeal to a variety of particular demands and embrace them under the populist subject. The common denominator of these particular demands is the exclusion from, or the unresponsiveness of the political system (Laclau 2007: 96). Thus, the populist discourse employs two strategies: emphasising the distinctiveness and particularity of certain social demands; and claiming the sameness and equality of the demands. Laclau describes the former strategy, based on othering, as the 'logic of difference', and the latter, resting on a common identity, as 'equivalential logic' (Laclau 2007: 96). Both logics facilitate the construction of the populist subject, which signifies the people and its enemies.

The AKP's political discourse invokes the historical legacy of the Turkish centre-right. Its central tenets are identical to what constitutional historian Bülent Tanör dubs the 'populist constitutional development theses'. According to Tanör, 'the common point of these theses is to explain [Turkish] constitutional development in terms of a 'contradiction' between a social stratum or class defined as 'bureaucracy' and another social group defined as the 'people'. In this explanation, the 'bureaucracy' plays the roles of the 'dominant actor' and the 'oppressor'" (Tanör 2010: 107). These views are rooted in the political theses of the centre-right Democratic Party (DP) of the 1950s. Tanör studies the arguments of two DP advocates: Ahmet Hamdi Başar, a founding figure of the Association of İstanbul Traders; and Celal Bayar, the head of the DP, who served as the president from 1950 until the military coup in 1960. In Başar's view, the Kemalist revolutionary cadres can be regarded as the descendants of the *kapıkulus*, Ottoman soldiers receiving a salary from the sultan. The basic political contradiction in Turkey is therefore not 'between employer and employee, but between these two and the *kapıkulu* in power' (Tanör 2010: 108). Bayar rests his argument on two basic assumptions: first, that 'the most correct idea springs from the fountain of the people';[4] second, that the people exercise their sovereignty through the majority party in the Turkish Grand National Assembly (TGNA). In Bayar's view, the Ottoman sultan shared his sovereignty with the army and the *medrese* (Islamic institutions of higher learning), specifically the jurists graduating from the *medreses*. Although Mustafa Kemal Atatürk abolished this mode of power-sharing with the 1924 Constitution, Bayar claimed that his historical political nemesis, İsmet İnönü, had reinstated the powers of these two institutions: the armed forces and the university. The coup on 27 May 1960 continued an old Ottoman tradition by appointing members of the armed forces, university professors and judges to rule over the legislature and the executive. The 1961 Constitution limited the sovereignty of the nation by creating power-sharing institutions such as the Senate, the Constitutional Court, autonomous universities, the National Security Council, the State Planning Agency, the Turkish Radio and Television Corporation etc. (Tanör 2010: 109–110).[5] The AKP's discourse criticising military guardianship, 'juristocracy' and the dominance of intellectuals recycles these rhetorical topics to construct a populist subject in the context of neoliberal transformation.

In this regard, the AKP's political discourse presents a narrative that responds to the particular imperatives of the period. The most significant achievement of the AKP has been to forge a coalition of both the winners and losers of neoliberalism: the rising Anatolian bourgeoisie and the urban poor (Hale and Özbudun 2010; Öniş 2006a; Tuğal 2007b). The AKP's ability to legitimise neoliberal reforms, which necessitates the centralisation and concentration of political authority to implement the policies for dismantling a social regime, lies at the core of its political success.[6] As with other state formation efforts in history, neoliberal reforms both require and contribute to a strong political subject (Roberts 2010). The AKP's anti-establishment discourse has both legitimised the implementation of neoliberal reforms and constituted the AKP as a populist subject fighting for the political empowerment of the people against the bureaucratic elite.

The AKP's success in absorbing popular demands should partly be attributed to the experiences of its cadres in municipality management in the 1990s under the Welfare Party. As Turkish society became urbanised to an unprecedented extent, the AKP articulated a discourse based on efficiency and service (Doğan 2011/12).[7] According to the AKP's foremost ideologue, Yalçın Akdoğan, the party emphasised 'efficiency in providing services rather than a specific identity' and the party's 'developing sense of identity is . . . predicated on normalisation of the current Turkish political system' (Akdoğan 2006: 52). The claim of passing from an identity to a service politics combines the neoliberal definition of politics as a technical process with the populist discourse of serving the people. However, it also contains a serious contradiction. For Akdoğan, 'political legitimacy is . . . based on the common acceptance of a national identity that expresses itself in commonly held norms regarding action, rules, and collective worth' (Akdoğan 2006: 50). Yet, the AKP's approach to political legitimacy oscillates between a conservative definition of public good and a liberal definition of legal procedures allowing the aggregation of individual preferences.[8]

Populism is an integral symptom of liberal democracy (Taggart 2000; Laclau 2007; Panizza 2005; Laclau 2005; Mouffe 2005b). It is distrustful of representative politics, but also makes use of the opportunity structures created by it when organising as a political movement. This leads to an institutional dilemma for populist movements: as the movement organises itself as a political party, the movement either becomes less populist, splits up or disintegrates completely. On the one hand, populism rests on the direct relation between the leader and the masses without the mediation of cumbersome party machinery. On the other hand, as a political movement, especially as a party in power for more than a decade as in the case of the AKP, it requires institutionalisation (Panizza 2005; Taggart 2000). Arguably, the AKP will increasingly face having to make a trade-off between the institutionalisation of its rule and its populist appeal (Kumbaracıbaşı 2009).

Contemporary strategic ideas in Turkey are formulated in the context of the emergence of the AKP's new ruling bloc, which facilitates the integration of Turkey into the global economy, defines a new collective identity, and a new role for Turkish foreign policy in regional as well as global affairs. As the analysis of Ahmet Davutoğlu's book on Turkish grand strategy in this chapter will demonstrate, the AKP's foreign policy discourse rests on its domestic populist discourse.

The Davutoğlu Doctrine: The Populist Construction of the Strategic Subject

The foreign policy discourse of the AKP follows the same narrative as neoliberal populism in domestic politics. Ahmet Davutoğlu, who has served as advisor both to Abdullah Gül, who was the AKP's first Prime Minister until he was appointed Minister of Foreign Affairs in 2009, and to the current Prime Minister, Tayyip Erdoğan, presents this discourse in systematic fashion. The Davutoğlu Doctrine is a self-styled critique of the so-called Kemalist foreign policy tradition. In the preface to his popular book, *Strategic Depth*, Davutoğlu asserts that Turkey needs a new alternative strategic vision. Referring to the emergence of German, English, Russian and American strategic thought, he argues that every major transformation needs a strategic approach that can turn resources into power (2008: v–vi). The Davutoğlu Doctrine is thus presented as a grand strategy for Turkey to rise again as a great power in international politics.

Davutoğlu's doctrine is an extension of the AKP's populist discourse in international politics. His main concern is the emergence of the strategic subject, that is, a proactive, ambitious and rational Turkey. Like the AKP rising in a state of transformation in Turkish society and politics, Davutoğlu formulates strategies for a rising Turkey at a time of transformation in world politics. In Davutoğlu's view, self-confidence and identity are the preconditions for a proactive Turkish strategy, and the lack thereof is attributed to the lack of self-confidence and identity of previous Turkish regimes. Davutoğlu outlines three approaches towards a globalising world politics: first, a defensive, do-nothing attitude; second, a clueless, go-with-the-flow attitude; and third, an assertive, pro-active, strategic attitude. The variation in these foreign policy choices is explained by the level of self-confidence and sense of identity of the actors. For Davutoğlu, societies undergoing a dynamic transformation in a dynamic environment have three strategic alternatives based on three psychological attitudes. In the first, actors lacking self-confidence and fearful of the dynamism of their own societies invoke a static outlook. They suspend their need for reformulating foreign policy, preferring to wait until the international environment loses its dynamism and reaches stability. Their strategic vision preaches a policy of letting time pass and avoiding dynamism. Thus, they want to keep the dynamism of their own societies under control and protect their countries from the effects of global changes as much as possible. Second, actors undergoing an identity crisis go with the flow without interpreting the power resources of their own dynamism. Failing to redefine themselves as subjects, they adopt an attitude that turns them into passive objects in the international system. Actors in this strategic vision want to forget about time. In their haste to adapt to new global trends, they alienate themselves from their local context and are caught in global currents without any direction. The third group, of self-confident actors, turns its dynamism into power in a changing environment. In this strategic vision, every second counts and every new situation presents new opportunities. They are confident in, and make use of, the dynamism of their own societies. They link the local and the global contexts to construct a new, self-confident generation. Neither avoiding chaos nor getting caught up in chaos, actors with this strategic vision actively engage with the chaotic environment to create a new order (Davutoğlu 2008: 10–11).

Despite the abstract and theoretical language of Davutoğlu's formulation, the target of his criticism and the subject of the new Turkish strategic vision are clear. Davutoğlu criticises two attitudes within the Turkish elite of the 1990s: the Kemalist elite, sceptical of globalisation, and the pro-globalisation liberal elite. The former lack self-confidence because of their lack of popular support; therefore, all they can do is to adopt an introverted, defensive strategy, which is bound to lose. The latter, on the other hand, have no sense of identity and embrace the imperatives of globalisation with no strategic vision whatsoever.

Thus, underlying Davutoğlu's book is a critique of the foreign policy strategy of the Turkish republic. The main problem of Turkish foreign policy, according to the Davutoğlu Doctrine, is the same problem in Turkish domestic politics identified by the AKP's populist rhetoric: the decadent elite. It reflects the basic contention of the AKP that, throughout the history of the Republic, it has been subjected to the dominance of a bureaucratic, culturally alienated and politically predominant elite, to the detriment of the people.

Davutoğlu's strategic formulation of the AKP's populism also informs his understanding of power in international relations. Davutoğlu analyses the components of power in international relations according to a formulation, which he calls a 'power equation'. The power equation consists of the sum of fixed data (history, geography, population, culture) and potential data (economic capacity, technological capacity, military capacity) multiplied by strategic mentality, strategic planning and political will. Fixed data are elements that cannot be changed in the short and medium term by political will. However, conjectural changes can lead to changes in the specific weight the fixed data carry in the power equation. They can be accurately defined as parameters and quasi-parameters.[9] Potential data can be changed in the short and medium term. They can be identified as variables of the equation. The data, however, do not make a state powerful in themselves. Strategic mentality, planning and political will turn these resources into power. They are the multipliers. Strategic mentality is a product of the historical legacy encompassing cultural, psychological, religious and social values, and the self-consciousness of a society reflecting on its place in the world. Thus, strategic mentality rests on both a perception of space and a perception of time. It varies from society to society because different societies perceive the world differently with regard to time and space. A robust strategic mentality enables a society to devise new concepts, instruments and forms to deal with the changing environment and increase its capabilities within the international distribution of power. Davutoğlu contrasts an active strategic mentality with a rupture in mentality and an isolation of mentality. Societies undergoing an identity crisis due to a radical break with the strategic mentality endanger their own historical existence. Societies excluding other societies by ossifying their strategic mentality close themselves off from the rest of human-kind and its common consciousness. Strategic planning denotes the harmony between short-term tactics and long-term strategy. Confusing tactical goals with strategic goals might lead to an obsession with short-term goals to the expense of long-term goals. In Davutoğlu's view, harmonising tactics with strategy requires a strategic conductor, a political will with self-confidence and initiative. Societies lacking political will allow their foreign policies to depend on con-jectural changes, becoming reactive and defensive rather than proactive and assertive. Elites with an identity crisis are risk-averse, passive and avoid taking the initiative. Their timid and fickle attitude oscillates between avoiding respon-sibilities that will increase the prestige of the country and fearing not being taken seriously. They are willing to make endless concessions in their values and priorities to get closer to the centre in the international system. For them, the historical legacy is a burden, and the country's geostrategic significance is a bargaining chip with great powers (2008: 17–34).

In Davutoğlu's view, the problem of the Turkish strategic mentality since the dissolution of the Ottoman Empire and the foundation of the Turkish Republic is the psychological tension deriving from a difference between the continuity of time and space perceptions and the location of Turkey in the international distribution of power (Davutoğlu 2008: 30). There are three reasons explaining the dearth of strategic theories in Turkey. First, there is a dearth of institutional settings fostering strategic thinking. Strategic theorising is underdeveloped due to institutional shortcomings in the Ministry of Foreign Affairs, the National Security Council, the Joint Chief of Staff, the political parties and think-tanks. Second, the poverty of strategic thought might also be attributed to the historical trajectory of the Turkish republic. During the nineteenth century, when great powers were developing their grand strategies of expansion, the Ottoman Empire was mainly preoccupied with preserving its territories. Thus, the elites of the empire remained on the defensive. Invoking an attitude that Davutoğlu calls 'neither absolute sovereignty nor absolute disengagement', these elites broke all ties with lost territories to focus on maintaining the current borders. However, they failed to create a sphere of influence and to protect their borders through trans-border diplomatic manoeuvres. They did not maintain ties with the elites in lost territories who could identify with Ottoman strategies. Nor did they create a tactical manoeuvring space by exploiting the struggles among great powers. The elites of the Turkish Republic continued this legacy, narrowing the horizons of Turkish foreign policy with diminishing tactical options and no influence abroad. Thus, foreign policy came to be dominated by domestic political struggles and external threats. More importantly, a dissonance developed between foreign policy imperatives and domestic political culture. This dissonance is related to a third point. Drawing on the work of R.D. Laing's *Divided Self*, Davutoğlu claims that Turkish elites have been burdened by an identity crisis that has debilitated their capacity for active strategising. Laing argues that the differentiation between the embodied self and the unembodied, inner-self leads to alienation and ontological insecurity. In Davutoğlu's view, the republican break with the Ottoman past and the subsequent Westernisation process led to ontological insecurity and alienation among the Turkish elite. Thus, in line with the AKP's critique of Turkish modernisation, Davutoğlu blames this historical experience for the lack of Turkish strategic vision (2008: 47–63).

Bill McSweeney, who discusses Laing in the context of international security, points out that 'ontological security relates to the sense that the social order as practically conceived is normal, consistent with one's expectations and skills to get along in it. It is a security of social relationship, that is to say a sense of being safely in cognitive control of the situation' (McSweeney 1999: 156). Contrary to Davutoğlu's usage of the concept, however, ontological security is not just a problem for Kemalism, but a challenge to every hegemonic political project: 'What is rendered insecure in a condition of ontological insecurity is fundamentally our common ties and shared knowledge with others involved in the interaction in which it occurs: our identity' (McSweeney 1999: 157). However, by assuming a trans-historical Turkishness, Davutoğlu essentialises the AKP's populist identity, upon which the new concept of national is predicated. This move consolidates the AKP's hegemony by securitising the populist identity.

This matters because, as Buzan, Wæver and de Wilde (1998: 23) point out, 'Security is the move that takes politics beyond the established rules of the game and frames the issue either as a special kind of politics or as above politics'. 'Securitisation is constituted by the intersubjective establishment of an existential threat with a saliency sufficient to have substantial political effects' (Buzan, Wæver and de Wilde 1998: 25). By locating populist identity at the core of ontological security Davutoğlu's analysis implies that any threat to this identity is a threat to security.

In Davutoğlu's populist discourse, the critique of elites is accompanied by a reassertion of political will based on popular sovereignty. Sounding almost like a German romantic of the early 19th century, Davutoğlu asserts that 'a state's depth, which fails to reach the depth of its nation and to provide the spiritual unity emerging from this depth, will only result in turning into brute force' (2008: 37). The importance of strategic mentality, planning and political will demonstrate that the most important problem for a country's strategy is the human factor. A qualified human factor can invent new ways of turning history and geography into power capabilities, while an unqualified human factor can turn the same elements into weakness. In this regard, the most significant issue in a country's strategic initiative (açılım) is the legitimacy of political will in civil society. A state without confidence in its own people cannot take strategic initiatives and the human factor alienated from the political decision-making process can neither lead nor enforce strategic planning. Strategic power can only be achieved through confidence in the nation (2008: 34–37). The main goal of Davutoğlu's book is to contribute to strategic mentality, strategic planning and the political will of Turkey in becoming a major power in world politics. Davutoğlu's analysis implies that the precondition for this revival is the AKP rule, concluding from this that any threat to its rule is simultaneously a threat to Turkey's security.

Turkish Strategy in the Post-Cold War World

Davutoğlu's book also contains specific strategies and tactics for Turkish foreign policy. For Davutoğlu, Turkey occupies a unique position among both regional and extra-regional states. It is the heir to the Ottoman Empire, the only non-European civilisation that both directly confronted Europe and dominated part of it. The foreign policy of the Turkish Republic, however, seems to have failed to make use of this unique position. Rather than becoming a weak but independent centre of a *sui generis* civilisational basin, the republican elite opted to become a regional power under the security umbrella of the strong Western civilisation basin. Overtime, this preference came to be perceived as a fixed parameter of foreign policy.

Davutoğlu identifies four kinds of states in the current international system: superpowers, great powers, regional powers and small powers. The strategies and tactics of states are constrained both by the strategies and tactics of their peers and those of more powerful states. Thus, whereas superpowers are constrained only by the strategies and tactics of other superpowers, great powers are constrained by both superpowers and other great powers, and so on. Regional and smaller powers enjoy tactical flexibility only so far as their policies are congruent with the strategic plans of superpowers and great powers. Regional powers can enhance their tactical manoeuvring space by taking advantage of these congruent policies through dynamic diplomacy. Davutoğlu criticises Turkish foreign policy during the Cold War. The international system after the Second World War was dominated by two superpowers: the USA and the USSR. Britain, France, Germany, China and Japan were great powers, while countries like Turkey, India, Brazil, Egypt, Argentina and Iraq are categorised as regional powers. During the Cold War, the Turkish political elite substituted short-term tactics, defined within the strategic parameters of superpowers and great powers, for long-term strategic plans. In Davutoğlu's view, the fall of the Soviet Union ushered in a new epoch of transition. The first transition period was marked by a discourse of the 'new world order' under American leadership and universal values. The second period, however, is a transition to a multipolar structure which unleashes the dynamics of balance of power politics. This period has been marked by non-ideological, issue-centred diplomatic manoeuvres and short-term alliances. The characteristics of this new structure increase uncertainty but enhance the prospects for tactical flexibility. For Davutoğlu, this new era offers new opportunities but also challenges those countries that have been predicating their own strategies on the strategies of others (2008: 74–79).

The most important consequence of the end of the Cold War, in Davutoğlu's view, has been the retrenching of the Eurasian (Soviet) power and the emergence of tactical manoeuvring spaces, which he calls 'geopolitical vacuums'. Turkey is located at the heart of one of these vacuums. Davutoğlu warns, however, that geopolitical location should not be regarded as an instrument in a defensive strategy for preserving boundaries, but as an instrument in a proactive strategy for turning regional influence into global influence, and for a gradual opening to world politics. A strategy geared to preserving the status quo in this dynamic era of world politics will not even be able to preserve the political boundaries of Turkey. For what he calls a 'gradual opening' to world politics, Davutoğlu asserts that Turkey needs to base its strategy on three tactical priorities in three geopolitical spheres of influence: the proximate land basin (the Balkans, the Middle East, Caucasia), the proximate sea basin (the Black Sea, the Adriatic, the Levant, the Red Sea, the Persian Gulf, the Caspian Sea), and the proximate continental basin (Europe, North Africa, South Asia, Central and East Asia) (2008: 109–118).

In Davutoğlu's view, Turkey should not alienate itself from the proximate land basin out of a temptation to integrate with Western Europe and to form trans-regional alliances. Turkish global influence depends on its regional influence. In the Balkans, Turkey should act as the protector of Muslims and seek to acquire a right to intervene as a guarantor in issues regarding Muslim minorities. Turkey should also pay close attention both to interactions between Russia and Germany and between Europe/Russia and the USA, Japan and China. It should pursue a balancing strategy to increase its ability to reach its tactical goals. In order to balance Russian influence, Turkey should push for building regional and extra-regional security institutions and prepare a plan to ensure the territorial integrity of Albania, Bosnia and Macedonia. In addition, Turkey should become a coordinator in land and maritime transportation as a basis of its regional economic strategy (2008: 119–124).

For Davutoğlu, Caucasia is Turkey's door to Asia. Global powers such as the USA, Britain, Germany and Japan are interested in this region for the transportation of Asian energy resources. Parallel to this competition among global powers, regional powers have also been competing for influence. For instance, the Russian-Armenian and the Turkish-Azeri alliances have compelled Georgia and Iran to pursue their own balancing strategies. The resulting rapprochement between Georgia and Turkey on the one hand, and between Armenia and Iran on the other, has implications for interregional strategies in that Turkish-Iranian relations in the Middle East or Turkish-Russian relations in the Balkans and the Black Sea are directly influenced by the interactions of these countries in Caucasia. In this context, securing Azeri territorial integrity is a priority for Turkish foreign policy. While Albania is essential for enhancing Turkish influence in the Adriatic, Azerbaijan is indispensable for gaining influence in the Caspian Sea. However, Turkey cannot reduce its Caucasian strategy to the Armenian-Azeri conflict. Rather, it should seek to solve this conflict within a wider regional context. Davutoğlu warns against the artificial borderlines imposed by the Cold War, emphasising the integrity of the Northern Middle East region, including Caucasia, Eastern Anatolia and the Levant/Persian Gulf. From this geopolitical viewpoint, Azeri oil reserves, Eastern Anatolian water reserves and Northern Iraqi oil reserves should be linked together. Thus, Turkish regional policy needs a strategic vision for Western Asia, the area stretching from the Persian Gulf to Northern Caucasia (2008: 124–129).

Davutoğlu defines the Middle East as Turkey's 'unavoidable hinterland.' He claims that Islamic civilisation made the region acquire a geocultural unity that extends far beyond the region. In contrast to the stability in the Balkans and Caucasia during the Cold War, bipolarity in the Middle East led to crises as the region became a stage for superpower rivalry. The region was part of what Spykman called the 'rimland', constituting a cornerstone for the containment of the Soviet Union. Consequently, Cold War ideological cleavages disturbed the geocultural unity of the region causing a divide between socialist-inspired Baathist and Nasserist dictatorships and Western-allied monarchies. This ideological polarisation, together with the oil-driven geoeconomic strategies, geopolitical alignment reflecting global power rivalries, and the intra-regional cultural/political conflict arising from the foundation of Israel, constituted the main dynamics of regional politics in this area. After the Cold War, the concept of the 'new world order' was first applied in the region during the First Gulf War, which also revealed inconsistencies between the strategies of the European powers and the USA in their approach to Iran and Syria. The main problem, however, remains the incompatibility of postcolonial borders with the actual geopolitics determined by physical geography. Crises between Turkey and Iraq, Turkey and Syria, Iraq and Kuwait, Iraq and Saudi Arabia, Saudi Arabia and Yemen, Egypt and Sudan reflect this problem. In particular, Turkey needs to revise its regional policies in order to prevent the emergence of a geopolitical vacuum in Northern Iraq, which could serve as a base for the Kurdish guerilla forces of the PKK. It also needs to reconsider its relations with Israel in a way that would not alienate it from the region. Turkey has the potential to lead in the region where the ideological and geocultural alignment of the Cold War has been replaced by a religious and civilisational alignment. Against Huntington's designation of Turkey as a 'torn-country', Davutoğlu claims that Turkey can serve as a model for sustaining territorial integrity with cultural and civilisational plurality (2008: 129–142).

According to Davutoğlu, Turkey is still regarded as a political centre by the people living on the proximate land basins. However, while Turkey needs to take up the responsibilities of the Ottoman Empire, it lacks the cultural and institutional instruments to live up to these responsibilities since the Ottoman legacy has been denounced by Republicans. The first step towards developing this regional influence is the elimination of problems with neighbouring countries, or what came to be known as the 'zero problem policy'. Alliances with countries beyond Turkey's borders can only be useful if they are not blocked by neighbouring countries. Similar to Germany's simultaneous initiative in the Helsinki Accords and its *Ostpolitik*, Turkey needs to move on two fronts: regional security and cooperation, and economic and cultural integration. Policies that increase interdependence though transportation, border commerce, mutual cultural exchange programmes, and mobility of capital and labour will benefit countries with consistent foreign policy projections. The main obstacle to this effort will be the cultural and institutional shortcomings in Turkey's preparedness to make use of its Ottoman legacy (2008: 143–149). Davutoğlu also asserts that the proximate sea basin is an indispensable sphere for Turkey located on the Anatolian-Balkans axis. For example, he is critical of Turkey's decision to decline Germany's invitation to invade the Dodecanese Islands in the Aegean Sea in 1944. Instead, Turkey's quest for British authorisation and its passive stance following Britain's refusal is presented by Davutoğlu as an example of Turkey's reactive foreign policy in the Republican era.

Davutoğlu's proposed strategies and tactics are designed to make Turkey a great power through the incremental projection of power in its region. The Ottoman legacy is invoked as providing an opportunity for this project. Assessing the feasibility of such a project lies beyond the scope of this chapter, the main purpose of which has been to demonstrate the centrality of the AKP's domestic populism in its foreign policy discourse. However, both discourse analysis and identity theory are limited in their ability to explain the actions of social actors pursuing their interests (McSweeney 1999: 210). In this regard, a complete analysis of the AKP's populism needs to go beyond the discursive level to explain the economic, social and political dynamics of the AKP's rule, and the limits to its populist discourse. Such an analysis in international relations has to start with the analysis of Turkey's relation to the world system.

Turkey's position in world politics has been conventionally defined as that of a 'middle power' (Oran 2001a). Examining Japanese politics, Robert Cox questioned the possibility of a middle power challenging the hegemonic world system (1996 [1989]). Given the attachment of the AKP to neoliberal populism, it is highly unlikely that the party will challenge the current capitalist world system. Thus, the AKP's foreign policy discourse cannot be described as revisionist. On the contrary, it follows the same arguments laid out by Chase, Hill and Kennedy (1996) and by Henry Kissinger (2001: 165) or by a 1991 issue of *The Economist*, which designated Turkey as the leader of 'the Turkic world from the Adriatic Sea to the Great Wall of China'. The phrase immediately became a motto for Suleyman Demirel (Oran 2001a: 230; Aydın 2001: 380).

Davutoğlu's emphasis on Turkey's geopolitics and its role as a bridge between civilisations is not novel either. The Turkish Joint Chief of Staff, Necip Tortumtay, argued back in the 1990s that Turkey, as a 'bridge among three continents' and as 'a nation with historical and cultural ties to the surrounding countries', was moving forward to improve its relations with its neighbours. He argued that Turkey presented a model of democracy and stability in a region marked by instability and upheaval, and that its power, culture and democracy entitled it to have a say in any future-looking regional strategy (Torumtay 1996: 15). İsmail Cem, the social democratic Minister of Foreign Affairs between 1997 and 2002, also articulated a similar foreign policy to Davutoğlu's (Cem 2009). The affinity of these foreign policy discourses articulated by these different actors suggests that, in order to evaluate the Davutoğlu Doctrine, one needs to go beyond the presuppositions of the AKP's populist discourse. This chapter presents a starting point in this regard.

NOTES

1 Erdoğan was calling on the Turkish Industry and Business Association to take sides regarding the referendum on constitutional changes on 12 September 2010. 'Erdoğan: Bitaraf olan bertaraf olur,' *Milliyet*, 18 August 2010, http://www.milliyet.com.tr/erdogan-bitaraf-olan-bertaraf-olur/siyaset/sondakika/18.08.2010/1277904/default.htm.

2 The Democratic Party's failure to do so is demonstrated in Ergil (1975).

3 These devices are metaphor, metonymy, synecdoche and catachresis (Laclau 2007:12).

4 Bayar paraphrased by Tanör (2010: 108).

5 These have also been influential on the socialist left and center-left (Tanör 2010: 111–134).

6 For other examples of neoliberal populism in Latin America, see Weyland (2003).

7 For the significance of the AKP's experience in the municipalities, see Doğan (2011/12).

8 I examined this paradox in the AKP's political theory in Birdal (2013).

9 For the distinction between parameters, quasi-parameters and variables, see Greif (2006: 167–170).

CHAPTER FIVE

The AKP's Three-Faceted Kurdish Policy: Tenders for the Rich, Alms for the Poor, Bombs for the Opposition

İrfan Aktan

Recently, we have witnessed people rising up against a number of authoritarian Middle Eastern and North African regimes, such as those of Tunisia, Egypt, Syria and Libya, during the process known as the 'Arab Spring', the violence of which intensified in 2011. One of the main characteristics of these uprisings has been the lack of an ethnic background. Hence, it is not possible to say that a striving for 'national liberation' lies at the core of these uprisings; they are not comparable with the rebellion of blacks against whites in South Africa or Kurdish people against the Turkish regime. Besides, the 'Arab Rebellions', which started suddenly and died down just as quickly, were openly supported or strengthened by international powers, primarily the USA and its regional ally, Turkey. There has also been a 30-year Kurdish rebellion in Turkey, although it has never qualified as a 'spring' according to the international community. My aim in this article is to provide an overview of the methods by which the Justice and Development Party (AKP), the ruling party of Turkey for more than ten years, has tried to suppress this rebellion. Before doing so, I should note that the Kurdish rebellion led by the Kurdistan Workers' Party (PKK) is not supported by international powers primarily due to three characteristics of the movement that distinguish it from other uprisings in the Middle East. First, Kurdish people are not rebelling against their own rulers but against a regime which is, in many respects, an imperialist state. Second, unlike the other movements in the Middle East, their rebellion is not based on Islamist principles, but on Marxist and other secular references, in opposition to capitalist regimes, particularly the USA. Third, the majority Kurdish populations in specific regions of Iran, Turkey, Syria and Iraq have been suppressed by all four countries' ruling regimes as part of a traditional alliance that suits the purposes of international powers. These three main factors have prevented the Kurdish uprising in Turkey from turning into a 'spring' and caused it to last for decades. This process has transformed Turkish state policy, on the one hand, and led to a significant transformation of Kurdish people and the Kurdish movement, on the other. This article evaluates the transformation that has happened in the past ten years of the AKP power.

Transformation of Kurdish Society

In order to understand the reasons for the rise of the PKK as an active force, it is useful first to remember the traditional structure of Kurdish society and the changes that it has undergone. The Kurdish people have always remained in touch with each other despite living in different states thanks to their relationships in agriculture, animal husbandry and illegal cross-border smuggling. Their smallest organisational unit is the 'tribe', often organised as villages, with each tribe having a representative or ruler. These representatives or rulers are subject to the chief or '*agha*' of '*ashiret*', the larger tribal organisation. Until 30 years ago, the state was the top rung in this hierarchical chain, so most tribal chiefs ultimately made their decisions after 'consulting' with the civilian authority, i.e. the state, and guided the tribe accordingly in terms of political orientation. Because of this form of social organisation, Kurdish people in any of the four states do not really need a state mechanism. Moreover, because they have to use the official language of the state they are subject to (Persian in Iran, Arabic in Iraq and Syria, Turkish in Turkey), for Kurds, the state represents a force from whose oppression one must escape, rather than a usable resource.

Born in the late 1970s, the PKK based itself on the idea that this hierarchical order was a source of exploitation for Kurdistan, making it oppose the state as well as the tribal chiefs. Gültan Kışanak, the Peace and Democracy Party (BDP) Co-chair and Diyarbakır MP, summarise this process as follows:

> Although the people were long convinced that 'this state could never come to reason', the organisation started to win their support when the people saw the PKK's determination to use arms. What's more, the PKK not only targeted the Turkish state but also the *aghas*, sending a message to poor Kurds that 'we are not fighting for our identity only; this is also a class struggle'. In contrast, other Kurdish organisations could not reach the poor masses, being instead rather stuck in elite circles, which, just like everywhere else in the world, are more conciliatory because, unlike the poor, they have something to lose. (Kışanak 2013: 8–9)

During the 1960s and 1970s, Kurds organised demonstrations, although participation was low, with attention capturing banners, such as 'Em tîne, Em Birçîne, Bê Kes û Bê Xwedîne' (We are hungry, we don't have water, we don't have anyone helping us). Up until then, every uprising by the Kurds against the state had been brutally suppressed but, finally, the Kurds started to hope for a change in their fortunes by supporting leftist-socialist movements in Turkey. In other words, one of the main reasons why Kurds tended to join the Turkish leftist movement instead of their own organisations was to avoid the rage of the state.

By the 1980s, several new Kurdish organisations, born within Turkish socialist movements, had started to kindle new hope in Kurdish society. In contrast to these movements, which mostly hoped to alleviate the state's oppression by means of dialogue and diplomacy, the PKK relied directly on armed struggle. It is known that the main group that refused to yield to brutal torture in Diyarbakır Prison following the 1980 military coup comprised the PKK militants and sympathisers. The PKK members' resistance to torture and its armed struggle against the state and the *aghas*, combined with the accumulated fury of the Kurdish people, enabled the organisation to reach large masses of Kurdish society. After moving to Syria following the 1980 coup, the PKK prepared for ideological and armed struggle until the mid-1980s, when its forces undertook large-scale actions in 1984 in Şemdinli, Hakkâri, Eruh and Siirt, which further increased the popularity of the organisation among the oppressed Kurdish society. By the 1990s, the PKK had established a tangible influence over Kurdish people in Turkey. Until the early 1990s, both the state and governments made a clear distinction between the PKK and Kurds, for example by spreading propaganda that the PKK was founded and controlled by Armenians, who were enemies of the state and, hence, the people of the region. However, this method was doomed to fail because Kurds called upon by the state to oppose the PKK knew exactly why the organisation had been founded and what it was trying to achieve; the organisation's militants were their own children, relatives or acquaintances. Therefore, the state soon recognised the 'reality of the PKK' and started to take action accordingly, including all kinds of interconnected military and economic measures taken without distinguishing the people from the organisation. Economic measures included the assassination, imprisonment or blackmail of Kurdish businessmen suspected of supporting the PKK, using secret funds for a counter-guerilla war that governments could utilise without being held to account, and increasing the salaries of military or police personnel working in the region as part of an officially declared regional state of emergency.

The military coup of 1980 had targeted all leftist-socialist movements in Turkey and to a large extent succeeded in suppressing such movements. Yet, the 1990s was marked by renewed military action against the Kurdish people in which, unlike the 1980s, the military now worked hand-in-hand with the government in the management of this process. During the 1990s, the state suspended rule of law and human rights in the region in order to use the strongest military methods available to fight off the PKK's actions and contain the Kurdish rebellion.

Before 1980, when the state's neo-liberal policies and village evacuations had not yet gained momentum, Kurds living in rural regions lived close to the land, making their living from traditional production methods using traditional tools, particularly in agriculture and animal husbandry. However, from the 1980s onwards, agriculture and animal husbandry rapidly declined as a result of the state's direct interventions. In the 1990s, thousands of Kurdish villages were evacuated by the state in order to isolate poor Kurdish villagers from the PKK and assimilate them. Hacettepe University's Institute of Population Studies has estimated that 953,680–1,201,200 people migrated 'for security reasons' between 1986 and 2005 (HUIPS 2006: 106). However, *Göç-Der* (Migrants' Association for Social Cooperation and Culture) reports that 1,464 villages were evacuated by the state and 4 to 4.5 million citizens of Turkey, who spoke Kurdish as their mother tongue, were displaced during this process (see GÖÇ-DER 1999–2001). This enormous forced migration can be seen as a modern '*tehcir*' (deportation) in that it was assumed that millions of Kurds exiled to Turkey's large metropolitan cities after their villages were burnt down would provide cheap labour, become assimilated and Turkicised in Turkish society and most importantly, keep away from the PKK. However, this plan went all wrong. The Kurds, concentrated in large cities, quickly created their own ghettos in certain neighbourhoods such as Türközü (Ankara), Tarlabaşı (İstanbul) and Kadifekale (İzmir), and started to live together. This type of socialisation did not allow assimilation, and these people, who had been abandoned by the state since it had burnt down their villages, continued to express their anger at the state under the Kurdish movement and maintained their support for the PKK. While it can be argued that these people partly met the demand for cheap labour (see Yörük in this volume), the cheap labour provided by the poor Kurdish masses also contributed to increasing unemployment among the ethnic Turkish urban poor. This proved to be another source of tension between the Turks and Kurds which still exists today. To alleviate this tension, the Housing Development Administration (TOKİ), controlled by the government, built new settlements under the scope of 'urban transformation projects', and people living in the slums were distributed among such settlements. The primary purpose of these efforts to break the communication between Kurds living in such neighbourhoods as Tarlabaşı (İstanbul), Kadifekale (İzmir) and Türközü (Ankara), who were victims of forced migration, was to destroy the social environment created in the slums.

The AKP's 'Solution Attempts'

This was the background against which the AKP government undertook one of its main missions, to produce new anti-Kurd policies to remedy the failure of the state's existing Kurdish policy. The 'new policy' which the AKP tried to exercise aimed not to resolve the problem by granting Kurdish people their rights but to sustain the guardianship system by using other actors and a different language. According to the AKP, it was not the military but the civil power that should be the primary actor in curbing the Kurdish movement. The Turkish Armed Forces (TSK) should remain just a tool that could be mobilised for war when necessary, and the government should have the control of that tool. According to the AKP, this would not only secure their power but also facilitate the resolution of the Kurdish question and, over time, this new approach became state policy. It is significant in respect that the Kurdish movement began sometimes referring to the AKP as the 'AKP State'. However, although the AKP has shaped the state's Kurdish policy in a new way because of its particular political characteristics, it would not be correct to think of the state and the AKP as two different actors. In fact, the approaches of the state and the AKP have become increasingly integrated.

This was not an easy process. The military elite, wanting to sustain previous failed state policies, never adopted the 'AKP's new policy'. During this process, a structure or organisation called '*Ergenekon*', which actually comprised the core of the state, allegedly largely run by the military elite, attempted to organise several coups to overthrow the AKP and sustain the state's traditional Kurdish policy. Tens of army officers, including the retired Chief of General Staff, were arrested and prosecuted in lawsuits against *Ergenekon*. Having conducted several coups previously, with the support of the USA, the TSK gradually tended to remain silent since it was no longer supported by international powers during the AKP's term in office. Consequently, the TSK was forced to 'submit' to the AKP government, which made it possible for the AKP to try to 'solve' the Kurdish question using its own methods.

The originality of the AKP's solution involved bringing certain civil actors into the foreground. These civil forces can be divided into two main groups: religious sects (primarily the Fethullah Gülen community) and new capital holders supported by the government. These two actors sometimes converged and their missions were supposed to complement each other. While the TSK and traditional state policy had used oppression, persecution, torture and other repressive methods against Kurds, the AKP wanted to win them over by means of '*devshirme*' (gathering) policy. This included strategies like trying to get the support of the middle class living in Kurdish regions and the devout community who had kept their distance from the PKK. The AKP's election tactics were shaped based on these two dynamics. During their first term in office, from 2002 to 2009, the AKP listed Kurdish *aghas* or prominent tribe members as mayoral or parliamentary candidates in local and general elections, while in their second governing period starting from 2009, middle-class doctors, engineers and lawyers were chosen for the parliament instead of tribal leaders, who had lost their representative power. The AKP also managed to win the support of religious populations of the lower class via religious sects. Regarding the latter group, religious sects began distributing basic commodities (clothes, food, coal, etc.) to poor Kurds, while the anti-PKK propaganda was used in mosques. However, as well as attempting to increase its credibility with the Kurdish lower class by using religious references, the AKP was also attempting to attract the middle class, which made up the base of the Kurdish movement, with its economic policies.

Even though, after 2011, Prime Minister Tayyip Erdoğan began an anti-propaganda campaign by claiming that the Kurdish movement embraces Zoroastrianism, the government did not base its regional policy on this method. Rather, the Fethullah Gülen community, trying to gain esteem and power in the Kurdish regions, attempted to spread a discourse of 'the brotherhood of Muslims' among the lower social classes in parallel with its economic support packages. Thus it is clear that the Gülen community and its discourse, or propaganda, of economic welfare, quality education, etc. was the primary tool that the AKP government used to spread its presence in Kurdish regions, specifically among the Kurdish lower-middle class. The government largely supported this policy of the Gülen community, and chose to strive to make the community's 'sweet talk' take hold in the region instead of acting coldly towards the Kurds. However, when the AKP government found that this strategy of using teachers, charitable institutions and the '*mele's* (imams, the religious guides in a mosque) instead of the police in order to gain influence among the region's population was insufficiently successful, they reverted to a policy of oppression, with operations against the KCK (Union of Communities in Kurdistan) to strike at the Kurdish movement. During 2013, the Gülen community played a significant role at this point in that the police and the judiciary, within which the community has significant power, arrested and imprisoned around 7,000 Kurdish politicians, activists, lawyers, journalists, mayors, MPs and students, who were accused of being part of the illegal Kurdish movement.

Meanwhile, the ongoing political transformation, occurring in parallel with the Kurdish people's struggle, was increasingly eroding the traditional organisational form of the Kurdish people. Constantly active, both politically and militarily, Kurds were gradually changing as a side effect of this process. Especially because of the secular structure of the Kurdish movement, Islam was also losing its influence on the process, although it used to shape the traditional social relations of Kurdish people to a large extent. Thus, even though the state has been trying to stimulate the Islamic sentiments in the Kurdish society by means of various religious communities, there has been a transformation in the masses mobilised by the Kurdish movement which makes it difficult to go back to the past. In reaction to the propaganda of the state and religious communities, with imams urging Kurds to obey the state, there have been campaigns calling upon Kurds to perform their religious duties outside mosques that have attracted mass participation. Hence, realising that their previous policy of excluding religion had created a negative effect, the Kurdish movement has started to include religion in its own political discourse, particularly since 2009. This has rendered the state's own attempts to organise or position devout Kurds against the PKK on religious grounds ineffective.

Invention of a Kurdish Entrepreneurial Middle Class

The efforts to strengthen a state-supported entrepreneur class through networks of relations in the Kurdish region shows the class basis of the AKP's project. State infrastructure tenders have been awarded to those businessmen who are influential in Kurdish tribes that have managed to survive. A new upper-middle class has been rapidly created in the region that not only submits to the AKP but also works for its interests or acts politically as part of the AKP. This class may be seen as a 'modern' version of the tribes who allied with the state against the Kurdish movement. There is one difference though: Kurdish tribes allying with the state continued speaking Kurdish and living the Kurdish culture. In contrast, the new upper-middle class is, to a large extent, made up of people who have adopted the consumption habits of the Turkish upper-middle class, both speaking Turkish and living a Turkish lifestyle.

It should be noted that Kurdish class structure has been directly and indirectly shaped by state policies. The decisive actor for the Kurdish upper-middle class in Turkey has been the state or governments. One of the ideological tools of the state or governments has been to make Kurds a part of the system by including certain classes in their own policies. This started with *agha*s, the ruling elite of the tribal system in Kurdish society, being supported economically and politically in specific periods, and continued from the 1980s onwards with certain tribes being transformed into village guards, a paramilitary force, led by tribe chiefs. Meanwhile, rich urban Kurdish businessmen have been subsidised by the AKP government. Thus, it can be said that the AKP has been implementing an updated version of the traditional policy of the Turkish state.

One of the most important conditions for Kurds to 'move into higher social classes' concerns how they position themselves with regard to the familiar policy of the state, or rather governments. Though the Turkish bourgeoisie has been able to make a fortune through the policies of the 'laissez faire' approach, the Kurdish bourgeoisie has not been treated with such a 'liberal stance'. Consequently, the 'Kurdish bourgeoisie' gets stronger or weaker depending on its relationship with the state. Recently, it has become possible to talk about a flourishing Kurdish 'middle class' that earns tenders by staying close to the AKP. However, this class cannot go far without subsidies, and the primary condition for getting subsidies is turning its back on the Kurdish movement, and even functioning as a Trojan horse to enhance the state's power in the region (Aktan 2010). According to Fırat Aydınkaya, the traditional state elite has been suspicious of any sense of belonging within Kurdish society, and has kept a close watch over the traditional Kurdish middle class, so the AKP's rise to power in 2002 marked a significant change of strategy in that the objective conditions for a new Kurdish middle class was created through an economic policy of state aid:

> Traditional tradesmen were turned into medium-scale businesses by means of microcredits. Special funds were transferred from the World Bank and the Provincial Bank (*İller Bankası*) for the creation of a middle class. KOSGEB (Small and Medium Enterprises Development Organisation), KÖYDES (Support for the Infrastructure in Villages) and other social development agencies were designed to help create a middle class. Also, İstanbul-based national capital holders opened branch after branch in Kurdistan, taking advantage of the 'no conflict' policy. Distributorship, franchising and branch opening spread about in the region. Thus, the network of national capital, in other words national capitalism, reached Kurdistan. Kurdistan was rediscovered for both cheap labour and cheap raw materials. Of course, this was not an incidental process. In a sense, the AKP-ruled state aided the new Kurdish middle class within a certain concept. So the economic and social foundations were laid for a political movement that could contend with the Kurdish movement. Therefore, in one respect, this new middle class shows the powerful symptoms of a political project. (Aydınkaya 2011: 152)

However, the expression 'Kurdish bourgeoisie' needs to be used in quotation marks for quite some time. First, the 'Kurdish' bourgeoisie is being shaped in a 'Turkish' way to a large extent. This section of society often does not identify itself with a Kurdish identity. Its members do not speak Kurdish; they take a pragmatic approach towards the Kurdish question, just like the Turkish bourgeoisie, so they align themselves closely with the AKP. Actually, this class had already been close to previous centre right parties like the Motherland Party (ANAP) and the True Path Party (DYP) before the AKP. In that respect, one cannot talk about a 'national bourgeoisie' with an original character. According to Aydınkaya, an important distinction should also be made between the new and traditional Kurdish middle class:

> They have a very different understanding of the word 'Kurdish' and their perspective on struggle is quite different from that of the Kurdish movement. The new Kurdish middle class highlights being a 'Kurd' as primarily an ethnic difference while for the Kurdish movement, a 'Kurd' is a dissident whose rights have been usurped and who has been forced to fight for their rights. The new middle class has a pragmatic approach to the concept of 'Kurdish'. In this re-creation, the word 'Kurdish' has lost its dissident nature and turned into a mode of search for power and status. In this way, the concept of 'Kurdish' loses its content of rebellion and is transformed into a 'side dish for a class', becoming tragically part of the system. (Aydınkaya 2011: 163)

The new Kurdish bourgeoisie has also been included in the new business networks developed with the Kurdistan Regional Government in Iraq as a result of the AKP's policy in the region. Sinan Çelebi, Ministry of Trade and Industry in the Kurdish Regional Government, revealed in January 2013 at the 'Business Opportunities in Iraq Summit' in Mersin that an average of three Turkish-based companies have been registered in Kurdistan every month since 1999. Çelebi also reported the following message of Nechervan Barzani, Prime Minister of Kurdistan: 'You should give Turkey priority above everyone else. Turkey must be prioritised in all relations, whether they are political, social or economic.' Speaking at the same summit, Mustafa Sever, Assistant Deputy Minister of Economy of Turkey, highlighted that the volume of foreign investment in Kurdistan exceeded 20 billion dollars, and that Iraqi Kurdistan has become a kind of meeting point for Turkish and Turkish-based Kurdish capital-owners. Even though this 'meeting' enhanced the similarities between them, the fact that their trade relations are conducted with the Kurdish government naturally creates a new perception of Kurdishness in Kurdish capital owners. According to this perception, the PKK's emphasis on class equality not only prevents Kurds from 'opening up to the world' but also damages the Kurdish nationality. In fact, the Turkish state and Turkish capital owners have an issue with the PKK rather than with Kurdish national identity because the PKK demands freedom and equality for Kurds and intends to establish this equality not only between Turks and Kurds but also among the Kurds. This intention of the PKK naturally draws a reaction from the Kurdish upper-middle class, most obviously in its attitude towards the section on the 'Economic Dimension' in the draft autonomy model presented by the Kurdish movement to the Democratic Autonomy Workshop organised by the Democratic Society Congress on December 18–19, 2010. Galip Ensarioğlu, at the time President of Diyarbakır Chamber of Commerce and Industry, commented about the Kurdish movement's anticipation of 'economic equality among Kurds': 'People who never ran a store in their lives are recommending an economic model for Kurdistan. Without having a clue about the global economic system, they are able to recommend an economic model for a huge region like Kurdistan. These have no connection with reality; they are not feasible; they are completely unrealistic.' On the other hand, Ensarioğlu did not object to the identity-based demands highlighted in the autonomy model and was elected Diyarbakır MP as an AKP candidate in the following general elections.

Generally speaking, it is difficult to say that the Kurdish upper-middle class in Turkey has a serious problem with the identity aspect of the Kurdish question highlighted by the PKK. In one interview, the Kurdish writer Muhsin Kızılkaya frankly stated that the Kurdish problem concerns Kurds who are not financially secure more than the urban upper-middle-class members of the Kurdish society like him:

> Actually, I don't have a big problem with this order, except for mentality. I am benefitting from so many things: I am living in a very good neighbourhood of İstanbul; I have a very beautiful house, a very nice wife; I have very good friends; I can go on vacations; I can spend time abroad. These weren't given to me by the state or the Republic of Turkey. I won all of these at the expense of being scorned. Some Kurdish politicians really despised me, but nevertheless I have earned my present condition only by my pen. So I can stay comfortably at home and say, 'I'm just fine, politics is nothing to me'. But I have never done that. (Aktan 2006: 250)

Different Kurdish Questions

When issues within the general Kurdish question are analysed, it can be seen that there are class differences within Kurdish society leading to different perceptions and approaches towards the problem. In particular, there is an increasingly obvious distance between the masses who, by participating in the Kurdish rebellion, have gained an awareness of their rights as a result of their grievances and the experience of uprising, and other sections of Kurdish society which have remained aloof from the rebellion while not holding back from demanding their identity rights.

In this respect, one can argue that both the war of the last 30 years and the 'civil initiatives' mentioned before, which have intensified during the AKP's rule, have created radical transformations in the Kurdish region. The foremost of such transformations is, without a doubt, the dissolution of traditional hierarchical relations in the past 20 years, specifically a serious weakening of Kurdish tribal chiefs. This group had dreamed of becoming the 'governors of the Kurdish people' if Kurdish freedom were won. According to them, if those fighting in the mountains could manage to found a state one day, they would seek their help as *agha*s who know how a state works, make them their rulers and follow their orders. Thus was the atmosphere felt in the halls (the '*divanhane*') and '*agha*'s houses' in the region from the second half of the 1980s until the last quarter of the 1990s. The propaganda used by the *agha*s against their own people was the inevitable way of keeping a foot in both camps. While the state was trying to keep this attitude of the *agha*s alive in order to weaken the PKK and manipulate it when necessary, those tribal members who were on good terms with the PKK were soothed by the idea of a state possibly being founded one day. In any case, the *agha*s also managed to maintain their image as a power above both the state and the PKK. However, while the social and political transformation in Turkey slowly destroyed the traditional image of the *agha*s regarding both the state and the PKK, the importance of the '*mala agha*' (agha house) in Kurdish society rapidly diminished. Consequently, while the *agha*s, acting more from identity concerns than class-related motivations, and dreaming of rising to local power, became marginalised, new upper-middle-class Kurds started to take their place.

The ongoing war in the region has played a fundamental role in the weakening of the *agha*s. Having been denied permission to conduct military operations, the TSK no longer needed the village guards previously used by the state as a paramilitary force under the *agha*s' control. Instead, village guards hung their weapons on the wall at home. Meanwhile, the Kurdish movement started to reach out to the guards and include their families in its base. As a result, the influence of the *agha*s, having previously acted as leaders of guards and ruling their people in alliance with the state, gradually diminished. In fact, few *agha*s in the region preferred to describe themselves as a 'guard leader' since the source of their continued power over their tribe was bound to the perception that this power came not from the state but from the tribe itself. Thus, when the state forced them to do so, the *agha*s had to choose sides. Those *agha*s that submitted, or rather continued submitting, to the state gradually lost their subjects because, having knelt before the state made it impossible for them to maintain the image of an *agha* who 'took orders from no one and only commanded others'. Ultimately, those *agha*s who accepted the state's patronage also started to lose their subjects due to the dramatic fall in the region's population because of forced migration when the majority of Kurds, who had been rapidly impoverished during the war, had migrated to large cities, whether forced by the state or their desperate economic conditions. These large masses also included former village guards who could not subsist on a guard's salary or were uncomfortable with being a guard. Those who could not migrate sent their children to the cities where they steadily lost their loyalty to *agha* and tribe. On the other hand, those *agha*s that approached the PKK naturally had to give up the idea of controlling their subjects through traditional methods of ruling. Thus, the Kurd's tribal structure began to dissolve independently of political tendencies.

As the traditional tribal structure collapsed, an increasing number of families 'began living like Turks', particularly in Kurdish cities. Not all Kurds exiled to the cities were living in desperate poverty, as some families had been able to sell land or animals to buy an apartment in the city, and paid to educate their children privately and send them to university. Such families, who could 'stand on their own two feet,' had no need to follow either the *agha*s or the PKK. Thus a new Kurdish middle class emerged, rooted in those formerly poor village families who had been able to avoid becoming a party to the conflicts from the late 1980s onwards. This development has opened up new politicisation dynamics since a significant share of the young, educated people growing up in such families has not chosen to keep away from politics. On the contrary, many of these people, particularly lawyers, have naturally become part of the continuing political polarisation. Being a lawyer in the Kurdish region often means being involved in political activity because the state's anti-democratic legal practices comprise one of the main issues between the state and Kurds. Some have entered politics; some have died while trying to fight the destruction caused by the state; and some have been imprisoned.

At the same time, the same processes have also made the new middle class increasingly more visible in Kurdish cities in its pursuit of wealth. For example, there are lawyers known to have earned large amounts of money from compensation cases paid to thousands of Kurdish villagers under the scope of the Act on Compensation of Damages Occurring Due to the Fight against Terrorism. While these lawyers have become rich thanks to the serious earlier violations of rights, engineers have also gained wealth from the AKP's neo-liberal policies, by means of various tendering opportunities, such as TOKİ housing projects and highway upgrading.

However, while some middle-class Kurdish professionals may have gained, the AKP policies appear to have further impoverished those lower Kurdish class groups that continue to support the PKK. Many statistics show that Kurdish cities are still systematically becoming poorer (see Sönmez 2007), and their impoverished populations are also increasingly becoming more politically active. Because the PKK militants have remained outside Turkey's borders since 1999 as instructed by the organisation's leader, Abdullah Öcalan, the region has no longer seen significant armed conflicts in the 2000s. Throughout the 1990s as well, although they sometimes organised mass demonstrations, Kurdish people were not directly involved in the conflict. To a large extent, this can be explained by the region's oppressive state of emergency administration. Instead, during the time when the PKK remained outside the country, the Kurdish masses making up the PKK's base started engaging in various civilian activities, especially the *Newroz* celebrations, which have become an annual event. This demonstrates another way that class-based differentiation within the Kurdish population has gained a political character. In opposition to the large lower class, which has nothing to lose, supports the PKK in every way and has become an increasingly more political actor, a new group has emerged which supports the government and condemns or criticises the violent policies of the PKK. This can be seen as part of an operation to spread a new 'discourse' against the Kurdish movement and the lower class that sustains it in order to prioritise political demands over economic ones. However, it must be emphasised that this polarisation has not completely served the interests of the state. For example, particularly in cities like Diyarbakır, the BDP still wins more votes than the AKP from upper-middle-class neighbourhoods, even if these people do not participate in mass demonstrations.

The AKP has chosen to penetrate the Kurdish ghettos through religious sects in order to prevent the secular Kurdish movement from reaching more supporters in the Kurdish lower class, sending a message that 'those who stand close to the party can move into a higher class' or 'at least survive'. In fact, the AKP has always followed a cautious policy about Kurds. Therefore, although those upper-middle-class Kurdish people that have accepted the government's authority are thriving, the government is nevertheless making sure that this prosperity is kept under control. That is, the AKP takes care that the opportunities provided to this group do not allow them to achieve continuous and independent prosperity. Similarly, it can also be argued that the AKP has subjected the Kurdish poor to a policy of controlled sustainable impoverishment, in that just enough aid is provided to the poor so that they can survive. The most important such aid includes fuel aid for winter, the opportunity to benefit from healthcare services free of charge provided that the person has no criminal record related to the PKK, and the allocation of a small bursary for primary school students. Thus, to reverse a catchphrase of development, the AKP government gives a fish to lower class Kurds rather than teaching them how to catch one. With reference to both classes, the state can now point to Kurds who have 'secured themselves' or at least 'survived' in order to send a message to the rebelling Kurds: 'If you toe the line, these opportunities are always there for you too'. Thus, a Kurd has to be 'reasonable' in order to gain wealth, to get a 'Green Card' for free access to healthcare services, to have their child placed in a sought-after boarding school, to live comfortably in their village, to get away with stealing electricity, or to benefit from any of the other many instances of 'positive discrimination'.

What Happened to the *Sarmaşık* Association?

In response, the Kurdish movement has also been trying to come up with some answers to the radical transformations occurring in the region. Shortly after its rise to power, the AKP put into effect various mechanisms to 'solve' the Kurdish question in favour of the state, as discussed above. It has tried populist economic tactics to make urban lower-class Kurds submit to the state's authority. Religious communities affiliated to the AKP have opened various education institutions in the Kurdish region, offering free services to successful Kurdish children, and distributed food, clothing, coal and healthcare support to their families and other poor urban populations under the guise of 'charity'.

Against these moves by the state, the Kurdish movement has also attempted various 'measures', with many BDP municipalities, particularly Diyarbakır Metropolitan Municipality, setting up social facilities for the urban poor. For instance, to decrease women's housework burden, free laundries were opened in Diyarbakır; activities were organised for children who had been victims or witnesses of violence; the poor were provided with some support, however small. Yet, these 'measures' have never reached a satisfactory level, except for one organisation: the Sarmaşık (Ivy) Association for Sustainable Development to Fight Poverty. Şerif Çamcı, President of the Sarmaşık Association, working to provide food aid to the Kurds who had been forced to leave their villages and migrate to cities, summarises their differences from other charity organisations as follows:

> We never defined ourselves as a charity organisation. This is an institution which does fieldwork, carries out socioeconomic research, questions the traditional understanding of aid in the fight against poverty, shows the correct way and shapes public opinion. Others are completely traditional charity organisations. They are agents that take from one side and give it

to the other. They are partly practicing their religion and partly acting out of conscience. Now they are after political gains through the AKP. When we started out, what bothered us most was the way in which poverty was completely exploited. Especially the AKP, this regime or the state is doing nothing serious to reach the Kurds in Kurdistan. This is just a culture of alms. The state and the AKP have no serious commitments or projects for the resolution of the Kurdish question. But they are reaching the people with alms and making them dependent. And they hope that the city and individuals, increasingly more impoverished each day, will become even more dependent on the state. The state is continuing to use this as blackmail.

When, as a group of journalists in 2008, we visited the food bank established by Sarmaşık to provide food to poor families, we saw a practice that was unique in the region, and differentiates this organisation from the charitable approach of religious sects in the region. The food bank was simply a market where the poor came and loaded shopping trolleys with basic foodstuffs from the shelves without paying anything and returned home. Coupons were distributed to the families identified previously by Sarmaşık and the families did their shopping in the market up to an amount determined for them, only they did not have to pay. Through this practice, Sarmaşık aimed to prevent such families from being humiliated, being seen as beggars or becoming dependent on charity.

Supported by the Kurdish movement, primarily upper-middle-class Kurds and the BDP municipalities, Sarmaşık, shortly after its foundation in 2006, had to face obstructions created by the state. Of course, the reason behind the obstacles created for the Sarmaşık Association is the concern that the policy of earning the poor people's support for the state, through the almsgiving culture of religious sects, could be interrupted. The religious sects supported by the state or even part of it, must have been quite disturbed by the economic support given to poor Kurdish populations by organisations other than their own, particularly those close to the Kurdish movement. One of the results of this disturbance was a vetoing of the partnership with Diyarbakır Metropolitan Municipality, the most important supporter and partner of the Food Bank Project, by the Governor of Diyarbakır in 2012, despite the unanimous resolution of the Municipal Council in favour of the partnership. The unanimous resolution of the Diyarbakır Provincial Council in favour of providing monetary support to Sarmaşık was also blocked by the veto of the Governor's Office. Administrative fines were also imposed on the association's president on the order of the governor's office on the grounds that small foreign donations made to the official accounts of Sarmaşık had not been reported to the state. The official application for an apartment that the association was trying to purchase for its headquarters, for which approval of the Governor's Office was required, was blocked for weeks. An official investigation was also started into the founders of the association on the grounds that they were related to the KCK. Fines were then imposed on all the board members of Sarmaşık who had collected aid for the victims of the Van earthquake, and 76,000 Turkish Lira was confiscated from the association. After the imposition of these administrative fines, the Diyarbakır

Governor's Office had Sarmaşık's 23 accounts with 11 different banks blocked. Ultimately, the State Council resolved that the partnership contribution paid by Diyarbakır Metropolitan Municipality for the Food Bank Project was not legal and ruled that the payment of around 1 million YTL should be returned to the municipality.

Conclusion

What happened to Sarmaşık is already enough to expose the reality of the state and its supporting religious sects' Kurdish policy. However, they did not stop at this; instead, the AKP enacted a very controversial law in 2013 to eliminate those rich Kurds who were close to the Kurdish movement. According to the Act on the Prevention of Financing of Terrorism, which came into effect after being published in the Official Gazette of 7 February 2013, the state can confiscate any money and all kinds of movable and immovable, tangible and intangible property, rights and receivables, the value of which can be represented in money, and all kinds of documents representing such valuables which are used for the 'financing of terrorism' (Official Gazette, 16 February 2013). Given that it is obvious that justice in Turkey works in parallel with government policies and is not independent of the state's Kurdish policy, it is not difficult to conjecture how the Act on the Prevention of Financing of Terrorism will be interpreted by judges. Clearly, based on current state of politics, it is now possible to prosecute all Kurdish business people or other rich Kurds who are not a member of the new, state-aided Kurdish middle-upper class, and who remain close to the Kurdish movement in order to confiscate their assets.

In conclusion, it must be emphasised that its ability to cover up various atrocities differentiates the AKP from previous governments. For example, in the 1990s, Kurdish business people were targeted directly by the government of Tansu Çiller and assassinated. In contrast, instead of risking damaging its image by killing business people, the AKP has opted to bring them into line by threatening them with confiscation of their assets. Whereas Kurds were gunned down by the police or soldiers in the middle of the street in the 1990s, today those Kurds that oppose the state are tried and sentenced to extremely heavy prison terms. The same applies to journalists: tens of Kurdish journalists were killed during the 1990s, while today, Kurdish journalists are arrested in groups, and even the news they make can be used as evidence of a crime.

On the other hand, although military methods of oppression were used less often against civilians in the first period of the AKP's rule (2002–2006), the magnitude of oppression and violence has subsequently become increasingly marked. Several examples can be given. In March 2006, more than ten citizens, including children, were shot during demonstrations in Diyarbakır's streets, organised to protest about the deaths of 14 PKK militants who had allegedly been killed with chemical weapons in the countryside around Muş. At the same time, an amendment in the Prevention of Terrorism Act made it possible to arrest children, since when countless Kurdish children have been tried under the Prevention of Terrorism Act (TMK), with many being sentenced to years in prison just for participating in street fights with police. Many children have died in police or gendarmerie shootings during the AKP's term in office, including 12-year-old Uğur Kaymaz, who was executed with his father in front of their home in Kızıltepe, Mardin in 2004. In December 2011, 34 Kurdish villagers were killed by Turkish military aircraft near Roboski Village, Uludere, Şırnak. Almost none of the investigations started after these killings have led to the punishment of those responsible. This suggests that such practices against civilian Kurds have intensified even more during those times when the AKP's '*devshirme*' (political recruitment) policies have started to fail, when the AKP has turned to the Turkish state's traditional oppressive means as their primary method.

Even though the AKP has tried to eliminate the Kurdish movement and win Kurds over to the state's side by means of 'white oppression' rather than the previous violent oppressive state policies, the increasingly massive growth of the movement has not been prevented. This suggests why several serious killings have taken place, such as the Roboski Slaughter mentioned above. Although not as large as those in the 1990s, several military operations have been conducted against the PKK, although the AKP failed in these too. The government has been equally unsuccessful in using the military to try to control the Kurdish mountains with high-tech weapons, chemical weaponry and high-impact bombs. Other non-military methods, including the launch of the 24/7 Kurdish language TV channel, TRT-6, by the official state TV broadcaster, TRT, and elective Kurdish courses at schools, no longer appear to be attracting Kurdish people because they are insufficient to meet Kurdish demands for equality. On the other hand, on 20 February 2013, the AKP government allowed the BDP MPs to meet the imprisoned the PKK leader, Abdullah Öcalan. The government initiated negotiations with Öcalan via different channels and started to make various statements to improve the negative image of Öcalan in the eyes of the nationalist Turkish population. This represents a public admission that the state's attempts since the 1980s to suppress the Kurdish movement with various tactics have completely failed. As for the future, the state's attitude towards the Kurdish movement may well be determined by the fate of negotiations with Öcalan.

CHAPTER SIX

The Media in Turkey: From Neoliberal Militarism to Authoritarian Conservatism

Uraz Aydın

It is unnatural to expect capital, which is able to reify everything it touches with its magic wand so as to assimilate everything to itself, to exempt cultural production and mass communication from this phantasmagorical experience. Of course, it would be an untenable assertion to presume that once upon a time there used to be a golden age when the media of mass communication was independent from the centres of economic and political power, but it should also be stressed that the process whereby money brings news and information under its own domination is a gradual one. In the mid-19th century, Balzac spoke of journalists as 'sentence merchants', while Marx did not deny the capacity of the press – provided it was free – to be the 'ubiquitous vigilant eye of a people's soul'. However, as long as the kingdom of capitalist expansion widens, and capital itself subordinates mass communication to its own rationality, the existential and effectual possibilities of a fourth estate existing that is willing to swim against the current dramatically fall. One critical stage in this commodification of communication is undoubtedly the neoliberal phase of capitalism. From its property structure to its ideological function, from its labour relations to its language of narration, there is now a 'media industry' that is much more integrated into capitalism.

In this chapter, the relationship between the construction of liberalism in Turkey and the transformation undergone within the sphere of the media will be basically discussed in terms of two axes. On the one hand, I will inquire into the restructuring process based on the tendency to competition and concentration in the realm of the media as a corollary of the adoption of neoliberal economic policies and the inevitable impact of this process on content production. On the other hand, I will discuss the role of the media in the formation of neoliberal hegemony. That is, the chapter will analyse both the objective and subjective positions of the mass communication media. These changing relations and ideological functions of media will also be considered by singling out two historical-political sequences. Regarding the first period (from the 1980s to 2000s), characterised by the formation of the free market economy and the interventionism of the military, the chapter will examine the role of the media, organised as a modern sector, in legitimising neoliberalism and the internalisation of market values by individuals. In addition, it will also evaluate the nationalist and laicist stance of the mainstream media in the face of the Kurdish rebellion and Islamic movement, both perceived by the neoliberal militarist regime as a threat. Regarding the second period, from the Justice and Development Party's (AKP) coming to power in 2002 till the present day, the chapter will offer both a take on the change in the power relations within the realm of mass communication and on the formation of a mainstream conservative media, and also an analysis of the publishing strategy of this media, which is compatible with the AKP's strategy of neoliberal authoritarian conservative hegemony.

The Media Industry and the Soul of Capitalism

Undoubtedly, one cannot consider the convergence of the structural transformation that the publishing field in Turkey underwent and the formation of a media industry in the 1980s as a mere coincidence. These years also correspond to a phase when there were fractures at economic, political and social levels, beginning with the 24 January 1980 'stability programme' and the 12 September 1980 coup d'état, through which a total restructuring took place within a neoliberal axis. In a context marked by the aim of integrating with global capitalism, celebration of the free market, the shattering of the socio-political power of organised labour, the transition to a model of export-oriented capital accumulation, and the accompanying project of hegemony labelled the 'New Right', the media, and the cultural field of production in general, were subjected to a restructuring process under the domination of capital.

Structural Transformation Under the Domination of Capital

Before this time, the traditional property structure of journalism in Turkey depended on a classical pattern of the journalist-boss, in which the editor-in-chief of each newspaper, which was in fact a family enterprise, was also the owner of the newspaper itself. Even though the mass press that emerged in the 1950s started to draw the attention of those who had accumulated capital outside this profession, it was only in the 1980s and 1990s that a media-capital fusion occurred in real terms (Kaya 2009).

This process, known as the 'penetration of holdings into the media' after the 'conglomeration of the media' from the 1960s onwards, can be read as a product of a double dynamic. On the one hand, such factors as the necessity to keep up with technological innovations, the curtailment of state subsidies towards newsprint paper as part of deregulation policies after 24 January 1980, and the astronomical rises in the cost of producing newspapers made publishing them exceedingly costly for family enterprises. On the other hand, in the eyes of capital groups, there were various advantages of owning a media organ, even if it was not a profitable investment, in a period when the economic field was being restructured in accordance with free market conditions. These external benefits included strengthening one's hand in the face of political powers, whether to reach an agreement or fight a conflict, gaining a stronger position against competing groups, winning state tenders, cashing in on credit and incentives, and advertising companies within the body of the group (especially banks) that operated across different sectors. All these advantages stimulated non-media capital to enter into the media sector (Sönmez 2004).

These groups, which had previously invested in sectors like energy, banking, finance, tourism and construction, took their first steps into the press sector although, once the state monopoly imposed on television broadcasting was repealed, they expanded into TV as well. Thus, in accordance with the operational laws of the neoliberal phase of capitalism, a 'modern' media industry began to take shape, accompanied by rather violent competition.

The principal and decisive consequence of this process was the rapid concentration of property ownership. From the mid-1990s onwards, as a result of horizontal, vertical and traversal processes of integration, the media industry came under the control of just a few actors. As Turgut Özal, who was not only the architect of the 24 January decisions that symbolised the transition to neoliberalism, but also the first Prime Minister and later President of the postcoup period, put it: 'Now, there will only be two and a half newspapers in Turkey'. According to 1995 figures, two major capital groups (Doğan and Sabah) controlled 70 per cent of the total circulation of newspapers and 87 per cent of magazines (Adaklı 2001; Ekzen 1999).

In the 1990s, there were various conjunctural convergences aimed at establishing distribution and/or TV advertisement cartels to prevent other groups joining the ranks of the major market groups, and some agreements to control the labour market in terms of anti-unionism, and wage and transfer policies. Nevertheless, despite such collusion, on the whole this period was characterised by constant competition between Dinç Bilgin, owner of the *Sabah* group, and Aydın Doğan, owner of the Doğan group. Through the agency of their managers and columnists, these two groups waged an intense war to expose each other's alleged administrative infractions concerning tenders and incentives (Adaklı 2006; Dursun 1999; Seçkin 1999a).

One of the most visible moments of this competition was when the practice known as 'promotion', distributing 'gifts' (whether earned through collecting coupons or won in a lottery) to the readers to increase a newspaper's circulation, became widespread, or even indispensable. During the late 1980s and the first half of the 1990s, there were veritable wars of promotion as rival newspapers distributed a wide array of gifts, ranging from detergents to paper playthings and encyclopedias, from automobiles and supermarkets to villas with swimming pools. As newspapers were now often being bought only for the products they gave or promised, a specific process of commodification in the Turkish press took place within the body of the major groups: that is, newspapers became publications lacking a staff of professional correspondents, with just a few pages filled with photographs, and oriented only towards promoting and distributing products. While this strategy did increase sales and profits for some time, agreements made in 1996 and 1997 limited promotions only to cultural products, after which circulations returned to their previous levels (Koloğlu 2006; Adaklı 2006; Seçkin 1999b).

Although economically weaker than Doğan, since it did not have much investment in non-media sectors, the Bilgin group was still able to determine the tone of newspaper publishing in various respects, especially thanks to its daily, *Sabah*. As the first newspaper to make use of computer technology, *Sabah* took a ruling position within the field by bringing in managers and columnists from rival publications, offering high transfer payments and rapidly increasing its circulation. Mustafa Sönmez, who studies the political economy of the Turkish media, argues that Dinç Bilgin 'was the wind that shook the traditional balances [of journalism] and continually forced sectoral growth knowing no bounds' (Sönmez 2004). Within this framework, *Sabah* was the organ mainly responsible for the introduction of a sensationalist tabloid discourse into the narrative structure of Turkish news, and for the increasing generalisation of this style, all just for the sake of increasing the number of readers/consumers. At *Sabah*, which its editor-in-chief called the 'newspaper of rising values', 'one can find almost precisely everything marketed in the name of change, all new values, all social tendencies in the direction of the wind' (Kozanoğlu 2004).

Another of Dinç Bilgin's strategies was, in 1990, to move his own newspaper and magazines (and later television channels) from Bab-ı Âli, the historical location of newspaper bureaus, situated in İstanbul's city centre, to giant plazas built on the city's periphery. Other groups then also rushed to these modern, chic-looking 'media factories' constructed far from the places where news generally happened. However, this was not only a symbolic manifestation of the transition from craftmanship to professionalism but also set off a series of transformations in areas ranging from labour relations to news-making practices (such as journalistic interviewing over the phone rather than face-to-face). Among these transformations, one could also mention that the staff working in sterilised towers overlooking İstanbul's peripheral slums developed a salient illusion with regard to their class positions (Atlas 1999; Nebiler 1995; Adaklı 2006).

The operation of newspaper publishing within the logic of a capitalist enterprise also affected relations between media bosses and workers. In the early 1990s, on Aydın Doğan's initiative (justified in terms of competing with other media groups who already prevented labour unions organising in their newspapers), an eventually successful campaign of deunionisation began. The resulting erosion of the consciousness and feelings of class belonging, and the destruction of the organised power of labour in the media industry, both represented constitutive factors of neoliberal restructuring. These developments not only caused devastating harm to reporting practices and the moral codes of journalism (including concepts such as public interest or editorial independence), but also contributed to the use of flexible (that is, precarious) forms of employment, which have reached a peak in today's media sector.

Hegemony and the Manufacturing of the Neoliberal Individual

The contribution of mass media communication to the construction of neo-liberal hegemony occurs at several levels. One of the fundamental axes of the publishing policy of the mainstream media, when increasingly integrated with capitalist relations of production, is the rationalisation of neoliberal counter-reforms and the naturalisation of the free market economy. One can see this particularly in media productions related to the privatisation of publicly owned enterprises (Dursun 2001). During this period, the rhetoric of the 'modern' and 'dynamic' market, positioned in contradistinction to the 'spendthrift' state and 'clumsy' bureaucracy, was frequently put into effect. Publications were produced in order to legitimise the transfer of state enterprises, presented as a 'burden' to the state, to private capital, and generally appeared to have a dissident and libertarian aura. However, they were actually articulated into another discourse, which gained a hegemonic character with the transition to parliamentary democracy after the 1980 coup d'état and the subsequent adoption of a free market regime. According to this conception, the Turkish state, on account of its repressive quality, had historically inhibited the development of civil society and the market, defined as the fields in which individual freedoms flourish and, therefore, the dynamics of democratisation (Yalman 2002; Akça 2006). Thus the state needed to be, and was, transformed into a minimal form by jettisoning the supposed burdens on its shoulders, while the expansion of those fields with dominant market relations was presented as stages leading towards Turkey's transition to a more libertarian and modern democratic structure.

In addition to those publications oriented towards manufacturing the public's consent by means of rationalising these New Right practices, the media also made a much more permanent contribution to the production of neoliberal hegemony. This was the establishment of a model of the individual compatible with the neoliberal era. One of the prominent vehicles for this was the tabloidisation of media content, mentioned above, with its concentration on sensationalism, the private lives of celebrities, individual success stories, and stories about the misfortunes befalling ordinary people (known as 'page 3 news' in Turkey). This style, pioneered by *Sabah*, but inevitably followed even by those newspapers that identified themselves as intellectual, rapidly became the dominant narrative form (Ergül 2000). This development can be explained in several ways. First, in the years following the 1980 coup, it was risky for the media to deal with socio-political issues due to severe threats of censure and closure, so this threatening atmosphere played a role in the development of reporting based on sensationalism and individual stories. In addition, the media's transformation of private life into a spectacle was one of the fundamental consequences of commercial publishing's search for profit, which is, of course, not intrinsic to Turkey. Finally, the need for the print media to compete with the attractions of commercial television broadcasting led to the weakening of the content and quality of written news and to the strengthening of drama and use of visual materials.

Turning to the ideological function of the generalisation of this new style of journalism, it is possible to argue that, after the 12 September coup, which had aimed to put an end to radical class politics, the media reinforced this de-politicisation at the social level in several ways. First, news content appealing to the most banal emotions and impulses took over (or trivialised) the space that should have been reserved for different news and information that would have enabled citizens to form their own opinions in order to take part in the democratic process. Second, by separating personal disasters from their political, social and economic contexts, the media prevented the audience or reader from realising how relations of power and domination, and even the audience and readers themselves, have a role in the formation of this context. Finally, by stimulating simple psychological or emotional reflexes, they led the audience or readers to be content with their current situation (İnal 2010).

In terms of the internalisation of neoliberal values, one of the functions of the media throughout the last two decades of the 20th century had been to celebrate wealth, luxury, and elite lifestyle. One of the first steps taken down this road was the effort to amend the image of the 'boss', which had been damaged in the 1970s, an era characterised by worker struggles and a radical socialist movement. That image of the boss, driven only by profit, and using every means possible in order to multiply profit, was gradually replaced by an image of the 'employer', an intellectual, art lover, having refined pleasures and conscious of modern urban culture, a socially responsible social-democrat. By the end of the 1990s, some of these employers were even being invited to become newspaper columnists through which they were presented as sages to be consulted for their advice on Turkey's social-political problems, such as human rights, the Kurdish problem or foreign affairs (Bali 2002).

Another primary aim of this period when the free market economy took shape was the production of consumers. The media's marketing of an elite, refined, 'Western' way of life changed the practices of individual identity construction, thereby making a decisive contribution to the formation of identities over patterns of consumption. The marketisation of the lifestyle itself was materialised through different media contents: tabloid magazine programmes and publications and weekend newspapers supplements (which for a time became an enormous site of competition), all featuring the private lives of the celebrities of the business world and show business; newspaper pages where news and advertising intertwined with each other, such as introducing favourite restaurants and entertainment venues under headings like 'gusto', 'lifestyle', and 'trend'; the plethora of magazines about decorating, fashion, women and men; and newspaper columns (Dağtaş 2006).

Newspaper columns in particular become decisive producers of content due to their ability to manufacture opinion and act as the shop window of newspapers. This development makes it possible to argue that a new form of class differentiation in terms of both economic and symbolic capital developed within the Turkish media, as actual professional journalists lost value and fell out of favour. Replacing them, columnists, considered by some analysts as the new aristocrats of the media, acquired a new elevated status as a result of the changes in the structure of the media industry (Bali 2002).

In Turkey, columnists, one of the primary factors affecting newspaper readers' preferences, correspond to the mediatic intellectuals that Bourdieu labelled as 'fast-thinkers' (Bourdieu 1996). In an age of fetishised speed and live broadcasting, opinion is no longer an intellectual product to be published only after a rigorous practice of reflection; instead, there is a need for 'opinion technicians', able to present ready-made opinions (Göker 2009). There are about 20 to 40 columnists per newspaper, performing this function by way of presenting their own interpretations on a variety of topics, ranging from the economy and football to politics and everyday life. Particularly in the 1990s, these columnists gained a disproportionate coverage to become the carriers of a universe of values based on individualism and conspicuous consumption as they discussed their private lives, their travels, the 'interesting' meals they ate, the cigars they smoked, the products they consumed, and the time they spent with elite people. In short, the way this genre, based on lifestyle pedagogy, has gained such importance and legitimacy makes it necessary to consider column writing not only as a product of the neoliberal intervention into the field of journalism, but also as a means to manufacture a neoliberal model of the individual.

Ideological Articulations: Neoliberalism, Nationalism, Militarism

The logo of *Hürriyet* newspaper, owned by the Doğan group, is composed of a silhouette of Mustafa Kemal, the indispensable icon of the Turkish Republic, over the Turkish flag. Below the logo, there is the newspaper's motto, which would generally be identified in other countries with the extreme right: 'Turkey belongs to Turks'. The newspaper's self-designated title, which expresses its assumed role as the Turkish media's vanguard, is also remarkable for its 'peaceful' emphasis: 'Flagship of the Turkish Media'. It would perhaps be impossible to find elsewhere a clearer expression of the simultaneously statist, nationalist and militarist spirit of the mainstream media in Turkey.

The Popularisation of Liberal Nationalism

From Kemalism to new right conservatism, from Islamism to some leftist currents, nationalism has always been an element of Turkey's political landscape. However, a new kind of nationalism began to emerge towards the 1990s. This westernist-liberal nationalism, based on the modernisationist vein of official Kemalist nationalism, developed as an expression of the pride taken in Turkey's economic dynamism that was emerging through the implementation of neo-liberal policies, integration with global capital and transformations in con-sumption patterns. Now having a modern capitalist economy and a cultural environment afforded by such an economy, Turkey was beginning to set itself apart from its Middle Eastern neighbours and move much closer to Mustafa Kemal's original aim of reaching the 'level of contemporary civilisation', or the 'World's Premier League', as the media elites put it. The primary vehicle for disseminating this new-found pride and self-confidence that fed a new nationalism, was the media, especially the columnists. The 'New Nationalism' commentary of Ertugrul Özkök, the editor-in-chief and columnist of *Hürriyet*, represents a clear example of this understanding. Özkök praised the new Turkish youth for feeling unobliged to 'grow a moustache to be a Turk', wearing blue jeans, 'getting their hair cut just like a typical USA soldier', yet still not refraining from planting a flag outside the entrances of bars and hanging pictures of Mustafa Kemal: 'For this generation is discovering for the first time in the history of Turkishness a feeling of 'nationality' without any complex. They are preparing to be registered as the representatives of a generation making Turkey into a "World state"' (Bora 1995).

One should also not underestimate the effects of the culture industry and, especially, young pop stars, in the popularisation of such a nationalism. During the 1990s, they performed while wearing necklaces with the star and crescent shapes, or containing pictures or letters of Atatürk, thus making them fashionable. Later on, newspapers also distributed these as promotions. In addition they stated, on every possible occasion, that they were Atatürkist, laicist and nationalist. These were significant indications that nationalist ideology was also mediated via consumption and entertainment, just like neoliberal values themselves (Kozanoğlu 1995; Konyar 2001).

Kurds and 'The Media with Epaulets'

In addition to such a nationalism finding favour among urban middle classes, another emergent nationalism with a much more ethnicist-chauvinistic emphasis was gaining currency among the social strata suffering from the devastation engendered by capitalist globalisation and neoliberal policies. This development also resulted from the attenuation of feelings of class-belonging that contributed to the rise of this kind of nationalism, the major spokesperson for which was the sports media. With the increasing importance of the Kurdish question, and the perception of this problem as a threat – in the state's own language – to 'the Turkish state's indivisible unity' (as laid down in the constitution), chauvinism also began to add its own colour to other nationalist (Kemalist, liberal, conservative, etc.) discourses.

In the early 1990s, it became clear that the Kurdish movement, which emerged in response to state policies of denial, extermination and assimilation, was not just made up of a few rebels. This led to the reconfiguration of the state's national security conception, to the consolidation of the militarisation of state apparatus under civil war conditions, and to the increasing involvement of the military in the political field (Paker 2010; Öngen 2002). During this period, the southeastern region of Turkey remained under a state of emergency, Kurdish villages were burned, Kurdish parliamentarians were sent to prison after being stripped of parliamentary immunity, Kurdish intellectuals, businessmen and journalists were openly killed on the streets by the paramilitary powers of the state, and the offices of the Kurdish-supporting daily *Özgür Ülke* were bombed after having been pointed out as a target by the Prime Minister Tansu Çiller.

The media played a decisive role in this perception of the Kurdish problem as a security problem to be solved not through democratic and peaceful means, but with arms. It functioned as an active psychological war device by taking for granted the information given by the Turkish General Staff and even publishing fabricated news, using a manipulative language or resorting to disinformation.

In terms of describing the warring parties, the media did not refrain from taking a stand by violating the minimum rules of journalistic objectivity. Successful military operations were described as a 'great cleansing', and Turkish soldiers were characterised as 'heroes', 'brave' and 'rambo'; PKK militants, on the other hand, were presented as 'cowards', or 'duped young people living on mountains under conditions of hunger and misery'. The invariable formula used to describe the PKK was the 'divisive terrorist organisation', and the leader of the movement, Abdullah Öcalan, was the 'head of the separatists'. Thus, instead of the phrase 'separatist', which in other contexts is used to denote ethnic rebellions aiming at achieving independence (e.g. Basques, Tamils), here there was an emphasis on the 'whole', trying to signify that this was an attack to divide or split 'our' wholeness or unity.

Another frequently used rhetorical device, which was in complete accordance with the state's discourse, was the thesis that the PKK was 'the pawn of foreign powers'. This thesis articulated with both the republican national struggle story and an older historical narrative that can be traced back to the Ottoman Empire: Turkey is always surrounded by enemy states desiring to 'divide' it; Turkey's national unity is always under threat. Another device used both to condemn the PKK, backed by a considerable segment of the Kurdish people, and to discredit it in the eyes of (Muslim) Kurds was the thesis that this organisation is the 'Turkish extension of the Armenian ASALA'. This fictitious connection was elevated to a racist level, with Öcalan described as an 'Armenian bastard' or 'Armenian offshoot'. There was a frequent circulation of 'information' that the 'baby killer' leader (Öcalan) of this 'terrorist organisation feeding on blood' had heroin farms, a weakness for young women, or that a cross was found in the grave which he prepared for himself (Ayaz 1997; Laçiner 1999). Another generalised formula based upon de-legitimising, even denying, the existence of the PKK was the use of the phrase 'so-called', sometimes to nonsensical degrees: 'the so-called conference of the terrorist organisation', 'the so-called flag', 'the so-called anthem', and so on. This same linguistic strategy of denial is also intensively used with respect to the the the 'so-called Armenian genocide'.

The epithet of 'the media with epaulets', coined by Ragıp Duran to denote the mainstream media's self-identification with the Turkish Armed Forces in its reproduction of official state discourse, is pertinent for our purposes, and this ascription is not just metaphorical. During the 'Journalists' Expedition to the Southeastern Region' organised by the General Staff at the end of 1997, many journalists and columnists preferred to wear military camouflage and boots, despite the fact that it was not necessary to do so (Duran 2000, 1996). Perhaps this was because of their concern to make a coherent link between appearance and content.

The Civil Basis of the Military Intervention: The Authoritarian Laicist Media

With the establishment of the belief in the legitimacy of the free market after 1980, the internalisation of competitive and individualist values, the modernisation of consumption patterns and the construction of a consumerist society, neoliberalism began to take root at both ideological and cultural levels. At the same time, the neoliberal strategy of accumulation also excluded wide segments of society by causing poverty, unemployment and economic insecurity. This meant that, during the 1990s, neither the centre-right nor centre-left parties, who intended to carry forward the neoliberal project, could comprehensively represent all segments of society.

In the midst of this crisis of political hegemony, the Welfare Party (RP) imposed itself as a political actor by becoming the leading party, first in the 1994 municipality elections, and a year later, in the general elections, following which it became part of the goverment as a coalition partner in 1996. Thanks to its discourse of the 'just order', with its anti-neoliberal resonances, an emphasised religious identity, and its anti-Western and anti-EU rhetoric the RP managed to unite social segments with different class interests under an Islamic identity. In response to the rise of this Islamic movement, the urban classes constituted a bloc around the Turkish Armed Forces, grounding itself on the defence of laicisism. This social bloc incorporated the big bourgeoisie, some segments of the working class, universities, professional chambers and the judiciary, and one of its major agents was the media. As a result of this conflict, which was as much based on identity politics as it was on different forms of articulation with global capitalism, the coalition goverment was given a warning by the Presidency of the General Staff on 28 February 1997 that forced it to resign after a few months (Akça 2009; Doğan 2010b).

During the process leading up to this intervention, defined by some as the 'postmodern coup', the media had a decisive function in the intensification of tension. In briefings given by the General Staff, not only to representatives of institutions (such as the judiciary and university) but also to media members, it was stated that 'reactionary' activities had become the country's principal threat, and that citizens should be aware of this issue. In parallel with this discourse, the Turkish mainstream media also set about demonstrating that there was a threat posed by sharia. Thus, scenes presenting anti-laicist speechs given by RP parliamentarians years ago were put back into circulation; news that pump-action rifle sales had increased in certain regions was presented as if this was the harbinger of a preparation for an Islamic revolution; the repression undergone by women in those Muslim countries with which the coalition government was affiliated was frequently highlighted. For sure, a number of provocative acts by RP administrators (including a dinner with religious sect leaders at the Prime Minister's officially secular residence, and Prime Minister Erbakan's ruminations as to whether Islam 'would come to force either by blood or without it') also contributed to this process, leading them to be continually retained on the agenda.

The dynamics of the media, with its tabloid style and tendency to personalise social issues, were also involved in the mobilisation for protecting the secular republic. After the RP took power, various religious sects increasingly became visible in crowded demonstrations organised in front of mosques following Friday prayers. The adherents of one of these sects in particular, the Aczmendi, attracted the media's attention, with their beards, gowns and batons. Müslüm Gündüz, the sect's sheikh, became something of a mediatic figure on account of his appearance, and the radical statements he made on every TV channel to which he was invited. However, after a while, he was caught in a sexual affair with a young woman, and it then was revealed soon afterwards that the same woman had previously been 'duped' into having an affair with a sheikh of another sect. This time, the cuckolded wife of that sheikh, the daughter of a rich İstanbulite family, became another mediatic figure, with her 'revelations' into the wealth of the sects, their 'corrupt' relations and connections with Islamist political leaders (Arıkan 2001). Years later, Dinç Bilgin, the owner of the *Sabah* group, referred in an interview to this event by stressing how the media had formed an alliance with the military during the 28 February process:

> On 28 February, the newspapers all had a common headline. For they took their nourishment from the same place; news was coming from the same sources. For instance, regarding the news about the Aczmendi sect, we were served from the same sources, just like *Hürriyet*, *Milliyet*, *ATV* and *Star*. (Düzel 2010)

During this process, the media reflected the armed forces' disquiet, sometimes expressed very heavily. However, it also covered up its journalistic policy by claiming that the military did not want to stage a coup, that it respected democracy, but there would be no tolerance to those aiming to destroy the democratic-secular regime. Therefore, the argument continued, there was no point in trying the military's patience anymore. That is, having taken lessons from the devastation wrought by the 1980 coup, it foregrounded a discourse that emphasised how there was now a need for 'unarmed forces' to mobilise. Thus, it actually tried to legitimise its civil contribution to militarist practices aimed at reorganising the political sphere.

Apart from applying social pressure on the government by reinforcing the perception that the secular regime was under threat, another 'success' of the media during this period was to channel another kind of social reaction in an anti-RP direction. A few weeks before the 28 February memorandum, towards the end of 1996, the hidden relations between the state and the mafia were unexpectedly revealed as the result of a car accident. While it was already well known that the state had previously made use of criminal nationalist cadres to carry out state-sponsored assassinations, this accident was the first time that it was revealed with such clarity because a police commander, a mafia leader and a parliamentarian from a centre-right party were all in the same car. Led initially by the socialist movement, the 'One Minute of Darkness for Constant Light' campaign (based on supporters turning off their lights every evening at a certain time) was a powerful expression of the demand for clarification over political murders. The centre-right wing of the governnment tried to protect the mafia murderer who died (and who was being sought after by Interpol at the time); the Islamic wing, on the other hand, preferred to make fun of them with a classic statist reflex. The government's dismissiveness was one thing, but there was another side to the issue: the concept of 'light' (or Enlightenment) was being coded in the republican-laicist imaginary as the opposite of religious obscurantism, so, based upon this coding, the media obscured the original content and demand of these demonstrations, masterfully shifting them to an anti-RP vein. Hence, not only was the political desire for the revelation of the secrets of the deep state inactivated, support was also gathered for military intervention as well.

Both before and after, the 28 February process was a period when the media came under tight monitoring and control. As well as the General Staff briefings, some generals attended the editorial meetings of newspapers; the Islamic-conservative press was not invited to the General Staff's meetings as they were not 'accredited'; the names of those journalists whose point of view was not in accord with that of the Turkish Armed Forces were kept in secret records and their bosses received complaints about them. However, the most dramatic event in this context was undoubtedly the publication of the statements of Şemdin Sakık, the second-in-command of the PKK, after being arrested. According to his statements, there had been colloboration between the PKK and a number of parliamentarians and other politicians, NGO administrators and journalists. As a consequence of the fact that the journalists in question were employees of *Sabah*, the names of these journalists were unveiled in the rival *Hürriyet*, in a commentary by the editor-in-chief titled 'Let's Get to Know the Scoundrels', and in the main news bulletin of *Kanal D*, also owned by the Doğan Media Group. The named journalists were either fired or had their professional credentials temporarily suspended, while another person named in Sakık's statements, the human rights activist Akın Birdal, was nearly killed in an assassination attempt at his office a few days later. Two years later, it was revealed that within the framework of the 'Powerful Action Plan' organised by the General Staff in April 1998, these names had been deliberately added to Sakık's statements before they were passed on to selected newspaper owners, columnists, and TV channels in order to 'discredit' and 'mobilise public opinion' against them (Yüksel 2004).

The Media in the Era of Neoliberal Authoritarian Conservatism

In the ten-year period that has passed since the AKP came to power in 2002, a radical upheaval has been experienced in the ownership structure of the media industry and its power relations. The start of this was the financial crisis of 2001, which deeply shocked the media sector, and allowed the AKP to unwittingly acquire the necessary ideological-cultural means of production to establish its own hegemony when it came to power a year later.

Liquidation of the Mainstream Media

In the 2001 crisis, the deepest in Turkish history, there was an approximately 10 per cent recession in the economy, accompanied by a huge fall in advertising revenue, from 1.1 billion dollars in 2000 to 550 million dollars in 2001; that is, a 51 per cent decrease from the previous year. In particular, media groups lost the advertising revenue from banks (of which there were about 80), and nearly all of them had also made investments in the financial sector prior to the crisis. In the face of this economic pressure, some groups managed to survive but only staggered out of this recession, while others were completely destroyed (Sönmez 2004).

The group to be first liquidated after the AKP came to power in 2002 was the Uzan group, which had become among the biggest media groups, having taken the risk of challenging Doğan and Bilgin. In addition to interests in banking and football, the Uzan family also had a considerable share of the energy sector, although their names were regularly involved in corruption speculations. Perhaps taking inspiration from Silvio Berlusconi, the Uzan family laid hands on nearly every sector, paying little attention to the contracts they signed. They wanted to crown this economic expansion by entering politics (perhaps also taking into consideration possible parliamentary immunity) and, on the eve of the 2002 elections, had established a party, the Young Party (GP), with a nationalist-populist discourse that harshly opposed the AKP. Mobilising every media tool available during the elections, the party's leader, Cem Uzan, obtained nearly 7 per cent of the votes, a very suprising achievement in such a short span of time, especially at a time when all the other parties' votes collapsed. As a result, the GP became one of the two new parties that gained prominence in the election, the other, of course, being the AKP. However, in mid-2003, more than 200 companies belonging to the Uzan group were confiscated due to various infractions and breaches of contract, entirely erasing the group from the economic, political and media fields. This was interpreted by various analysts as a statement from the AKP government directed to all the mainstream media.

Indeed, some assets of Dinç Bilgin were also confiscated (and he was himself imprisoned for a while on remand while awaiting trial) for illegally providing extra credit for his other companies via the bank he had purchased in 1997 from the Privization Administration, in order to increase his competitive capacity against Doğan. *Sabah* newspaper and *ATV* channel (and other media belonging to the group) were first put under the control of the Saving Deposit Insurance Fund (TMSF) before being bought by another group, the Ciner group. Later however, the TMSF again confiscated *Sabah* and *ATV* for various further infractions, before a deal was reached at the end of 2007 after a long and complicated tender process. Only one group participated in this tender, Çalık Holding, whose CEO was the son-in-law of Prime Minister Erdoğan. Until then, the Çalık group had not been well-known, apart from its investments in the construction and textile sectors. Yet, within a few years, it increased its total assets from 1 billion to 4.4. billion dollars, taking on such giant projects as the Samsun–Ceyhan Pipeline. As such, it was one of the major examples of Islamic capital's ability to expand under the patronage of the AKP government (Mavioğlu 2012; Adaklı 2010).

Unlike Bilgin, the Doğan group managed not to collapse. Despite the losses it made from its activities in the media sector after the 2001 crisis and subsequent general recession, it managed to survive, especially by means of its investments in the energy sector. Initially, the Doğan group approached the AKP with caution, just like the other factions of the big bourgeoisie. After the government's early statement of commitment to IMF programmes and the EU integration project, that is, after it was sure that the AKP would not act in government like the RP had, it tried to develop orderly relations with the government, even if its media organisations also sometimes maintained a low-profile opposition towards it. Withdrawing in this period from the banking sector, Doğan wanted to take over its arch-rival *Sabah–ATV*, but Dinç Bilgin refused to consent to Doğan's offer. Instead, it enlarged its media group by purchasing Uzan's confiscated TV channel (*Star TV*), incorporating the daily *Vatan*, which had actually been established by journalists who left *Sabah*, and added digital publishing. According to 2008 data, it was still the biggest group, controlling the 34 per cent of total daily newspaper circulation, 23 per cent of TV ratings, and 43 per cent of total advertising revenues (Adaklı 2010).

However, between 2007 and 2008, that is, in the second period of its rule, the AKP abandoned its defensive position in favour of engaging in conflict with the military-bureaucratic forces. In the resulting tense environment, previous orderly relations deteriorated when publications owned by the Doğan group readopted their historical militarist roles. When the newspapers belonging to the Doğan group then reported allegations, by the leader of the main opposition party, of Erdoğan's involvement in a fraud that had happened in an Islamic charitable foundation, the remaining ties between the AKP and the Doğan group were completely broken. Erdoğan asserted that Aydın Doğan had allowed the publication of the allegations because he had not given him permission over some commercial business (supposedly including a petroleum refinery, and modifications to the Hilton hotel). The debate rapidly turned into a harsh battle of words between the conservative press and the Doğan Group media, and soon afterwards, all companies in the Doğan group were taken under strict fiscal administration by state inspectors. In the beginning of 2009, the Doğan group was officially notified of an increased tax fine of 4.8 billion TL ($3.22 billion), whereupon Doğan engaged in stragetic downsising, selling the daily *Milliyet* (his first investment in the media sector), *Vatan*, *Star TV* and the Hürriyet Media Towers. In parallel with this downsizing, the group's tax debts also decreased (Mavioğlu 2012).

However, the group was not content with this orientation, and either removed or pensioned off those columnists and managers who had been the architects of *Hürriyet*'s statist-laicist line, to make way for new 'democratic' columnists, of an Islamic background and close to the government. This self-imposed penalty can also be regarded as intimidation, or in Mustafa Sönmez's harsher expression, a 'hostage-taking' operation, not only towards other media groups but also towards the big bourgeoisie as well (Sönmez 2012). Consequently, the rest of the laicist mainstream media also showed some signs of alignment during this period, by means of bringing in conservative writers, sacking the anti-AKP opinion technicians and qualified (therefore, critical) journalists, and generally toning down its anti-government discourse.

The Conservative Mainstream Media Bloc

In its second term of government, the AKP increased its efforts to establish its own domination over the key institutions of authoritarian laicist republicanism, namely, the military, the judiciary, the universities and the media. In parallel with the weakening or disintegration of the laicist media, and by means of the decisive role of strengthening the Islamic capital under the patronage of the AKP government, a conservative media bloc took shape. From this period onwards, the conservative media started to abandon its critical attitude towards the current power apparatuses and, instead, became the new mainstream media, thanks to the fact that the ruling party also began to establish its own command over state institutions that had, until then, been controlled by laicist forces.

Islamic-conservative ideological-cultural production began to develop, particularly in the mid-1990s, in parallel with the political and economic strengthening of the Islamic movement. For example, there was a significant increase in the number of daily newspapers (*Zaman, Türkiye, Milli Gazete, Yeni Asya, Vakit* and *Yeni Şafak*) and television channels (*TGRT, Kanal 7*), some of which were owned by a specific religious community, and also a growth in the number of public-speaking independent Islamist intellectuals (Doğan 2010; Gülalp 2002). At this time, on issues such as the Kurdish problem and the Turkish Armed Forces' domination over political life, there was some convergence between these intellectuals and some liberal leftist circles and intellectuals. It can even be argued that, for these liberal and liberal leftist intellectuals, whose views had been dismissed after the 28 February 1997 memorandum and the 2001 economic crisis, the Islamist media became a refuge (Aydın 2009).

Thanks to the AKP's power, there were further additions to this Islamic-conservative media after the 1990s that allowed a hegemonic media bloc to be created that included tens of newspapers, television channels, journals, radios and websites, both large and small. For sure, *Sabah-ATV* was one of the main elements, but the state television company, TRT, whose five channels came under increasing government control, and the state news agency (Anadolu Ajansı), also adopted a decisive role in providing ideological support for the AKP in its power struggle against the institutions of the Kemalist regime. One should mention the following in particular: the daily *Zaman*, known as the mouthpiece of the Fethullah Gülen Community, controlling (thanks to subscriptions and free distribution by Gülen members) nearly 20 per cent of total daily circulation; *Star*, previously an aggressively nationalist tabloid daily within the Uzan group, but transformed by its new owner into a liberal-conservative intellectual newspaper, along with *Kanal 24*; the daily *Yeni Şafak*, published by Albayrak Holding, one of the capital groups most loyal to the AKP, particularly to Erdoğan; and the liberal-oriented daily *Taraf*, founded specifically with a mission to struggle against military tutelage.

The Cement of the New Hegemony

As a result of the weakening of the institutional-material foundations of authoritarian republicanism and the subsequent break up of its ideological monopoly, together with the AKP's limited moves, whether actual or discursive, it seemed possible for a time to discuss such taboo issues as the criticisms of the armed forces' traditional interventions in politics, the recognition of Kurdish identity and democratic solutions to the problem, which had previously all been contained behind the red lines of the National Security Council. This provided an atmosphere that fed the 'democratisation discourse', which was an indispensable ideological element for the construction of the AKP's hegemony. In the 12 September 2010 referendum, organised to amend certain constitutional clauses, the AKP obtained overwhelming approval, which led to the crystallisation of a nationalist-authoritarian-conservative turn in its politics. In the wake of such a turn, it became clear that the process carried out under the name of democratisation was actually a move by the governing party to inactivate all kinds of opposition, and to limit the ground for opposition as far as possible.

The year 2007 was one of sheer turmoil. First, the General Staff published a threatening memorandum via its website to counteract the AKP's effort to secure the presidency, one of the key institutions of the republican regime, for one of its party members. Second, there were several legal attempts to close down the AKP. Third, it was revealed that, between 2003 and 2004, there had been some planning within the military for a coup against the government. Hence, even while it refrained from overtly responding to these challenges, the AKP began to prioritise the struggle against military tutelage. The fundamental and most important site of this political struggle to push back the military was the Ergenekon case. The matter in dispute was the 'Ergenekon Terror Organisation', alleged to have developed various coup plans against the AKP, carried out activities to harm the party in the eyes of the domestic public and Western countries, and organised various attacks and murders (particularly those targeting minorities) in order to foment the sense of disorder needed to justify a new military intervention. This case was met with enthusiasm by wide segments of society, as it was also seen as the ultimate opportunity to settle accounts with past coup perpetrators and with organisations like the Special War Department, counter-guerillas and branches of the Operation Gladio, which were strongly believed to have been involved in a long series of provocations, assassinations and massacres over a period of 40 years.

Regarding the media response to Ergenekon, two newspapers, *Hürriyet* and *Cumhuriyet*, which were still fundamental ideological mouthpieces of Kemalism, sometimes took an indifferent or sceptical attitude towards the operations and arrests and sometimes pursued an editorial policy aiming to discredit the case. The conservative media, on the other hand, dealt with the case process within a discourse of democratisation and of settling accounts with the country's dark history, often publishing, without subjecting them to any kind of journalistic scrutiny, documents and formal criminal charges leaked from inside the judicary or the police.

However, various irregularites in the prosecution process, inadequate proof for some arrests, allegations of the involvement in Ergenekon of people with very different political views, the limitation of the inquiry to crimes perpetrated under the AKP's rule, and the unification of 16 separate cases under a single Ergenekon Terror Organisation case (which made the whole process very complicated), all led to a vanishing of the public's initial excitement. Meanwhile, these developments also strengthened perceptions, which substantially weakened the credibility of the case, that it was being used, in at least one respect, by the ruling party in order to eliminate those factions with whom it was uncomfortable (Şik 2012). Nonetheless, the Ergenekon case fulfilled a significant ideological function in terms of authoritarianisation, which is one of the main foundations of the AKP's neoliberal-conservative hegemony project. In the legitimisation of the AKP's 'security oriented governing technique', carried out in order to transform the political sphere into a secure one, to depoliticise social issues and crimininalise all sorts of opposition and resistance, the construction of a discourse by the conservative media and new opinion technicians around the 'Ergenekon Terror Organisation' played a dominant role (Türk 2012). Although the AKP was now bringing all state apparatuses under its own control, and high-ranking military officers, including the ex-Commander of the Turkish Armed Forces, politicians, academics, mafia leaders and journalists were being arrested, the new mainstream media managed to hegemonise the discourse of threatening 'pro-coup, totalitarian, terrorist' forces *versus* civil politics and democratic forces, by means of bringing into the discussion on every occasion the allegation that, deep down in the state's basement tunnels, the Ergenekon organisation was staying on alert to overthrow the government.

This stigmatisation of all sorts of people who dared to resist, or at least oppose, in the face of the AKP's unbridled neoliberal orientation, became the ideological reflex of the conservative media. However, despite their best efforts, neither the AKP politicians nor their intellectual supporters in the media could credibly associate with Ergenekon the range of opposition to the government's neo-liberalism: student protests against the marketisation of higher education, peasant resistance against hydroelectric plants, actions by workers who were victims of privatisations, farming unions organising against the industrialisation of agriculture, socialist movements, and, of course, the Kurdish movement.[1]

The AKP backed down from taking steps towards a democratic solution of the Kurdish problem, turning back instead to the archaic nationalist-statist position of previous Turkish ruling elites. In this old-new road, thousands of Kurdish local administrators, party spokespeople, party members, lawyers and journalists were jailed, making it physically impossible for them to engage in politics. In addition, the media encouraged a new mobilisation for the criminilisation of the Kurdish movement. To do this, the new hegemonic discourse's reservoir of democratic arguments was consulted in order to allege that the 'so-called' civil Kurdish opposition had in fact a totalitarian structure; that it was intolerant of pluralism and dissenting voices; and that it was under the full domination of the PKK military wing. From these allegations, one is thus expected to infer that it is the justifiable task of the Turkish state to 'rescue' the Kurdish people from this 'military tutelage'. It is possible to see a typical example of the criminalisation through homogenisation of different elements of the anti-AKP opposition in Şamil Tayyar's[2] book *Kürt Ergenekonu* (Kurdish Ergenekon). Subtitled as the 'Secret Codes of the Deep PKK', this book tells us that the organisation was established by the National Intelligence Organisation; that it marched 'hand in hand' with the army during the 28 February process; and that it is now under the command of the 'Global Ergenekon' (though it is impossible from the book to learn what that really is). The author explains his purposes in writing such 'analytical' research as follows: 'I hope this contributes to the peace process. I hope Turkey, just like it cleared the way for democratisation by judging Ergenekon, will speed up this process by eliminating the PKK, the blood brother of the same organisation' (Tayyar 2011).[3]

Conclusion: Continuity of the Neoliberal Security Media from February 28 to the AKP

'The road to liberal hell is paved with democratic good intentions'. This observation provides a clue as to the 30-year history of Turkey in the wake of the last military regime, especially to the 'democratisation' adventure experienced under the AKP's rule. This includes the establishment of the legal and institutional framework of a liberal democratic order by making Turkey a candidate for full EU membership, the breaking of the Turkish military's power over political life, and the expansion of the market's sphere of domination in order to 'lighten' the clumsy bureaucratic state. The AKP's road to the new neoliberal–conservative regime, in which all kinds of political and social opposition have been deemed a security problem and duly suppressed, was paved with these 'democratic' intentions.

The results of a 2011 survey on censorship, carried out with journalists of different political views and different positions, enables us to read the new security-based authoritarianism through the media. The percentage of those who thought that the military's role in news content was 'very important' or 'important' was 57.2 per cent. On the other hand, the percentage of those who saw the police's intervention as either 'very important' or 'important' was 73.7 per cent (Arsan 2011). These results clearly describe the 'forces of coercion' hierachy within the AKP's security paradigm. The police forces are increasingly taking the place (and following the example) of the 1990s military. They function not only as a coercive apparatus, but also fulfil a key role, by means of the mainstream conservative media, in manufacturing consent for authoritarian security policies. There are even some police columnists who have developed an intellectual profile, making, for example, predictions about prospective operations. Although this is a dramatic example of collaboration between the media and the police, we see it only in the supposedly liberal daily *Taraf*. In a very organised, almost institutional, fashion the police forces now send investigative information about targeted people to selected newspapers and columnists almost in the form of a press release, suggesting beforehand the headlines, preparing the spotlight, underlining the significant parts. Thus, the police forces have become, as it were, a new actor in the media industry (Şık 2012). The fact that the information in these texts almost literally figures in the columns of conservative opinion technicians and newspaper headlines shows that some 'professional values' are still maintained, regardless of changing powers and regimes.

Other results in the survey mentioned above also show that journalists often resort to self-censorship with respect to criticising the government, that religious communities intervene to provide news content more than the police, and that there is a real fear of being jailed for writing critical news. For example, after Ahmet Şık, a socialist journalist, investigated the Fethullah Gülen community's organisation within the police forces, he was put into custody for a year, for allegedly carrying out his research on Ergenekon's instructions. The offices of a newspaper and a publishing house were raided and the computers located there were seized in order to find the digital copies of this yet unpublished book. Most probably, this process had a salient effect on the results of this survey.

After the 1990s, self-censorship thus became a professional reflex again, probably because, following the dismissal of the authoritarian laicist columnists and critical journalists, it was now time to remove those liberal columnists and Islamist journalists directing the slightest criticism at the authoritarian orientation within the AKP. Within the context of dismissals, arrests, self-censorship and conformism, the Turkish media is becoming a monolith, based on a neoliberal-conservative consensus, being a complete substitute for the neoliberal-nationalist monolith of the 1990s. The moments when this is broken are limited to conflicts within the conservative power bloc, though it is certainly possible to predict that the conflicts between the new owners of the state will grow further in the years ahead. However, this does not make us hopeful, either for a pluralist and free media system guarding the public good, or for a general democratisation of Turkey.

NOTES

1   Upon the declaration by Paul Auster, American author and director, that he would not come to Turkey due to restrictions imposed on freedom of expression and the arrests of journalists, the Vice President of the AKP stated that Auster was under the influence of the 'Neocon-Ergenekon'. I think this is a fair illustration of the severity of the situation.
2   The *Star* newspaper columnist Tayyar became an AKP MP in 2011.
3   In order to demonise Kurds further in the eyes of religious-conservative people, the new mainstream newspapers and Islamic-militarist TV series (a new genre in its own right), circulate a body of 'knowledge' about the 'fact' that PKK members worship fire, eat pork and engage in homosexual practices in the caves where they hide. In doing so, these media followed in the footsteps of the Prime Minister and the Minister of Internal Affairs. See Göker (2012).

CHAPTER SEVEN

'We'll Come and Demolish Your House!': The Role of Spatial (Re-)Production in the Neoliberal Hegemonic Politics of Turkey

Erbatur Çavuşoğlu and Julia Strutz

In the coming years, the Turkish state, through its Housing Development Administration (TOKİ), plans to evict six million households nationwide. 'We'll come and demolish your house' is what Prime Minister Erdoğan has proclaimed (Ntvmsnbc 2012). This article tries to solve the puzzle of why it is not *despite* its spatial politics, but rather *because* of them, that the Justice and Development Party (AKP) is able to sustain its neoliberal hegemony in Turkey. It raises three claims. Firstly, since the 2000s, the re-production of space in Turkey has become the single most important economic accumulation model. Like any hegemonic project that needs to control and reproduce its space, the AKP's political project, too, is built upon growth and the re-production of space. The new quality of this re-production in the last decade has been the regime's frantic exploitation of non-commodified spaces: privatising the large state-owned stock of former industrial and public buildings, forests, rivers and informally urbanised land, and creating a set of laws to expropriate property from the current owners of valuable inner city neighbourhoods. Secondly, and interconnected with this new vigor concerning the re-production of space, the construction sector in the 2000s has grown immensely compared to other sectors, so that it now employs large parts of the population that were made redundant by sectoral change over recent years. The construction sector is no longer an assemblage of small to middle-sized construction firms, but monopolised by a few large constructors and developers with close ties to the regime. Thirdly, the AKP's neoliberal hegemony is – like most other regimes in Turkish history – founded on corporatism. The AKP, however, has an advantage in comparison to the other corporatists: it can add Islamism as an overarching identity that transcends class differences, while it continues to use nationalism in a period in which nationalism has reached new heights. The fact that the neoliberal hegemony of the AKP has received such widespread support since 2000 is related to these three overarching political strategies which have made the AKP the moral leader of a national-popular project – a leader that can produce consent and, when it cannot, does not shy away from using force.

This chapter starts out by unraveling the process of the re-production of space with the help of the theories of Antonio Gramsci. To contextualise and underline the spatial character of the AKP's neoliberal project, we will sketch out four hegemonic periods in Turkey since the 1920s, before focusing on spatial re-production since the 1980s. The final part will try to explain how spatial politics today functions as a hegemonic tool. Most examples in this article will be drawn from İstanbul as it includes one-fifth of the population of the country, produces 27 per cent of the national GDP, 38 per cent of total industrial output, 50 per cent of services, and 40 per cent of tax revenues (OECD 2008). We believe that it is possible to observe the general trends of the country in İstanbul, while at the same time İstanbul is itself the creator of these trends. Nevertheless, we are also aware that this article ignores certain other developments in the provinces, although, regarding the question of hegemony production, we think it is legitimate to write only from the centre.

Reading Spatial (Re-)Production from a Gramscian Perspective

Neomarxist analysis no longer considers space as a superstructure or background of social relations in capitalism, but as an integral element (Harvey 2006; Lefebvre 2007; Soja 1989). A finite resource like space can only be produced as if it were a commodity by increasing its quantity (e.g. through height and density) or quality (e.g. shopping malls, boutique hotels and gated communities). However, instead of conceiving of space as simply a box structured by capitalist society, where the height of skyscrapers mirrors capitalist development, space itself is structuring capitalist society. Thus, capitalist society not only commodifies space and extracts its land rent, but also makes space into a means of production itself, actively involved in putting and keeping everyone in his or her place. Gramsci, likewise, refuses to understand space only in its Cartesian three-dimensionality, but treats it as:

(a) the territorialisation of political power and processes of state formation,
(b) the spatial division of labour between town and countryside (. . .) and
(c) spatial imaginaries and the representation of space. Gramsci did not believe that space exists in itself, independently of the specific social relations that construct it, reproduce it, and occur within it. (Jessop 2005: 425)

Gramsci's idea of the historic block can be understood as 'historic-geographic constellations of state and civil society' (Kipfer 2002: 126) that achieved hegemony because they were able to fuse and balance out base and superstructure, micro and macro level, and fractions of society. The most important medium to achieve the balancing act necessary for the formation of a historic block is everyday life, or, as Gramsci calls it, 'popular culture' (Hall 1979). In order to become and stay hegemonic, every historic block needs to produce its own everyday life embedded in its own (urban) space, since it is (urban) space where the everyday 'takes place' and where hegemony is mediated (Goonewardena 2005).

Neo-Gramscian state theory thus opens up new perspectives for understanding the role of the production of urban space in shaping a capitalist hegemony (Kipfer and Keil 2002: 234; Loopmans and Decker 2010). While the 'absorption' of rural immigrants into the city by Islamic municipalities and their constitutive role for new capital groups has been identified as a passive revolution in a Gramscian sense (Tuğal 2009), the role of space for balancing out consent and force is often underestimated or disregarded in the literature. As we will show below, in the Turkish context, space has been used throughout the 20th century as an important means to create consent and make the force of the state both visible and tangible. What is new in recent developments is that, while spatial policies used to be a method to *strengthen* hegemony, the AKP's neoliberal hegemony is *constituted* through their use of space. Since the 2000s, the AKP has invented governance models to commodify spaces that, on the one hand, allow them to allocate surpluses to their own budgets and networks while also supporting the enormous growth of a government-allied construction sector on the other. Their ideology of building more and more, again and again, is not only a most welcome source of income for many, but also integrates the modernist-developmentalist and corporatist convictions of former historic blocks. This construction ideology has indeed developed into a national-popular project that, while creating both victims and winners, integrates many members of society via property relations.

Key Concepts of Spatial (Re-)Production in Different Hegemonic Periods

Changes in the production of space in Turkey have often been both triggered and maintained parallel to historic blocks. We identify four of these: the redistribution of rural land between 1923 and 1950; the redistribution of urban land between 1950 and 1980; the redistribution of construction rights between 1980 and 2000; and the redistribution of non-commodified space since 2000. This periodisation is only an attempt to describe dominant tendencies. That is, it does not imply that some phenomena outlined here cannot be observed across all four periods.

1923–1950s: Redistribution of Rural Land

When the Republic of Turkey was created in 1923, it found itself deprived of most of its (port) cities, which had previously sustained the economy of the

Ottoman Empire, and left with a citizenry of 13 million, of which 80 per cent lived in rural areas (Köymen 1999). İstanbul was not seen as a suitable capital city for the new nation as it symbolised the former historic block, with its mosques, Ottoman palaces, and its non-Muslim infrastructure of schools, banks and businesses. The national project of the Republic was the creation of a new society, free of the social and class distinctions passed down by the Ottoman Empire, and based on the peasantry and a new capital founded in Ankara. Ankara was to symbolise the life of the new national elite, who were to live in apartments with cubic, modernist architecture, accessible by car via broad avenues (Bozdoğan 2001). As rural land had been largely owned by the imperial family and former elites, it was nationalised and then redistributed. The big challenge, however, was to integrate the rural majority of the new nation, which mostly lacked basic infrastructure like schools, hospitals or transportation and, in particular, the potentially dangerous landless peasants needed to be resettled (Scott 1998). In response, the state both redistributed resources to the rural population by assigning appropriated arable land and abolishing tithes on agricultural products (aşar), and also tried to stimulate the industrialisation of the Anatolian hinterland. Emblematic of this period was the establishment of state-owned factories and people's houses (halkevleri) in the new provincial centres, where the people would go to work, receive basic education and become acquainted with the new nation's ideology, Kemalism. In short, the state aimed to produce consent in a Gramscian sense. Graduates of the people's houses (Halkevleri, a sort of educational community centre) would travel to even more remote areas to set up village institutes (köy enstitüleri) to educate the peasantry (Karaömerlioğlu 1998). However, the Republic was only partly successful in these attempts, as evidenced by the increasing amount of force used against Kurdish, Roma and non-Muslim populations, and the violent resettlement and dispersal of these dissident groups. By 1945, the historic block consisted mainly of landlords, organised within the Republican People's Party (CHP) and opposed to the redistribution of rural land (which they owned). Eventually, only a small proportion of public land was redistributed (Köymen 1999), which may explain in part the failure of the historic block to integrate the Anatolian hinterland into the Kemalist project and the increasing dissent of these strata of the population against the regime.

1950s–1980s: Redistribution of Urban Land

In the 1950s, the CHP's single-party hegemony started to falter, eventually being replaced by a multiparty system. However, as the coup d'états of 1960, 1971 and 1980 show, it was never replaced by a new, stable historic block. This inability to stabilise was strongly linked to spatial changes. With the end of the Second World War, Turkey became eligible for the American Marshall funds, which made enormous numbers of agricultural workers redundant due to the mechanisation of agriculture with 'Marshall tractors'. Many of these workers ended up migrating to the major cities. This push-factor for urbanisation was coupled with the pull-factor created by the state's import-substitution policies, which required labour for new industries. As a result, during this period, cities like İstanbul,

Ankara and İzmir began to grow, and had to grapple with an influx of rural migrants arriving to work in the new urban industrial centres.

As the state was unable to provide housing for this new population, the newcomers settled informally on publicly owned land, building their own shelters – the *gecekondu* (Karpat 1976). The *gecekondu* was a consent-producing solution: by constructing their own *gecekondu*s, industrial workers acquired cheap housing in the vicinity of their work places, and could sustain life in the metropolis, despite their low wages. Although the city authorities paid lip-service to opposing this illegal squatting, for them it meant urbanisation on the cheap, because it freed them from having to provide social housing for the new urbanites, and solved the accommodation question simply by redistributing unused urban land; industry was provided with a cheap workforce that was even able to consume the new, domestically-produced goods, and the newly emerging political parties' interests could be served by an electorate through clientelistic networks reaching into the informal settlements. In order to protect their shelters, *gecekondu* settlers had to trade their votes for protection from demolition and to ensure the provision of basic urban infrastructure like water, electricity and roads. This constellation of factors required political organisation on a neighbourhood level, which meant that many political careers began through achieving legalisation of a settlement and gaining official neighbourhood status as mayor (Erder 1999). The new urbanites were not only loyal to their parties; they also introduced new values and claims into the political establishment.

1980s–2000s: Redistribution of Construction Rights

The military coup of 1980 terminated the struggles for hegemony that had dominated the years before through a restoration of Kemalist law and order. Following a return to civil authority, the Motherland Party (ANAP) heralded a new neoliberal historic block that put an end to import-substitution. As an armada of new imported products started entering the market, the low-quality products previously produced in Turkey no longer found customers, so factories closed and real wages dropped. The new historic block dutifully followed neoliberal World Bank directives to de-industrialise Turkish cities and develop a service-based economy. İstanbul, not Ankara, became imagined as a world city, a node in a global network of cities trading financial services, knowledge and technology (Sassen 1991).

As previously, this historic block was also confronted by an increasingly redundant population – this time of low-skilled industrial workers. To counter increasing socio-economic segregation and decreasing purchasing power, between 1984 and 1988, the duo of Prime Minister Turgut Özal and Mayor of İstanbul Bedrettin Dalan issued six amnesties to make the city's informal settlements legal. In addition, they increased the maximum legal building height in the settlements, from one or two storeys, to four storeys. To obtain the necessary support for these policies, the historic block redistributed construction rights to the losers of neoliberalism, who could thereby compensate for their loss of employment by adding several floors to their *gecekondu*s, which could then be sold or rented out. Alongside the amnesties, Özal and Dalan also legalised unofficially constructed industrial and commercial buildings, which extended the production of consent from the workers to the capitalists themselves. This densification of the city generated a new and lucrative sector of housing production and construction. In particular, a four-storey house could usually not be self-built by the *gecekondu* owner. Instead, in many cases, small-scale professional developers undertook the task. For example, in the *yapsat* (build and sell) system, the *gecekondu* owner, having no other capital than the title to the *gecekondu* itself, collaborated with a developer, who built the new apartment block and was paid by being allowed to re-sell parts of it.

While these developments, continuing until the beginning of the 1990s, marked a turn to neoliberalism and a change in the logic of spatial reproduction, they did not aggregate into a long-lasting, stable block. They did, however, pave the way for the neoliberal hegemony of the AKP today, in several ways. Firstly, in 1984, the Mass Housing Administration, TOKİ was established as a belated state response to the housing question. Although it only produced a small amount of housing in the 1980s and 1990s, TOKİ was to become one of the most important actors in the production of space in the 2000s. Secondly, Dalan and Özal launched an era of forceful, state-led urban transformation. In order to de-industrialise the centre of İstanbul and redevelop it as a world city, small-scale factories alongside the Golden Horn were displaced and highways cutting though historic inner-city neighbourhoods like the Tarlabaşı Boulevard were constructed. During the 1980s, as part of this transformation, a wave of speculative high-rise buildings, shopping malls, gated communities and 5-star hotels flooded the city. Thirdly, in the early 1990s, the religious and conservative Welfare Party (RP) and the Virtue Party (FP), the predecessors of the AKP, became the voice of the masses left out of İstanbul's global city project. These parties were able to capitalise on an anti-global city discourse (Bora 1999), gaining their first electoral successes in the early 1990s.

2000s: Redistribution of Non-Commodified Spaces

In 1999, the Marmara earthquake exposed the vulnerability of self-built and low-quality constructions like the *gecekondu* in İstanbul's extremely dense urban structure. In addition, cities like İstanbul had far exceeded their ecological limits. Consequently, the AKP's spatial policy could no longer depend solely on handing out further construction rights, even though an important part of their constituency was people employed in the construction sector. The solution was that new space needed to be created.

The AKP's strategy was to create and distribute spaces that had not been commodified so far: spaces below and above buildings, former industrial sites, state-owned land, forest areas around the city, historic and *gecekondu* neighbourhoods. The commodification of these spaces required the ratification of a whole body of new laws. Among the most important was Law No. 5366, 'Preservation by Renovation and Utilisation by Revitalisation of Deteriorated Immovable Historical and Cultural Properties', which enabled municipalities to 'urgently expropriate' the property of any owner of a historic or heritage-listed building, on the pretext of preservation. As the cases of the neighbourhoods of Sulukule,

Fener-Balat, Süleymaniye and Tarlabaşı (Kuyucu and Ünsal 2010) show, this law was in reality a tool designed to revalue central areas of İstanbul, built-up until the 20th century, by total demolishing and reconstructing them. Through this law, and another announced in 2011, the remaining non-commodified spaces, namely more than 26,000 rural areas, like meadows and mountain pastures, were opened up to development and added to the real estate market. The latest step in this process is the 'Law on the Transformation of Disaster-Risk Areas', passed in spring 2012, which enables the central government to declare almost any building as 'at risk'. The owner of the property is then forced to sell it to the municipality and demolish it at their own expense. Depending on the financial strength of the property owner, they can get themselves relocated to a project of the same or a smaller size, closer or farther away from the original location. The rights of tenants are completely disregarded in the process, and even owner-occupiers have no legal way to protect their houses from demolition; they can only sue for higher compensation. Through this 'national policy', as the Minister of Urbanism, Erdoğan Bayraktar calls it, 6 million housing units will be demolished in the first stage, starting in autumn 2012 (*Milliyet*, 18 May 2012).

The main actor in these urban transformation projects is TOKİ, which takes on a variety of roles, from constructor and developer to planning authority, often in cooperation with private sector subcontractors. Since the 2000s, TOKİ has become the driving force behind national development, and part of a strategy to keep the pace of national economic growth at between 6 and 7 per cent by re-producing and redistributing space. After legal changes in 2004, TOKİ took over the public land and property formerly owned by a variety of other state institutions, and was also legally empowered to expropriate private property. TOKİ can buy these plots at any price it wishes, without having to consult the privatisation administration; it has authority to make development plans itself for any housing and infrastructure project. TOKİ's mass housing and urban transformation projects are exempted from taxes and duties, in contrast to all other building constructors. It is also not subject to controls by the investment programmes of the state planning agency, by the court of auditors, or any other form of independent financial oversight. According to the mortgage laws, TOKİ also has the authority to take on credit commitments, just like other private financial institutions (Geray 2010). Since TOKİ's extraordinary competences not only include housing, but also office space, shopping malls, schools, hospitals, prisons, mosques and police stations, it has turned into a very important producer of urban infrastructure. It can therefore determine and steer urban development more than any municipality, without being controlled financially and without regard to building quality, let alone any control mechanisms that would include the public – TOKİ is only directly responsible to the Prime Minister.

TOKİ is an instrument for revenue creation through both the development of projects in areas with high land rent and increasing land rents by developing construction projects which it can share with subcontracting construction firms like Kuzu, Biat, Aksa, Ağaoğlu, Taşyapı, Albayrak, İhlas and Çalık (Gürek 2008). These firms, the 'TOKİ princes', belong to the historic block. Thus, based on its extraordinary authority, TOKİ creates unfair competition in the market as a state institution and has acquired a monopoly position through which it can direct the market.[1] In light of the massive scale of the resulting evictions, displacements and systematic destruction of natural and living environments, in other words, TOKİ's employment of the means to commodify space, one cannot help asking why there has been so little dissent and opposition to its policies.

Developmentalism, Modernisation and the AKP's National-Popular Project

If we understand hegemony as political, intellectual and moral leadership, which produces consent via a national-popular project (Jessop 1990b), we can argue that the AKP's hegemonic project is very much based on an ideology of growth and development. This directly affects urban policies.

To reach the development level of the West has been the prime target, almost the *raison d'etre*, of the Turkish Republic since its foundation in 1923, and without much alteration through subsequent historic blocks and hegemonic periods. The most popular political figures were and are modernisers; believers in progress and development; omniscient engineers that get things done (Göle 1993). In particular, Prime Ministers Atatürk, Menderes, Demirel, Özal and Erdoğan have all been decisive developmentalists, heroes of developmentalist ideology, whose projects have been appreciated without much questioning. Their investment projects have aimed to increase production and re-production, and any doubts about their rationale, effects, or even their ideology of distribution and redistribution have been almost perceived as high treason. That is, these 'father(s) of the state' (*devlet baba*) have always known what is best for the country and its cities (and often behaved as if they were their mayors) without the need to consult others. This has meant that planning, which would at least require these leaders to publically explain their proposals, has never been an accepted tool for development; rather, it has been very much perceived as a barrier to it. Neither nationalism, Kemalism, corporatism, conservatism, liberalism nor Islamism has ever managed to seriously challenge this modernist and developmentalist ideology; they have only been able to accommodate their convictions within modernism and a belief in development.

The AKP is widely perceived as an Islamic party, and criticised by Kemalists and leftists for being backward and dangerously traditionalist. However, this view totally loses sight of the brutal developmentalist ideology shared by all parties, which partly explains the electoral success of the AKP. As an AKP MP once claimed, in order to legitimise the party and challenge the Kemalists, 'If Atatürk were alive, he'd join AKP'. Indeed, their rhetorical similarities are quite astonishing: in 1933, under single-party rule, the slogan for the tenth anniversary of the Republic was 'Let's not stop, we'll fall down' (*Durmayalım, düşeriz*), while in the 2000s, the the AKP's slogan reads 'No rest, move on' (*Durmak yok, yola devam*).

Linked to the belief in progress and development, the vision of İstanbul as a global city has been shared widely by all political groups since the 1980s. However, it was the AKP that implemented the policies and massive, concrete investments necessary for this vision to become a reality. Firstly, the AKP's hegemonic project is more comprehensive than the earlier project of Özal and Dalan, in terms of its urban policies. Dalan suspended the Planning Office of İstanbul, declaring that 'the future plans of İstanbul are in my mind' (Cumhuriyet 1986). He shared these plans with capital groups, while amnesties for illegal constructions provided the compensation for the low and middle income groups. The AKP, by contrast, re-established the Planning Office, as the İstanbul Metropolitan Planning Office (IMP), and appointed a large committee of academics as advisors. Although the plans made by IMP are totally disregarded and contradict many flagship projects announced by the Prime Minister personally, and although the municipality continues to plunder the remaining non-commodified spaces, especially in the north of the city (IMP's Master Plan was designed to prevent this), a 'plan' now officially exists, in addition to a process that makes the whole procedure appear scientific, almost democratic.

Now, armed with a legitimate master plan, the vision of 'İstanbul as a World City' predicts a rapid structural change from agriculture and industry to global service sectors like finance, real estate and insurance, with 10 per cent of agricultural and industrial workers envisioned to change to service jobs in the next 10 years. The master plan itself, however, does not say a word about how this structural change is to happen: there is no concrete programme of job training, re-education or state subsidies to deal with the social consequences of this decision. What is clear, however, in the context of spatial politics and urban transformation, is how this aim will be achieved. Poor quality inner-city neigh-bourhoods are to be displaced to the periphery, while the centre will become unaffordable for the poor, and their living conditions in İstanbul increasingly difficult. They are to be replaced by highly-educated service workers, repre-senting a new type of global citizen. As the Prime Minister put it, 'There is a price for living in İstanbul' (*Milliyet*, 2 December 2007).

Although this global city project is widely supported, the policies required to implement it have produced some resistance. However, the AKP has cleverly countered this by a consent production it calls 'social local governance' (*sosyal belediyecilik*), often taking the form of charity for the city's poor, such as fridges in summer and charcoal in winter. The city's Islamic-oriented municipalities have also designed and invested in non-alcoholic common spaces, formed horizontal aid networks, and established people's assemblies and complaint points, in this way establishing bodies for negotiation in cities (Yavuz 2009: 60). Although such examples cannot be considered as democratising local politics, but rather as policies meant to produce consent, they have certainly been successful in producing an illusion of democracy among the masses.

As Gramsci reminds us, a passive revolution is a process of the absorption of revolutionary movements into the historic block, which results in only the illusion of revolution. In this sense, the AKP, as a political movement approved by both the Muslim and the Western world, has managed to absorb both the radical Islamic movements opposed to the capitalist system and the global city dream (Tuğal 2009) as well as some nationalists, liberals, capitalists, democrats and other believers in progress. The AKP offers a little bit of everything: alms, local democracy, good macro-economic performance, a global city and neoliberalism.

At the same time, nothing has really changed. The AKP's rule – especially since the elections of 2011 – has been overshadowed by numerous human rights violations, while the gap between rich and poor appears to have widened, although no official statistics have been published on this issue since 2000. In short, the AKP's project is thus a classic example of a passive revolution.

Construction Ideology as a Hegemonic Concept

The construction sector is often identified as the motor of the Turkish economy. Its contribution to the development of the country not only includes the landscapes of reinforced concrete, but also the creation of employment. In the 2000s, the construction sector developed into a sector without alternative. The economic politics determined by the IMF prompted disinvestment in many sectors, such as agriculture, animal breeding, mining, energy and manufacture. While an alternative promising sector for Turkey is tourism, because of the country's risky geopolitical position, it cannot guarantee to be a safe haven for tourists. The finance sector is constantly susceptible to crisis due the country's huge foreign debt and inflation, although Turkish economists still imagine that services, especially finance and insurance, can be future growth sectors. In this situation, only the construction sector can provide the jobs needed for low-qualified former workers in agriculture and manufacture. The construction sector can also participate in international economic contracts, can be exported, and is rapidly growing. In fact, while the Turkish economy has grown by an average of 5 per cent since the economic crisis in 2001, the construction sector has achieved an average growth rate of 7 per cent (TÜİK 2012), with a peak of 22 per cent in the second quarter of 2010. However, the variations in the construction sector's performance in times of economic growth and crisis are almost twice as extreme as the growth and decline rates of the Turkish economy in general.

Ideologically, the construction sector serves as a national-popular machine for consent production. In the 2011 election campaign, the AKP used the slogan 'Our aim for 2023: Stability shall continue, Turkey shall grow'. The campaign pledges included a secret 'crazy project' for İstanbul, which gave way to much speculation in the press. The Prime Minister eventually disclosed a project called 'Kanal İstanbul', a second canal running parallel to the Bosporus, and two 'New İstanbuls' on the shore of the Black Sea north of the city to house several million people. He also reiterated a number of his other favourite projects: a third bridge crossing the Bosporus, a third airport, a car tunnel under the Bosporus, and the registration of protected forest land as urban land, if it had already been urbanised informally (so called 2B areas).

The construction sector is thus satisfying the masses, both ideologically and economically. Finally, Turkish cities are becoming modern, starting to look very much like cities in the developed countries, and becoming spaces for unlimited consumption. Many people have taken advantage of the chance to benefit from the process of integrating non-commodified spaces into the real estate market.

As always in less regulated capitalist environments, the bigger get the bigger share. While a member of the middle class gets a plot of forest land legalised to build an apartment on, a larger investor can easily make a fortune out of a plot. For example, the investor behind Sapphire İstanbul, a 260 metre-high skyscraper in the heart of İstanbul's central business district (CBD), was able to get an extraordinary building permit to build 135,000m^2 above the permitted density and height for that area. With square metre prices ranging from €8–10,000 in the area, it is easy to estimate the amount of (untaxed) money this investor earned (Çavuşoğlu 2011).

Before the 1980s, the construction sector was locally based, with many small- and middle-sized, often family, enterprises[2] and only a very small number of international actors like Koç and Zorlu based in İstanbul. However, this began to change with the liberalisation of the market. In the 1980s, Anatolian-based small- and middle-sized enterprises in the construction sector started to open offices in İstanbul, growing bigger in size until they out-competed the smaller firms. The growth and continuation of their business depends on their ability to win public bids for rail, dam, public building, mass housing or other infrastructure projects. To be able to maximise their profits from such projects, specific political networks and contacts are necessary. TOKİ, the biggest bidder in the business, most often distributes to contractor holdings belonging to the 'TOKİ princes', all of which have very close ideological and family relations to the AKP. This mode of re-production of space became a popular accumulation model, with more winners than losers, and has helped the AKP, we claim, to gain more than half of the total votes in recent elections.

Corporatism and the Production of Consent

Corporatism can be defined as a state form within capitalism (Jessop 1979) that imagines society as an organism where everybody depends on each other. As a hierarchical and authoritarian societal model within the mode of capitalist production, corporatism supports the principle of private property and economic ventures. However, it also creates practices and institutions that negate class differences and class struggle, so that groups depend on, are compatible with, and essential to each other like the members of a family. It is a strategy that hides the conflict between labour and capital by creating institutional linkage mechanisms, most prominently the trade unions. In the case of Turkey, one can speak of an exclusionary form of state corporatism that aims at eliminating working-class demands. Typical trade union demands, such as the improvement of working and living conditions, health services, housing and a minimum wage, are instead ratified and implemented by the state alone (Cizre-Sakallıoğlu 1992). Parla and Davison (2004) shows that the dominant political ideology in Turkey is corporatist, with fascist characteristics from time to time, and sustained by a line of parties since the 1940s: Democrat Party (DP), Justice Party (AP), Right Path Party (DYP) and Motherland Party (ANAP). One can reasonably add the AKP to this line, possibly even to the extent of describing it as the strongest representative of corporatism so far.

For many years, mainstream Turkish Islamic ideology used to focus on religious issues within a concept of worldly asceticism and modesty, rather than secular issues. However, the AKP's rise has been characterised by an integration of Islamic policies with neoliberalism. Thus, getting rich is claimed to be a mission to make Muslims able to deal with and be successful in a capitalist world. Inequality is perceived as existing between Christians and Muslims, believers and non-believers, but not as a class struggle. This has prepared a very suitable climate for corporatism to be reinvented and re-popularised.

Both corporatism and the Islamic societal vision, especially that of the AKP over the last decade, tend to imagine society not as a struggle between different classes, but as a fabric made up of different groups that are functionally differentiated. Both therefore perceive class struggle as a threat to social peace, claiming that differences between rich and poor, or employee and employer, are unimportant. Such differences, their argument goes, can be overcome by an amicable spirit that includes various rights and duties, and can be prevented by Islamic mechanisms of solidarity, brotherhood and harmony. From this perspective, the antagonism between capital and labour appears as one between pious and secular, or a struggle between national-conservative capital and imperialists. However, this ethic also obfuscates important issues like bad working conditions and exploitation; it turns society into an otherworldly panopticon and makes any kind of resistance or class-based solidarity unthinkable. Instead, as Durak (2011) shows, class relations are imprisoned in a language establishing the legitimacy of the religious-conservative bourgeoisie, using the magical formulaic concepts of patience, ordeal, gratitude, and trust in god and destiny. Instead of being improved through union membership, which among Islamists is extremely low and labelled as shameful and sinful, job security and the improvement of working conditions are to be achieved through membership in religious communities or other religious hierarchies (Durak 2011).

We argue that, together with the increasing class differences of the 2000s, an Islamic corporatism has developed that renders these inequalities invisible. Furthermore, this is in no way inadvertent; rather, there is an ontological relationship between corporatism and Islam. That is, besides regulating everyday life and the economy, Islam in Turkey also aims to establish social justice, but without including a class strategy. In this way, it is extremely compatible with the solidarity model of corporatism. Thus, we are dealing again with a passive revolution: the adoption of a secular tradition of corporatism and capitalism by its former opponents, and their integration with Islamism, without challenging existing social structures or solving social problems.

Conclusion: The Results of Force and Consent in Spatial Policies

In this article, we have tried to focus on the emerging modes of accumulation by the re-production of space in the AKP era and to explain the role of non-commodified space, the role of the construction sector, and the developmentalist and corporatist ideology of the AKP's hegemonic project. The 'objective conditions' of the AKP's spatial politics have already led to the eviction of many from the houses they live in and rapidly destroyed their basis of livelihood, using an enormous amount of force. Yet, the majority gives its consent to these policies. Most of the current literature explains this success through a variety of factors: the absence of an effective centre-right party, the deficiencies of Turkey's leftist opposition, the general rise in popularity of political Islam, Prime Minister Erdoğan's charisma, Turkey's new regional leadership, the distribution of charity to the urban poor by international and national funds, combined with populist forms of local governance, and the AKP's reform of the insurance and the health sectors (Akça 2011; Buğra 2008; Tuğal 2009). In this article, however, we have offered an alternative or additional explanation to understand how an Islamic neoliberalism, reconciled with developmentalism, has used the construction sector to form a national-popular project, how this Islamic neoliberalism has been able to achieve this via space, and how it has used corporatism against the victims of this process. The AKP has created such massive land rents through its introduction of urban transformation projects that, even if the resulting revenue has been shared unequally, a majority still feel that they benefit from this process. Urban transformation projects on average double the value of a property, which often equals a greater benefit than 20 years of an average family's income. Thus, although İstanbul's transformation projects have caused massive evictions and create a more socio-economically segregated city, there has not been any sustained opposition by landlords. The main losers from these projects are tenants. Only in some cases can they gain some compensation, such as the right to become a landlord in a TOKİ project through relatively affordable, at least for some, monthly payments. TOKİ promises that tenants can fulfil their dream to become homeowners by offering long-term credit schemes with monthly down payments as if they were paying rent.

These factors help explain why there has been so little opposition to a politician informing everybody that the state 'will come and demolish your house'. As Erdoğan has said, 'I call out to my whole nation to make our job easier. We will not leave you in the street, but make our job easier' (Ntvmsnbc 2012).

NOTES

1 It is therefore not surprising that TOKİ regularly intervenes in private sector projects that have come to a deadlock. For example, TOKİ stepped in when the Tarlabaşı Renewal Project was heavily criticised by a local initiative. Using its extraordinary authority, TOKİ began to evict the householders affected by the project one by one. The bid for the rebuilding process then was won by Çalık Holding, owned by the Prime Minister's son-in-law.
2 Emblematic is the 'yapsat' system explained earlier.

Part II

Re-orientation(s) of the Social Question(s)

CHAPTER EIGHT

The Transformation of Social Welfare and Politics in Turkey: A Successful Convergence of Neoliberalism and Populism

Barış Alp Özden

This chapter aims to analyse the radical transformation of the social welfare regime in Turkey over the last decade in terms of its effects on state–society relations, as well as on the guiding normative principles of the political order. This transformation reflects a shift in political rationalities from the welfare state structuring which involved interventionist and protectionist economic policies to that of a neoliberal state which promotes competition and decentralisation while calling for personal responsibility and self-help to keep under control socio–economic insecurity aggravated by the expansion of market relations. The current episode of neoliberal transformation in Turkey, this chapter suggests, is hard to understand without a proper assessment of the role new poverty alleviation strategies have played in co-opting, assimilating or appropriating potential opposition to market reforms. In other words, the combination of a political reorientation regarding poverty alleviation and a discursive shift regarding the inclusion and empowerment of the most destitute have made the neoliberal project more stable and consensual. The innovative welfare transfer mechanisms and poverty reduction techniques pursued by the AKP government have also implied a new way of governing through multiple and competing administrative practices, which epitomises neoliberal state restructuring in Turkey (cf. Luccisano 2004).

Needless to say, this type of governing is very much in line with global trends in social policy making and shaped to a great extent by the spirit of the conceptual categories developed by international agencies such as the World Bank and the United Nations Development Programme (Yalman 2011). However, the timing, design and specific operationalisation of the reforms reflect the particularities of Turkish politics. This makes it all the more important to analyse Turkey's specific welfare policy mix during the last decade within the wider context of neoliberal transformation. Furthermore, it is necessary to keep in mind that, as elsewhere in the world, this particular policy response has been played out against the backdrop of the welfare regime that Turkey established in the post-Second World War period (see Esping-Andersen 1990).

As highlighted in many chapters in this volume, the AKP's ascent to national power in the November 2002 elections, coming after a series of economic-cum-political crises throughout the 1990s, was a watershed in Turkish politics that brought along a radical reordering of state–society relations. After the twin crises of 2001 and 2002, which swept all the three veteran parties out of the parliament and paved the way for the AKP's victory as the only electoral alternative with a 'clean' record, poverty and widening socio-economic inequalities emerged as major issues in Turkey within the context of a prolonged process of structural adjustment over the previous two decades. Once in power, the AKP proved to be a loyal follower of neoliberal macroeconomic strategy. It was able to stabilise the economy and establish an appropriate environment for capitalising on the benefits associated with the transnationalisation of the economy, thus managing to open new paths for private capital accumulation, which, in turn, allowed the party to make progress on addressing the social problems of the country that previous governments had not been able to. Successive AKP governments have extended welfare programmes to previously excluded individuals and implemented new assistance programmes aimed at ensuring the most basic levels of social protection. Their innovative social assistance programmes and the new development discourse based on notions of integration and inclusion also reflect Turkey's encounter with the emerging post-Washington consensus in this period.[1] This policy consensus is also evident in the government's practice of implementing active state policies addressing the most basic needs of the poor while showing its commitment to rolling back neoliberal policies in public finance, industrial relations and the labour market.

The specific aim of this chapter is to explain how the AKP's social policy approach, while proving very successful in depoliticising the longstanding social problems of the country, turning poverty and inequality into an administrative problem, has also closed off the possibility of any meaningful transformation of social relations. It can therefore be argued that the AKP's approach to social policy represents a strategy of what James Ferguson astutely describes as 'anti-politics', which marginalises and obscures the spheres of political contestation (Ferguson 1994). Unlike previous governance programmes determined by structural adjustment, the AKP's strategy has helped the party manage social tensions in new ways that bypass and further undermine ideas of representation and those institutional structures that have historically been linked to collective action and organisation.

Framed in these terms, I argue that the policies and the programmes instituted by the AKP, led by the charismatic figure of Recep Tayyip Erdoğan, represent a new form of populist politics that bears comparison with the policies of Lula da Silva in Brazil (see Chodor 2010; de Oliveira 2006) and Thaksin Shinawatra in Thailand (see Phongpaichit and Baker 2008; Jayasuriya and Hewison 2004). Such neoliberal populism shares some features with the populism of previous decades: a personalised and paternalistic pattern of political leadership, a multi-class coalition, an amorphous and eclectic ideology, and the distribution of material gifts to consolidate political support (Roberts 1995: 88). However, neoliberal populism also differs in important ways. First of all, as one prominent scholar of Turkey's political economy suggests, it is a 'controlled populism' that steers the economy according to the neoliberal macroeconomic policy agenda set by international financial institutions (Öniş 2012). Secondly, while the analytical core of both 'historical populism' and neoliberal populism is based on 'the constitution of the people as a political actor' (Panizza 2005: 3), neoliberal populism attempts to create 'new non-class forms of identity and representation that attempt to disarticulate social conflict from material relations of power and re-embed social relations within increasingly moralised notions of community' (Jayasuriya and Hewison 2004: 574). That is, neoliberal populism is closely affiliated with a conservative understanding of society that features membership in a homogenous and amorphous community or nation. This feature of neo-liberal populism, its forging of non-class forms of identity and representation, also explains its appeal to the most unorganised, dislocated segments of the society, namely the new urban poor and informal sector workers (cf. Weyland 2003).

This chapter provides a case study of the Turkish welfare regime and its transformation within the wider context of the transition to neoliberalism. The object of the chapter is not merely to analyse the path that Turkey has embarked upon with the recent reform packages under the AKP government. Nor does it aim to diagnose the ills or offer prescriptions for possible alternative social protection programmes. Rather, its object is to identify the processes and strategies that have enabled the neoliberalism project to become hegemonic in Turkey by focusing on the implications of the social welfare transformation for changing state–society relations. In doing this, the chapter is divided into four parts. Part one briefly outlines the main pillars of the social policy environment in Turkey before the AKP came to power in order to explain the nature of the social welfare crisis in which the country found itself in the 1990s. Part two suggests that the erosion of Turkey's traditional welfare regime, and the initial policy responses of governments in the post-1980 period, not only produced a new kind of widespread poverty but also provided the conjuncture for the AKP to introduce deep-seated structural changes to the country's welfare regime. Part three examines the social policies of successive Erdoğan governments, revealing the continuities and departures from the economic and social projects of the coalition govern-ments of the previous decade, and their significance in solidifying consent for neoliberalism in Turkey. The chapter concludes by way of suggesting that the neoliberal populist strategy pursued in the last decade in Turkey could not have been possible without the weakening and near-disappearance of many organised actors in society (especially the labour movement).

Turkey's Old Welfare Regime

Turkey's social security system epitomised the corporatist and elitist nature of the social security systems that developed in the aftermath of the Second World War. The state's provision of free education at primary, secondary and tertiary levels formed the backbone of formal social policies, although the commercialisation of public schools and the proliferation of private education ventures since the 1980s have substantially undermined its previously egalitarian dimension. Health and old age insurance schemes were established mainly as a privilege for workers in the formal sector, civil servants and Turkey's assorted middle class, whose capacity to resist reforms has proven considerable. However, the considerable portion of the labour force employed in the informal sector and agricultural workers were excluded from the system, and even for the small stratum of the labour market included in it, the social benefits provided varied considerably according to occupationally defined status differentials. Various social security institutions were introduced in Turkey. The Retirement Chests, founded in 1949, provided combined health and pension services to both civil and military personnel employed in the public sector. The Workers Insurance was established in 1945 for workers, and later transformed into the Social Insurance Institution (SSK) in 1964, while Bağ-Kur was established in 1971 to cover self-employed and agricultural workers.

The privileges offered to civil servants covered by the Retirement Chests are demonstrated by the fact that the health care benefits accruing to those covered by this institution were the highest, whereas those of SSK were the lowest (Buğra and Candaş 2011: 518). These social insurance institutions relied on a state administered pay-as-you-go system in which each generation paid the pensions of the previous generation, with the government's role being mainly limited to guaranteeing deficits. The fact that the state was not a contributor to the system until the mid-1990s, when these institutions faced gradually increasing deficits, was another factor that curtailed the access of many people to social welfare.

Besides these social insurance institutions, a number of services were established to provide social protection to certain targeted groups. For example, a means-tested old age pension was made available in 1976 for those people over 65 who had low living standards, did not receive any other income, and had no-one else responsible for their care. However, since its inception, the monthly allowances provided by this social programme have been extremely low by any standards. According to OECD, it is equal to just 6 per cent of average earnings, making it the lowest means-tested pension in the OECD (2006: 146). In 1992, a means-tested scheme called the Green Card was organised to provide free health care services to low-income citizens falling outside the health care coverage provided by the social insurance schemes. As Ministry of Health statistics reveal, since its inception, the number of Green Card holders has fluctuated significantly between 8 and 14 million citizens because political parties seized on it as means of exerting political patronage and clientelism. Cards were most likely to be distributed prior to elections, but in the immediate aftermath many of them would be cancelled (see Altınok and Üçer 2009: 4). It is noteworthy that, against the backdrop of Turkey's employment-based social security system, the Green Card scheme was novel in allowing a significant portion of society, for the first time, to access doctors and hospitals within the social security system (Yoltar 2009). However, the scheme ended in 1 January 2012 when it was replaced by the General Health Insurance (GHI) scheme.

The social welfare system in Turkey lacked a social assistance pillar until 1986 when the Fund for the Encouragement of Social Assistance and Solidarity (reorganised as a general directorate in 2004) was created to provide benefits on a discretionary basis to those in need. The foundation of the fund implied the recognition of the need to respond to emerging forms of poverty in the context of the neoliberal adjustment process that the country was passing through during this period (Bugra and Keyder 2006). However the fund turned out to be poorly financed and improperly administered[2] until, as we shall see, the AKP government turned to the organisation as a key instrument in its project of building hegemony.

Turkey's 'minimalist' formal social policy provisions (Arın 2002; Özdemir and Yücesan-Özdemir 2008) were backed up by indirect social integration mechanisms and informal networks of support (Buğra and Keyder 2003, 2006). This informal welfare regime essentially rested on the ideal of a woman's role in society being mainly as mother or wife. According to this patriarchal model, women are seen as care providers, whereas men are the principal bread-winners, so women receive benefits such as healthcare on the basis of the labour market status of their fathers or husbands. Nurseries and publicly funded care facilities for the disabled and the elderly remain very limited while the pre-school education schooling rate is still only slightly above 15 per cent (Akşit 2007: 131). The main effect of this aspect of Turkey's welfare regime has been women's low involvement in the formal labour market, which makes it impossible for many women to gain access to health and social security systems as independent citizens (Dedeoğlu 2012; Kılıç 2008). Female labour force participation is roughly around 23 per cent, although this ratio is even lower in urban settings than rural areas since small-scale agricultural production still depends very much on unpaid family labour in Turkey (Buğra and Yakut-Çakar 2010: 524; Özbay 1995).

Given high female inactivity rates coupled with the importance of unregistered informal work, the extended family has been the central pillar of the Turkish welfare regime (see World Bank 2003). While a familial ideology manifested in the concept of 'protecting and strengthening the integrity of family' has always prevailed in the discourse and actions of Republican governments, it has taken on a much more conservative tone in recent years, as manifest in the new General Directorate of Social Services and Child Protection (SHÇEK) initiated project called 'Return to the Family' (Aileye Dönüş), which aims to substitute familial care for the state's institutional care of children (Yazıcı 2008). A salient feature of this normative family model in Turkey has been the low level of state penetration into the private realm to foster the function of the extended family as the only safety net for many individuals (Grüjten 2008).

The symbiotic relationship between agricultural and urban livelihoods was another pillar of the informal welfare regime development in Turkey. Until recently, agricultural production and rural life played a significant role in the Turkish economy and social structure.[3] The high percentage of the rural population involved in subsistence agriculture and the abundance of non-wage labour (sharecropping, peasant agriculture, family labour etc.) implied that new immigrants in urban centres did not have to sever all ties with the countryside, but, on the contrary, could count on these relationships as family support mechanisms that combined different livelihoods (Buğra and Keyder 2006: 220).

Moreover the growing influx of workers to the urban areas in the immediate aftermath of the Second World War was pursued through the networks of kinship and *hemşerilik* (the institution of fellow-townsman relationships) in the city. For the newcomers, such primordial relationships could be put to use for finding work or shelter, and often provided crucial security nets for workers to buffer the uncertainties of the urban market environment.

If those possessing land had some insurance since they were not completely wage dependent, those with a house in the city were equally fortunate since home ownership could provide an opportunity to climb the social ladder. Relatively easy access to the *gecekondu*, a form of irregular housing in Turkey, constituted an important means of integration into urban society. For at least some of the new immigrants, the *gecekondu* was not only a source of security, but became an instrument for generating income and accumulating wealth since continued urbanisation and valuation of urban space provided an opportunity for many dwellers to replace their single-storey shanty houses with small gardens, with multi-storey apartment blocks to capture a portion of urban rents (Işık and Pınarcıoğlu 2001; Erder 1999). This was made possible, above all, by the populist and patronage-based nature of Turkish politics. What was at stake was an implicit settlement between the urban political authorities and the dwellers, in which the latter, in exchange for their votes, were allowed to occupy mostly public land and sooner or later obtain title to their plots, and be provided with municipal services. For the business class as well, *gecekondus* were beneficial, as they lowered the costs of the reproduction of labour power.

The Crisis and the Neoliberal Label

The redistributive mechanisms and informal safety nets outlined above were strongly associated with Turkey's import substitution industrialisation (ISI) strategy. They started to be targeted in the 1980s, and the post-1980 period represents a radical transformation in the logic of economic and social policy making in favour of orthodox neoclassical assumptions that optimal distributional outcomes are realised through the free interplay of competitive market forces.

Turkey's small-scale peasant farmers and its agriculture sector experienced a grave crisis during this period. What had made Turkey's agricultural structure sustainable was a long tradition of state sectorial support by way of direct price subsidies, subsidised agricultural bank credits, non-taxation of rural incomes and guaranteed state purchases of strategic commodities. Sometimes governments entered the market as both suppliers of inputs and purchasers of products in order to regulate agricultural production. However, this policy started to change in the mid-1990s to be replaced eventually by market reforms aiming to eliminate the distortions resulting from direct government interventions in the agricultural sector or the inefficiencies of agricultural cooperatives (Doğruel, Doğruel and Yeldan, 2003). These market reforms made it increasingly difficult for the small-scale peasant agriculture to survive, precipitated the dissolution of existing agrarian structures,[4] and undermined the complex safety networks and relationships that many immigrants to Turkey's cities had previously relied on in times of hardship. Furthermore, the forced expulsion of Kurdish villagers in the early 1990s during the most heated period of armed conflict between the PKK and the Turkish armed forces in the east and southeast of Turkey uprooted at least one million people from their land, and thus from their livelihoods, virtually overnight. Such developments made it all the more impossible to contain poverty within the countryside and maintain the invisibility of abject poverty to the established middle classes of Turkey's urban centres.

Exacerbating these changes was 'the radical transition in the governance of urban land and housing markets from a populist to a neo-liberal mode' (Kuyucu and Ünsal 2010: 1479). Two major developments accelerated this process which intensified socio-economic and spatial segregation. One factor was the rapidly growing private construction corporations who were becoming increasingly eager to capitalise on the commodification of urban space, which was being used beyond its ecological limits. The second development pertained to institutional changes in the governance of housing, which enabled the executive power to use the legal, coercive and financial powers of the state to transfer property forcibly from politically and economically vulnerable inhabitants to stronger 'urban entrepreneurs' catering to the middle-class demands of luxury housing. This ended the period in which the urban poor could compensate for their falling incomes by easy access to urban land (see Çavuşoglu and Strutz's contribution to this volume).

The most visible effect of Turkey's re-orientation towards neoliberalism has been the impact of adjustment on employment and labour market structures. During the ISI period, state economic enterprises (SEEs) had been the critical tools available to the state in pursuit of industrial targets. They were also instrumental in absorbing a significant portion of the country's domestic labour surplus.[5] The acceptance of the 24 January 1980 economic package, which aimed at making economic strategy more outward-looking, with more emphasis on the private sector and market forces, and successive stabilisation attempts, implied that the important role played by the SEEs in employment creation was over. Employment and labour market structures changed more profoundly after the critical decision was made to open the capital account fully in 1989. After this move, growth in the Turkish economy followed directly the direction of flows of foreign financial capital which, according to many economists, stimulated a vicious circle of capital inflows and financial excesses that ended with successive deep-seated crises experienced over a short interval in 1994, 1998, 2000 and 2001 (see, inter alia, Yentürk 1999; Yeldan 2006; Alper and Öniş 2003).

Under these conditions, labour markets became the main absorber of the shocks of these crises. Suppression of wage incomes was the prominent response of capital after the 1980 coup d'état. However, during the 1990s, it was labour shedding policies that became more widely used, when squeezing wages was halted by a new wave of labour activism aiming to restore the income losses of the previous decade. Thus, one of the major characteristics of labour market adjustments throughout the 1990s was widespread layoffs in the private sector,[6] accompanied by the intensification of marginalised labour through various tactics such as outsourcing, job flexibility and deregulation of labour relations.

By the mid-1990s, roughly half of Turkey's labour force in private manufacturing was informally employed, indicating the formation of a dual labour market with widening gaps between the earnings of workers in different labour categories (Boratav, Yeldan and Köse 2000).

High informality and low labour participation rates turned out to be the principal reason for the crisis of Turkey's social security system. Ratio of insured to overall population reached as high as 85.3 per cent in 1997. However, half of the working population was still left out of social insurance programmes and the proportion of active premium payers to the total labour force was 51 per cent. During the 1990s, the need for reform of the existing social security system came onto the agenda, mainly through the pressure from International Financial Institutions (IFIs), who were concerned with the growing deficit within the social security system. According to Labor Ministry figures, the total amount of deficit of the three social security institutions increased dramatically from 39 trillion TL in 1994, to 335 trillion TL in 1996 and 2.4 quadrillion TL in 1999. Ratios of the deficit to GNP increased to 2.2 per cent in 1996 and 3 per cent in 1999 while it was only 0.3 per cent in 1990 (İTO 1999: 144).

For both the World Bank and leading business organisations in Turkey, the issue at stake was not simply managing the structural defects of the social security system, but was, equally importantly, coming to terms with a solution that would also provide leverage to the economy by developing the Turkish financial system so as to integrate it more closely with global financial markets (World Bank 1994; TÜSİAD 1997; İTO 1999). The terms of this discussion were set by the World Bank-sponsored multi-pillar system of benefits: a couple of mandatory and voluntary fund systems that are both privately owned and managed along with minimal benefits that are publicly provided through the existing pay-as-you-go systems. A multi-pillar system was also seen as a requirement to adapt to the flexible work patterns that were penetrating swiftly into Turkish labour relations (TÜSİAD 1997: 108).

Whether this reform agenda was appropriate for the Turkish setting, given its social welfare history of haphazard development, experience of rampant inflation and fragile financial markets, was of little concern to the proponents of reform since they were more occupied with the problem of the low capital accumulation path that the Turkish economy had found itself on during that decade. With its mini boom-and-bust cycles, the Turkish economy was not able to increase the private investments which could have provided a sustained stimulus to the overall economy. In 2001, per capita income stood at the same level as in 1991, leading many scholars of the Turkish economy to describe the 1990s as 'the lost decade' of the country (Yeldan 2001b). Furthermore, the 1990s proved to be unstable in both political and economic terms. The nine successive fragile coalition governments between 1991 and 2001, none of which lasted in office more than two years, lacked the political power to undertake any drastic stabilisation measures that would hurt large segments of society. For many observers of the Turkish economy during the period the 'populist cycles' of intense distributional pressures were directly associated with those weak and unstable coalition governments that desperately held on to a populist agenda in order to establish broad electoral support, despite the country needed structural reforms to curb the growing macroeconomic disequilibria (see Öniş 2003; Cizre-Sakallıoğlu and Yeldan 2000). Several pension reform proposals were presented in response to the losses suffered by the social insurance system. However, due to the political climate of the 1990s outlined above, only a comparatively modest reform was enacted in 1999, which aimed to expand the contribution period by raising the minimum retirement age (see OECD 2006).

The AKP's Reform Agenda: An Uneasy but Successful Convergence of Neoliberalism and Populism

The AKP came to power in 2002 in the immediate aftermath of one of the most grievous crises in Turkey's history. Against the initial suspicions and reservations on the part of the major capital groups about the policy orientation of the AKP cadres, who had recently split with the Islamist Felicity Party (SP) and its pragmatic and populist social programme, the AKP largely continued with the preceding coalition government's neoliberal macroeconomic strategy. The party adhered strictly to the prescriptions of the on-going IMF programme, especially with regard to fiscal austerity and privatisation. While undoubtedly helped by a favourable global economic climate, especially a global commodities boom, the government was able to stabilise the economy, reduce inflation to single digit numbers, and fuel growth. This provided the opportunity for the party to generate deep-seated structural changes in Turkey's welfare regime.

In particular, the labour market and labour market institutions once again became the target of adjustment policies. Already a grave problem, unemployment reached record highs during the crises of 2000 and 2001. The official rate of non-agricultural unemployment (widely recognised as a gross underestimate) escalated to 14.5 per cent (5 per cent above the pre-crisis level) in 2002 and remained around 13 per cent until 2009 when the global financial crisis shot this rate up to 17.4 per cent. Simultaneously, the proportion of workers without social security reached a peak of 53 per cent in 2004 (World Bank 2009: 13). In the face of these challenges, the government's major policy approach was to promote labour market reforms to expand flexible employment relations and enhance active labour market policies. As a matter of fact, employer organisations had also continually complained that labour market rigidities due to Turkish labour laws were the main obstacles decreasing Turkish firms' competitiveness with their Chinese and European counterparts.[7]

It is in this context that the new Labor Law was adopted in 2003, which introduced a legal basis for flexible employment relationships, namely part-time and temporary employment schemes. In particular, this enabled employers to draw up successive contracts and sub-contract labour more easily, though without providing sufficient measures to protect part-time and fixed term employees. The law also limited job security by excluding from its remit all firms employing less than 30 workers, which was an important step towards meeting the demands of employers since roughly 90 per cent of manufacturing establishments in Turkey, and the majority of enterprises in the trade and services sectors operated below this threshold (Taymaz and Özler 2004: 23–24; Özkan 2009). In 2008, an

Employment Package was announced that included a temporary measure to reduce the burden of social security premiums on employers for newly hired female and young workers, as well as active labour market policies. Another step in the direction of labour market flexibilisation and activation was taken in 2011 with the launch of the National Employment Strategy. The Strategy defined new flexible work forms like temporary work through private employment bureaus, tele-working, on-call work, home-working and job sharing, and suggested the replacement of job security with 'flexicurity' in Turkey's employment regime. According to the new strategy, established links between employment security and social security should be severed, with employment security only being provided by increasing the employability of the population through active labour market programmes of vocational education and life-long learning (intended to enhance the human capital) (KEİG 2012).

While employability training programmes were being slowly developed, workfare programmes were introduced through microcredit projects, mainly directed at supporting small entrepreneurial initiatives (Buğra and Adar 2008). The idea that the 'latent micro-entrepreneurialism' of individuals could be used to create a new economic development strategy was introduced by an AKP deputy for Diyarbakır, Aziz Akgül, out of his belief that conventional social policies and unconditional social assistance programmes posed the risk of creating 'dependence on aid' or a 'beggar culture' (Kandemir and Aktaş 2011: 258). Akgül's project of building microfinance institutions, inspired by the Grameen Bank project of the Bangladeshi economist Muhammed Yunus, was embraced immediately by the government, and two state-owned banks implemented microfinance development as part of their operations. In addition, two NGOs were established to initiate microcredit projects. One of them, the Turkish Grameen Microfinance Program (TGMP), which started operations by disbursing credits to poor women in the southeastern cities of Turkey, now has more than 60,000 members (TGMP 2012). These NGOs have enjoyed the full support of the government so far. Indeed, cooperation between the government and the TGMP has grown so strong that the central office of this institution in Diyarbakır is located inside the governor prefecture (Günel and Aytülün 2006: 158). However, the actual impact of microcredit programmes in terms of poverty alleviation is doubtful: as revealed by several studies, these programmes have proved to be more successful in subjugating the poor into market discipline, which is evident in the figures for high repayment rates (Gürses 2009).

The first striking feature of recent labour market reforms that should be emphasised is that they represent a radical change from traditional social welfarism in their explicit rejection of the concept of full-time formal wage labour as the 'normal' frame of reference for social policy. Unsurprisingly, this is in line with the new 'transnational social policy' that valorises atypical work patterns and the productive capacities of the poor (Ferguson 2007). According to this view, as contemporary conditions under which the national economies are operating have closed off the prospect of employment creation through growth, only self-managerial, self-entrepreneurial agents can secure their own survival. Therefore, so the argument goes, the role of the developmental state has to be redefined within the contours of regulating and maintaining the legal and institutional infrastructure on which the capacities of the market agents, including the poor and the precarious, can unfold. In the shared language of the government and the new bureaucracy promoting the new social policy agenda, this line of thinking is reflected in the motto of 'teaching people how to fish rather than giving them fish' (Gürses 2009; Yalman 2011).

Secondly, these labour market reforms have revealed the salience of neoliberal populist jargon in the way they are asserted to be targeting the alleged labour 'rigidities' and the 'privileges' of the formal, organised segments of the labouring classes. A recurrent theme emphasised by policy makers has been that labour reforms work in favour of the disadvantaged segments of the population, especially unemployed youth and women, as the new programmes and policies ease labour market rigidities and increase the private employers' demand for labour. On a number of occasions, Prime Minister Erdoğan has reminded people that his sympathy is not with degenerate public sector workers, who are organised in the strong unions and are still complaining about their deteriorating working conditions and eroding job security. Rather, his sympathy lies with those unemployed masses that are ready to work harder without complaining for a far smaller income.[8] In effect, the government has successfully used the hierarchical and inegalitarian nature of the established social welfare regime in Turkey as a pretext to pit one sector, whose alleged privileges it is abolishing, against the other that it continues to support through clientelism and social assistance programmes – a primary condition for making possible the desired transformation of the welfare regime.

As suggested at the beginning of the chapter, the AKP's social policies represent a new way of governing through multiple and competing administrative practices that combine neoliberalism and neopopulism. Social security and health reforms epitomise a venture that adopts seemingly contradictory policies, yet still manages to address the material aspirations of the disadvantaged segments of Turkey's population. The leading motivation for the government's 'managerial reforms' in the area of social security and health care was attaining fiscal discipline through a new system of welfare delivery which emphasises neoliberal notions of efficiency, competition, markets, consumerism and customer care (see Clarke and Newman 1997; Pollit and Bouckaert 2000).

The recent health insurance reform, for example, reflected this new neoliberal rationality, which deploys market or market-like mechanisms and models within the terrain of the public service itself.[9] The introduction of efficiency-driven, customer-oriented measures and performance management tools have changed the workplace culture in public and university hospitals and promoted competition among health care professionals (TTB 2009). Recent changes in the financing and organisational structures of public hospitals (i.e. the establishment of Public Hospitals Unions) have further blurred the boundaries between public and private by turning them into autonomous business institutions competing with private hospitals (Sütlaş 2012). The reform has also precipitated the privatisation of health care service so that private hospitals and clinics have become a booming sector and private insurance companies have flooded the market (Eder 2010). One immediate result of the reform was that the private health expenditure of Turkish households tripled between 2002 and 2010 (Sönmez 2011: 66).

The government claimed that the reform would benefit the most disadvantaged segments of society who, up until then, had been excluded from the social security system. The Health Transformation Program (the document that drew up the framework of reform) was presented by the Ministry of Health as a necessary step for the 'social state' to take (Ağartan 2012: 463). The General Health Insurance (GHI) scheme, which emphasised universalism as one of its major priorities, aims to cover every Turkish citizen through a unified package of health-related services. The law unified three separate public health insurance schemes under one GHI Scheme, thereby dismantling the previous hierarchy between state employees, workers and the self-employed. Consequently, public coverage has increased rapidly since the reforms to implement universal health insurance began in 2003 under the ten-year Health Transformation Program, with the proportion of the population covered rising from 70 per cent in 2002 to 83 per cent in 2010 (WHO 2012: 118).

The health reform had obvious appeal for the poorest segments of the population (namely the unemployed and 'marginal' sector workers), and helped the AKP to win wider credit. According to the Turkey Life Satisfaction Survey, satisfaction with health services increased from 39.5 per cent to 73.1 per cent between 2003 and 2010 (Karadeniz 2012: 19), and different surveys conducted over the last ten years reveal that popular support is greatest for the AKP's health policies. It even seems to be the case that the mounting grievances of health professionals and haphazard increases in the levels of insurees' co-payments have not changed public opinion, given the significant improvements achieved in terms of accessibility to health insurance. When the original reform proposals were met with strong protests by physicians' associations and trade unions, who justifiably argued that the new system of health care provision was unsustainable and would face a fiscal crisis in the near future, Erdoğan managed to whip up mass support by depicting the opponents as agents of the status quo. In this way, Erdoğan was able to marginalise the opposition and reinforce his charisma and self-image as the leader of the silent masses attacking the established elite and its special interests.

A third example of the AKP's neoliberal populist strategy is found in the party's innovative social assistance policy (see Yıldırım 2009). A remarkable feature of the social policy environment in Turkey over the last decade has been the creation of a complex web of social assistance involving local municipalities, faith-based charitable organisations and public poverty reduction programmes. Welfare governance under the AKP, in other words, has brought together public, semi-public and private efforts to alleviate the worst excesses of poverty in a new way that disarticulates social relations and conflicts within civil society (cf. Jayasuriya and Hewison 2004: 575).

Any observer of the development of welfare provision in the last decade would acknowledge the increasing visibility of local municipalities and charities in the social assistance regime. A series of municipality laws passed in 2004 and 2005 enhanced the power of local governments, providing ample room for patronage politics. Hence, more municipalities, small and large, have become involved in charity-type programmes. A recent survey showed that more than 70 per cent of municipalities in Turkey provide social assistance, especially in-kind

(Aydın 2008), and there is growing evidence that such social aid activities have become indispensable tools for gaining electoral results for these municipalities (Eder 2010: 178). Local governments controlled by the AKP have been especially successful in mobilising charitable donations and channeling them to the destitute.

Similarly, the rise of faith-based charitable associations and philanthropic activities over the period are not independent of their mutually beneficial relationship with the ruling government, although they are not directly supported by the AKP financially. For instance, *Deniz Feneri* and *Kimse Yok Mu*, two major charitable organisations of Islamic character, have become giant NGOs controlling hundreds of millions of dollars in donations having been awarded the status of Association of Public Interest by the Council of Ministers. This status, enjoyed by only 11 other associations in Turkey, guarantees important privileges, such as the right to collect donations without prior permission from the state and tax exemptions (Şen, Aksular and Samur 2009). By 2012, according to its own accounts, *Deniz Feneri* had supported 500,000 families. It has around 400 professional employees and more than 50,000 volunteers (Deniz Feneri, 2012). The fact that these entitlements only became possible during the AKP's time in office, as Mine Eder puts it, 'highlights how these NGOs are actually considered as new instruments of state's political power' (2010: 180). Put differently, the state's sub-contracting out of some of its social responsibilities represents a novel development, where the reinforcement of local governance through decentralisation proceeds in parallel with an extension of state power through voluntary associations.

This same tendency of exercising and extending state power through private actors is also evidenced in the social assistance schemes organised by the Social Cooperation Foundations. These foundations were established in 1986 under the Fund for Encouragement of Social Cooperation and Solidarity. Over 900 Social Cooperation Foundations located in each province and sub-province supply, on a means-tested basis, food, heating, education and health support to vulnerable families. Although such foundations have been assisting poor households in different ways for nearly 20 years, Turkey was denounced by international development agencies for not having developed a well-targeted and designed social safety net programme for vulnerable households (IFPRI 2007). Important changes in the structure and function of the social assistance system came in the aftermath of a major crisis in 2001, preceded by the 1999 Marmara earthquake, which caused a series of bankruptcies and major lay-offs in almost every sector. Consequently, the numbers of people at risk of poverty climbed to around 26 per cent of the population in 2003, while child poverty rates reached as high as 34 per cent, according to Eurostat (Buğra and Keyder 2007: 11).

This was the context when the World Bank began to contribute to Turkey's social assistance provision through the framework of the Social Risk Mitigation Project (SRMP). Initially, the project was conceived of as a 'complementary part of structural reforms' to diffuse potential social discontent through selective subsidies (Zabcı 2006). However, it made a lasting impact on social welfare provisioning in Turkey. As widely noted, since the 1990s, the World Bank has started to promote more seriously pro-poor public spending in developing countries. Accordingly, the SRMP was designed to increase the resources available for developing the kind of social assistance schemes that could produce visible, concrete and immediately beneficial results in terms of alleviating the worst excesses of poverty. This new approach to social policy was also enthusiastically embraced by the AKP cadres, who were aware, from their earlier experience in the municipalities, that targeted social aid produces greater electoral returns and far wider credit for the politicians. The establishment of the General Directorate of Social Assistance and Solidarity (SYDGM) in 2004, which was demanded by the World Bank as a condition for its loan agreement, enhanced the operational capacity as well as the autonomy of the directorate, which derived a growing portion of its resources from extra-budgetary funds (Şener 2010).

Since 2003, the directorate's flagship programme has been Conditional Cash Transfers (CCTs). The programme includes the provision of money subsidies to targeted households living in extreme poverty, provided they ensure their children attend school and participate in periodic health-related activities. Over two million families are estimated to have received cash, meaning that the programme reaches approximately ten million people every year. As Marcie J. Patton suggests, '(f)rom a neoliberal perspective conditional cash transfers are a relatively low budget way to provide immediate assistance to indigent families, in this case costing only 0.3 per cent of GDP' (2008: 15). Nevertheless, its political impact has been huge, not only because it has helped, to a certain degree, to reduce poverty and stimulate demand in the most afflicted regions of the country (see Köse and Bahçe 2009; Akan 2011) but because it has also delivered the symbolic message that the government and the state actually cares for the poor. Consequently, there is growing evidence that the CCT programmes have proved their ability to earn the approval of a wide cross-section of public opinion.

Going beyond the provision of short-term relief for the most destitute, the CCT programmes have been promoted by the 'international developmental apparatus' because they provide both the incentives and disciplinary measures necessary to change the subjectivity of the poor from passive welfare recipients to 'empowered' market subjects who are 'responsibilised' to rationally make investments in the education and health of their children in order to increase their 'human capital' (cf. Luccisano 2008; Ferguson 2007). For example, the World Bank Project Appraisal Document on the Social Risk Mitigation Project describes the aim of the cash transfer programme as being 'to ensure families are proactive in seeking their welfare' (quoted in Taştan 2005: 125). In this way, the new cash transfer programme seeks a double achievement. First, by putting emphasis on the theme of 'investment in human capital' the programme aims to persuade poor families to invest in themselves through education and healthcare, which in turn provides, as recent World Bank reports suggest, a 'springboard' for development and productivity gains (Hall 2006). Secondly, the programme neatly conforms to neoliberal strategies of governance through creating self-governing subjects (Dean 1999). Thus, the poor are cast as personally responsible for the decisions they take. The individuals who receive cash are expected to make rational and responsible choices of investing in the basic capacities of their children to break the intergenerational cycles of poverty, but without the policy compulsions and surveillance of the traditional welfare state. In this way, the programme ushers in a new conceptualisation of social justice to be understood in individual terms.

Evidence on the performance of the CCT programme has yet to be systematically gathered, although in terms of numerical achievements, its record is already positive in some respects. CCT payments have increased over time, with the least developed regions and provinces receiving the bulk of the benefits. Even though no accurate data has been provided, many officials and foundation staff consider that the programme has had a positive impact on school attendance and increasing preventive healthcare. Moreover, for a considerable number of destitute families who have no regular income, CCT support has become a vital factor in their lives, which they use for providing food and other basic needs (IFPRI 2007; Kudat 2006). This is very much in line with several Latin American countries' experiences with cash transfer programmes, in the sense that they may have 'some limited impact in terms of human capital formation, but they are not a panacea against social exclusion' (Yalman 2011: 239; see also Hall 2006).

The CCT programme has come in for criticism, particularly regarding doubts over its selection procedures, the function of conditionality, accountability and transparency, and the role of clientelism and patronage. A recurrent concern is the regular occurrence of targeting errors due to poor coordination. Critics of the CCT approach also claim that there is convincing evidence that the foundations define the 'deserving poor' arbitrarily. Other, more far-reaching criticisms of the programme concern the lack of transparency of social transfers and the manipulation of these funds for political purposes. Some critics allege that cash support is essentially a politically-driven strategy for holding down increases in the legal minimum wage. For others, the registration and selection of beneficiaries is tainted by high levels of clientelism and patronage (Buğra and Keyder 2006; Eder 2010).

The apparently blatant politicisation of these cash transfer programmes, however, suggests that they may retain a long-term role in Turkey's social policy agenda. Certainly, it is evident that the AKP government has come to depend heavily on the programme to strengthen political support and Erdoğan's official image as the 'father of the poor' who grew up amongst them and is still one of them. Furthermore, local politicians have developed similar cash transfer schemes to build political support among the urban poor.

Conclusion

This chapter has discussed the current transformation of Turkey's welfare regime in the context of worldwide contemporary developments in social policy processes. It has demonstrated that this transformation, under the constraints of globalisation and neoliberalism, has involved a change from a welfare regime that placed labour at its centre, albeit in an inegalitarian and corporatist way, to a new system of welfare governance that aims to keep under control the socio-economic insecurity aggravated by the expansion of market relations. The defining characteristic of this new system of welfare governance is the combination of disciplinary macroeconomic policies with more expansionist and interventionist social policies targeting those disadvantaged segments of the population that had been hitherto excluded from state welfare services. The new approach to social policy is more concerned with human capital development and responsibilising the poor, and thus has the effect of insulating the structures of social and economic power from political struggles and bargaining. Consequently, the major accomplishment of the social politics of successive AKP governments in the last decade has been to depoliticise the social issues of the country, such as inequality and unemployment, by turning them into an administrative problem.

Populism has proved to be a remarkably resilient feature of the Turkish political landscape. Since the classical era of Turkish populism that emerged with the introduction of the multi-party regime in the post-Second World War period, populist parties from both left and right have repeatedly managed to gain substantial support. However, the argument made in this chapter strongly suggests that the latest version of populist politics, deployed by the AKP over the last decade in Turkey, has managed to fill the void between the economic-political project of neoliberalism and the actual mundane techniques of neo-liberal governance in the area of social policy. The AKP's neoliberal populist strategy has proved to be very capable of accomplishing deep-seated market oriented reforms in a number of critical policy areas, such as labour markets and health care, while still managing to address the material aspirations of the most destitute. Therefore, the Turkish state's multiple and seemingly contradictory administrative practices in social policy should not be ascribed to supposed vacillation by the government 'between conservative-liberal trends and a universalist, rights-based approach to social policy' (Bugra and Keyder 2006: 211), but should rather be seen as a political strategy that is quite appropriate to the new type of neoliberal governing in the historical context of the post-Washington consensus.

The current success of this neoliberal populist strategy was not guaranteed, however, by the favourable global economic climate, although this undoubtedly helped fuel the growth that enabled the government to raise financial resources to fight poverty. Nor can this strategy's success be explained by referring to the populist inclinations of Turkey's political party system. Rather, the fundamental factor that made this political strategy possible, and even successful, is the decades-long weakening and near-disappearance of many organised actors in society (especially the labour movement). The situation for labour unions in Turkey has become very precarious for various reasons, some of which are discussed in Dogan's contribution to this volume. While trade unions organised 35 per cent of the labour force in 1980, today the figure is barely 6 per cent (Özuğurlu 2009: 347). Moreover, an ideological breakthrough has been achieved after the 1980 military coup, whose leaders denounced any form of collectivism while heralding the market as a sphere of freedom and of voluntary relationships between supposedly independent and free agents. These seismic changes have strongly affected how populist appeals are made to the masses, who are no longer easily reachable through labour organisations. In particular, neoliberal populism appeals to these new generations of unorganised informal labour and the urban poor, whose psychology is moved by the 'hope that the state might moderate equality' and the 'fear that social movements might create disorder' (Anderson 2011). That no comparable social and labour activism has yet challenged the AKP's neoliberal approach casts doubt on any expectations that the power of its neoliberal populist outlook will weaken in the near future.

NOTES

1   The shift that came with the post-Washington consensus era in the global social policy agenda has been discussed comprehensively in a still growing literature. See, *inter alia*, Porter and Craig (2004) and Ruckert (2010).

2   The total expenditure of the two main public assistance schemes (the Social Assistance and Solidarity Fund and Old Age Pensions) represented as little as 0.37 per cent of GNP in 1998 (State Planning Organization and World Bank 2009). Moreover, most of the tiny resources of the fund were plundered to finance public deficits in the aftermath of deep crises in 1994 and 2001 (Şenses and Koyuncu 2007).

3   As Eric Hobsbawm noted in his classic account of the 'short' twentieth century, Turkey was an exceptional case in world history, where rural livelihood retained its importance until recently. The urban population in Turkey outnumbered the rural population only after the mid-1980s (1994: 291).

4   The share of agricultural employment in total employment fell from nearly 50 per cent in 1988 to 30 per cent in 2005 and then to 25 per cent in 2010, according to the Turkish Statistics Institute, TURKSTAT (2010).

5   By 1980, these enterprises employed nearly one-third of the entire manufacturing work force.

6   The index of private manufacturing employment in medium to large enterprises was 30 per cent lower at the outbreak of the 1994 crisis than its 1988 level (Boratav, Yeldan and Köse: 2000:4).

7   For a critique of 'the myth of rigidities' in the formal labour market in Turkey, see Onaran (2002).

8   A good example is Erdoğan's reaction to the Tekel (Turkey's biggest public producer of alcoholic beverages and tobacco products) workers' long-continued resistance, which began on 15 December 2009 and continued until late May 2010, against the government decision to close 12 Tekel factories and redeploy the workers in other public sector jobs on 11-month temporary contracts. The Prime Minister said the government would not dole out money to workers, who he claimed were being influenced by 'ideological groups and extremists', for not producing anything and challenged the protestors to start their own businesses as freestanding and able citizens. See *The Guardian*, 'Turkish Tobacco Workers Get Upper Hand in Bitter Dispute over Jobs', 29 January 2010; *Radikal*, 'Erdoğan Tekel İşçilerine Savaş Açtı: İstemezükçüler', 2 February 2010; *Radikal*, 'Erdoğan: Tekel İşçileri Açız diye Ajitasyon Yapıyorlar', 22 January 2010.

9   Recent scholarship on welfare reform suggests that the transformation of public services in the last three decades signifies a process of subjecting the control of public service to the principles, powers and practices of managerial coordination. See Ağartan (2007, 2012). In other respects, however, it might be argued that the managerialist rhetoric of reform has helped to disguise the political agenda of the government, to co-opt and assert control over health care professionals and the bureaucracy, in the process of creating a more effective instrument for partisan rule. See, for example, TTB (2012), BIANET (2007). However, these issues are beyond the immediate concern of this study.

CHAPTER NINE

Domesticity of Neoliberalism: Family, Sexuality and Gender in Turkey

Ece Öztan

The articulation of neoliberal and conservative policies in the Justice and Development Party (AKP) period has led to a new hegemony in terms of the citizenship in Turkey. Familism is an important component of the AKP's hegemony. In this chapter, I aim to analyse the AKP's discourses and policies concerning reproduction, sexuality and family in the context of neoliberal governance. Firstly, I look at familistic indicators of the gender regime and familistic legitimisation of state authority. In the second part, I specifically focus on the biopolitical framework of the AKP's familism. The state apparatus and discourse on the family give us a rich basis for analysing the hegemony construction process of political projects. Family and caring relations are vital, not only for economic reasons, but also for community relations and political hegemony. It is also a cornerstone for understanding citizenship formations in terms of gender.

Modern citizenship is obviously not simply an inclusionary construction; rather, it is an exclusionary system based on cultural, ethnic and class-based dominations and sexual orders in which discourses on reproduction, sexuality and gender play a key role (Mayer 2000; Yuval-Davis 1997). Miller sees reproduction as one of the most basic attributes of modern citizenship (Miller 2007). Reproduction as a political duty and the family as a political entity have both been recognised by modern states, whether liberal or authoritarian. For instance, while modernisation was the prominent element in the definition of the modern Turkish female identity proposed by republican and pro-modernisation elites, female citizens of the Republic were identified with the contrasting images inherent to modern citizenship. That is, Turkey's modernisation did not eliminate a preoccupation with sexuality and women's chastity. Rather, as Parla underlines, it attributed a new significance to honour and shame by incorporating them into a 'national order of things' (Parla 2001:75). Biopolitics means the penetration of the state's political power into vital processes of life, such as reproduction, human sexuality, parental and familial relations, or health and disease (Rose 2001). Reproduction, sexuality and the body are the primary geography of the neoliberal hegemony since neoliberalism typically hands over certain kinds of welfare notions and disciplinary functions to the family. Although the policing of family is a key issue in the Foucauldian literature, we need more empirical cases to analyse the forms of neoliberal hegemony in terms of interrelated forms of different rationalities. The politics of sexuality and family provides a suitable example to analyse how religious morality, neoliberal subjectivity and market rationality can be closely interwoven and how neoliberal hegemony can penetrate at different scales of politics and into every facet of social life, including bodies, sexualities and families.

Familism and the Gender Regime in Turkey

Familism as an ideology or value system, relates the centrality that it gives to familial relations to certain forms, functions and values. Familism refers not only to the normalisation of heterosexuality, marriage, maternalist morality, the gender division of labour (Song 2009; Goddard 1996) and certain marital reproductive behaviours (Dalla Zuanna 2001), but also to the legitimisation of specific political frameworks including the organisation of welfare (Esping-Anderson 1999; Yang 2006). However, Yang differentiates familism from 'familialism'. Familism is an ideology which refers to family solidarity and normative family patterns (Heller 1970), while familialism, as introduced by Esping-Anderson (1999), is more concerned with family-based policy orientations (Yang 2002). Accordingly, familism includes both practical and material dynamics, and a process of cultural construction and state intervention, in which religious, conservative and national moralities and neoliberal rationalities intertwine. The role and importance of familistic solidarity, and the implications of familialism for social services and the welfare regime in Turkey, have been noted by several studies (Buğra and Candaş 2011; Buğra and Keyder 2006; Yazıcı 2008).[1] In the 1980s, the socio-economic and spatial transformations accompanying Turkey's entry into the global economy eroded the non-formal component of the welfare regime, including the traditional caring function of the extended family. Researches indicate that women's unpaid care labour in the nuclear family, and thus the conservative family-preserving features of welfare, have become highly salient during recent neoliberal transformations (Buğra and Keyder 2003, 2006). Before discussing the AKP's familism and biopolitics, I look briefly at marriage and divorce patterns, reproductive behaviours, maternalism and the gender division of labour which, taken together, constitute the familistic framework of the gender regime in Turkey.

Republican modernity and urbanisation have affected demographic and family patterns in Turkey. Declining fertility rates, increases in divorce and age at marriage, greater independence among young people, and more egalitarianism in gender roles have generated hybridisation in family systems and cultural heterogeneity in society (Kavas and Gündüz-Hoşgör 2010; Nauck and Klaus 2008). According to the Turkish Demography and Health Survey 2008, the total fertility rate has almost halved during the last 30 years (from 4.33 in 1978 to 2.15 in 2008). For the first time in Turkey's history, its population growth rate is decreasing, mainly due to the lower birth rate. However, despite some changes in demographic trends and family life, Turkey is still largely a familistic-oriented society. Although the modernity project paved the way for women's access to the public sphere in terms of education, employment and politics, it neither spread evenly throughout the country nor challenged the prevalent family ideology, which assigned the domestic role to women and the breadwinner role to men (Özbilgin and Healy 2004: 366). Since the early Republic, social policies have placed women within the male-breadwinner family model rather than as a basic component of the labour force. Consequently, Turkey has one of the lowest female labour force participation rates, which has been described as the 'Turkish puzzle' (State Planning Organisation and World Bank 2009). According to the World Economic Forum's 2012 Gender Gap Report, Turkey is one of the worst performing countries in terms of the economic participation sub-index (129th out of 135 countries): only 26 out of every 100 women participate in the labour force (WEF 2012: 340). The withdrawal of women from the agricultural sector has not resulted in a growth in their participation in paid work. The female labour force participation ratio decreases in urban areas and among married women. Although Turkey's modern Republican regime encouraged the involvement of elite women in public life, a doubly contrasting pattern has occurred in women's lives. Statistical data reveals a highly polarised female population in terms of socio-economic status, employment, educational attainment, fertility rates, average marriage age, etc. The overall very low level of female labour force participation masks a strong polarisation among employed women. Almost 43 per cent of total female employment is agricultural while around one-third of working women are employed as unpaid family workers (TURKSTAT, 2011b: 18). In contrast, only a small group of highly educated women occupy white collar jobs in the formal economy (Gündüz-Hoşgör and Smits 2008). Because of the strong intra-family division of labour, even if women are employed professionally, they are still expected to give precedence to their domestic roles. Studies show that the main factors behind the low employment rates are critical phases in the life courses of women, especially marriage and childbearing (Memiş et al. 2012). This picture becomes even worse when social security patterns are taken into account. Due to women's low employment levels and higher unregistered employment rates, they benefit less from retirement rights and social security in general: only 24 per cent of working women have health insurance (Benli 2008: 17), while old-age pension rates among elderly women is only 8 per cent. Even women who have paid insurance premiums throughout their entire working lives are likely to receive a lower pension (Karadenis 2012: 11–13). All these patterns make both married women and single women (up to the age of 18 or up to the age of 25 if they continue to higher education) dependent on their insured husband or father. Thus, the family can still be seen as the primary social security net for women in Turkey.

Marriage and parenthood are the norm and almost universal in Turkey. Eighty-six per cent of all women aged 20 and over are married (ADNKS 2012). Mean age at marriage is 23.3 for women and 26.6 for men, while the time between first marriage and first birth is less than two years (TURKSTAT 2011c: 13). Both divorce and separation, and childbearing outside marriage, remain uncommon and socially discouraged. More than 60 per cent of people in all age groups older than 25 years old reported that they do not approve of cohabitating couples (TURKSTAT 2006: 23). The proportion of divorced or separated women aged 15–49 is approximately 2 per cent. Not only marriage but also the gender division of labour in households is almost universal in Turkey. The day-care of more than 90 per cent of 0–5-year-old children is done only by their mothers (TURKSTAT 2006: 66). According to the Time Use Survey 2006, while women on average spend more than five hours daily on 'house and household care', men spend less than one hour. Even when women participate in the labour market, there is only a minor reduction in their hours of household care. One in every two women joining the labour force does not retain their position after their marriage, pregnancy or childbirth (Korkut and Eslen-Ziya 2011: 408). Scholars have also shown that marriage and childbearing have asymmetric impacts on the time usage patterns of women and men (Memiş at al. 2012). In particular, while men's participation in household production increases in couples with one child, it decreases in the case of the second child or further children. Egalitarian dynamics in gender relations remain weak since there is no institutional or political support behind change. Women are significantly affected by the number of their children in terms of both their working hours in household production and the labour market (Memiş et al. 2012: 175–176). In short, marriage and having one or more children has an increasingly negative impact on a woman's working life. Turkish society almost unanimously supports the withdrawal of working women from their jobs when they marry and/or have a child. Taken together, these indicators show that the traditional gender division of labour and family structure are still the prevalent pattern in Turkey.

These inequitable and discriminative social patterns are also supported and legitimised by policies and legislation (Ecevit 2012: 15). For instance, according to the Labor Law, if a newly-wed female worker terminates her contract voluntarily within a year of marriage, she is entitled to a severance payment (Turkish Labour Act 1475: Article 14 and 4857: Article 120). The provision considering female workers as 'potential mothers' and supporting their traditional roles has been in force for several years without being questioned. Turkey's social policy framework also mostly supports inequitable gender relations.

On the other hand, paternalist protectionism and familial dependency have been eroded to some extent by neoliberal reforms in the social security system. These have introduced gender-neutralisation in the marriage allowance, and ended the differential treatment of women in schemes for retirement, invalidity benefits and healthcare. Kılıç indicates that these changes can be seen as a move away from the 'male-breadwinner family' model towards a model of 'universal breadwinner' (Kılıç 2008: 493). This trend can also be seen as the individual-isation of the social as some writers have pointed out (Ferge 1997). However, unless the gendered division of both paid and unpaid labour patterns changes, these reforms make women more vulnerable, both in the face of present risks in the labour market and in the home (Lewis 2001). Although the trend since the mid-1980s has been towards a more egalitarian view of women's participation, especially in the labour market and politics, the main political parties remain committed to preserving traditional family structures and the gendered division of labour. However, the AKP's familism has distinct features at both discursive and operational levels, in which religious, conservative and neoliberal rationalities intertwine.

Familism and the Neoliberal–Conservative Hegemony

Familism has always been an important component of the discourse of the Turkish political centre, with recognition of women mainly for their reproductive roles and family responsibilities being very common in mainstream politics. This has also been the case for centre-left parties. Arat notes how the approaches of Turkish political parties toward women developed from complete omission of women in the 1920s to their recognition as citizens in the 1930s and to the reluctant acceptance of women's access to economic life in the 1950s, continuing throughout the 1970s (Arat 2009), to the more pro-women and egalitarian approaches of the 1990s. Compared to the approach of post-1980 period political parties, such as the Motherland Party (ANAP), the AKP's programme takes a more comprehensive and progressive approach in terms of women. However, despite its comprehensive approach, the context is always the family. The article titled 'Women' in the AKP programme begins by emphasising reproductive feminity: 'Not only because women make up half of the population, but also because they are individuals and first and foremost effective at raising a healthy future generation, women's issues have priority in our party' (AKP Program 2012).

The establishment of the Prime Ministery Family Research Institution in 1989 was the initial step towards conservative familism in the post-1980 era. During the ANAP period, all managerial cadres of the institution were filled by nationalist/Islamist and conservative representatives of the party (Atılgan 2000: 145–146). However, the institution had not yet become operative in terms of policy. In 2004, however, during the first AKP government, the status of the institution was changed to a General Directorate and its functions and personnel structure enlarged. From the working commissions of the Family Councils organised by the Family Research Institution since 1990, it is obvious that there was a thematic shift to a specific social policy approach in the 2000s. For instance, 'Poverty' and 'Family Support Services' were the specific themes of the Fourth and the Fifth Family Councils held in 2004 and 2008. The abolition of the state ministry previously responsible for women's issues followed by the establishment of a new ministry named the Family and Social Policies Ministry (ASPB) exemplified the AKP's marginalisation of women's rights and the centrality of familism in the party's politics. More recently, the family was also the main locus for social policies in the booklet declaring the 2023 political vision of the AKP in reference to the 100th anniversary of the Republic of Turkey:

> The driving force behind our social policies is to protect and support families that are the strength of our community and builders of our future . . . In fact, it is our strong family structure that sustains our community

despite all difficulties and social and individual traumas . . . AK Party considers the family unit as the most important factor in raising the mentally and physically healthy citizens with strong moral and ethical values that the new Turkey needs. As such, we will work towards creating 'social awareness' in all segments of our community in order to protect and value the family unit. One of the ways to achieve this will be developing an effective social policy that strengthens the institution of marriage, protects the unity of the family and maintains family values. (AKP 2012: 32–33)

The family is vital for the AKP, not only for socio-economic reasons, but also in terms of ideological legitimatisation, including moral, spiritual and religious values. The party identifies a strong family structure as a distinguishing characteristic of Turkish society. The AKP projects itself as a society-centred project covering all segments of society in line with moderate Islamism, conservatism and nationalism. Especially after 2007, the AKP has increasingly referred to its identity as part of the dominant centre-right tradition in Turkey that started with the Democrat Party in the 1950s. This definition of the party's identity as 'conservative democrat' not only distances the AKP from previous Islamist stances but is also an effort to reconfigure various strands of the Turkish political right (Şen 2010: 59). In its political vision for 2023, called *Great Nation, Great Power*, the AKP identified conservative democracy as 'a political identity and a political style shaped by Turkey's socio-cultural characteristics and local dynamics'. Presentation of conservative democracy as an identity, not an ideology, refers to a closing distance between the party and society in the AKP's discourse.

The family is also both an important metaphor and an operational ground for the AKP's neoliberal conservative hegemony. For example, a recent state commercial released by the Family and Social Politics Ministry (ASPB) shows the symbiotic and symbolic meanings of the family for the AKP's conservative democracy. In a three-minute clip, accompanied by a touching melody, we are shown a small girl, a disabled youngster, a single mother with a baby in her arms, a war veteran with a medal and a lonely old lady, all with worried faces, who are lost in the dark corridors of a labyrinth. Then we see how all the desperate faces are changing as they start to see images of happy extended family dinners, marriages, children, husbands, grandmothers and fathers on the labyrinth's wall, before the video informs us that these images can be realised. Finally, the images are crowned by the slogan 'We do not allow anyone to be lost; we are all a huge family' (ASPB 2012). The AKP's most frequently used banners demonstrate similar sentiments: 'We are all Turkey together', 'We are all one huge family' and the 'Great Nation-Great Power'. Such formulations combined with the party's conservative democratic self-identification show that the AKP sees itself as the father of the family, society, the nation and even the region, backed by fantasies and desires of a new Ottomanism. The neo-Ottomanism is not only the geo-strategic vision that the AKP's Middle East policy is largely based on (Yeşilyurt and Akdevelioğlu 2009), it is also 'an alternative source of shared identity' (Yavuz 2009: 95) and an 'alternative national history, unsettling secularist constructions of Turkey's national history centred around the Kemalist/Republican era of the twentieth century' (Çınar 2001: 365). Besides its traditional-religious conservative references, the 'we are all one huge family' discourse includes the mobilisation of the emotions and empathetic sentiments of society, which some scholars have described as the 'economies of empathy' or 'emotions of the market' (Pedwell 2012; Cleminson 2012).

The AKP's vision of a nurturing extended family based on the gender division of labour and pronatalism is set against idealised images of the nuclear family and the state's previous family planning policies. Prime Minister Erdoğan's repeated public calls for women to have at least three children (*Radikal*, 8 March 2008) must be understood on the one hand as a reaction against centralist-regulating forms of family-planning and as a message announcing the beginning of new pronatalist population policies to stimulate the economy and 'the great nation' on the other. Lately, the Prime Minister has also harshly criticised past birth control campaigns, accusing those who introduced such policies as 'having launched a "sterilising" drive in Turkey to decrease and contain its power' (*Hürriyet Daily News*, 21 January 2013). The parallels between the pronatalist discourse of the early years of the Republic and the AKP's 'great nation-great power' formulation are striking.[2]

This formulation and definition of conservatism as a political identity shaped by Turkey's socio-cultural characteristics overlaps with the AKP's opposition to radical or top-down change. While a bottom-up approach does not in practice entail an anti-authoritarian stance in relation to different political demands, it does favour the societal mainstream, in which family values, morality and traditional sentiments are central. Despite all the emphasis on tolerance, civility, dialogue, difference, plurality and compromise, the AKP's approach to democracy is explicitly majoritarian. Its opposition to all '-isms' provides the grounds for the party to denigrate all oppositional movements. Thus, the AKP's anti-feminism stems from both its self-identification and its notion of equality. For example, the party's approach to gender equality was clarified by the Prime Minister's response to feminist criticisms in a meeting with women's organisations: 'Women and men cannot be equal. They are complementary. I do not believe in female–male equality. I am for equality of opportunity' (*Gazete Vatan*, 20 July 2010). The basic components of the AKP's anti-feminism include marginalisation of women's rights, the domination of familism in place of rights-based policies and the party's gradually rising authoritarian tone against feminist groups.

Although the party takes a comprehensive approach to women's issues, the context is always the family. Of course, marginalisation of women's rights and anti-feminism is not the only characteristic of the AKP's gender policies. Neoliberalism represents a gradual backlash for the feminist movement worldwide. However, in contrast to post-feminist familism in the West, the AKP uses rhetoric about 'the strength of the Turkish family' rather than 'family decline'. Finally, although there have also been some positive developments regarding women's issues, especially through legislation introduced during the AKP's rule, anti-feminist sentiment has always been decisive in practice. For instance, in 2009, instead of forming the long-demanded gender equality parliamentary commission, the AKP's cadres changed its name and restricted its terms of reference to 'equality of opportunity' (Coşar and Yeğenoğlu 2011: 562).

Furthermore, the party's attitude towards women's organisations has gradually become significantly more confrontational.

The AKP's Biopolitics: Sexuality, Reproduction and Familism

Families and communities are seen as the intermediary mechanisms and societal spaces into which neoliberal policies penetrate. Thus, the family is also an operational site for implementing social policies. Neoliberal redistribution strategies are based on the family, community and market. Accordingly, the family serves not only as an ideological foundation but also an operational unit for welfare governance. As mothers, women are the core demographic focus of state or community intervention. Familism facilitates the penetration of contractual relationships and self-help ideology into the daily lives of citizens. This is why the family, together with other intermediary mechanisms, such as charitable organisations and NGOs, have become the new instruments in welfare programmes from poverty reduction to social assistance. The AKP favours the involvement of multiple actors in the private sphere as a moral obligation to society. For instance, the Family Social Support Initiative (ASDEP) launched by the ASPB aims to implement a 'case and context specific' approach for governance of the disadvantaged.

The strength of the Turkish family motto is crystallised in social policies encouraging home-caring of the elderly, the disabled and children. For instance, the Return to the Family Project aims to send children in state residential homes back to their families (Yazıcı 2012), while the recent programme of conditional cash transfers to poor mothers and financial support for widowed women is based on a highly normative definition of the family and needs. Thus, although poor divorced women share similar vulnerabilities to widows, the government chooses to assist only the latter. In contrast, divorced women are seen as threatening the 'ideal family' so they do not deserve assistance (Yılmaz 2012; Özar et al. 2012). The AKP government's de-institutionalisation approach in its current social policies regarding care of the elderly, the disabled and vulnerable children is also based on the party's 'strength of the Turkish family' rhetoric (Yazıcı 2012).

In October 2011, a protocol between ASPB and the *Diyanet* (Directorate of Religious Affairs – DRA) was signed in order to develop counselling, education and social services targeting families. The aims of the cooperation are as follows: 'to inform families about psychological, sociological, economic, legal, cultural and religious issues for a responsible and healthy family life'; 'to minimise the effects of problems causing the fragmentation of families, such as migration, divorce, illness'; and 'to organise activities to improve religious and national sensations'. Under this framework, Family Development and Guidance Offices within the provincial organisation of the Directorate were also established.

Through this new family-community-market cooperation, every facet of family life can be monitored, recorded and/or organised. For instance, the ASPB has recently signed a protocol for a 'family education programme', called the Family Academy, with a private Turkish bank. The programme covers management of the family budget, saving methods, credit card usage, etc. Following recent legislation to establish Private Family Counseling Centers, the ASPB also signed a protocol with the Turkish Sexual Health Institute (CİSED) to provide training for a family counselling certificate. However, CİSED is also an organisation that spreads propaganda that homosexuality is a psychological disorder through seminars, booklets and other publications. Since its foundation, the association has been criticised by LGBTT organisations fighting homophobia (Altınal 2011: 57).

The AKP's familistic discourse is based on an explicitly heteronormative-patriarchal family notion, biological determinism and disciplining sexuality. The AKP's discourse on sexuality, reproduction and gender coincides with the party's consolidation of political power and its rising authoritarianism. In 2010, Aliye Kavaf, the minister responsible for women and family affairs, said in an interview that she believes homosexuality is a disease and should be treated (*Hürriyet*, 7 March 2010). Kavaf's alarming words were neither the first nor the last by the AKP cadres regarding sexuality. Furthermore, all such homophobic, sexist and anti-feminist utterances have been the precursors to a series of initiatives, legislation and projects for disciplining sexuality and women's bodies in particular. I will just give a couple of examples to display the centrality of sexuality within the AKP's familism and neoliberal conservative notion of citizenship.

Marriage, Adultery, Abortion and Assisted Reproduction Technologies (ARTs)

Debate over adultery and abortion, the new legislation on assisted reproduction technologies and projects on families demonstrate how the AKP's biopolitical governance re-produces dominant gendered, sexualised and classed hierarchies in society. Preservation of family values and opposition to abortion were already declared as principles of conservative democracy in 2003. A range of programmes targeting 'healthy family life' initiated by the government are strictly based on a highly rigid definition of the family, disciplining sexuality and religious morality. In accordance with anxieties over family values, a project supported by the prime ministry, called 'My Family Turkey', was initiated in 2004 in which a series of booklets were sent to municipalities to be given as gifts to couples on their wedding day. The booklets contain quite detailed advice on different facets of family life including sexual life. For example, the advice on the first night after the wedding is as follows:

> When the wedding date is arranged, the bride's menstruation date has to be considered. Couples should avoid alcoholic drinks. Alcoholic drinks are the enemy of a sexual relationship. The girl should also want the sexual relationship as the man wants it, and she should not feel that she is forced ... The man should psychologically prepare his partner for sexual intercourse. He should encourage her and explain the futility of her anxieties ... The man should successfully arouse the feelings of his wife. In these

conditions, the woman does not feel almost any pain. Excitement and pleasure wipe out the pain. (Sarıkaya and Özcan 2005)

This is a clear example of how intimate sexual relations can become part of the governmental agenda. Recently, the ASPB has launched new programmes, such as pre-nuptial courses and family courses, and also released a series of booklets which aim to offer couples counselling on almost every facet of family life, including the wedding night and sexual life (see ATHGM 2012).

Other examples include the prime minister's proposal in 2004 to re-criminalise adultery during the Penal Code reform and the nationwide debate on sexuality. The adultery proposal was harshly criticised, both domestically and internationally, creating a major political crisis between the EU and the Turkish government, and even a financial crisis as the markets fell drastically. Erdoğan claimed that criminalisation was necessary for gender equality, stating that it was meant to protect wives from cheating husbands (*Milliyet*, 4 September 2004), while the Minister of Health announced that it would help in the fight against AIDS (*Milliyet*, 11 September 2004). The State Minister for Women and Family also defended the proposal, stating that 'just because we want to join the EU, we cannot give up our values' (*Zaman*, 28 August 2004). Women's organisations organised a march under the slogan of 'our bodies and sexuality belong to ourselves' in front of the parliament. Due to strong reactions at both international and national levels, the bill was withdrawn. However, only a day later, Erdoğan angrily referred to the march and its slogan: 'There were even those who marched to Ankara, carrying placards that do not suit the Turkish woman. I cannot applaud behaviour that does not suit our moral values and traditions . . . A marginal group cannot represent the Turkish woman' (*Zaman*, 25 September 2003). Such statements about opponents of the government show how the AKP's conservative democracy could become authoritarian and how the party's hegemonic strategy relies on a disciplinary biopolitics for citizens. Besides, it clearly shows how sexuality has become a central issue in terms of international relations, national borders and definitions of citizenship.

Another example of the AKP's biopolitics concerns the 2010 legislation on assisted reproduction technologies (ART). The legislation, which had been slipped through without any debate in parliament, introduced significantly stricter regulations covering the opening of new treatment centres, funding of treatment, principles of cryopreservation and donation, and the number of embryos to be transferred (BBC News, 15 March 2010). The first ART legislation had been introduced in 1987 and amended three times. Following the introduction of ARTs in Turkey, legislation limited its use to married couples. Although third-party assisted reproduction (the use of donor spermatozoa and eggs/gametes or embryo donation) was forbidden, people were free to access such treatments in other countries. In fact, ART centres in Turkey cooperated with centres in other countries, especially Cyprus and Greece, to facilitate such trips abroad for artificial insemination through mutual arrangements. However, the 2010 legislation specifically banned trips for third-party assisted reproduction. Alongside the explicit prohibition on cross-border travel for third-party assisted reproduction, what is very interesting about the new legislation is that doctors, medical personnel and clinics that encourage, advise or direct their patients to centres performing these treatments stand to lose their ART licences and face further criminal charges. In addition, a woman who conceives through gamete donation will also face charges. These regulations were presented as 'protecting the racial purity of the nation', although I consider the main reason for this legislation to be the AKP's heteronormative familism and governance of sexuality rather than such racist fears. Officials also justified the new regulations by reference to another law forbidding the concealment of a child's bloodline. However, it is clear that the new legislation is definitely not concerned with the inheritance rights of children; rather, it is intended to restrict women's autonomy over their bodies and sexuality, apart from being another clear example of the AKP's authoritarianism. While the married-couple-only approach of the ART legislation represents the heteronormative familism and sexuality rooted in Turkish politics, providing public funding opportunities for these treatments alongside prohibitions and sanctions on cross-border travel for gamete donation signify the AKP's neoliberal populism and authoritarianism.[3] Authoritarianism and populism can be intertwined in a neoliberal agenda controlling the scope of emotions such as hope, desire, anxiety and empathy, the scope of religious values and traditional sensitivities, and the scope of liberal notions like self-actualisation, competition, freedom of choice and self-help.

The most recent debate over women's sexuality and reproductive rights concerned the AKP's anti-abortion agenda. Actually, opposition to abortion had already been declared as a principle of the party's conservative democracy in 2003. According to the AKP's monthly publication, *Turkey Bulletin*, abortion is a practice that erodes families and violates children's rights. Religious sensitivities can also be seen as legitimising the party's anti-abortion stance (Akdoğan 2003: 31). At the AKP's 2012 women congress Prime Minister Erdoğan announced plans to ban abortion, saying that 'every abortion is an Uludere, every abortion is a murder'. Such a comparison of abortion to the massacre at Uludere, in which Turkish warplanes killed 34 civilians, sent a multiple message to the government's opponents, to the media, to feminists, to women and to Kurds:

> I am a prime minister who opposes Caesarean births, and I know all this is being done on purpose. I know these are steps taken to prevent this country's population from growing further. I see abortion as murder, and I call upon those circles and members of the media who oppose my comments: You live and breathe Uludere. I say every abortion is an Uludere. We have to know that it is an insidious plan to eliminate a nation from the world stage. Turkey needs a young and dynamic population that constitutes the basis of its economy. (*Radikal*, 27 May 2012)

Following Erdoğan's words, the AKP cadres continued to declare their anti-abortion stance in similar alarmist tones, while the anti-abortion campaign was extended even for rape victims. For instance, Health Minister Recep Akdağ stated that unwanted babies born out of incidents of sexual assault should be protected by the state. He also proposed punishing hospitals that carry out elective cesarean sections, stating that he believes they lead to lower birth rates.

Another AKP politician and Chairman of the parliamentary Human Rights Committee, Ayhan Sefer Üstün, called abortion a 'crime against humanity' (*Sabah*, 29 May 2012). The current abortion regulation in Turkey was introduced in 1983 by the country's then military rulers. In their anti-abortion campaign, the AKP cadres refer to the current abortion law and family planning legislation as the product of a militarist, Jacobin mentality.

In response, thousands of women and activists have staged demonstrations throughout the country, carrying the placards that the prime minister has deemed not suitable for Turkish women. When these reactions combined with survey results published in the Turkish media to indicate that curbing abortion rights would cause the AKP to lose votes, even among its female supporters, the government backed away from its initial plans to ban abortion. However, although the government gave up its plans, according to information leaked to the media, the draft abortion bill grants health care providers the right to refuse to perform abortions, introduces a counselling service to dissuade women from seeking abortions, and increases the fines for those who exceed the 10-week time limit on abortion. Besides, the new legislation will only allow abortions to be performed in hospitals, not in clinics. Already in practice, hospitals mostly seek the approval of husbands before performing abortions, and it is already impossible for a single woman to have an abortion in a public hospital, which is also the case in primary reproductive health service centres. Although health legislation declares that everybody is able to get free primary public health services, studies indicate that primary reproductive health programmes initiated by the public sector, universities or even non-government organisations solely target married women (Akın et al. 2006). All these legislative initiatives in the name of 'children's rights', 'fetus' rights' or, as we see in the new ART legislation, in the name of revealing a child's bloodline, are related to both the socially conservative moral character of Turkey's present gender regime and the moral economy of neoliberalism.

Conclusion

The creation of a biopolitical space in the bodies of modern female citizens is absolutely central to the creation of public and private spaces in both liberalism and neoliberalism (Miller 2007: 355). The difference in the AKP's familism is based on its capacity to penetrate societal spaces in which family, community and the market intertwine. Neoliberalism represents a restructuring of the interaction between the state, society and the economy, between the public and the private, thus a restructuring of citizenship formations. The emergence of a neoliberal state apparatus implies a re-articulation of the spaces of citizenship formation and the emergence of new forms of identity and subjectivity. The family, market, community and responsible individuals are the active components of neoliberal welfare regimes (Ilcan and Basok 2004; Brodie 2002; Raco, 2003). However, perhaps an even more significant characteristic of the AKP's family policies is the articulation of Turkish Islamism and conservatism with neoliberal governmentality. Religious conservatism and the politics of emotions serve as a normative terrain balancing neoliberal subjectivity within the market's moral governance. Pre-nuptial courses, family counselling services, parenting schools, in-vitro fertilisation funding for poor families, conditional cash transfers for mothers, family ombudsman services: all these projects and programmes of the AKP exemplify new modes of familism based on an articulation of neoliberal and conservative forms of patriarchy. Spaces of intimacy, family and sexuality have been reshaped both by neoliberal notions, such as competition, self-interest, freedom of choice, contractualism, and religious and conservative moralities and patriarchy. Within this discourse concerning policies and projects related to caring relations, families are seen as the ideal place for care, whether for the disabled, the elderly or children. These policies are highly likely to reinforce women's roles in the household division of labour as the primary caregivers. Actually, the government is most certainly aware that the family is not necessarily a warm safety net full of compassion. All the conditional cash transfers and income assistance programmes for the unpaid care labour are signs of this.

This new normativity places women as citizens on the front line of accountability for the provision of care in both community and family. Neoliberal economic thought is connected to the socially conservative moral character of the family and gender regime. 'The case and context specific approach' to social policies that target groups such as vulnerable widows, infertile families and socially deprived neighbourhoods informs the changing notion of citizenship. Family and community-based policies of governance and the notion of active citizenship are the distinctive characteristics instead of a rights-based politics of inclusion and a notion of equality. In this context, the notion of social cohesion substitutes for social justice. Risk-based social policy is a key element for creating cohesion. One of the key aspects of the AKP's neoliberal hegemony is their politics of marginal spaces in which gender, sexuality and class based inequalities are central. The AKP's rhetoric, based on religious and traditional sentiments, allows for both governance of marginal spaces and also welfare policies based on the mobilisation of emotions such as compassion and empathy. Wide-ranging neoliberal welfare strategies aiming especially at specific groups are the main components of a biopolitics that tries to control and minimise all the 'risks' of population. From maternity to nutrition of children, from management of the family budget to organisation of leisure, analysis of all these strategies is essential for understanding gender and citizenship regimes within the intersectional class, ethnic and gender-based relations of power.

NOTES

1   For the centrality of the family in Turkey's welfare regime and the role of family support mechanisms, see also Barış Alp Özden's chapter in this book.

2   One of the prominent figures of the early years of the Republic, Şevket Süreyya Aydemir's concerns on the quantity of the population provides a relevant example: 'Our population should be as many as to crowd the whole world . . . Our nation should reach the far ends of the world; it should expand to all countries – just like the old great Turkish Nation' (Aydemir 1941: 50, quoted in Zeybek 2007). 'We want a lot more people [in Turkey]; we want people well-fed, blissful and rich. We bear a

growing grudge against our past, which left Anatolia [AsiaMinor] empty, poor, old and ruined' (Aydemir 1932, quoted in Zeybek 2007). Of course, the 1930s and 40s were also the heyday of eugenics and eugenic discourse coincided with the new regime's ideological consolidation. Nevertheless, the great nation discourse of the past and the AKP's new version share common characteristics: the recurring reference to the near past and to undefined 'others' who prevent 'the nation' from realizing its potential; and fantasies and desires about the 'golden age' of the nation.

3   For instance, the recent protocol between the ASPB and one of the biggest hospital chain groups in Turkey's health sector offers public funding opportunities for in-vitro fertilization (IVF) for poor couples (see 'Hopes Become Real' http://www. umutlargercekoluyor.com). In 2004, the AKP government had also provided limited funding for in-vitro fertilization (IVF) cycles in couples where all other treatment options had been exhausted.

CHAPTER TEN

The Deradicalisation of Organised Labour

M. Görkem Doğan

The neoliberal onslaught has pushed back the organised labour movement more or less everywhere and in every respect. Not only have union membership figures dropped but also the political wing of the movement, the reformist or radical left-wing political parties, have lost ground, both ideologically and electorally, along with the political importance of labour unions. According to Greg Albo, it is impossible to separate, analytically or politically, the emergence of neoliberalism from the defeat of working-class politics and the retreat of the labour unions (Albo 2009: 4). It seems that the ruling class, by adopting neoliberal policies, has successfully damaged the social, economic and political power of organised labour in order to solve its problem of falling profit margins.

The Turkish experience is no exception to this; after the forceful suppression of labour militancy in the 1980s, the labour movement witnessed a brief but significant period of vitality at the end of the 1980s. However, the accommodation of this movement to the emerging neoliberal logic, facilitated by the reliance of Turkish union leaders on their political links in Ankara, led to its downfall. Union leaders were unaccustomed to involving themselves in political affairs that did not directly affect the interests of their members, so they did not do much to prevent the so-called 'reforms' of the labour market and large-scale privatisations during the 1990s. Therefore, many critical bills and other key institutional arrangements undermining the capacity of organised labour to maintain its very survival as a social and political force to be reckoned with were passed unchallenged. That era was, by and large, about the building a legal basis for privatisation and public sector reform, targeting state economic enterprises, which had been the bastions of union power in Turkey. Meanwhile, the Turkish economy became further engulfed in a deep crisis that shattered the very basis of the political system. As a result, under the auspices of the IMF, a severe austerity programme was implemented, including privatisations and other measures to both augment the flexibility of the labour market and reduce social spending's share of the national budget. These then were the political and economic developments leading up to the current era, marked by the hegemony of the Justice and Development Party (AKP).

The institutional changes brought by the neoliberal 'reforms' led to an acute erosion in Turkish unions' membership figures and their political and ideological influence over society at large, and also caused a massive shift in the composition of the labour force and its precarisation. The public sector's share of employment went down while those jobs that were still available in the public sector became increasingly non-unionised, either because of sub-contracting or the growth of contract staffing. These conditions created a vicious cycle for organised labour that further carried it towards the depths of oblivion: whenever a new reform project or a privatisation scheme was imposed, they received only meagre safeguards to protect their declining membership; but this in its turn meant even fewer members and increasing apathy for the cause of labour represented by the remaining privileged unionised few from the large swathes of the labour force facing new conditions of extreme precariousness.

All in all, the ascent of the market-oriented, conservative conception of society was built on the demise of working-class organisations through a process of institutional interaction between the organised labour movement and both the unstable neoliberal governments of the 1990s and the slowly consolidating government of the AKP. This interaction is the subject of this chapter whose aim is to evaluate this process of institutional dealings, along with the social trans-formation that the labour force went through, and to explore the reasons behind the deradicalisation of the labour movement after the early 1990s. That era was marked by both social dialogue policies on the part of trade unions, and by a conservatism which prevented them from adopting organisational strategies targeting the working population at large.

This chapter argues that the neoliberal reform package affecting organised labour was not implemented in the form of a shock therapy but realised gradually, reflecting the traditional wisdom of the Turkish political elite. As a result, the organised labour movement lived through a period of slow decay, starting in the mid-1990s, when it began losing whatever leverage it had previously over the working masses.[1] At first, the AKP followed tradition in this respect by never crossing certain, albeit ever-receding, red lines laid down by the labour unions. It was only after 2007 that the government showed an eagerness to complete its offensive to achieve full flexibility in the labour market and to erase any meaningful institutional safeguards protecting employees. Looking ahead, this chapter concludes that, although the established labour unions have seemed unable to counter this assault so far, the uncertainty of the present terrain may facilitate an unexpected revitalisation of the movement.

The Legacy of the 1990s for Organised Labour

Although a stark disparity divides the crisis-ridden 1990s from the more recent stable rule of the AKP, one must not ignore continuities that link these two periods. Firstly, the major political developments of the former era had repercussions in defining the political divides of the latter era. Secondly, and more importantly, the AKP government remained faithful to the economic policies prepared after the 1998 stand-by agreement with the IMF. That is why this author prefers to conceptualise the last few years of the 1990s and the first five years of the AKP in government as a transitional era, in which the structural transformation that Turkey went through was still a subject of political bargaining, where the power of organised labour could not yet be dismissed. However, the steady decay of the social power base of the organised labour movement that began in the 1990s accelerated during this transition era, and later crossed a qualitative threshold, after which it became negligible. To fully understand this process, we must revisit the path that the Turkish labour unions followed in the aftermath of the 1980 coup.

Presently, there exist three labour union confederations in Turkey, and three other main confederations representing civil servants. In both fields, one represents the centre and centre-right, one the left, and the other the religious conservatives. The largest and oldest confederation is the representative of the establishment, Türk İş (Confederation of Turkish Trade Unions), which has become an almost monopolist force in the public sector. To its left, there is DİSK (Confederation of Progressive Trade Unions of Turkey), a confederation primarily organised in the large private businesses of the greater İstanbul area and the municipalities controlled by leftist parties. Hak İş, a confederation with Islamist sympathies, strengthened during the last two decades, engaging in minor turf wars with the left-leaning Türk İş affiliates in two or three cases, enjoys shy governmental support.[2]

The Turkish organised labour movement first appeared in the mid-1940s, when the first attempt at unionisation occurred during Turkey's transition to multi-party politics following a half decade of grave hardships for the working class due to the previous one-party state's inability, or unwillingness, to shelter the urban poor and wage earners from the deteriorating living conditions of that era. From its start, the unionisation drives mainly originated in urban industrial workplaces under the close surveillance of the political authorities, who were ever-ready to purge radical elements from the movement. During the 1950s, the spread of state economic enterprises disseminated labour organisation into the countryside under the auspices of the Democratic Party government.[3] During this period, the organised labour movement vacillated between a submission to the political authorities and an autonomous vitality in organisational ingenuity that occasionally defied those same authorities (Çelik 2010).

During the period of import substitution beginning with the 1960s, Turkish labour unions primarily organised in the public sector, although they also operated in the new large private businesses established in the metal and chemical industries, thanks to the organisational and financial strength they developed from their power in the giant public sector corporations. However, despite gaining this foothold in the private sector during the 1960s they were unable to enlarge this breach in terms of membership. In Turkey, the institutional context of the regime of industrial relations was anyway designed for the public sector, and governments of all political allegiances were reluctant to regulate industrial relations in the private sector, thus weakening the power of organised labour there. This pattern became a massive liability for labour unions in the private sector following the crisis in import substitution, which hit the Turkish economy in the late 1970s. The result was lengthening strikes with no positive gains for the workers (Türkiye Denizciler Sendikası 1987: 41–43), and a deteriorating social atmosphere that ended in the bloody coup d'état of 1980, which undermined the campaign to unionise the private sector.

The coup enabled the ruling class to silence organised labour and lay the political and institutional foundations for the structural adjustment of Turkey to the changing demands of international finance capital. More specifically, the institutional setting of the regime of industrial relations was reconfigured according to the demands of employers. The militant tendencies in organised labour were criminalised so as to handicap unionisation efforts. Nonetheless, in the latter part of the 1980s, the workers reacted, both against their decreasing purchasing power and living standards, and the Özal administration's bellicose discourse against the moral economy of Turkish workers.[4] This mounting social opposition, led by the workers employed in the public sector, resulted in the end of Motherland Party rule and paved the way for the coalition governments of the 1990s, in the infamous 'lost decade'.

The early 1990s represented a high point for Turkey's organised labour movement, as its opposition to the neoliberal discourse of the Özal administration became the main pillar of social opposition to these policies, and probably contributed to the electoral success of the parliamentary opposition in 1991. Indeed, both Türk İş, the largest Turkish labour confederation, and the new coalition government included people of similar political affiliations. The new government reversed the decade-long decline in real wages, and seemed to want to appease the organised labour movement, though without discarding the previous government's agenda of structural adjustment, of which the main item was public sector reform and privatisation. That is the very reason why, just when it seemed strongest, the organised labour movement was in fact on the brink of its eventual failure.

When organised labour seemed secure and influential, it became undermined by three main dynamics. The first was the mentality, which had actually permeated the labour unions since their very beginnings in the late 1940s, according to which they are an exclusively workers' institution, hence involved only in affairs relating to their members, using primarily their lobbying power in Ankara as the main strategy for promoting their members' interests.[5] Although there were instances when the labour unions resorted to workplace militancy or raised issues pertaining to the whole working class, these were only exceptions to the norm. Their victory against the neoliberal discourse of the Özal administration had been partly a result of the strict adherence to these norms, by both the labour unions' leadership and the rank and file. In short, the protection of the rights and privileges of their members constituted the foremost concern of the labour unions, and this habit has undermined the wider stand of organised labour in the politics of industrial relations in three main ways.

First, it has divided the working class and alienated non-unionised workers from the labour unions, a problem that is likely to intensify as the labour force's situation becomes more precarious due to continued neoliberal reforms.[6] The labour unions' concern for their members, and neglect of other underprivileged wage earners, has made their cause less popular, especially among the urban poor. Meanwhile, Turkey's conservative governments, pursuing a neoliberal agenda, have successfully driven a wedge between sectors of the labour force, by pitting the precarious against the unionised through political propaganda. The AKP and its leader Recep Tayyip Erdoğan, as other neo-conservative politicians everywhere, has proved to be an enthusiastic follower of this strategy, especially when in government.

The progress made in privatisation constitutes the second dynamic undermining the organised labour movement. Although public sector reforms and the divestiture of publicly owned assets and enterprises was an issue that first entered the agenda of the Turkish governments during the crisis of the late 1970s, the 1980 coup d'état paved the way for its implementation, and its actual execution was delayed until the mid-1990s due to legal impediments.[7] However, the ideological legitimatisation of these divestitures was mostly undertaken during the Özal administration, and the demise of the Soviet Bloc somehow gave credibility to a discourse praising the self-regulating market, and viewing private enterprise as the most efficient social mechanism for distributing tangible and intangible goods among the polity. The labour union leadership failed to openly challenge this claim as they were afraid of being labelled as endorsing a pro-socialist world view, especially after the collapse of the Soviet Bloc. Instead, they were always eager for a negotiated settlement to protect the pension rights and employment opportunities of their members, but not their work places or the ethos of public service. As a result, as long as the acquired rights of the existing members were not threatened, or could at least somehow be protected with minor losses, organised labour refrained from resisting with determination the neoliberal policies challenging their power base. Their main strategy of struggle was legal action, sometimes backed by public demonstrations, which often found an approving audience among the statist elite.

While legal action against divestitures was successful in delaying them until the late 1990s, later governments successfully overcame the legal obstacles so that the end of the millennium saw a steep rise in state earnings from privatisations. As the process of privatisation lengthened, union opposition against privatisation became less vocal in order to minimise possible harm to workers employed in the public sector. The labour unions proved their pragmatism by merely pressing for employment guaranties for their members through their traditional lobbying methods in Ankara, either backstage of the parliament or in the streets.[8] The governments, on the other hand, learning from the lessons of the late 1980s when the neoliberal Özal administration stumbled in the face of labour opposition, did not push hard against the organised labour, instead pressing for reforms in an incremental manner until as late as the early years of the first decade of the new millennium. Nevertheless, their boldness increased with every victory along this process.

The third dynamic that needs to be remembered when evaluating the strategy of social opposition led by the labour unions against the neoliberal reform agenda has already been alluded to: the impact of the demise of the Soviet Bloc. The influence of the socialist left over organised labour has a peculiar trait in the Turkish case due to the lack of a reformist mass labour party. Moreover, the Republic's founding political faction, afraid of social mobilisation, also avoided establishing Nasserist or Peronist type official labour unions. Rather, they mostly tried to prevent the infusion of socialist ideals into the labour unions through harsh policing. Consequently, Turkish labour unions have been comprised almost exclusively of workers, although in some branches socialists have had sufficient weight that the leadership must take them into account. Indeed, this weight has made itself felt during some successful labour protests throughout the republican history. However, the widespread socialist agitation of the 1990s among industrial workers and public employees, emboldened by the mild successes of the late 1980s, subsequently lost their fervor and self-confidence after the demise of the Soviets. The same international political developments contributed also to the bureaucratisation of the relatively small number of leftist union managers.[9] The global crisis of the socialist ideals shattered the confidence of the socialist cadres, mostly rank and file militants, in the labour unions, and made the leadership of organised labour more confident in their strategy of social dialogue, a tendency also nurtured by their international links.[10]

As a result, intimidated by the new hostile environment of political economy, the labour unions focused even more strongly on the narrow interests of their members and the dialogue channels offered by the governments, even though this meant the dissolution of their power base in the long run. While the unions were still capable of organising mass demonstrations and mustering support from among the opinion makers, their ability to mobilise workers in the workplace, the real source of power for a labour movement, dwindled. All in all, the 1990s marked the end of the beginning of the decay of Turkish organised labour vis-à-vis the neoliberal hegemony.

The Retreat of Organised Labour

The coalition that replaced the Motherland Party government proved to be a disaster in terms of living up to its promises.[11] The new government neither realised a complete transition to democracy, instead paving the way for a brutal repression of the Kurdish insurgency, nor handled the economy better than its predecessor, leading to the disastrous economic crisis of 1994, that Turkey never really recovered from until 2002. From then on, the previously warm relationship between the main centres of organised labour and government soured because of cutbacks in public spending and hurried attempts at privatisation. Conditions during the following years further destabilised the ineffective political establishment and made international financial institutions the real supervisors of domestic economic policy, to the extent of ensuring the appointment of one of their own, albeit a Turkish national, Kemal Derviş, to steer the ailing Turkish economy in line with their neoliberal dogmas. In particular, he supervised the establishment of independent bodies to manage financial institutions and agricultural subsidies (Köymen 2007: 139). The deal reached with the IMF in 1998 for the close monitoring agreement determined the course of Turkish economic policy in the following decade, and paved the way for its neoliberal transformation (Bağımsız Sosyal Bilimciler 2007: 10).

The AKP was a new political force when it won in a landslide election victory in 2002, but it was nevertheless keen to stick to the policies set by Kemal Derviş. Indeed, it was only this clear victory that made it possible to implement these policies, though slowly at first. As the AKP's grasp of government strengthened, so did its audacity in pushing forward neoliberal reforms that resulted in the commercialisation of public services, widespread privatisation and flexibility in the labour market. Meanwhile, the labour unions lost prestige due to their association with the former political class, only struggling to protect the fortunes of their existing members, who composed less and less of the total labour force.

During the tumultuous years of the late 1990s, the labour unions teamed up with various chambers of professionals, and societies representing pensioners, to form the Platform of Labor. This body argued against pension reform and privatisation and supported a social platform composed of basic demands for the labouring masses. However, while the old school statist scholars ran the show, the union leadership was only interested in it in order to further their lobbying efforts in Ankara and it seems to have had some political significance until the rise of the AKP. Nevertheless, both privatisation and pension reform were implemented, albeit without turning out to be totally ruinous for unionised workers. For instance, parliament ratified Law no. 4447, which raised the age of retirement, and complicated other requirements regarding pension entitlements, just a week after the 1999 İzmit earthquake, which wrecked both the industrial Marmara region and the Turkish political establishment. While taking advantage of a natural disaster was an unsavoury tactic to evade a possible outcry, the bill at least included transitional exceptions regarding the benefit of senior workers and professionals who had been paying into the insurance system for a longer time.

This pattern of appeasing organised labour while pursuing an audacious agenda of neoliberal transformation continued until 2007 when the AKP gained their second electoral victory and selected Abdullah Gül from their own ranks to Çankaya.[12] For example, the government closed the paper monopoly (SEKA) in 2005, yet transferred its employees from its main factory to the Kocaeli municipality even if this did not match with their wider policy of cost-cutting in the public sector and outsourcing services.[13] On another occasion, they annulled the severance pay[14] and introduced a special fund for seniority payments as a stipulation of the new Labor Code, Law no. 4857 ratified in 2003, but postponed its implementation indefinitely.[15] Organised labour has harshly criticised this measure, citing it as a legitimate reason for general strike if ever implemented. A final example in this respect is the refusal of the Labor Ministry to publish the membership figures of the labour unions after they ceased using their own inaccurate figures and replaced them with more accurate statistics from the Institution of Social Insurance. This measure, if implemented, would have barred many important labour unions from the negotiating tables where they represent their members in collective agreements because the relevant law at the time, a legacy of the 1980 coup, required each union to organise at least 10 per cent of a sector in order to have the right to represent workers in collective bargaining or organise industrial action. Thus, the AKP, like its predecessors has not been interested in mounting an all-out assault on organised labour, but rather has been always ready to create exceptions to ease tensions, especially for the privileged unionised few.

Such compromises did not, however, facilitate the struggle of organised labour, since their power base continued to shrink slowly but steadily, and their moral authority, whatever it had been, eroded even faster. Viewed in the general context of precarisation of the labour force, the labour unions more and more seemed to be only interested in defending the interests of their privileged members. According to Adaman and others, this traditional short-sighted policy, which also has corresponding examples elsewhere, based on defending the privileges of union members in an ocean of underprivileged workers, is unsustainable (Adaman, Buğra and İnsel 2009: 179). Indeed, this period of transition was marked by two phenomena: one new and the other expected. The novelty was the spread of precarious employment to become the primary form of employment, which has meant a rapid decline in union membership. The expected development was the replacement of old labour union leaders from cadres associated with the collapsed centre parties with new leaders close to the AKP. These two developments require further analysis.

The Spread of Precarious Employment

Traditionally, Turkey's organised labour movement stems from two sources. One is the public sector, composed of state economic enterprises and the institutions delivering public services; the other is the privately-owned large industrial establishments. The latter is a legacy of import substitution, but reinvented itself to match the needs of the new era from 1980 onwards, when Turkish industry began to put more emphasis on exporting. The opportune regional climate of the 1980s, marked by the war between Iran and Iraq, made the Middle East a trading partner where Turkish import substitution industries could sell finished products. After the collapse of the Soviet Bloc, Turkish capital found further new opportunities around the Black Sea region, although after this brief interval Europe returned to its place as the main trade partner of Turkey. The customs union agreement signed in 1995 certainly played a major part in this shift, by providing a strong stimulus to the private sector to decrease their production costs to compete with other potential competitors in penetrating European markets.

Thus, under the pressure of both the economic crisis, for which the international financial institutions imposed their standard neoliberal prescriptions, and the new export-led economic strategy, Turkey's labour market began to transform itself significantly from the late 1990s onwards. Public sector reform has been the focus of political bickering for the last three decades. However, more important have been other factors, primarily the rapid dissolution of rural areas due the harsh effects of neoliberal policies on Turkish agriculture, and of course the use of state terror to curb the Kurdish insurgency, which together have made available large swathes of poor migrants ready to enter the job market, hence providing the necessary structural input for the neoliberal transformation.[16] A large portion of the Turkish labour market was already made up of informal employment, but the intrusion of total flexibility into formal employment was achieved first through the spread of outsourcing and sub-contracting in both the private and public sectors. In the public sector, the privatisation of various large state economic enterprises, which for years had supplied manpower and income to the labour unions, undermined some of the traditional powerhouses of the organised labour affiliated to Türk İş, such as Yol İş after the closing of the general directorate of village services (KHGM), and Tek Gıda İş after the privatisation of the state monopoly on alcohol and tobacco production (TEKEL). Apart from outright closures or privatisations, another policy pursued in public sector reform has been outsourcing, which means sub-contracting certain auxiliary duties of the remaining publicly owned production units to private businesses.

For adherents of flexibility, this sub-contracting turned out to be the decisive factor in shaping the labour market in the new millennium, though this had not been their main intention when ratifying the new Labor Code. Outsourcing has had a similar critical effect on public services: in line with the neoliberal policy of the commercialisation of public services, the government defined a core set of services to be provided by public institutions and outsourced all other duties deemed supplementary.[17] This policy has deeply transformed public services in Turkey, and has also been the main course of action in the commercialisation of the country's healthcare system. From 2007 onwards, the AKP became more assertive and discarded whatever conciliatory tone it may have had in this domain.[18]

Sub-contracting, as already mentioned, directly moulds the labour market to suit neoliberal interests in the context of rising unemployment and a fading labour movement unable to recover from the loss of its powerbase in the public sector. Sub-contracting has developed and spread like a weed, as part of the neoliberal transformation of Turkish industry, with its focus on low-cost exports and soaring small entrepreneurs outbidding each other in the organised industrial zones that fill the margins of urban areas. Legally, no firm can sub-contract its main line of work, yet many firms, including those that are still publicly owned, break these rules, which are ever permeable due to the traditional unwillingness and inability of governments to enforce the labour code on private businesses. This was recently underpinned with a commitment to operate the public sector according to a market mentality as well. In no time, therefore, sub-contracting has become synonymous with many malpractices that harm workers, including very high rates of work-related accidents, including those that result in the gruesome deaths of employees.[19]

In the Turkish context, sub-contracting seems to have two important advantages for the neoliberal regime of industrial relations. Firstly, it divides the labour force into a hierarchy of at least three types of employment: at the top, those who represent the employer, like engineers or middle managers; in the middle, the privileged, better paid workers directly employed by the company owner; at the bottom, those who are deemed disposable, the flexibly employed, easily hired and fired workers provided by sub-contractors. In addition, some labour unions, including Tes İş (operating in the sector of energy production and distribution), which presently occupies the presidency of Türk İş, have been known to refuse to organise the sub-contractor employees, thus contributing to this divide. Although recently this tendency has been reversed as a reaction to small radical labour unions attempting to organise these precarious workers, the damage was already done. The AKP government, relying on its authoritarian populist discourse that pits underprivileged sectors of society against those in formal employment, was able to play on this division to further weaken the conditions even of the formally employed. The privileged employees, meanwhile, have never hid their contempt for those employed by sub-contractors contributing to the success of the government's strategy. In one extreme instance, for example, the formally employed miners in the Amasra coal pit even protested against the attempt by their own unions to organise the workers of the biggest sub-contractor mining firm in their region (Adıgüzel 2012).

The spread of sub-contracting has also had some unintended consequences that have further helped bolster the neoliberal social transformation at a societal level. Firstly, by creating small entrepreneurs from among the master workers, the new regime not only coopts potential union organisers into its own ranks, but also enhances its capacity to control and ideologically manipulate the working masses, both by lowering the theatre of supervision to the immediate vicinity of the employee, and by feeding their vain hopes of social advancement. Secondly, some ex-union organisers have used their earlier acquaintance with large employers to obtain contracts for the firms now owned by themselves or their close relatives, which has further discredited unionism and unionists in the eyes of the populace. In the Turkish case, it seems that the discourse of popular capitalism, which was one of the main pillars of the discursive strategies of the authoritarian populist political agenda, has benefited significantly from the spread of sub-contracting. That is why, currently, the Labor Minister made clear that his ministry has begun to work on draft amendments that will facilitate sub-contracting.

The Unionists of the AKP

As has already been noted, Turkish labour unions are traditionally adept at conforming themselves to the political establishment. Since their foundation, the labour unions have been infiltrated by the governing parties of the era, and benefited from this close connection to organise in state economic enterprises. After the mid-1960s, a somewhat more political relationship developed since labour unions operating in private businesses also established ties with left-wing political groupings, as initiated by the Turkish Workers Party and DİSK. However, those labour unions that were active in the public sector preferred to retain close bonds to the establishment parties of the centre with the exception of the Motherland Party that tended not to reciprocate the support of Türk İş. The Islamist labour unions grew stronger and began to act like genuine organisations during the early 1990s.[20] The merger in March 1991 of Çelik İş, which was operating in the two important steel mills of İskenderun and Karabük, with Özdemir İş, affiliated to the Islamist Hak İş confederation, was an important event in this respect. Along with DİSK, Hak İş then became the junior partner to Türk İş in representing Turkish organised labour.

At the end of the 1990s, the demise of the former political establishment and the rapid rise of the AKP were not matched by a similar transition in labour unions. For all unions, except those unionising public employees, it was hard to recruit new members, and harder still to protect their overall membership figures, especially in sectors like textiles or foodstuffs, whose public monopolies were shut down or privatised. Nevertheless, with its power base in the public sector, Türk İş successfully protected its dominance over DİSK and Hak İş, with only a change of staff in its higher echelons. One must also note that the power balance within Türk İş also changed in that Türk Metal, already strong in private sector automobile and consumer electronics giants such as Tofaş and Arçelik, and Tes İş, unionising public workers employed in energy production and distribution, have clearly become the major forces in the confederation now, while the power of once dominant public sector unions, such as Yol İş, Tek Gıda İş or TEKSİF (operating in the state-owned textile industry), dwindles due to privatisation. From the mid-2000s onwards, in a series of extraordinary congresses, the pro-AKP union bosses, most of whom were the former financial managers of those unions, took the lead in Türk İş. Thus, Mustafa Kumlu became first chairman of Tes İş then also Türk İş, Ergün Atalay, a classmate of Tayyip Erdoğan, was elected to the presidency of first Demiryol İş (the railway workers' union) and then to the board of directors of Türk İş, while in Türk Metal, the previously unchallenged leader, Mustafa Özbek, charged with conspiracy against the government in the Ergenekon plot, was forced to hand over the presidency to his right-hand man, Pervul Kavlak. Since Özbek was released from detention, no one has heard from him, while the union he once led has been able to maintain its position in the sector.

Overall, it seems that the AKP has preferred to avoid a frontal assault against labour unions whenever possible, apart from some individual cases like the infamous incident in the official news agency (AA) when the minister himself encouraged the establishment of a rival union to be adhered to Hak İş. The labour union leadership has also proved to be a reliable social partner for those implementing neoliberal structural reforms, so long as they are not too hasty, and are ready to compromise to protect the acquired rights of existing union members. Türk İş headquarters complained loudly only against the annulment of severance pay, the establishment of private employment agencies and the introduction of the regional minimum wage and got what it wanted.

The Era of the Confrontational AKP

The previously mildly confrontational attitude of the AKP government began to intensify in the aftermath of its 2007 election victory. The governing party, emboldened both by its electoral success and the neutralisation of the challenge of the old elite of the political establishment, decided that it had delayed too long over various neoliberal reforms regarding labour market flexibility and the commercialisation of public services, and attempted to abandon this deferral. However, as already discussed, the consensual relationship between organised labour and all governments since 1991 has rested on a mutual understanding that the unions accept the necessity of adjustment to the changing market-friendly international circumstances of the political economy while, in return, governments avoid crossing certain well-defined red lines, which mostly relate to the vital interests of the senior members of the labour unions. This reciprocal concord somehow worked smoothly, notwithstanding three exceptions: the sporadic demonstrations held when needed to show the force of the organised labour movement; the constitutional or administrative lawsuits that were the labour unions' main strategy of opposition against the government's policy of privatisations and greater flexibility in the job market; and the annual confrontations over May Day celebrations.[21] Obviously, those labour unions known for their leftist leanings, such as those affiliated to the public sector confederation KESK, DİSK or left-leaning Türk İş associates such as Petrol İş (operating in the oil extracting and chemical industries) provided more confrontation during this era, yet they did not break the general pattern.

The overall result of this mutual understanding was a slow but steady deterioration of organised labour in Turkey as a part of the global crisis hitting the union movement from the 1980s onwards. Nowadays, labour unions represent no more than 5 to 7 per cent of Turkey's total formal workforce, disregarding public employees; their influence in governmental circles is now very low; and their appeal among the informal labour force and non-unionised formal workers is even lower.[22] The AKP, in its recent assaults on the labour movement, has clearly benefited from this, and felt free to ignore the labour unions by pressing forward with neoliberal reforms that had previously remained in limbo, either due to court rulings or vocal union opposition.

Earliest concrete steps in this direction came in healthcare, when the government decided to implement its commercialisation plans, which had been delayed by previous court rulings backed by opposition from both the chamber of doctors and leftist medical sector labour unions. In addition, complaining, as always, about the lack of flexibility in the labour market, the government drafted a bold legal reform in this respect, yet downgraded its original aims when promulgating the amalgamated law no. 6111 in February 2011, contented itself with stipulating some measures of flexible employment in the public sector, easing workplace inspections in the private sector and facilitating the plunder of the unemployment fund by greedy businessmen.

The government also drafted a law allowing the establishment of private employment agencies that would sever the employment relationship so as to make it impossible to unionise. Surprisingly enough, in a rare instance of defiance against his former party, the President of the Republic vetoed the bill after heavy lobbying by government-friendly labour unions. However, three years later, in June 2012, the same president did not even bother to hear union leaders when accepting a hastily drafted law banning strikes in the air transportation sector. This law marked a new height in the confrontational attitude of the government against organised labour by punishing a sector where a radical company union (Hava İş) had for years managed to protect the income and social rights of its members while supporting progressive causes. This ban did not find its way into the recently ratified law on unions and collective bargaining, Law No. 6356, which essentially kept intact the spirit of its predecessors made after the coup. The organisational thresholds, although modified according to the shrinking union membership from 10 to 3 per cent, were kept, along with a restrictive legal framework concerning strikes, collective bargaining and union structures. Moreover, the legal safeguards of unionisation in small businesses were lifted. DİSK Research Bureau complained that, as a result of this law, 29 of the 50 qualified unions might lose their right to collective bargaining (DİSK-AR 2012).

The increasing intransigence of the government has been only slightly reciprocated by signs of vitality from within the labour movement. Firstly, there has been a renewed, even if feeble, interest in unionisation, especially from the employees of medium-sized firms specialised in sub-contracting from large national or international companies. Secondly, innovative organisational forms are being tried to organise the non-unionised formal work force, such as ad-hoc platforms for white collar workers, or solidarity groups with specific aims, such as platforms against workplace accidents and the like. Thirdly, the traditional centres of labour have also showed some signs of vitality, beginning with demonstrations against the commercialisation of healthcare.

The single most important incident in this respect was the resistance of the remaining workers of the once giant state alcohol and tobacco monopoly, TEKEL, to protect their employment rights after its closure.[23] The profitable parts of TEKEL had already been privatised, and the workers in the Adana factory even continued to be paid after production ceased to ease the unrest. However, in the new era, the government proposed the remaining workers only insecure jobs in the public sector. The workers retaliated by organising a sit-down protest in the centre of Ankara, from November 2009 to April 2010, which enjoyed widespread popular support. This event turned into a cause *célèbre* for organised labour, and a political nuisance for the government. Although the resistance eventually ended without any tangible gain, it created a rift in the heart of Türk İş. Furthermore, since 2008, May Day parades have become more crowded, and the customary mass protests organised by public employee labour unions have also become more successful.

★ ★ ★

To sum up, Turkish governments have rarely pursued their neoliberal agenda in the form of shock therapy, and the AKP has been no exception. During the first part of its reign, it continued to follow the path set by its predecessors, avoiding alienating the leaders of organised labour which, in turn, accepted the need to reform the public sector and the labour market. Consequently, neoliberal reforms were pursued at a slow pace that, while stimulating some protest marches, a lot of lobbying and several court rulings, did not create any staunch opposition from organised labour. All the while, new forms of precarious employment, privatisation and commercialisation of public services became the norm for the Turkish regime of industrial relations. At the end of the first decade of the new millennium, the unions seem completely unable to mobilise the workers for industrial militancy, and remain totally overpowered by the deviousness of the AKP, which on the one hand has carefully and gradually implemented its neoliberal reforms so as to not alienate the working masses, while also remaining firm in its belief in markets by relentlessly seeking ways to further the reform process. The AKP is not the first government to march down this road, ever since the mid-1990s, the Turkish ruling class has opted for this strategy. The current government has merely elaborated this scheme and enriched it with a healthy dose of religiosity to make it look indigenous.

Lately, however, emboldened by various political and related judicial developments, and faced by a deepening global recession that necessitated harsher measures against potential social demands from popular sectors,[24] the AKP government has seemed to be in more of a hurry than before to implement its neoliberal agenda. In turn, to confront both this mounting threat and its own slow decomposition, the working-class movement has shown sporadic but ephemeral signs of revitalisation. The political opportunity structure created by the deepening global recession, and mounting political hostility in Turkey, may yet pave the way for more intense social struggles against the market-oriented conservatism of the AKP. If so, then a new cycle of protest that unshackles the power of organised labour may yet emerge.

NOTES

1 The public employees who began to unionise in this period followed a different trajectory, in the end losing only some of their combativeness but not their prestige. Their story also relates to the perception of the Kurdish liberation struggle among the working class since, from its inception, the militants of this movement came from the cadres of socialist groupings and sympathisers of the Kurdish liberation movement.

2 The story of public employee unions is different though. The AKP's favorite religious conservative organization, Memur Sen, has, thanks to overt governmental support, become the leading union recently over the right-wing Kamu Sen – once the darling of the old establishment – and the leftist KESK.

3 For a general account of the Turkish trade unionism under the multi-party politics, see Makal (2002).

4 For an account of this cycle of protest, see Doğan (2010).

5 The globally praised institutions of social dialogue fit well into this habit and, in this vein, the AKP resorted to the newly founded Economic and Social Council, making it a constitutional body, to bring governance into the regulation of industrial relations, in line with its neoliberal creed.

6 For an evaluation of the rift existing between unionised and precarious workers and its actual consequences, see Adaman, Buğra and İnsel (2009).

7 For an account of the governmental attempts of divestiture up until the AKP government, see Ercan and Öniş (2001).

8 For instance, this author personally witnessed the workers employed in the general directorate of village services demanding the chair of their labour union find them a job in another public sector institution, rather than struggle militantly for the survival of their work place, during the very demonstration organised to protest against its closure in 20 November 2004 in Ankara. For the details of this demonstration, see Birleşik Metal-İş Gazetesi (2004: 8–9).

9 For an evaluation of the leftist unionists policy positions in the former part of the 1990s, see Oğuz (1995).

10 For an exposition of the perceptions of union leaders concerning the transformation of capitalist production relations in the neoliberal era, see Yazıcı (1993).

11 For an evaluation of the first three years of the coalition government, see Saybaşılı (1995).

12 The seat of Turkish President of the Republic. Gül's election was, for some, a symbol of the AKP's takeover of the state apparatus.

13 The workers were registered to Selüloz İş, an affiliate of Türk İş in SEKA, though they were registered to an affiliate of Hak İş, the labour confederation known for its Islamist leanings in the municipality.

14 Roughly speaking, severance pay in Turkey is triple the OECD average.

15 Severance pay may be the unique domain where Turkish employees enjoyed an advantage compared to the other OECD countries, hence the labour unions were reluctant to negotiate away this benefit, although international financial institutions and the AKP government cited this reform as essential to achieve labour flexibility. This code, apart from introducing various forms of flexibility, also stipulates the applicability of some labour-friendly measures, but solely for establishments employing more than 30 workers.

16 For a detailed analysis of the transformation in the labour market, see Mütevellioğlu and Işık (2009).

17 This policy of defining a core and outsourcing the rest of the public services was first applied in Europe. See Halimi (2004).

18 For the transformation in healthcare, see Aydın (2012).

19 The shipbuilding industry in Tuzla became especially infamous in this respect, see Tuzla Tersaneler Bölgesi İzleme ve İnceleme Komisyonu (2008).

20 For the establishment of Hak İş, see Koç (1994: 40–46).

21 Turkish governments are always reluctant to allow May Day celebrations. Thus the level of police presence on this day is a good indicator of the nature of the relationship between the authorities and organised labour.

22 For a discussion of the crisis of labour unions in the Turkish case, see Sazak (2006).

23 For a detailed analysis of this episode, see Türkmen (2012).

24 One must note that the 2012 ILO meeting was blocked because of the employers' reluctance to discuss concerns over strike bans.

CHAPTER ELEVEN

Flexible and Conservative: Working-Class Formation in an Industrial Town

F. Serkan Öngel

The Justice and Development Party (AKP) has been a fortunate party, so to speak, because the political, economic and social agendas of Turkey were almost 'cleaned' or stabilised thanks to the effects of the 2001 economic crisis. In particular, before the AKP came to power in 2002, the radical neoliberal transformation programme imposed by the IMF had been put into effect by the previous coalition government, whose members were then eliminated from the political scene of Turkey in the 2002 election. This chapter deals with the third premise that paved the way for the reconstitution and consolidation of the neoliberal hegemony during the AKP era, namely the social defeat of the working class through the 2001 crisis, which both preceded and accompanied the AKP's political victory. However, it was not just the devastating effects of the crisis but also the integration of certain sectors of Turkish manufacturing capital into global production chains that caused a deep transformation of the working-class formation both in terms of working conditions and class consciousness, particularly by accelerating the fragmentation of work processes. Thus, this chapter focuses on the transformation of working-class consciousness in relation to the neoliberal hegemony established in Turkey, particularly in the 2000s, in parallel with these two overlapping phenomena. The study is based on a profile survey carried out with metal industry workers in 2008; in-depth interviews performed in the Gebze region, one of the most important industrial centres of Turkey; and transformations observed in electoral behaviour in the Gebze region.[1] The reason for focusing on this region is its rich experience of the fragmentation of production processes and the construction of neoliberal hegemony. Gebze is a county of Kocaeli, located on the periphery of İstanbul. In the 1960s, it was a medium-sized city that required heavy capital investment, with a population of 30,000. Large-scale national and foreign companies started to establish themselves in the region during this period. By the 2000s, the city had become a large industrial centre with a population of nearly 500,000, producing for the global market and hosting the production units of multinational companies (MNCs) and their dependent suppliers.

The Gebze region has a tradition of working-class organisation, with support for left-wing social democratic parties being higher than the Turkish average until the mid-1990s, when the economic and social transformations in the second half of the 1990s, and particularly after the 2001 crisis, laid the foundations for undermining its distinctive forms of working-class culture and solidarity. The chapter explores the transformation of working-class consciousness in the region, together with the rise of the AKP, which has Islamist roots, and the Nationalist Movement Party (MHP), which represents a continuation of the fascist movement, and investigates the organisational dynamics of the neoliberal hegemony.

The New International Division of Labour and Global Production Chains

The new international division of labour is mainly characterised by the beginning of globally organised developments in production after the crisis of the 1970s, the shifting of production units from traditional industrial centres to neighbouring underdeveloped or developing countries to benefit from certain cost advantages, and the global market-oriented production carried out in these new units (Fröbel et al. 1982: 91–92). These new units became known as 'global market factories'. Although Fröbel generally describes the regions where 'global market factories' are located as 'free production zones', other industrial areas can also be considered under this scope. An almost inexhaustible potential workforce pool emerged during this period, with the number of people employed in non-agricultural sectors increasing from 833 million to 2.49 billion in the developing world. There are significant differences between advanced industrial countries and newly industrialising countries in terms of their workforces. The first is the very large difference in wages. The second involves several factors in newly industrialising countries, including frequent irregularity and lack of control in employment, long working hours, night shifts, overtime and inadequate paid leave, which cause workers to face an intense working life (Fröbel 1983). Third, the presence of an irregular and flexible labour market creates a workforce that can easily be hired and fired, thereby being forced to adapt to the intense work life. Fourth, non-typical employment forms, such as getting work done at the employee's home or unilateral contracts, are common in these countries. Fifth, productivity is quite high because of work discipline and the prevalence of intense ways of working. As a result, it has been observed in the last 30 years that, under the influence of a climate of competition, working conditions have deteriorated not only in newly industrialised countries, but also in the industrial world.

One of the main mechanisms which made this possible was the model called the multi-level sub-contracting system, developed first by Japanese capital. Compared to other models, its key distinguishing feature is that it is based on a far less centralised production structure, and has a tendency to reproduce itself. The essence of this structure is the use of numerous levels that depend on a widespread network of sub-contractors. A chain then forms from the bottom to the top or primary layer, which comprises those employed directly by the top layer. Secondary sub-contractors work for primary sub-contractors, and tertiary sub-contractors work for secondary sub-contractors, and so on, with the mechanism spreading to the bottom in this manner. At the bottom are house-holds having their simple domestic chores done by other people (Arrighi 2009: 504–505). This kind of production structure, based on multi-layered networks of sub-contractors, appeared in Gebze, particularly in the 2000s.

Gebze became an important production base for the global market thanks to its location on the periphery of İstanbul, Turkey's largest industrial centre. In fact, it is increasingly undertaking the latter's industrial functions. In the 1960s, the region was considered as a whole with İstanbul and came to be seen as the new location for İstanbul's industry. Production industries became concentrated there due to government incentives offered under a specific plan (İİB 1963: 51–52; TBMM 10/254: 18; Tümertekin 1997: 45). In this process, the region's industry was constructed as part of the producer-driven global commodity chains in industries such as metal-working and chemicals. The spatial organisation of production, in parallel with its fragmentation, took the form of networks of suppliers with different types of relations to the commodity chains.[2] The rela-tionship between the suppliers and the head office or primary company is very similar to, and sometimes reminiscent of, an integrated company. The steering force of the production chain, which is the absolute decision maker, is located in the MNC's head offices. By forming contractual relationships, it creates a network of suppliers around the area in which the MNCs have decided to invest. This leads to a structure in which the lower layers of the value chain are designed centrally within a vertical integration. For example, the Gebze region, other counties of Kocaeli, and Sakarya (the neighbouring province) each currently host the production units of two major automotive companies (MARKA 2010: 59), employing around 15,000 employees. The 251 member companies of the Association of Automotive Parts and Component Manufacturers (TAYSAD), with their production units located in other regions employing 72,000 workers (127,000 including suppliers), provide services for these companies. A very high proportion of these jobs, 30 per cent, are provided by the Gebze region (TOSB 2009; OSD 2012: 32–35).

The Working Class Trapped by Crisis and Unemployment

The South-East Asia crisis of 1998 had a strong effect on the construction of neoliberal economic policies in Turkey. Under the influence of this crisis, a convention named the 'Memorandum on Economic Policies' was signed to give the IMF powers to closely monitor and control the Turkish economy. Over a ten-year period, these policies served as guidelines for the implementation of neoliberal economic policies that expanded their influence and scope through standby arrangements and the Transition to the Strong Economy Program. After an IMF-initiated exchange rate-based deflation programme was implemented in the first years of this programme, two severe financial crises occurred in December 2000 and February 2001 (Yeldan 2010: 10; Sönmez 2009: 55). Times of crisis are characterised by inter-class and intra-capital struggles that are more severe than normal so that all the contradictions of capitalist production become visible. Such crises enable the transformation of both inter- and intra-class conflicts, with the state playing an active role in this process. As Öztürk and Ercan put it, crises 'encompass using new production organisations and new technologies, increasing the oppression of labour by capital, searching for different valuation forms for capital, mergers, elimination of capital that is unable to survive, layoffs and new legal/organisational transformations related with these changes. This transformation is realised with organisational and legal regulations by the government' (2009: 62). Periods of crisis are thus critical times for the dominating classes to strengthen their hegemony.

The crisis of 2000–2001 represented an unforgettable defeat for the Turkish working class. Unemployment rates increased from 6.9 to 9.1 per cent in 2001, while employment decreased by 7.7 per cent in state manufacturing establishments and by 8.6 per cent in private companies. In 2001, the real wages of private sector employees declined by 25 per cent compared to 1993 figures (Yeldan 2010: 10; Öztürk and Ercan 2009: 84). The crisis also paved the way for the transition to a *de facto* flexible working order. Persistently demanded by capital on the grounds of global competitiveness, this flexibility gained a legal base by the new Labour Act of 2003, which brought in flexible and temporary employment forms that imposed precariousness on workers for the sake of global competitiveness (Öztürk 2009: 356). Considering that almost half of employment in Turkey was already unregistered and depended on extreme flexibility, this meant a further loss of rights, even for workers employed in regular jobs. As the United Metal Workers Union emphasised, many employer organisations, especially the Turkish Employers' Association of Metal Industries (MESS), and individual employers started to push for the inclusion of flexibility provisions in collective bargaining agreements, and reduce the rights of unionised workers to the level required by the new act by means of collective agreements (Birleşik Metal-İş 2006: 28).

The enactment of these new labour laws was the first step taken to equalise the conditions of registered and even unionised workers with those of flexible or unregistered ones. In the period following the crisis of 2000–2001, the Turkish economy could not create the expected level of employment despite high growth and increasing exports. Unemployment increased from 6.5 per cent in 2000 to 10.3 per cent in 2002, with the number of unemployed increasing by almost one million to reach 2,464,000 from 1,497,000 (TURKSTAT 2011b). Meanwhile, from 2002 to 2006, an average 7.2 per cent real increase was achieved in Turkey's gross national product (GNP). However, this growth proved to have a very limited capacity to create employment so that unemployment never decreased below 9 per cent up to the end of 2007, just before the collapse brought about by the latest global crisis (see Figure 11.1).

The global crisis started to damage the Turkish economy in October 2008, following a slowing growth rate in 2007. GNP growth fell to 0.9 per cent for 2008, with a further decrease of 6.8 per cent in just the first half of 2009. The crisis was felt particularly acutely in industrial sectors and cities (Yeldan 2010: 17). The number of people drawing unemployment insurance, according to data

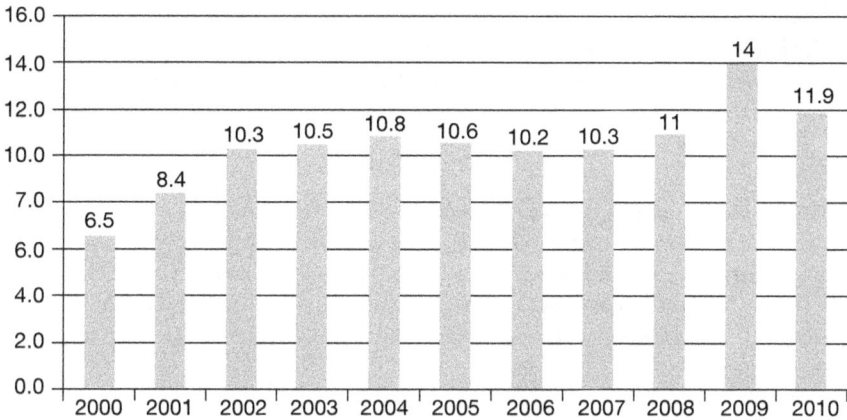

Figure 11.1 Unemployment Rates in Turkey by Year (%)

Source: TURKSTAT Labour Force Statistics (Data for 2000-2003 are from the 2000 series and data for 2004-2010 are from the 2005 series.

from the Turkish Employment Institution (İŞKUR 2011) and the Social Security Institution (SGK 2008), can be taken as an indication of the number of layoffs in this period: although the conditions for benefitting from the unemployment insurance fund are very strict, the number of people becoming eligible to use it between 2008 and July 2009 reached 609,000 nationally. Gebze's province, Kocaeli, had the fifth highest number of layoffs, behind İstanbul, Bursa, İzmir and Ankara. According to SGK statistics, a total of 23,807 workers were laid off during this period, meeting the conditions to apply for unemployment allowance, meaning 7.95 per cent of people working in Kocaeli. The actual number of layoffs, however, was even higher.

Thus, the crisis had a devastating effect on the working class of the Gebze region. Ahmet (survey conducted in 2010), a union-member worker employed at the F1 company, one of Ford's suppliers, points out that the 'last in, first out' rule, which had been widely implemented in the industrial sector until the crisis, was no longer sufficient, so companies preferentially laid off higher paid workers instead to cut down costs.[3] At Ahmet's company, which had nearly 300 employees, 30 workers were laid off due to the crisis, but over 60 others resigned voluntarily because of loss of income due to unpaid leave[4] and the resulting decline in wages. That is, many workers preferred to resign and receive their severance pay in order to pay their accrued debts. Subsequently, however, many could not find another job,[5] and those who could do so had to work in informal sectors, flexibly and without being part of any union organisation:

> These people [who resigned] couldn't find jobs either. They are in a wretched condition. Many returned to their villages. The workers who had come to the region with hope returned to their villages. When I speak with my friends who quit their jobs in that period and are now working in other companies, for some, Dostel was their first working experience;

they say they find their new workplace rather strange. One can appreciate how good it is to work as part of a union organisation when one works at a workplace with no organisation. There are no rules: you know when to start work but can't know when to leave. There is no overtime pay. (Barış, survey conducted in 2010)

In the Gebze region, unemployment reached serious levels in parallel with the region's incorporation into the global economy. Union branch head Özer (survey conducted in 2010), who started to work in the Gebze OMTAŞ factory in 1984, describes how job search practices and cultural behaviour forms changed in the period up to the end of the 1980s, based on his own working experience:

What was good for workers in that time was that there was a sign in front of every factory saying that workers were to be hired. When I first came here, I went to the employment agency. They told me to pick the one I liked. I asked around which was the best place and they said OMTAŞ. I went to OMTAŞ. They only asked: 'What do you do? Who are you?' They never asked if I was qualified.

Özer explains that those days are over and the new situation powerfully fed into the fears of losing one's job, so that people tended to be more preoccupied with their own problems, and feelings and practices of solidarity were thereby weakened. Özer claims that Gebze retained the characteristics of a medium-sized Anatolian town until 1988–89, in that feelings of solidarity were not corrupted and friendships were not as self-interested as they are today.

Before 1990, if anyone had a problem at the factory where I worked, it meant everyone had a problem. If someone was moving, both the truck and the men who would carry the stuff would turn up in front of that person's house one morning. All of them were our friends from the factory. All were permanent workers. We would do the removals until noon and be guests at that house in the evening. After 1990, people started to compete with each other.

Özer thinks that this weakening of solidarity and strengthening of individuality also had a negative impact on union organisations. This kind of relationship between unemployment and individualisation and the weakening of the foundations of solidarity helps explain the damage caused to the consciousness of workers in times of crisis. This weakening of class-based solidarity also prepares the ground for the creation of 'other' types of solidarity and organisational relations against crises, which should be considered as an important factor in the establishment of the AKP's hegemony over Turkey's working class.

Based on these deteriorating conditions of employment, workers were introduced to the concept of competition, and the effort to sustain business in conditions of crisis resulted in the erosion of class consciousness. Oddly enough, workers tend to develop a sense of 'ownership for businesses':

Now, time is measured in seconds, and costs with pennies. We see our workplace as our own. The capital owner uses this. He says to the worker, we need to work hard in order to compete. The worker is worked to death, really. For example, the bosses say, 'we need to fix the costs'. If the workplace is not unionised, the worker works free for 10/20 hours of overtime.

This intense competitive pressure felt by the workers has caused actual working hours to greatly exceed legal limits. While the legal weekly average working time is 45 hours in Turkey, this rises to 53.8 hours with overtime, which is 12 hours more than the EU average (EUROSTAT 2009: 31). According to the Labor Act No. 1475, which was in effect before 2003, overtime work was subject to the approval of regional labour directorates (article 35), who were also authorised to suspend production (Overtime By-Laws), and any violation of this provision could result in penal sanctions (article 99, paragraph 2). However, these provisions are replaced by the new Labor Act No. 4857, which left the implementation of overtime to the discretion of employers as long as the workers agreed (Ataman 2003: 20).

Today, intense work is considered as the normal way of working. According to the labour law, the working week should not exceed 45 hours and daily working time should be 8 hours, but not more than 11 hours (Ataman 2003: 95–96). However, in many industries, workers have normal working days of 12 hours. Such intense working life means the end of social life for workers. Özer (survey conducted in 2010) summarises the situation clearly:

In organisational procedures, we ask them how long they work, and they say they work normal hours. We ask how. They say from 8 am to 8 pm. When asked if they are paid overtime, they answer, 'What overtime? I already said we work normal hours.' So 12 hours' work a day is now seen as normal work. A person working 12 hours a day cannot have a family life. They can't have friendship relations. They don't have the chance to go somewhere and participate in a social activity. They have to get up with the morning call to prayer and go to bed with the night call to prayer.

Barış (survey conducted in 2010), a worker at Dostel, makes this summary:

The worker has to work very hard to be paid more. Legal work time can go up to 11 hours a day. There are workers doing double shifts. Some work 16 hours a day. Some cannot do overtime-work because of the workplace. So they work at weddings, at weekends. There is no life but work. They can't take their family and go visit somewhere.

The main reason for the widespread implementation of overtime in unionised workplaces is the level of wages that are too low to live on. The majority of the workers included in the site survey working in the Gebze region (59.5 per cent) are paid 500–900 Turkish Lira (TL) per month, while the monthly average household income of 84.7 per cent of workers is below 1,700 TL.[6]

Another issue is the annual paid leave. According to the labour law, annual paid leave varies between 14 and 26 business days, depending on the terms of employment. However, in non-unionised establishments, annual leave can only be used to a very limited extent, and the time of leave is determined at the discretion of the employer.

Especially in non-unionised companies, 8–10 days' annual leave is allowed on average. Workers think their annual leave is 10 days until the third to fifth year of employment is completed. Some think it is 12 days. The employer says, 'I fix the time as I want to'. The worker is sent away for leave when he is not needed, at a time which is not suitable for him at all. (Özer, survey conducted in 2010)

Thus, workers struggle under hard conditions to survive, and work under circumstances where there is limited opportunity to reproduce themselves. Besides not having the proper time for their private life, working conditions also make it difficult for them to become a part of an organisation. Thus, their organisational relations remain limited to their workplace, which creates problems in terms of establishing lasting and solid relations, even for workers in unionised workplaces. For a worker employed at a non-unionised business, meanwhile, it is almost impossible to come across such an activity.

Sub-contracting and Its Destructive Effect on Class Consciousness

In Gebze, according to site survey results, the number of people changing jobs is higher than in other regions (Table 11.1). In addition, the duration of unemployment is shorter in Gebze. Specifically, the proportion of previously unemployed workers who remain unemployed for more than six months was 43.4 per cent in Gebze versus 57.5 per cent in other regions. This indicates the presence of a more flexible employment structure in the Gebze region and this structure is closely related to the penetration of sub-contracting into the region.

In Turkey, sub-contracting was included in the labour law with a description limited to the relationship between primary employer and sub-employer. In this relationship, one main aspect of the definition of 'sub-employer' is the requirement for the sub-employer to employ its workers only for work undertaken at the premises of the primary employer. This means that a sub-contractor relationship includes in-house sub-contracting activities (Şafak 2004: 123). However, *de facto*, the sub-contractor relationship encompasses both sub-contracted com-

Table 11.1 Distribution of regions by number of job changes

	Number	Gebze %	Other %
How many times did you change your job?	0–3	69.9	74.4
	4+	30.6	25.7

Source: Results from the survey conducted with United Metal Workers Union members in April–June 2008.

panies doing their activities on the contractor's business premises and suppliers that provide input to the primary companies producing the final products. In order to distinguish between these two types of sub-contractors, the terms 'in-house sub-contractor' and 'supplier sub-contractor' will be used respectively.

The aim of both types of sub-contracting is to reduce labour costs, the elimination of workers' rights with regard to unionisation and collective bargaining, and thereby to increase competitiveness. The extraordinarily widespread implementation of sub-contracting causes fragmentation of the labour market and makes union and collective bargaining rights unusable (Şafak 2004: 111). That is to say, working conditions at sub-contractor workplaces are subject to pressure from the primary company, thereby becoming significantly harsher. An officer from Dostel, one of the primary suppliers of Ford, summarises this situation as follows:

> There is a significant supply industry because of the outsourcing activities of major companies and this supply industry has emerged from inside the main industry. This system is considered by primary companies because it is more flexible. The primary company focuses on value-added activities. And low value-added tasks are transferred to companies like ours. We are not independent. (Yücel, survey conducted in 2011)

The workers in such companies undertaking low value-added tasks are naturally subject to pressure. As Barış (survey conducted in 2010) describes:

> In the past, a person could start working in the factory and retire from there, but now there is a crisis in every 5–6 years. Staff renewals, layoffs and factory closures are common. Collective bargaining is also subject to great pressure in this process.

Barış (survey conducted in 2010) also explains that 'employers do not accept unionisation easily, and unions can only hold on when the workplace is resistant'. After unionisation though, sub-contracting employers put more pressure on workers due to pressure from the primary company. Employers thus pass onto their workers the competitive pressure they encounter because other suppliers of the primary company are not unionised. In the Gebze region, this becomes a factor in almost every collective agreement, particularly in the supply industry, creating significant pressure on unionisation:

> During the crisis, most factories became non-unionised. Wages and hourly rates were reduced even in unionised companies at the time of crisis. This did not happen where we [the United Metal Workers Union] were organised. And this creates a problem for the employer. Because hourly rates are higher in unionised workplaces, employers put more pressure for more productivity. (Barış, survey conducted in 2010)

Sub-contracting brought about two main types of fragmentation among the workers that deeply transformed the working-class formation. First, it has divided the working class with regard to age. In Gebze, 42 per cent of workers younger than 35 have worked for a sub-contractor, compared to only 34.4 per cent of workers older than 35. This shows that young workers work for sub-contractors more than the previous generation despite their shorter working experience. In Gebze, the average working experience is ten years for workers younger than 35 and twenty years for workers older than 35. This also points to an age-dependent rupture in the working class that makes it inevitable for differences to emerge between the work experience and class consciousness of older workers with previous knowledge of organisation and young workers, who only have the experience of working for a sub-contractor.

Second, it works through 'contractual' fragmentation, even among workers in the same premises. Özer (survey conducted in 2010), branch head of the United Metal Workers Union, which has long been the central actor in union organisation in the region, describes the sub-contracting system as follows:

> After the mid-90s, we began to see sub-contractors at factories. Sub-contractors were doing the cleaning. Then they entered the staff canteen. Then security was given to them. And then, starting from the lower levels of production, warehousing, packaging etc., they came up to the very centre of production.

The increasingly common existence of multiple companies in workplaces makes union organisation more difficult. On the one hand, unions have to find out the structure and number of separate companies in the same business. On the other hand, they have to deal with the artificial divisions that employers try to create among workers: 'You are employees of x company; others are none of your business', or 'You are our workers, don't develop relations with others'. The union organisation process at F2, a global supply company for the automotive industry located in Gebze, is an important example in this regard:

> In the first organisation period, there were six separate businesses in the F2 company. We were able to bring these six businesses together only after two years. There seemed to be two factories in Gebze. There were four companies at the factory in Kartal. Almost all staff go to work on foot. There were no shuttles in Kartal, thus, all workers go to work on foot. Workers from different companies gathered in different coffeehouses. Those from company A went to Hasan's coffeehouse, those from company B to Mehmet's. They didn't even come near each other. And this also started to kindle corruption in society. (Özer, survey conducted in 2011)

The sub-contracting system causes workers to become increasingly individualistic. the fragmentation of the social structure becomes more marked after every crisis so that the crisis of 2001 proved to be more destructive to the solidarity and social behaviour of the working class. During the 2001 crisis, he adds, 'the idea came up that the less people one knew, the less one would be harmed'. In this sense, the crisis of 2001 was different. Workers thought that keeping a distance from workers' leaders and unions, while staying close to the employer instead, could guarantee their jobs. In this regard, the atmosphere of defeat created by this crisis is one of the most important aspects of the hegemony established over the working class.

In fact, it seems that the dissolution of solidarity among the working class, thanks to the above-mentioned fragmentation and individualisation practices, has been replaced by the increasing effects of practices organised by religious sects. Sub-contracting has also played a role in this regard in that the increasingly common use of sub-contracting has coincided with the increasing activity of religious sects, to the extent that piety appears to be one step in the transition to a permanent job, with relations with religious sects acting as a factor for being hired by sub-contractor companies. Mehmet (survey conducted in 2012), a leftist worker with 15 years' experience in the region, who was born and raised in Gebze, summarises this process as follows:

> There is no more supporting of fellow townsmen;[7] everyone is looking after their own interests in their relations. And this works over political power. This is very common in Gebze as well. Sub-contracting is very instrumental in this . . . In the past, mayors, district governors or people of power would recommend people to companies; they were their 'townsmen'. Now, they send these people to the sub-contractor, not the main factory. From there, they somehow pass to the primary company. But they manage this through Islamic references. And this is experienced most commonly in Gebze.

The relations that workers maintain with their co-workers outside work can be taken as another indication of the 'isolationist' tendency among the working class. It appears that, nowadays, workers in the Gebze region have more limited relations with each other. For instance, 21.9 per cent of the survey respondents in Gebze said 'I do not meet my co-workers outside of work', compared to 14.1 per cent in other regions. While more than a third of the workers in other regions (35.6 per cent) met their co-workers outside of the neighbourhood they lived in, this proportion was only 29.5 per cent for Gebze (Table 11.2).

Table 11.2 Comparison of regions by location of meeting outside the factory

	Gebze		Other	
	N	%	N	%
I don't meet my co-workers outside of work	61	21.9	60	14.1
We meet at homes with our families	48	17.3	79	18.5
There are places in the neighbourhood where we come together	82	29.5	152	35.6
We meet at the union	18	6.5	26	6.1
We arrange to meet in the city centre	24	8.6	42	9.8
We meet at the village association	8	2.9	16	3.7
Other	37	13.3	52	12.2

Source: Results from the survey conducted with United Metal Workers' Union members in April–June 2008.

Thus, it appears to be difficult for workers in the Gebze region, because of the severe conditions that they work under, to come together outside of their family lives. Instead, relations are only sustained within neighbourhoods or at home, while life in the neighbourhood and daily practices are increasingly shaped by religious sects. Mermer (survey conducted in 2012), who attended high school in the 1990s, recalls that Islamic elements were not very active in Gebze at that time:

> In the 1990s, there was a village culture in the community. Families would sit together in the street, visit each other; there was the spirit of neigh-bourliness. Now, no-one would open their door to the other . . . But if there was a (religious) conversation meeting, they would. In the 1990s, people sustained simple relations like simple solidarity acts, doing one's work together, looking after one's neighbour, solving the problem when someone's child had an issue etc. Now relations are sustained by the sect.

This transformation shows that daily practices outside of working life are becoming defined by relations with religious sects that replace previous neigh-bourhood and friendship relations as a form of social network. 'If one is part of a sect,' Mermer claims, 'doors are opened more easily':

> When you knock on somebody's door, you visit them once, but they don't come to you, although your visit should be returned. But they always welcome the sect. The sect has penetrated there. They influence the family with their stories. Workers at factories meet their co-workers in sect houses. Family visits take place. The Quran is read. They have started to act as advised by the spiritual leaders in the sect.

Workers and the Construction of the Neoliberal Hegemony

The defeat suffered by the working class through the fragmentation of produc-tion processes and successive crises runs parallel to a process of conservatism and organised daily practices. From 2002 on, a political approach built through the AKP that synthesised Islamic tradition culturally, and neoliberalism economi-cally, became more powerful in the region. In Table 11.3, MMS stands for nationalist conservative right, which consists of fascist and radical Islamic movements (MHP, MSP, SP etc.). Legal parties of the Kurdish political movement and radical left parties are represented under the heading of radical left and Kurdish movement. The AKP achieved a major leap in the elections of 2002 while the centre-left lost 15 per cent. However, this defeat was not limited to the left, as there was also a significant shift of the centre-right and nationalist-conservative voters to the AKP. After the crisis of 2008, the AKP achieved its highest ever share of the vote in the Gebze region in the elections of 2011, which is noteworthy considering that this increase occurred despite the severe damage caused in the region by the crisis.

Table 11.3 Changes in voting behaviour (in percent) in the Gebze region

Years	AKP	MMS	Centre Right	Centre Left	Radical Left/ Kurdish Movement	Other
1969		1	61.3	31.2	2.8	3.7
1973		12	47.1	38.2		2.7
1977		11.8	38.7	48.2	0.4	0.9
1983			54.9	45.1		0
1987		13.9	43.2	43		0
1991		24.3	35.9	39.3	0	0.5
1995		37.9	26.2	30.4	4.9	0.6
1999		40.1	18.4	33.5	7.1	0.9
2001	42.2	15.3	16	18.5	7.6	0.4
2007	53.2	18.8	5.9	17.3	4.2	0.6
2011	56.7	17	0.6	21.2	3.9	0.8

Source: Calculated by the author using TURKSTAT data.

One of the factors that have allowed the AKP government to find support from workers is religion. In the Gebze region, 65 per cent of metal workers who define themselves religiously also support the AKP government or find it acceptable. Together with the other regions included in the survey, the proportion is 58.5 per cent, although this falls to 35 per cent among those defining themselves in social class terms.[8] Overall, 35.2 per cent of the metal workers surveyed described themselves as religious, while the proportion for metal workers in Gebze specifically was 42 per cent.

As seen in Table 11.4, the proportion of respondents finding the AKP government successful or acceptable is directly connected with their relationship with

Table 11.4 Religiousness and proportion of respondents offering favourable opinions on the success of the AKP government

		How religious are you?								
		I perform all of my religious duties		I perform my religious duties as often as possible		I sometimes perform my religious duties		I am a believer but I don't perform my religious duties		I am not really interested in religion	
		N	%	N	%	N	%	N	%	N	%
Do you find the AKP Government successful?	Yes	16	23.2	25	13.7	30	8.9	4	4.5	0	.0
	Not successful	30	43.5	83	45.4	200	59.2	66	74.2	26	92.9
	Acceptable	23	33.3	75	41.0	108	32.0	19	21.3	2	7.1

Source: Results from the survey conducted with United Metal Workers' Union members in April–June 2008.

religion. That is, there is barely any support for the AKP government among those who stated that they were not really interested in religion, whereas 56.5 per cent of all religious respondents and 65 per cent of those in the Gebze region had a favourable view. According to results from the same survey, 60 per cent of respondents defined themselves in religious terms compared to only 23 per cent who defined themselves in terms of social class, which shows how the AKP has been able to organise on the basis of religious conservatism.

When we look at the views of metal workers voting for the AKP in the general elections of 22 July 2007, we see a difference between their votes and their views on the AKP policies regarding economic issues and the problems of the working class. The most typical example of this concerns the social security act, which increased both the retirement age and the period of premium payments, and made payment of contributions mandatory. As Table 11.5 shows, the percentages of respondents agreeing or disagreeing with these regulations vary dramatically according to their political allegiances. In addition, Table 11.5 also reveals that there is no consensus of opinion within the AKP's electoral base. The overall proportion of metal workers who believe that the change in the social security system operates in favour of workers' interests is 13.3 per cent, although this increases to 24.58 per cent for workers who voted for the AKP. This compares to 58.1 per cent of the AKP voters in general who believe that changes in the social security system do not support workers' interests.

Although the United Metal Workers' Union, a left-wing union, conducted an effective campaign against the changes to the social security regulations, the AKP voters among its members did not change their political preference. One of the reasons for this, as Mermer (survey conducted in 2012) puts it, is the network of relations outside of the workplace:

> For example, the representative of the United Metal Workers' Union at company A supports AKP. He says, 'this is a struggle for rights, this is different for me.' I speak with young people supporting AKP; they say, 'We recognise the United Metal. We saw what other unions did'. But the guy supports AKP because the sects are very influential; he is not a part of it but his family has something to do with the sect, and so do his relatives. And he lives with them. But in the end, he visits the union every day.

Table 11.5 Opinions of workers on social security reform according to political views

	AKP		CHP		MHP	
	N	%	N	%	N	%
I certainly don't agree	52	29.05	86	60.14	64	51.61
I don't agree	52	29.05	42	29.37	40	32.26
I neither agree nor disagree	31	17.32	6	4.20	9	7.26
I agree	25	13.97	4	2.80	10	8.06
I completely agree	19	10.61	5	3.50	1	0.81

Source: Results from the survey conducted with United Metal Workers' Union members in April–June 2008.

Even though the workers who support the AKP react to negative develop-ments, they still defend the government by pointing out the good things it has done. Mermer reports how, in his conversations with his co-workers in the neighbourhood where he lives, whenever the implementation of any policy of the AKP government is mentioned that is seen as negative, other positive acts are persistently brought up to deflect attention. The result of this is the breakdown of the relationship between people's political preferences and class interests, thus making religious conservatism an important tool in the construction of neo-liberal hegemony. This process is also strengthened by the loss of unity of the working class in sub-contractor networks and the filling of this gap by religious sects.

By analysing employee-employer relations and religiousness in Konya, considered as the centre of piety in Turkey, Durak also details in his work how religiosity is used as an effective tool in disciplining labour. Workers' acceptance and acquiescence of inequalities is mostly realised through the employment of religious motives such as patience, trial, gratitude, faith and fate. These are expressed as 'the world as a trial' and hence the need to internalise the inequali-ties between classes, to be 'patient' with the challenge of harsh working condi-tions, to feel 'gratitude' for what one has without asking for too much, to have 'faith' under risky conditions and 'accept one's fate no matter what'. Such a discourse has proved to be influential on the working class, making it an important factor for obtaining their consent (Durak 2011: 98).

★ ★ ★

The AKP was built on a social organisation which is the continuation of a political movement that increasingly strengthened its influence in the 1990s, following a period of crises and heavy losses for the working class, when the confidence of the masses in politics had fallen to a minimum. For the working class, this period corresponds to a time of class disintegration, when class solidarity declined and personal relations, individualisation and relations based on self-interest became very common. The transformation that followed the economic crises, which included the organisation of religious conservatism with a neoliberal agenda, also saw the implementation of a legal framework for labour flexibility and increasingly widespread use of in-house and supplier sub-contracting. All in all, the determining factor behind the establishment of the AKP's hegemony was a combination of the increased organisational activity of religious conservatism and sect relations, particularly in workers' cities through social networks with the atmosphere of defeat created by the crisis and the transformation in the organisation of production. Due to the weakening of the foundations for solidarity resulting from the economic crises and the sub-contracting process, the working class began to base its political preferences not on class interests but under the guidance of religious sects and in line with the relations of interest built with the governing political power. This has played a critical role in sustaining the current political structure in Turkey.

NOTES

1   The site survey was conducted with around 1,000 workers at 78 factories where the United Metal Workers Union is organised, from which 806 valid questionnaires were collected. It was conducted in cities including İstanbul, Gebze, Bursa, İzmir, Kocaeli, Denizli, Manisa, Aydın, Mersin, Hatay, Gaziantep, Ankara and Eskişehir, where the metal and automotive industries have a significant presence. Regions where the survey was conducted include the İzmir Branch (İzmir, Manisa, Aydın, Denizli), Anatolian Branch (Ankara, Mersin, Hatay, Gaziantep, Kırşehir etc.), İstanbul Branch No. 1 (Anatolian side of İstanbul), İstanbul Branch No. 2 (European side of İstanbul and Thrace), Bursa Branch (Bursa), Eskişehir Branch (Eskişehir-Bilecik), Kocaeli Branch (Kocaeli, Sakarya, Düzce; except Gebze) and Gebze Branch (Dilovası, Çayırova, Darıca, Gebze). The majority of the survey respondents were blue-collar workers working in production. The data set obtained from the site survey is a valid source for comparing Gebze with other regions. The number of valid surveys for Gebze was 297.

2   The relationships of these supplier types were presented in the *Global Value Chains and their Spatial Effects* study, using data from 250 companies that are members of the Association of Automotive Parts and Component Manufacturers (TAYSAD).

3   As occasion requires, the names of the respondents and companies are coded, changed or left as they are.

4   During the crisis, companies tried to manage by sending workers away on unpaid leave, which inevitably led to a decline in the incomes of these workers.

5   A survey of union-member workers, registered but non-union member workers, and unregistered workers showed that experience of unemployment lasting more than six months is significantly less common among union-member workers. However, union-member workers also have the lowest chance of finding a new job in the three months after becoming unemployed. This is not surprising because it is more difficult for a union-member worker with a proper job to find a new job offering similar standards to the previous one. On the other hand, it is easier to find a similar job for an unregistered or non-union member worker (Adaman et al. 2009: 177–178).

6   According to data from the Ministry of Labor and Social Security, the minimum wage in that period (01/07/2008–31/12/2008) was 457 TL net. According to the results of TURKSTAT's Income and Life Conditions Survey, 2006–2009 (TURKSTAT 2011b), average household income in the Eastern Marmara Region in 2008 was 17,434 TL per year and 1,453 TL per month. Average income in urban areas is 12 per cent higher than the Turkish average. When this rate is applied to the data of the Eastern Marmara Region, average household income works out at 1,631 TL.

7   Supporting fellow townsmen means the forms of solidarity established between people originating from the same region within the larger population migrating from the countryside to the cities.

8   In the survey, respondents were considered 'religious' if they stated that they performed all "religious duties" or as many of them as possible.

CHAPTER TWELVE

The Rise of the Islamic Bourgeoisie and the Socialisation of Neoliberalism: Behind the Success Story of Two Pious Cities

A. Ekber Doğan and Yasin Durak

During the 1990s, various Anatolian provinces experienced a socio-economic transformation shaped by a new process of industrialisation. Although this process did not change the prevailing geography of Turkish industry, in which the Eastern Marmara Region, including İstanbul, still remains by far the most industrially developed region, as a result of their industrial growth, other provinces such as Kayseri, Konya, Denizli and Antep, which are now called the 'Anatolian Tigers', have been experienced a significant transformation in terms of both scale and economic and social structure. Of these provinces, which share a characteristic of conservatism, Kayseri and Konya have become distinguishable from the others for their profoundly conservative identity and Islamist municipal administrations since the 1990s.

This chapter aims to analyse two particular phenomena associated with the recent economic revival of these two provinces, whose growth has been fostered by the new industrialisation. The first phenomenon is the emergence of a pious or so-called 'Islamic' fraction within Turkey's capitalist class, while the second concerns the appearance of particular kinds of local labour control regime. These two phenomena are interrelated since the production and reproduction of a particular labour control regime has been one of the most critical factors underlying the accumulation process of this particular capitalist fraction. Related to this, along with the rise of both a pious bourgeoisie and Islamist politics, first locally, then nationally, a new kind of conservative framework of social reproduction, based mainly on religious elements, has emerged with the function of socialising neoliberalism in Turkey.

The Emergence and Development of Pious Capitalists

The Association of Independent Industrialists and Businessmen (MÜSİAD) was founded in 1990 by five İstanbul entrepreneurs as the first nationally organised business association based on religious sentiment and networks. The establishment of such an organisation reflected the need of pious capitalists to declare their interests and organise their business relationships independently from Turkey's major capitalists and their organisation, namely the Turkish Industry and Business Association (TÜSİAD). The emergence of the pious Anatolian bourgeoisie as a self-conscious fraction of Turkish capital dates back to the years of Necmettin Erbakan (end of the 1960s), who went on to establish Turkey's first Islamist party. While still General Secretary of the Union of Chambers and Commodity Exchanges of Turkey (TOBB), Erbakan came to be the spokesperson of the Anatolian small- and medium-scale bourgeoisie. He criticised the Justice Party (AP) government over its industrial and import substitution policies, accusing the government and its allies in TOBB of discriminating in favour of large capitalists in İstanbul and İzmir. He was elected TOBB Chairman in 1969 but, within a couple of months, the AP government forced his dismissal by issuing a decree. Soon after, Erbakan entered politics, winning a parliamentary seat in Konya in the 1969 general elections. This stage of Erbakan's political career ended when, along with other leading politicians, he was banned from politics for about seven years following the 12 September 1980 military coup. The ban was rescinded after a referendum in 1987 and, shortly after that, Erbakan became the head of the Welfare Party (RP).

During this post–coup period, another politician, Turgut Özal, emerged as the second notable figure in the rise of the pious bourgeoisie. Özal had been a member and parliamentary candidate for Erbakan's former party, the National Salvation Party (MSP), and had also been Chairman of the Trade Union of Metal Industrialists (MESS). After serving as deputy prime minister in the military junta government between 1980 and 1983, his party, the Motherland Party (ANAP), won the first elections after the coup, with Özal becoming Prime Minister. During the 1980s, he represented the alliance between the pious small- and medium-scale enterprises and large capital, in other words between the Anatolian and the İstanbul bourgeoisie. This alliance reflected a social consensus between liberal and conservative values, similar to contemporary neoliberal or new right trends in Western countries. More than half of MÜSİAD members started their businesses during Turgut Özal's administration between 1983 and 1991 (Yavuz 2005: 131). A significant portion of these owned firms that had thrived by taking advantage of the rising influence of Islamism, the urbanisation of capital and growing urban rents, and funding from various Arabic financial institutions during the Özal governments (Bulut 1997: 258–263; Yavuz 2005: 125).

The 1990s represented a breakthrough for these businessmen, due to the RP's electoral success in winning the majority of large- and medium-scale municipalities in 1994, and the emergence of industrialisation in certain Anatolian provinces. This capital fraction, formerly named in the literature as *Green Capital* or *Capital of Sects* and then as *Islamic* or *Islamist Capital*, continued to grow thanks to the above mentioned supportive policies and its gradually rising participation through subcontracting within new global production chains. By the end of the 1990s, certain business associations, particularly MÜSİAD, the Confederation of Businessmen and Industrialists of Turkey (TUSKON),[1] and the Anatolian Lions Businessmen's Association (ASKON)[2] were becoming stronger through their growing membership and their increasing effectiveness in both private business and government procurement.

During the second half of the 1990s, some of these emergent Islamist firms, such as Kombassan, YİMPAŞ and Jet-Pa, enlarged their capital accumulation and investment scales. Through their high levels of capital accumulation, the Islamist holdings that flourished between 1993 and 1997, during the brightest years of the RP in government, played a significant role in the subsequent diversification within Islamist capital due to differences in the scale of production and/or business and in types of investment financing. The two most dynamic segments within this capital sector were, firstly, the owners of small- and medium-scale enterprises (SME), who developed their businesses mainly by means of government subsidies and privileges for Organised Industrial Districts (OID), and, secondly, entrepreneurs in trade, services and construction, doing business with RP-led Islamist municipalities.

First Konya, and later Kayseri, became paradigmatic examples of the cooperation established between pious capital and these newly emerging Islamist municipalities. In both provinces, the number of OIDs has risen from one to three since 1990, and they are the two provinces which have experienced Islamic capital accumulation most intensively since the mid-1990s. Although a few firms, such as Kombassan and Yimpaş, have classical features that would categorise them as 'holding' companies, or a group of large-scale corporations, these so-called 'Islamic Holdings' played a significant role in Islamist capital accumulation. By 1996, the number of holdings based in Konya was more than seventy. However, over time, they have differed regarding the extent to which they have benefitted from the accelerated privatisation process during the current Justice and Development Party's (AKP) governing period; the amount of international business they have done; and the extent to which they have taken advantage of the wide opportunities offered by Islamist municipalities, such as the metropolitan municipalities of İstanbul and Ankara, which together represent approximately 30 per cent of Turkey's national income. This differentiation among the mid-Anatolian provinces during the mid-1990s developed to such an extent that many Islamist entrepreneurs, who had increased their own wealth, strongly lobbied for the exclusion of small-scale entrepreneurs from MÜSİAD (Özdemir 2006: 157). The following comment by one businessman, who is a member of one of the traditional religious circles, clearly reveals these tensions within Islamist capital: 'Up to this point we have been all together, but now conditions are significantly changed. We cannot go forward carrying the weak on our shoulders. God forbid; we may lose everything together.'

In parallel to this differentiation, some members of Islamist capital have ceased hiding their wealth and started to manifest it in public, with some even boasting of their luxury lifestyles. Consequently, various 'consumption patterns' of the newly enriched segments of the Islamist movement have gained visibility.

Understood in terms of class heterogeneity in the Islamist sociopolitical move-ment, this latter phenomenon has been important for the re-conceptualisation of the Islamist bourgeoisie. Certain figures, such as the founding member and ex-chairman of MÜSİAD, Erol Yarar, have become champions of this re-conceptualisation. Yarar, who claims that MÜSİAD members are the original bourgeoisie of Turkey, argues that, to a certain degree, the manifestation of wealth is necessary for such capitalists to be accepted as a societal role model: 'After giving 2.5 per cent of our wealth as alms to the poor, we can use our money for whatever we want; we shouldn't be embarrassed at showing our prosperity.' His response to criticisms about luxury lifestyles or consumption patterns is to argue that the 'ascetic/monastic life' is a moralistic fallacy (Özkan 2009; Altaylı 2009).

The military memorandum issued against the Welfare Party–True Path Party (RP-DYP) coalition government on 28 February 1997 was a key moment for this capital fraction. The rationale of the memorandum was to pre-empt 'the rising reactionary threat against the secular Turkish Republic'. Erbakan's RP, as the senior partner in the coalition government, was accused of actions leading towards this end. The memorandum had significant effects, including the fall of the RP-DYP coalition government and the banning of the RP, the party that had won the highest percentage of votes in the 1995 general election. In addition, Islamist capital was intimidated by police measures and fiscal operations launched against Islamic holdings operating on the basis of future dividends, while Turkey's mainstream media engaged in propaganda about the exclusion of Islamic capital from future public tenders. In 1998, a prosecution was launched in order to dissolve MÜSİAD, on the basis of a speech given by Erol Yarar, MÜSİAD's president, which had criticised the law passed to increase the minimum period of compulsory primary schooling from five to eight years for impeding İmam-Hatip schools (religious vocational education schools) and thereby promoting a 'specifically irreligious education'. During this period, MÜSİAD's membership decreased sharply from 2,800 in 1997 to 1,800 in 2002, and Islamic capital noticeably withdrew into a conciliatory stance. In particular, it distanced itself from the more radical reactions to this political crisis by some sections of the petty bourgeoisie, such as craftsmen and artisans. In the political sphere, after the RP was dissolved, the Virtue Party (FP) was established to take its place. After FP was closed, increased support by the Islamic capital fraction for moderate Islamists, specifically an emergent reformist wing in FP, was the most significant factor leading to the foundation of the AKP. From an Islamist perspective, Yasin Aktay (2004) argues that the priorities of the reformist group that founded the AKP reflected the rationality of the new social and class strata that had become so closely entwined in the current regime that they could no longer leave it, even if they wished to.

After the political turmoil of the 28 February period and the concrete impacts of the subsequent deep economic crises of November 2000 and February 2001, Islamic capital voluntarily changed from being an autonomous and rival actor against major İstanbul capitalists. As a class fraction, while they gave up some of their claims on an economic level and retreated to a more conciliatory line, the influence of Islamic capital on Islamic political actors increased dramatically after the FP's closure. One former FP MP, Mehmet Bekaroğlu, explained this in his book, *The End of Politics: From the Just Order to the Realities of the World* (2007), by arguing that Turkey's Islamic capital fraction had accumulated such a remarkable amount of capital that this accumulation had itself created constraints:

> They gradually entered the global market with the advantages they gained, they asked for the conditions required by the global market and the 'stability' which would pave the way for capital. And they regarded [Erbakan] Hodja and his group as the obstacle to stability and the neoliberal wave . . . From then on, Erbakan could not be the person to provide new opportunities and advantages for them. For this reason, they were necessarily reformists in terms of economics. What is more, they put effort, before everyone did, into changing the Virtue Party. (Bekaroğlu 2007: 223)

After the foundation of MÜSİAD, the AKP's coming to power as a single party government in 2002 was the most significant turning point in the history of Islamist capitalists. In order to understand how Islamist capitalists have advanced hand-in-hand with the AKP government, one should analyse the boost in the membership of organisations such as MÜSİAD and TUSKON after 2007, and how Islamist capitalists, such as Albayrak, Kiler, Çalık, Boydak, Sanko, Cüneyt Zapsu, Fettah Tamince and Ethem Sancak, who were close to the party's elite, achieved the status that enabled them to compete against TÜSİAD members. Especially during the AKP's second term (2007–2011), being a member of Islamic capital organisations became the safest way of surviving and doing business in the market. Consequently, capitalists of every persuasion rushed into these organisations and considered it necessary to attend their fairs, their organisations of *hajj* and *umrah*, their community meetings, and even to change their religious community affiliations in some regions. Underlying this rush, certain factors played a particular role in the growth and transformation of Islamic capital, particularly the public tenders for the Housing Development Administration (TOKİ), which had a total value of 20 billion dollars, the rapidly growing investment budget of the İstanbul Metropolitan Municipality, and the accelerated privatisation of public enterprises. The primary beneficiaries of these 'business opportunities' have mostly been entrepreneurs with close ties to the AKP government circles. Organisations of Islamic business circles have grown accordingly, and the increase in their membership indicates their empowerment during the AKP period: MÜSİAD has grown from around 1,800 to approximately 6,500 members, who together employ around 1,200,000 workers (MÜSİAD 2013). As a result, this capital fraction has gained the ability to control 15 per cent of Turkey's total national income. Similarly, TUSKON's membership has increased from 12,000 in 2009 to approximately 34,000 in 2012 (TUSKON 2009; 2012).

Labour Control and 'Cultural Hegemony' at the Workplace Level

A businessman from Kayseri asks a job applicant [worker]: 'How much money do you want?' The worker says the amount he wants to get. 'No way!' the businessman says, 'You ask for too much.' The worker decreases the amount of salary he asks for. The employer says again: 'No, that's too much.' The negotiation continues like this till finally the worker says: 'Let me work for peanuts.' The businessman says: 'No, that's too much,' so the worker gives in and says: 'Let me fast two days a week on your behalf.'

This joke was told by Ali Coşkun, the former Minister of Industry of the AKP government. Although it was told to point out the supposedly cunning style of Kayseri businessmen, it also gives many clues about the structure of the labour market and labour control mechanisms in mid-Anatolia's southern and eastern provinces, such as Karaman, Aksaray, Niğde, Nevşehir, Yozgat and, most importantly, Kayseri and Konya.

Historically, working conditions in these provinces were always handicapped by the prevalence of insecurity, low levels of registered workers, low wages and irregular pay, and high levels of informal temporary jobs (Ayata 2000: 222–224; Van Velzen 1978: 125–129; Yurt Ansiklopedisi 1983: 4740–4741 [Kayseri], 5206–5208 [Konya]). Leo Van Velzen and Sencer Ayata conducted significant case studies on small-scale industry in Kayseri in the 1970s and 1980s which provide concrete knowledge about the historical background of labour processes in many of the mid-Anatolian provinces. Van Velzen observed that almost all plants were employing workers at a wage lower than the officially required minimum wage, and entrepreneurs were performing their production through numerous workshops (which can be understood as analogous to today's sweatshops) in order to preserve their existing low-level wages while remaining immune to legal sanctions (1978: 127). Hence, for decades, the organisational capacity and the level of consciousness were low, and labour union actions, such as walk-outs, slow-downs or strikes, were fairly rare among Konya and Kayseri's working classes.

The capitalist classes of these cities benefited from these conditions by pushing flexibilisation further through such practices as subcontracting to small workshops, using home-based production in poor working-class neighbourhoods, and exploiting paternal or other hierarchical relations based on local traditional or cultural norms and values.

The Case of Konya

As a growing capital fraction, the Islamist bourgeoisie became the constituent of a new local social alliance by supporting the RP, which had the potential to bring their values and expectations to the political arena. The SME owners exerted a significant dominance in the administrative cadres of the party's local branches in Kayseri and Konya, reflecting an affiliation between local party administrators and SME owners, whose wealth was increasing. The majority of the party elite and members of the municipal councils consisted of SME owners with plants in the earliest OIDs in their provinces, together with entrepreneurs in construction or real estate (Doğan 2007: 193).

The gradual industrialisation of these provinces coincided with an attack on several historical gains by the working class, and on the collective urban rights of the middle and lower social classes. Hence, the rise of Islamist politics in Kayseri and Konya went hand in hand with this new industrialisation. Demirpolat (2002: 305) claims that, whereas the 'will to power' of the Islamic elites was mainly based on the idea of regaining power against the Western world, at the same time it caused new orientations to emerge within Islamic trends that were compatible with capitalism and the modern world. This was a problem which almost all modern religious-conservative movements have to deal with. The industrialisation process in the OIDs should be understood in this context. It was an updated conservative version of the gradual modernisation model for Turkey, first formulated by Ziya Gökalp at the beginning of the twentieth century with the motto of 'modernism within tradition' (Buğra 2004: 134). The main premise of this updated version was to bring about the revival of traditional cultural values, enable the disciplined collaboration of employees and employers, and thereby provide rapid development at local and national levels. Thus, the rationale of the labour control regime in SMEs has a special significance regarding the analysis of the rise of the conservative bourgeoisie as, through the practices of this regime, unequal social relations were legitimised, 'all possibilities' in terms of labour relations were defined, and the consent or obedience of the working class to poor working conditions was provided. In explaining these developments in labour relations, which have been completely overt in the cases of Konya and Kayseri, the concept of 'cultural hegemony' (Thompson 1991; 1963) is particularly appropriate.

Thanks to the strategies implemented by this labour control regime, on the one hand, conservative values have become effective in the work environment, while, on the other hand, the input provided through the growth of absolute exploitation has been guaranteed. A vision of the Islamic utopia desired by both employers and workers has emerged as a common world view. That is, the idea that the workers are on the same side as their employers shapes their imagination of their daily working life. Two main strategies are important in this process. First, the difficult conditions created by flexible employment structures and the informal work environment results in the workers' general tendency to respect the informal social security systems provided by employers. Besides, the efficiency of local and informal networks also plays an important part in manipulating the workers in order to control them, both in their work environment and in their private daily lives. This makes the life patterns of employees match the paternalistic expectations of the employers. Second, the sustaining of the cultural hegemony of the worker-employer relationship through Islamic rhetoric reveals a mystified comprehension of actual relations (recognisable through concepts such as patience, trial, gratitude, faith and fate). Thus, current relations are legitimised by divine references. Thanks to the Islamic rituals observed by employers and employees together, such as the breaks provided during work-time for prayer, employees' demands related to working conditions are reduced to a religious rhetoric, and the practice called *faith of labour*[3] can easily emerge (Durak 2011).

An Unequal Consensus: Pious-Conservative Utopia

As Demir (2005: 877) states, '[the] pious-conservative bourgeoisie grounds the legitimacy of chasing benefits on two bases, religious and national'. In this legitimising process, 'religious arguments are used against the pious grassroots, and nationalist arguments are used against the elites of country'. It is possible to find such a combined religious and nationalist emphasis in the expressions of most firm owners in the OID in Konya, as shown by the interviews conducted for this study.[4] These business owners do not distinguish the religious from the national; for them, the 'nation' symbolises a unity of religion. Moreover, they emphasise the exceptional importance of their businesses for the national economy and within the framework of legitimacy patterns, such as 'national responsibilities' undertaken in accordance with 'national interests' or public consciousness brought along with piousness.

Ernst Bloch evaluates the continuation of the 'selfish interests' of capitalist entrepreneurship in a bourgeois economy through such 'altruist excuses' as some kind of utopianism. In fact, this is 'the meeting of utopianism with false conscious' as a desire for a perfect world (2007: 190–193). He argues that the bourgeoisie needs 'a virtue to cover up its selfishness' in this way. Likewise, the belief of the pious-conservative business owners in honourable and honest profit depends on a utopianism described as the 'national interest', which means that the interests of these business owners 'have a utopian impact'.

> When the worker is fired, the following day he starts working at another place, but if this business goes bankrupt it won't be re-established the following day. And also many people cannot earn their daily bread . . . Nobody knows this. We are even accused of driving our own car but we have to have a car for our businesses. Let me tell you something. Businessmen should definitely have a chauffeur. What would have happened if I had had an accident while on my way here? We are watching over many people's daily bread. We have the weight of Turkey on our shoulders. (3. Businessman – Employer)

This utopianism does not just exist in the employers' mental world; at the same time, it is an imagination to be imposed by employers on their workers as part of creating an interclass consensus. Business owners tend to cover up or delay disagreements based on class contradictions by constantly emphasising the view that their own interests coincide with others' interests, especially of their employees.

> (. . .) Allah helped him [the boss] in the past . . . After all, he never misses his prayers; he never usurps somebody else's rightful share . . . We all had a crisis; most of the businesses here were shut down; we all saw it; people went bankrupt and became poor, but his business went well . . . Why? Because he did not reach for ill-gotten profit. I am not saying that all the bankrupt people reached for ill-gotten profit but if a man reaches for ill-gotten profit he suffers for that. (13. Interviewee – Worker)

Expressions revealing this utopianism, such as 'if everybody does his best, everything will be flawless', were repeated by the business owners interviewed for this study. This utopic impact focused especially on an Islamic imagination of the world, because the notion of the 'general interests of the nation' expressed by these business owners can be frequently transformed into 'the interests of Muslims' or 'the success of the Islam world'. The pursuit of interclass consensus to be maintained by this utopic impact was crucial for ensuring the accumulation of supposedly Islamic capital.

Peace at work, enabled by the pious-conservative utopia functioning as a shared world view, has important consequences for employers. As a result of the commitment to industrial peace, the majority of workers identify working without causing problems (or, as they put it, 'just working and not poking their noses into anything') as a quality to be proud of. Almost all of the workers interviewed started talking by specifying these features. Thus, in protesting the working conditions, causing problems or not meeting the employer's demands, a worker comes face to face with a 'moral principle' produced by the workers themselves. They consider their commitment to such a work ethic as providing a framework of legitimacy for their demands. On the other hand, employers make effective use of the implications of this accepted moral principle when they fire workers. That is, a worker who is disobedient, not working devotedly, or habitually coming to work late, is easily labelled 'immoral'. Firing such a worker is thus legitimised by the inconsistency of his world view rather than the inconsistency of his work discipline. Thus, the common feature of the interviewees who had been fired is their incompatibility with the religious moral sanctions of industrial relations in Konya, namely not sharing the world view that underpins the legitimacy of Konya's industrial relations regime.

Locality and Efficiency of Informal Relation Networks

As everywhere, the informal networks that generally influence working relationships in the neo-liberal era can be affected by the general norms of the dominant culture. As scholars have previously noted, the control of workers is maintained through the reinforcement of the 'hegemonic culture' (Lears and Jackson 1985) surrounding daily life and the 'manipulation of social relations' (Boissevain 1974). In this regard, informal networks and the basis of the legitimacy framework on which face-to-face relations develop, take on the task of providing labour control by virtue of being 'manipulation devices'. Acts such as finding a job, hiring or firing a worker, solving problems in the workplace, and ensuring the consent or obedience of the workers to poor working conditions are shaped considerably through these networks and frameworks.

> To tell the truth, we generally find a job via acquaintances . . . It is difficult to get a job via a job advertisement. You can also find a job via a job advertisement but you may be fired at any time . . . How can you trust these firm owners? He [employer] may tell you that he has registered you but he may not, perhaps you cannot get along with the people there, he may fire you in a few days . . . It is better if you get a job via acquaintances

> . . . After all, a man starting a job via an advertisement must have let his acquaintances know that he is looking for a job. When he gets a job through one of his acquaintances, he quits the previous one. There are so many people who do that. (12. Interviewee – Worker)

Almost all of the workers interviewed in Konya thought that it was 'safer' to work under 'known' employers, although this brought 'undesired' responsibilities for the workers. Fellow countrymen preferred to work with known employers or work in enterprises owned by relatives because 'the market conditions were very bad'.

In many situations, networks of informal relations function as a means of executing mutual compromises, alliances, compliances, pressure and consent. Although both employers and workers are able to manipulate these networks, the more effective manipulation of social relations is carried out by employers because the compromises they make are usually non-obligatory. The hegemonic relationship becomes stronger as long as the ruthlessness of the market is compensated for by the protectiveness of the employer. When employers are impressed by an adequate level of trustworthiness, they rapidly give a lot of privileges to their faithful workers. Thus, 'gaining the trust of the employer' becomes an essential target for many workers.

> I can give an example, but of course I will not give the name of that person. I mean, we do not like to talk about this very much. We do not say it . . . Almost eight years ago, one of our workers died . . . He had a wife and two children . . . He departed . . . So we sat down with our partners, talked and made a decision . . . You may not believe this but we have sent his salary to his family every month since his death. That is to say, when our worker shows himself to be reliable, we never let anyone down . . . Our worker died, his book of sins and merits is closed, but ours is still open. (6. Interviewee – Employer)

However, the level of such 'informal insurance' varies for each worker, because it depends on the closeness of their relationship with the employer. That is, not each and every worker can be trusted, which results in the use of 'clientelism' as an effective control strategy.

Ambiguous 'compromises' made by employers in certain situations, and the unstable informal relations based on face-to-face relations rather than workers' concrete gains, are not powerful and reliable enough. These 'manipulation devices' generally do not work without the 'theatres' in which the employers can perform. As might be expected, the obligations put on the employers' side by these networks of informal relations are not stable. Employers, upon realising instances which they call 'abuse', can keep workers at arm's length immediately. Therefore, it is quite significant that one business manager defined his authority as 'smiling seriousness', which explicitly demonstrates the complementarity of approaching and avoiding. Although, they may sometimes show great intimacy to their workers, simultaneously they have to remind them 'who is the boss' through other impositions.

Borders of Cultural Hegemony

As a control strategy, cultural hegemony also forces the authority to give some rights to the ruled people. Although such control defined 'the outside limits of what [is] politically, socially practicable, and hence influenced the forms of what was practiced' (Thompson 1991: 86), the manipulative power provided for the authority has been historically restricted by its 'legitimising elements'. Thus, the obligations generated by conventions or other legitimising elements provide the dominated population with an opportunity to use the rhetoric of hegemony in order to express their demands (Thompson 1991: 73).

The relations emerging in this way mean that the control defined within the context of cultural hegemony lacks structural features. Indeed, it is possible to claim that hegemony perfectly displays the characteristics of a relational variation. However, what can never be changed in this relational variability is a common world view accepted by both sides of this hegemonic relation. This world view 'appeals to a wide range of other groups within the society, and they must be able to claim with at least some plausibility that their particular interests are those of society at large' (Lears and Jackson 1985: 571). In Konya, this type of common world view, based in this case on piousness–conservatism, provides one of the basic foundations for the cultural hegemony seen in this city.

What are the borders of the actual relations of cultural hegemony? What could be the extent of the sustainability of a hegemonic control having pious-conservative characteristics, as in Konya? These questions can be answered through an analysis of this sacred legitimacy framework, because it is this framework that shapes the particular forms of 'everyday experience' (Lears and Jackson 1985: 577) and the public discourse. Therefore, marking out the borders of this legitimacy reveals the continuity of the hegemonic relation.

In the cases of Konya and Kayseri, the religious values of *Sunni Islam* constitute the language of hegemony by presenting the essential references of the hegemonic relations, while mystifying inequalities. Since actual relations are legitimised by divine references, the worker's commitment to the hegemonic culture may correlate with their commitment to God. Thus, 'bewitched' comments related to the unequal relations of employers' daily lives are quite common.

In an old story, it is narrated that a fire starts in a forest. While all the animals are running away, a single ant tries to put out the fire with a single drop of water. Our case is just like that. It is not likely that the system will improve nowadays. We only try to keep our hands clean, that's all . . . When we improve ourselves as individuals, when we live in accordance with Islam and in accordance with what we call Islamic, the society and the state will remain ordered. And of course this will not happen in a minute. (7. Interviewee – Employer)

While Azrael is destroying a clan he notices a person reading the *Kur'an*. He tells Allah, 'There was a person, he was citing your name; for this reason I could not kill him.' Allah says, 'kill him too.' Azrael asks, 'Why?' [Allah] commands, 'He is no good to anyone but himself.' That is, Allah does not need him . . . Therefore, we should appreciate our people. In other words, would it matter if I had a job or not? (21. Interviewee – Worker)

This religious rhetoric, emerging within the scope of cultural hegemony, has other effects. It legitimises both the sanctions of the employers and some demands of the workers. Conventional 'time-out for praying', which only became possible when workers turned the employer's pious-conservative rhetoric back on them, is the best example of this. Thus, the pious–conservatism of these business owners led to a compromise of three time-outs per day, which are given to workers within the working hours, with each lasting around 15 to 20 minutes. The criteria for the 'time-out for praying' theatre can reach such an extent that employers cannot control it. This small compromise made (reluctantly) by employers is exceptionally important in terms of the functionality of cultural hegemony. This is because removing such an overtly pious custom could cause the workers to resist, which in turn would reveal underlying conflicts that would destroy the employer's strongest ground, namely his piousness in this case. Conflicts of this kind increase day by day, along with exposure to the contradictions of the legitimacy framework of cultural hegemony. However, they do not cause radical separations; rather, they cause a form of subjection, namely 'conflicting subjection'.

Consequently, it is possible for actual relations, actual conditions and the experience of reality to make clear the nature of hegemonic control at any moment. Therefore, such hegemony cannot continue on its own forever, so the theatres and compromises of employers are critical for sustaining this process. In short, employees consent to the hegemonic culture constituting the conventional framework of working relations only so long as employers comply with the legitimacy criteria of this conventional framework.

Role of Laborers and Conservatism in the Rising Process of Pious Capitalists

Konya has played an important role in the rise in pious conservatism in Turkey, as the pious conservative bourgeoisie is primarily organised in Anatolian cities such as Konya. At the same time, pious-conservative workers have also become important through their production of surplus value during this growth. However, their importance has been generally ignored by sociologists due to the latter's lack of a social class perspective. That is, they could not see any differences within the pious conservative parts of Turkish society; they saw only a kind of homogeneity among pious conservative people. Consequently, despite only having a description of the pious conservative bourgeoisie, they analysed this process as indicating the rise of all pious conservative parts of society against the secular Kemalist elites.

Aktay (2000: 138) argues that the emphasis on 'indigenousness' in the story about the rise of the Islamic capital is a consequence of oppression by the secular elites and the state. Thus, a 'diasporic perception' of pious people emerged, which resulted in a 'horizontal solidarity' between Islamic entrepreneurs being seen as the most important factor in their ability to rise on their own. However, this basic solidarity pattern has been built effectively between the provincial conservative proletariat and the pious conservative bourgeoisie as well. As Tuğal (2007a: 102) points out, RP's well-known motto in the mid-1990s, the 'Just Order', emerged at the same time as a political call for unity. With reference to the idea of economic jihad, 'Just Order' implied the identification of the labourers' fate with that of the pious conservative bourgeoisie. Moreover, not only religion and the networks of religious communities, but also the local cultural values of various Anatolian regions and other informal networks, such as kinship relations, played a significant role in the emergence of this 'vertical solidarity'. Embedded within it, the workers have played an essential role in the rise of pious conservative capitalism since it is not purely economic in nature. Along with its economic-productive role as cheap labour, the labouring people of Anatolia have become a fruitful human resource for the constitution of a religious conservative social hegemony as well. For example, especially in the 1990s, many poor people worked for religious communities as volunteers, for Islamic political parties as volunteers or activists, if not for whatever they could be then at least 'for the sake of God'. All these people, the Anatolian proletariat, were and still are, even today, the invisible power behind this process of hegemony building. Hence, we can claim that the most important dynamic behind the rise of Islamic capital was the labourers 'running amok', feeling a 'union of hearts' with the pious conservative bourgeoisie in the 1990s.

During the 1990s, this 'union of hearts' was created through the grassroots activities of Islamic political parties and communities, particularly during election periods. With slogans such as 'one amongst us', as used by Islamist candidates in the 1994 local elections (Kurtoğlu 1998: 347), or through campaign techniques mainly based on house visits and face-to-face communication (Delibaş 2001), Islamist candidates successfully created links between the Islamic elites and the grassroots. They visited patients, attended funerals and weddings, displaying theatrical skills that persuaded people that they were 'one amongst them'. Through these practices, the poor peoples' 'will to respectability' and the pious conservative candidates' 'will to power' became connected with each other.

The successes in local elections since the mid-1990s of the RP and its successor Islamic conservative parties can be attributed to this well-constructed vertical solidarity. After taking local power, Islamists attempted to reshape social relations and daily life in the provinces. By integrating local cultural values with Islamic codes, the new Islamist urban administrations have developed a new system of social reproduction. Islamist municipal administrations in Kayseri and Konya, for example, directly or indirectly adopted a system of socialisation which enabled the coordination and cooperation of social actors through channels other than the markets, through practices such as organising weddings and circumcision ceremonies for families that could not afford them, organising massive dinner events in public spaces for breaking the fast during Ramadan, providing free bus services during religious festivals, distributing free coal packs in winter and starting new soup kitchens.

These practices can be regarded as practices of socialisation in being the non-profit and non-market activities of social, political and administrative bodies

(Gough 2002). In this sense, socialisation is not just an educational process for producing consent for the social system, but also a new type of public service provision. Those services provided by municipalities or Islamist groups to the urban poor have expanded into a wide range of activities, including soup kitchens, food aid, free school stationery, community dormitories, and other kinds of charitable activities. However, in drawing on religious, traditional and local values, they have worked simultaneously with the penetration of neoliberal policies into the provision of municipal services, the privatisation of municipal enterprises, and a sharp downsizing of personnel. Thus, we propose the term 'precarious' to describe the publicity created by these practices of the Islamist municipalities. They have adopted various neoliberal policies, such as minimising the collective production of services, purchasing all goods and services from private firms, and pricing all services according to market prices, which made such services much more inaccessible, especially for needy people. On the other hand, they have continued with the above mentioned social service practices, such as helping poor people, collective circumcisions and weddings, free bus rides for the elderly, student scholarships, free electricity for mosques, free health check-ups in poor neighbourhoods, and free coal distribution to religious sect student dormitories. Neoliberal policy choices have greatly contributed to the 'precariousness of the publicness' by weakening the public character of municipal services that were supposed to be based on the notion of citizenship rights. Meanwhile, the practices of 'pious socialisation' have gradually replaced them and consolidated the precarious publicity by calling people in need 'Muslims' rather than citizens of the province.

Conclusion

We can summarise the argument of this article by stating that the rise of religious and traditional socio-cultural ties, values and practices because of Islamism, as a social movement and political power, has been important in establishing a special local labour control regime that has transformed a number of SMEs into Islamic capitalists since the 1990s. We examined some phenomena which facilitate the establishment of reciprocities between capital and labour: the networks of informal relations, the paternalistic and corporatist values derived from Islam and local conservatism, and the role of the operation of Islamist socio-cultural hegemony in general. At the same time, a neoliberal-Islamist mentality has been dominant in local and central government levels for at least a decade in Turkey. It has changed notions of citizenship, publicness and urbanism with some social inclusion mechanisms, especially by distributing relief supplies and supporting the charitable activities of its benefactors while downsizing the social aspects of state. This can be called 'Eğreti Kamusallık' – 'Precarious Publicness' (Doğan 2007).

While reshaping residents' perceptions of urbanity, this system has sustained the functioning of the hegemony of local labour control mechanisms in small- and medium-sized production units. As previously discussed, these mechanisms are based on pious and conservative values that have created social consent for the workers' dependence on craftsmen, masters or the state in workplaces, as part of the continuation of the *Akhi* institution, a former guild organisation in Central Anatolian provinces. Both the system of socialisation and the local labour control regimes have been huge barriers blocking the development of any democratic publicness that might have arisen during the 1990s in response to the region's process of industrialisation and proletarianisation. Instead, they have caused the growth of a new kind of publicness and/or urbanity in these provinces.

NOTES

1   According to its internet pages, MÜSİAD was established in 1990 by five industrialists and businessmen, and today has '3,150 senior members and 1,750 young members representing more than 15,000 companies that invest overall 5 billion US dollars per year, contribute 17 billion US Dollars to Turkey's export revenue as well as employing 1,200,000 personnel. MÜSİAD has 31 branch-offices across Turkey with 94 allied contact points in 44 countries'. TUSKON was established in 2005 as a successor to İŞHAD – the Association of Business Life (founded in 1993 as a businessmen's organization of the religious circle of Fettullah Gülen). It claims that the confederation represents around 34,000 entrepreneurs in Turkey (TUSKON 2012).

2   The third important Islamist businessmen's association is ASKON (Turkish abbreviation of *Anatolian Lions Businessmen's Association*) founded in 1998. The founders and members of this organisation remained loyal to Erbakan after the 28th of February process as a result of a political split between MÜSİAD and the Welfare Party, later the Virtue Party. It had 691 members in 2009 but this later dropped to 594 because of a further split within the Felicity Party (the successor of the Virtue Party) (ASKON 2009, 2012).

3   Faith of labour is a term which describes the political practices of Anatolian pious-conservative workers. In Turkish, the word '*Tevekkül*' means putting oneself in God's hands but after the struggle against destiny.

4   In this study, 30 participants were included: 15 workers from Konya Organized Industrial Zone, 10 employers, and 5 unemployed people with previous experience of work in this zone.

CHAPTER THIRTEEN

Neoliberal Hegemony and Grassroots Politics: The Islamist and Kurdish Movements

Erdem Yörük

The construction of neoliberal hegemony in Turkey has depended on, among other things, the direction and extent of struggles among contending political actors to mobilise the popular support of grassroots groups. During the neoliberal period starting in the 1980s, the Islamist and Kurdish political movements became the main political actors managing to mobilise grassroots opposition to the neoliberal project. Since the 1990s, an informal proletariat has replaced the formal proletariat as the centre of grassroots politics and the main hegemonic struggle has shifted into winning the support of the informal proletariat in the struggle to de/legitimise neoliberal policies. The informal proletariat of Turkey's slums has become the main object of political party competition, being a vast source of popular support for contending political parties as well as the main political threat to the state due to the influence of Islamist and Kurdish radical groups. In this chapter, I will describe the structural processes that have both enhanced and undermined the social power of the formal and informal proletariat, and discuss both the mainstream and radical political actors that have mobilised and contained this grassroots power. In particular, I will refer to neoliberal export-oriented policies, the internal displacement of Kurds and the ways in which the Islamist and Kurdish movements have mobilised the informal proletariat. From this analysis, I will argue that, during the 1990s, it was the Islamists who mobilised anti-neoliberal grievances, while in the 2000s, because of the de-radicalisation of the Islamist movement that enabled the imposition of neoliberal hegemony in Turkey, it was the radicalisation of the Kurdish movement that became the main force resisting this hegemonic establishment. That is, the left-leaning Kurdish movement has replaced Islamists as the main centre of anti-neoliberal mobilisation targeting the informal proletariat. I will argue that these political mobilisations have become central for the establishment of neoliberal hegemony so that Turkey's governing parties, particularly the Justice and Development Party (AKP), only gained hegemony to the extent that the informal proletariat gave consent to government policies and lost power to the extent that the informal proletariat was mobilised by the opposition.

Grassroots Politics in the Neoliberal Era

Over the last four decades, grassroots politics in Turkey has undergone a transformation: its centre has shifted from the formal proletariat to the informal proletariat and from non-Kurds to the Kurds. By grassroots politics, I refer to the totality of social movements, including protests, riots, strikes, boycotts, occupations, armed struggles etc. In differentiating between different segments of the proletariat, I adopt the distinction that Portes and Hoffman make between the formal and informal proletariat. The formal proletariat consists of workers in industry, services and agriculture, protected by existing labour laws and social security, while the informal proletariat comprises workers without social security and 'those workers who are not incorporated into fully commodified, legally regulated working relations, but survive at the margins through a wide variety of subsistence and semi-clandestine economic activities'. The informal proletariat is 'the sum of own account workers minus professionals and technicians, domestic servants, and paid and unpaid workers in microenterprises' (Portes and Hoffman 2003: 54).

As in many other developing countries, prior to the 1980s, the formal proletariat in Turkey gained substantial structural bargaining power as a result of import-substitutionist developmentalism. Globally, this structural bargaining power was translated into associational bargaining power through trade union militancy and the mobilisation of the socialist left (Wright 2000; Silver 2003). In Turkey, moreover, intense political competition between the centre-left and centre-right provided the formal proletariat with extensive electoral power.

On 12 September 1980, the Turkish army staged a coup d'état that swiftly suppressed the power of the formal proletariat, creating a grassroots political silence for almost a decade. The junta closed the parliament and banned all political parties, arrested their leaders, and invalidated the constitution. During the seven years of martial law, 650,000 people (1.5 per cent of the population) were arrested; 1,683,000 people were blacklisted; 7,000 people were accused of crimes punishable by capital punishment; the main leftist trade union, DİSK, was closed and its leaders imprisoned; 23,677 associations were closed; 30,000 people were dismissed for their political activism; 14,000 people were deprived of their citizenship and 388,000 people were deprived of their passports; 30,000 left the country as political refugees; 50 people were executed; 171 people were determined to have died because of torture and another 300 people died in suspicious ways; police operations started against every leftist organisation; and a total of 98,000 people were put on trial accused of being members of illegal organisations. As this list suggests, although the military claimed that the coup was an act against terror, in reality the coup itself initiated a period of state terror (Cumhuriyet 2000).

The 1980 coup d'état created the political conditions to implement neoliberal structural adjustment policies. These swiftly established a new economic and social atmosphere that gave an overt advantage to capital vis-à-vis labour. As Keyder describes it:

The share of wages and salaries in national income dropped from around 30 per cent in the 1970s to roughly 20 per cent in the 1980s. Wages in manufacturing had increased, more or less in line with productivity, over the three decades after 1950; by contrast, the level of real wages remained in 2000 what it had been in 1980, having dropped below that for long periods in between. Manufacturing employment in the public sector fell from 250,000 to 100,000 between 1980 and 2000, due to downsizing and privatisation. Workers in the state-owned industries had constituted the core of the labour movement of the 1960s and 70s – organised trade unionists who received relatively high wages and good benefits. With privatisation, deregulation and flexible employment, the advantages they had enjoyed in a protected manufacturing sector rapidly eroded. Subcontracting, the spread of smaller enterprises and piecework became standard practices; especially as the service sector gained ground, informal and diversified conditions of work increased. (Keyder 2004: 66)

The coup was a measure not only against the socialist threat to the regime, but also against any possible resistance by the formal proletariat to the intended neoliberal policies. After the coup, the government immediately started to implement the so-called 24 January Decision policies to initiate a neoliberal transition from import-substitutionism to export-oriented growth, facing minimum resistance from the workers and the left, whose political power had been destroyed by the coup. This resulted in 58 per cent declines in real wages and a 51 per cent decline in private sector wage share between 1976 and 1986. Although a high economic growth rate was achieved after the 1980s, it did not result in formal job creation, and structural unemployment has kept increasing during the last three decades following the coup (Adaman and Keyder 2006). It is not surprising, therefore, that Halit Narin, president of the Employers Union Confederation of Turkey, acclaimed the coup by saying 'until now, the workers have laughed, from now on, we will laugh'. He made a good prediction. One of the first actions of the junta was to freeze wages and outlaw strikes. In a series of similar interventions, the military junta and the following neoliberal government of the Motherland Party (ANAP) dismantled Turkey's import-substitutionist industrialism and politically oversaw a deterioration in income distribution. These neoliberal economic policies have encouraged, and depended largely on, temporary and flexible employment schemes, with sub-contracted and informal labour becoming the crux of a new accumulation regime in manufacturing and services, in both the private and public sectors. By the end of 1990, sub-contracted workers represented a quarter of the work force in Turkey (Cam 2002).

Rapid urbanisation after the 1990s also contributed to the demographic rise of the informal proletariat. Turkey's major cities have absorbed waves of mass migration from Turkey's peripheral regions since the 1950s. However, it is important to differentiate between migration before and after the 1990s in terms of the conditions that caused them. Up until the 1990s, population movements to urban areas were primarily driven by economic concerns, particularly by employment opportunities in big cities. In other words, this migration wave was mainly a pull migration (Taş and Lightfoot 2005). However, migration after the 1980s was mainly a push migration caused by a combination of factors. First, there was a more rapid mechanisation of agriculture than before and a parallel decline in agricultural subsidies. As a result, between 1980 and 1997, the number of tractors tripled in the country and the number of livestock fell from 49 million to 32 million in predominately Kurdish areas, where the effects of neoliberalism were felt the most. This created an exodus of rural workers from all regions of the country who moved to the urbanised western parts of Turkey with poor fortunes and prospects (Adaman and Keyder 2006; Cam 2002).

The second source of rapid migration during the neoliberal era was the internal displacement of Kurds during the 1990s. Under the Emergency State Rule imposed in the southeast, Turkish military forces evacuated and burned more than three thousand villages in Kurdish regions and initiated a policy of internal displacement to block growing rural Kurdish popular support for the Kurdistan's Workers' Party (PKK). Millions of Kurdish peasants were forced to migrate, initially to the cities within their region, but later on to western parts of the country (Yükseker and Kurban 2009; Ayata and Yükseker 2005). According to a recent survey conducted by the KONDA Research Institute, 4.8 per cent of Turkey's population, and 23 per cent of its Kurdish population, was internally displaced during the 1990s. Considering the population of Turkey during this period, this means that approximately 2.3 million people were displaced (KONDA 2011, based on author's own calculation). This internal displacement of Kurds has been one of the largest internal displacement operations in the world since 1980, comparable to similar actions in Nigeria, Somalia, Sudan, Zimbabwe and Colombia.

While the internal displacement of Kurds was intended as a military measure against the Kurdish insurgency, it had unintended consequences in terms of the social, political and economic processes that would take place during the following decade. First, internal displacement has radically changed the class structure of Turkey and the ethnic composition of the working class. Second, it has urbanised the Kurdish movement and, ironically, made İstanbul the city with the largest Kurdish population in the world, with three million Kurds out of a population of twelve million. Third, this has transformed the pace and content of Kurdish migration, making it quantitatively and qualitatively different to previous migration waves (Keyder and Yenal 2011).

The newcomers to Turkey's major cities were pushed from their lands because of political and military-security concerns instead of being pulled by the cities' social and economic opportunities, unlike earlier generations of migrants. The Kurds were the most disadvantaged because internal displacement created a condition of dispossession for them. They were forced to leave their villages, houses and arable land behind, relying mainly on kin and community networks to survive under extremely unfavourable conditions in the economic and spatial peripheries of the cities (Ayata and Yükseker 2005). Furthermore, this forced migration occurred in a neoliberal economic environment in which there was very limited creation of formal permanent jobs. Constituting a cheap labour source, without professional qualifications and ready to work in any job they could find, displaced Kurds became a major part of the informal labour market in cities like İstanbul. Due to neoliberal policies, including the privatisation of state-owned enterprises and the rise of outsourcing, formal employment has declined as a social reality as well as an expectation for the new migrants. In addition, improvements in automation, and new management techniques introduced to minimise labour costs, reduced formal employment still further in non-agricultural sectors. Even between 1986 and 1996 when the neoliberal project was again slowed, 300,000 workers lost their jobs in public enterprises (Cam 2002: 100). Since the 1990s, the globally competitive sectors of the Turkish economy, for example textiles and clothing, construction, shipbuilding and electrical equipment production, have depended largely on sub-contracting chains based in the informal economy, and on an informal working proletariat crowding the slum areas of major cities. Overall then, the rapid proletarianisation of the Kurds and the growth of the informal proletariat have turned out to be two converging processes: the war in the southeast has changed the ethnic composition of the working class in Turkey by proletarianising the Kurdish population, and Kurdicising the expanding informal proletariat. As a result, slum areas in Turkey have grown dramatically, while gaining a new ethnic characteristic (Yörük 2012).

Urban Kurds have been increasingly included in the labour force as part of the informal proletariat that has replaced the diminished formal proletariat, whose structural bargaining power had been too strong to allow the neoliberal project to be implemented. The weak bargaining power of Kurds has made them a cheap and flexible labour source for the new accumulation regime so it is likely that this labour supply has been an important factor contributing to the immense success that the Turkish economy has recently achieved in the global economy. Turkey has done much better than other comparable countries, becoming an emerging economy and a centre of capitalist production and accumulation. Turkish exports increased from $3 billion in 1980 to $13 billion in 1990, to $50 billion in 2000 and $113 billion in 2010. Gross National Income (GNI) increased from $93 billion in 1980 to $235 billion in 1990, and from $580 billion in 2000 to $1,103 billion in 2010. This corresponds to a GNI per capita of $2,120 in 1980, $4,350 in 1990, $9,120 in 2000 and $15,170 in 2010 (World Bank 2011). In 2008, Turkey was ranked third in the construction business world-wide, and fourth in textiles and clothing. The internal displacement of Kurds is the most extensive and rapid dispossession and proletarianisation operation in Turkish history, supplying an excess of cheap, informal, insecure, disposable and fully proletarianised labour. It has created the material conditions for successful neoliberal accumulation by providing the backbone of the informal labour market for textiles, construction, food production, dock work and seasonal agricultural production that has led economic growth in Turkey. In sum, the unmaking of Turkey's formal proletariat and its structural and associational bargaining power, and the subsequent making through internal displacement of a significantly ethnicised informal proletariat without a structural bargaining power have rendered the Turkish economy an important zone of flexible accumulation in the world economy.

The Islamist Movement and Party Politics

During the neoliberal era, Turkey's burgeoning informal proletariat has replaced the declining formal proletariat as the centre of grassroots politics, becoming the main source of political support and political threat for governments. This has occurred, not unintentionally, but through the mobilisation of radical political actors. The Islamist movement was the first large-scale actor to radicalise the informal proletariat during the 1990s. Following the military coup in 1980, the political stage was set for the Islamic movement to flourish and mobilise broader segments of the population. By the 1990s, Islamism had been organised into a mass political movement led by a radical Islamist party, the Welfare Party. The effects of neoliberal structural adjustment policies, rapid migration (especially of Kurds), and the Islamic Revolution in Iran, together enabled the Islamist movement, organised around the new Welfare Party, to appeal to the growing informal proletariat of the slums (Öniş 2007; Tuğal 2009).

During the 1990s, centre-left and centre-right parties, as well as the radical left, were no longer able to mobilise the grassroots, despite their grievances emanating out of neoliberalisation. This failure to provide any democratic or left-wing solution to the political and economic turmoil surrounding the subalterns of the country, led the centre-left Social Democratic People's Party (SHP) to return to the rigidly secularist position of the early Republican People's Party (CHP). Despite being partners in various coalition governments, social democrats did nothing but watch silently what was happening to the disadvantaged sectors of the society, whose support had brought SHP to power in the first place (Öniş 2007). The Kurds were being suppressed by state terror, Alevis were massacred in Sivas in 1993, and the formal proletariat was being destroyed by neoliberalisation. As these developments increased the distance between social democratic politicians and their proletarian supporters, the social democrats sought refuge in their original elitist and secularist Kemalist stance. Meanwhile, the socialist left, smashed by the military coup, was still too weak to mobilise the informal proletariat. Islamists were able to develop as the main political power garnering the political support of the growing informal proletariat, using a powerful ideological framework called the Just Order (*Adil Düzen*) system. The Welfare Party embraced the slums with a rhetoric that combined justice and tradition, supported largely by welfare populism as well as by increasing the quality of urban services, especially in the long-neglected slums. This growing political power of the Islamists was translated into electoral success as the Islamist share of the vote increased from 8 per cent in 1987 to 16 per cent in 1991 and 22 per cent in 1995, bringing the Welfare Party to national office. After less than a year in power, however, the Welfare Party's coalition government was overthrown by a military intervention in 1997. Islamic political mobilisation continued to increase until the end of 1990s, but has undergone a sharp decline during the 2000s.

The AKP, which originated from within the banned Welfare Party, but in a reformed and politically more organised form, came to national power with the 2002 elections (Özler and Sarkissian 2009). After the military intervention in 1997, the country had been ruled by a series of weak coalition governments, ending with a deep economic crisis in 2001 when the currency was devaluated by 40 per cent, the stock market collapsed and overnight interest rates climbed to 7,500 per cent in a couple of days. Foreign liquid capital was swiftly withdrawn, leaving behind a chain of debt, bankruptcy and unemployment. The devastating effects, both of the crisis itself and the recovery programme imposed on the vast majority of people, included rising poverty, unemployment and political grievances with the existing political parties of the 1990s. This created a unique opportunity for the neoliberal Islamist AKP government to establish a long-lasting hegemony.

The AKP embraced a neoliberal economic agenda with the help of Islamist political mobilisation. During its three terms in office, it has deregulated financial markets, accelerated privatisations and layoffs, limited agricultural subsidies and liquidated the welfare rights of private and public formal sector employees. Its main agenda has been to demolish economic statism so as to attract international capital, but also to weaken political secularism in order to gain the popular support of the Muslim masses. As the governing party throughout the 2000s, the AKP has successfully implemented a process that Tuğal (2009) has called a 'Passive Revolution'. That is, the AKP government has managed to contain the religious radicalism, anti-capitalism and anti-Americanism that were previously mobilised by the Islamic movement in the 1990s. Meanwhile, religious conservatism has diffused into wider areas of Turkish social life: Turkey has become a more religious country, but with less religious radicalism, which has enabled the diffusion of neoliberal capitalism with less friction. The AKP explicitly displayed its neoliberal tendencies, claiming that it would become similar to the WASPs (White Anglo Saxon Protestants) of the USA (Tuğal 2007b).

The AKP represents a coalition of Turkey's new export-oriented provincial bourgeoisie and liberal/conservative intellectuals, and claims to fill the centre-right position left empty over the 1990s. Tuğal's assessment of this process is that 'Resistance to neoliberalism has now been removed, and there is a broader acceptance of 'market realities' among the popular sectors. One reason for the change is that, for the first time in Turkish history, practicing Muslims are spearheading the liberalisation of the economy; it is their religious lifestyle that wins them mass consent' (2007: 22). The AKP has undoubtedly gained the support of a large number of people who were economically and socially hurt by the harsh economic crisis of 2001. In particular, the party won the consent of Turkey's poor informal proletariat for the rising neoliberal power of the emerging bourgeoisies. A juxtaposition of neoliberalism, populism, conservatism and, more recently, authoritarianism, has been the defining characteristic of the AKP's rule.

The Kurdish Movement

During the 2000s, in contrast to the AKP's containment of the Islamist political radicalism of the informal proletariat, Kurdish political parties have managed to radicalise the informal proletariat of the slums against the AKP policies. Since the early 1980s, the PKK has led a Kurdish uprising against the Turkish state. Kurds constitute 18 per cent of the current population in Turkey (KONDA 2011). This is not, however, the first such uprising, as there have been intermittent nationalist rebellions involving Kurds since the foundation of the republic in 1923, though the current unrest led by the PKK since the late 1980s, has been stronger than the many previous armed insurgencies. The PKK's original goal was to create an independent, socialist Kurdish state in Kurdistan, a geographical region comprising parts of southeastern Turkey, northeastern Iraq, northeastern Syria and northwestern Iran, where the Kurdish population constitutes the majority. After the mid-1990s, however, the objective shifted to the attainment of Kurdish cultural and identity rights, which had been fiercely denied by the Turkish state since the 1920s. During the 2000s, the main demand of the Kurdish movement has become the de-centralisation of state power and the establishment of regional governments in a system called 'Democratic Autonomy' to secure the rights of Turkey's minorities.

The PKK started its guerilla struggle against Turkish armed forces in predominantly Kurdish areas of the country in 1984. The popularity of the PKK among the Kurdish people, who were then mostly a peasant population, rapidly grew during the late 1980s, allowing the PKK to become capable of mobilising the Kurdish masses in the 1990s in huge numbers. In 1987, the Turkish government declared Emergency State Rule in southeastern provinces and set up the Special Governorship of Emergency Rule, which would remain in effect until 2002. This meant that, including the period of martial law between 1978 and 1987, Kurdish regions remained under extraordinary security measures for a total period of 24 years. Between 1989 and 1993, the PKK was able to mobilise hundreds of thousands of Kurds in both armed and civil disobedience, with almost every city in Kurdish regions simultaneously staging mass protests against the state. The rebellion in Nusaybin, a town close to the Syrian border, marked the beginning of this Serhildan, the Kurdish intifada, and riots spread to other cities in the southeast, such as Mardin, Batman, Diyarbakir, Siirt, Şanlıurfa and Şırnak, before affecting other cities like Bingöl, Bitlis, Hakkâri, Muş and Van, spread across Turkey's Kurdish southeast provinces. Such persistent popular unrest, and the accompanying escalation of guerilla warfare, made it clear that the Kurds had become a serious threat to the Turkish State, which was also facing another major grassroots challenge of labour unrest in western Turkey, known as the Spring Actions. Although this was a coincidence, because there was no significant ideological or organisational link connecting Kurdish unrest in eastern Turkey and labour unrest in western Turkey, this historical coincidence has nevertheless drawn the trajectories of the working class and Kurdish movements alongside one another consistently since the late 1990s.

The development of neoliberal policies has created handicapping conditions for the movement of the formal proletariat, with the rise of sub-contracting and informality making it ever more difficult to organise workers through unions. However, it has also signified a new zone of struggle that is more difficult for the state to control, namely the informal proletariat. During the late 1990s, the largely Kurdish informal proletariat of the slums became the embryo of a political threat for the state. The Kurdish informal proletariat gained its asso-ciational capacity through the emerging urban, legal left-wing Kurdish political parties. Not only these Kurdish political parties, but also the radical left, recognised this shift in the centre of Turkey's social movements towards the slums. Therefore, as in many other countries, the slums in Turkey have turned into places that are unpredictably prone to social explosions, in which Kurds have become one of the main centres of grassroots political activism. The first signs of this development came with the Gazi Neighborhood Riots in 1995 and the May 1 celebrations in 1996, both in İstanbul. At the Gazi events, state security forces lost control of the Gazi slum, while on 1 May 1996, slum-dwellers started a massive riot in İstanbul's centre. Thus, Turkey's informal proletarians became the subject of riots, as would be the case in many other countries in the following years.

Since the 1990s, the informal proletariat of the slums, and particularly the Kurdish poor, became the centre of grassroots politics in Turkey, providing both potential threats as well as potential bases of popular support for political parties. First, 30 years of Kurdish armed struggle, urbanisation, proletarianisation and impoverishment expanded the Kurdish political movement into the slum areas of Turkey's major cities. These urban Kurds became increasingly radicalised, staging massive protests and uprisings since the 1990s, in both the Kurdish southeast and western cities. This ethnic threat to the regime was also expressed as electoral competition. Since the 1990s, the Kurdish movement in Turkey has been organised through both illegal and legal wings, in a similar fashion to ETA-Herri Batasuna in Spain and the IRA-Sinn Féin in Northern Ireland. However, it has been necessary to regularly re-form Kurdish political parties as each of them has been banned by Turkey's Supreme Court. The latest of these Kurdish political parties is the Peace and Democracy Party (BDP), founded in 2008.

During the 2000s, the governing AKP has been competing intensively with these Kurdish parties across the predominantly Kurdish regions of Turkey as well as in the slum areas of metropolises. A KONDA survey showed that the AKP and the BDP are largely competing for the support of Turkey's lower classes, while the CHP gains its votes mainly from the middle classes and bourgeoisie. More specifically, of Turkey's poorest 20 per cent of the population, 44 per cent vote for the AKP, 11 per cent for Kurdish parties and only 6.8 per cent vote for the CHP. However, 14.7 per cent of those who voted for the current Kurdish party in the 2002 elections switched their votes to the AKP in 2007 (KONDA 2007). Kurdish party support is twice as high among the unemployed and those unable to work as its overall national vote, while Kurdish party support among Turkey's richest 20 per cent and the bourgeoisie is zero. For both the AKP and the BDP, there is also a negative correlation between income and support. The KONDA dataset shows that voting rates for the AKP were 4.22 per cent higher in rural areas than its national average. In three successive elections, the AKP has won support from the national electorate to win an absolute majority in parliament, while the BDP, the current Kurdish party, managed to gain 36 seats with 6 per cent of the vote in the 2011 elections, and to win control of 98 municipalities, mostly in Kurdish regions. In part, the achievements of the BDP resulted from the formation of a series of successful electoral alliances with the socialist left. Since the 2007 elections, these collective electoral campaigns have worked very well, both in Kurdish regions and in the poor slums of the metropolises. Most recently, such alliances culminated in the foundation of a new political party, the People's Democracy Party (HDP), which brings together the Kurds, the socialist left, religious and ethnic minorities, environmentalists, feminists and LGBTs.

The legal and illegal wings of the Kurdish movement, together with hundreds of NGOs, youth and women's organisations, as well as political organisations of the Kurdish diaspora in most European countries, have together managed to mobilise Kurds, both to provide electoral support and to instigate frequent uprisings in Turkey's urban areas. Since the late 1990s, uprisings, protests and police interventions have become constant features of the Kurdish-populated city slums, both in the Kurdish southeast and western regions. The BDP has risen to become the governing AKP's main radical political rival in both areas, especially as the ceasefire agreed between the PKK and the Turkish state since the early 2000s has improved its chances of success in democratic politics. This growing power of the Kurdish opposition has become the main challenge to the AKP's neoliberal hegemony. In sum, during the 2000s, the AKP has competed with the Kurdish parties to win the support of Turkey's Kurdish proletariat. While socialist Kurdish parties have partly replaced the radical Islamists of the 1990s in responding to the grievances against neoliberalism of the informal proletariat, the AKP has turned Islamism into a force for containing the political activism of the slums.

The AKP's response to this rising Kurdish power has been inconsistent and ambivalent. The party first gained the support of the Kurdish masses by promising to bring about a democratic solution to Turkey's Kurdish problem. However, this was followed by a period of repression during the mid-2000s. Later, between 2007 and 2009, the AKP introduced both a discourse and a policy of democratic relaxation regarding the identity rights of Kurds in Turkey through a programme called 'the Kurdish Overture', which included state TV broadcasting in Kurdish for the first time and the legalisation of teaching the Kurdish language. Since 2009, however, the AKP has launched increasing numbers of police operations targeting the BDP. For example, the police have arrested more than 7,000 members of the BDP since 2010 and the governing AKP has withdrawn its 'Kurdish Overture' policies. For example, in March 2012, the AKP outlawed the Kurdish *Newroz* (New Year) celebrations organised by the BDP. Despite strict security measures taken by the government, hundreds of thousands of Kurds gathered in Diyarbakır on *Newroz*, ignoring the government's demands, and indicating the extent to which the BDP is able to mobilise its Kurdish supporters. Indeed, recent coercive policies more generally have only resulted in increasing Kurdish popular support for the BDP, leaving Turkey's weak and over-numerous centre parties sidelined by a binary competition between the BDP and the AKP. For example, the most recent opinion polls indicate that the BDP support has increased to 8 per cent from 6.5 per cent in the June 2011 elections. In short, the BDP, as a credible representative of Kurds in Turkey, has increasingly managed to mobilise Kurdish slum populations, making it a serious competitor in these areas for the governing AKP.

In order to understand how the Kurdish movement has mobilised anti-hegemonic social forces against the neoliberal policies of the AKP, one needs to consider the politicised interaction between class and ethnicity in contemporary

Turkey. As explained above, a combination of internal displacement and neo-liberal agricultural policies has led to a rapid exodus of rural Kurds to Turkey's expanding major cities, causing a rapid proletarianisation of the Kurds. However, the radicalisation of the Kurds, as a threat to the neoliberal hegemony of the AKP, occurred primarily because of the radical political stance of the Kurdish movement. Over the last three decades, the Kurdish movement has remained essentially structured and organised on the basis of a left-wing ideology, and this leftist tradition has been responsible for current anti-capitalist mobilisation among the Kurds. The Democratic Autonomy project of the Kurdish movement has been explicitly described as an anti-capitalist project, and one of its main aims is to organise the people from below, through grassroots institutions like councils, cooperatives and people's assemblies. The Kurdish movement presents Democratic Autonomy as a system aimed at 'building an anti-monopolist, egalitarian and solidarity-based economic system in which everyone is self-employed, female labour participation is privileged, the main objective is not profit but use-value' (BIANET 2010).

This anti-capitalist stance of the Kurdish movement has transformed the electoral competition between the AKP and the BDP into a political competition over the AKP government's neoliberal policies. The AKP's hegemonic project is based on a discourse that refers to its recent unprecedented economic and political success, while the Kurdish movement's political strategy is based on breaching this discourse by illustrating the AKP's economic and political failings. The BDP has challenged the AKP policies on numerous occasions regarding the Kurdish issue, thereby undermining the popularity of the AKP among conservative Kurds. This is significant because the governing AKP has failed to fulfil its promise to resolve the Kurdish conflict, which has come to be seen as the most important issue in Turkey, thereby creating legitimacy problems for the AKP, not only among the Kurds but also among nationalist Turks. In short, the AKP has been unable to establish and maintain the image of being the party that finally brought political stability to Turkey. This failure has also damaged the international hegemony of the AKP in its pursuit of neo-Ottomanist foreign policy in that, being unable to resolve Turkey's domestic Kurdish issue makes it much more difficult for the AKP to convince others in the Middle East that Turkey can bring political stability to the region.

The BDP has also criticised the AKP's neoliberal policies by revealing the expansion of poverty that has afflicted not only the Kurds and Kurdish regions but also the urban slums of the country in general. This has created another breach in the AKP's discourse that its liberal economic policies would bring prosperity for all in Turkey. In addition, the BDP has been able to resist the AKP's attempts to render invisible the ethno-political aspects of the poverty of Kurds by pressuring poor Kurds to choose being poor over being Kurdish in order to qualify for social assistance. Against this, the BDP has highlighted the Kurdishness of poverty in Turkey, pointing to the overlap of class and ethnicity in the production of poverty. This has made social assistance a central arena of political struggle between the AKP and the Kurdish movement, and forced the AKP government to direct social assistance programmes specifically to the Kurdish minority in an effort to contain Kurdish unrest (Yörük 2012). This is something that the Kurdish movement has achieved through mass organising, most clearly seen by the *Newroz* rallies of 2012, when close to a million Kurds demonstrated despite heavy policy repression. Another indication was the hunger strikes of Kurdish political prisoners in the fall of 2012, which mobilised not only the Kurdish masses but also a wide spectrum of leftist opposition groups and resulted in a massive and broadly-based wave of political protest against the government. It thereby rendered the Kurdish movement the centre of opposition to AKP rule.

Conclusion

It has been commonly thought that, in the neoliberal era, grassroots politics is generally no longer a central force shaping politics and policies. The political right in Turkey has claimed this situation signals the end of anarchy, while the left has remained lost in deep nostalgia for the era when a powerful and militant proletariat was led by an influential socialist ideology. However, during the 1990s an informal proletariat, created through the implementation of neoliberal export-oriented policies, emerged as the new grassroots political actor. Under the influence of Islamist and Kurdish radical groups, this informal proletariat of the slums has become the main object of political party competition as it represents a vast source of both popular support and political threat to the Turkish state. Specifically, from the 1990s to the 2000s, the Kurdish movement in Turkey has become the epicentre of political opposition against successive AKP governments that have been implementing neoliberal policies. This has occurred as previously radical Islamists have themselves been absorbed into neoliberalism by the governing AKP, while urban Kurds have been mobilised into radicalism by left-wing Kurdish political parties. As Tuğal argues, the Islamist Welfare Party of the 1990s adopted the strategy of mobilising subaltern grievances resulting from neoliberalism among Turkey's informal proletariat towards Islamic radicalism in order to capture state power. As this strategy was ultimately unsuccessful, the Islamist AKP of the 2000s replaced this radicalising strategy with an alternative strategy of containing the grievances caused by neoliberalism through the application of political patronage in order to maintain state power. While this has allowed Turkey's Islamist movement to capture state power, it has come at the expense of the movement itself becoming de-radicalised and neoliberalised, allowing the Kurdish movement to become the main oppositional force in Turkey, radicalised and anti-neoliberal.

Structurally, the Kurdish war and mass internal displacement during the 1990s proletarianised the Kurds and Kurdicised Turkey's proletariat. This facilitated the almost unprecedented 'success' of neoliberal capitalist accumulation in Turkey by creating a huge supply of cheap and informal urban labour. To maintain its political power, the AKP has endeavoured, first, to win the popular support of the lower classes in Turkey in its competition with the CHP and the military and, second, to contain the BDP and the political instability resulting from the pauperisation of Kurds. As a result, the Kurdish movement has emerged as the most significant competitor to the AKP in slum areas, which has impeded the AKP's capacity to win the support of the informal proletariat for its neoliberal agenda. Beyond this threat to the AKP's neoliberal hegemony, the Kurdish movement's search for a strategic alliance with the Turkish radical left, as well as its demand for democratic autonomy for the Kurds, has created the potential for furthering the anti-capitalist mobilisation of the slums. During the 1990s, the Islamists had been more radical and successfully responded to the grievances of the informal proletariat against neoliberal developments but, by the 2000s, they had become neoliberal themselves and merely sought to contain those same proletarian grievances, which allowed a succession of Kurdish parties to emerge as the main political subject mobilising the slums against the neoliberal economic and political hegemony. Nevertheless, because the current Kurdish party and its radical leftist allies are much weaker than the governing AKP, containment of proletarian grievances has taken precedence over mobilisation, which explains the relatively smooth path to neoliberal hegemony that Turkey has followed during the 2000s.

A Postscript: #resistturkey

İsmet Akça, Ahmet Bekmen and Barış Alp Özden

'It's as if revolution winked at us.'
(a placard in the Gezi Park)

Perhaps the greatest misfortune that can befall a new book is a simultaneous explosive and radical transformation related to its subject matter. But this can be a fortuitous development as well. Comforting us as editors is that our particular misfortune is directly connected with one of the largest and most widespread mass revolts in the history of Turkey, and that it provides a new and unexpected perspective on the analyses presented in this volume. In the context of the urban transformation of Taksim square in İstanbul, one of the most significant urban political spaces in Turkey, a group of activists resisted the uprooting of trees in Taksim's Gezi Park through pacifist methods. This resistance was met by brutal police violence that led to the kind of mass mobilisation and protest unprecedented in the history of modern Turkey. Over the course of roughly three weeks, tens of thousands of people poured onto Taksim square, adamantly resisting police violence, and transforming both park and square into a public space inaccessible to state authorities for two weeks. This development also resulted in mass marches in various neighbourhoods of İstanbul and many other cities, especially in other large cities like Ankara and İzmir. After a brutal police attack aimed at retaking the square and the park, the protesters continued to gather by holding daily forums in other parks all around İstanbul. These voices from the street were generally calling for liberty against oppression, targeting the ruling AKP, particularly the Prime Minister, Recep Tayyip Erdoğan.

Background

So how did the AKP, which had established a unique hegemony in the history of Turkey, especially with respect to the post-1980 neoliberal era, become the target of such mass protests? It was, of course, not just due to a few trees. Rather, the felling of a few trees in Gezi Park was the spark that ignited a long-standing social reaction against the AKP's neoliberal, authoritarian and conservative populism, analysed by İsmet Akça in this volume. The politics of neoliberalism, particularly its attempt to exclude dominated social classes and groups from the political space, both locally and globally, and its depoliticisation of the masses, have been articulated to the AKP's rightist-populist politics based on a majoritarian conception of national will. This combination gave rise to an authoritarianism that has blocked alternative and dissident voices from politicising their causes. This authoritarian aspect of the AKP populism, which began to become more evident after the 2007 elections, became completely determining in the wake of the 2011 elections. In 2007, the AKP successfully faced down the military-centred secularist socio-political bloc's challenge to Abdullah Gül's presidential candidacy by taking the issue to a general election. This allowed the government to strengthen its hold and impose its hegemony, already established in social and political spaces, at state level. The government moved beyond its previous 'war of position' to begin waging a 'war of manoeuvre' against the Kemalist military and civil bureaucracy, defined by the AKP populism as the true power bloc of the country. After 2007, this power bloc was expelled from the last citadels of the state over which it had held control: the Presidency, higher judicial bodies, the Council of Higher Education (YÖK) and the military. During this process, especially through the referendum of 12 September 2010 regarding constitutional amendments and in the 2011 elections, the AKP continued to implement its political strategy of widening its hegemony over those masses not favouring the party, particularly through a promise of democratisation. Thus, the 2010 referendum was politically framed as 'the struggle of the democratic bloc against the bureaucratic tutelage regime'. The use of such a political framing during the referendum was also a hegemonic move by the AKP to reverse the effects of the 2009 local elections, when it lost votes for the first time as a result of the repercussions of the 2008 economic crisis and the KCK (Kurdistan Communities' Union) trials, whose real aim was to weaken the Kurdish movement.

The AKP's authoritarian populism has a double nature. On the one hand, it recognises sociological differences but, on the other hand, it is, as it were, allergic to their politicisation. Accordingly, whenever any kind of social and political dissidence raises its voice, especially when street politics comes into play, it attempts to crush it through its newly authoritarian state power. At the centre of this stands the trinity of the police, the judiciary and the media, combining under the AKP's strategy of labeling any kind of oppositional politicisation as 'terror'. After its victory in the 2011 elections, the AKP set about constructing a new Turkey in its own image in a fashion that was increasingly indifferent and inconsiderate of oppositional groups. It introduced a kind of bio-politics distinguished by its articulation of neoliberalism and religious conservatism, including the increasing control of social life by means of a myriad of policies imposed in authoritarian ways. These included the following: significant restrictions on the right to abortion; pro-natalist promotion of families having at least three children; limitations imposed on the sale and consumption of alcohol; national education reforms aimed at producing the labour force needed by neoliberal capitalism and the formation of a conservative life world; the clear announcement of the target of raising a religious generation; the placement of unqualified cadres within the institution (ÖSYM) responsible for nation-wide school exams that led to repeated cases of exam fraud; severe pressure on the media, including the dismissal and/or arrest of dissident journalists; the proliferation of unlawful eavesdropping and other privacy violations, especially in political trials; various unwarranted interventions in cultural and artistic fields such as the aggressive criticisms directed toward state theatres, the demolition of a controversial sculpture in Kars over nationalist concerns; numerous ideologically inspired urban renewal schemes, such as the transformation of the historical Emek movie theatre in Taksim into a shopping mall, the decision to demolish the Atatürk Cultural Center in Taksim square, the conversion of the historic Haydarpaşa railway terminus; and the conversion of city centres into fields of rent and capital accumulation, such as the construction of the third bridge over the Bosphorus. All these actions have reinforced the view of a significant section of society that the AKP does not recognise any other will than its own, that it does not listen to others, and that it has an oppressive, patronising understanding of administration. In addition, due to the AKP's rapid positioning of its own cadres in public offices, many more people have begun to experience the coerciveness of this style of administration, not only as a potential risk but as a concrete reality in their everyday, professional and social lives.

It was probably Turkey's Alevis who first felt this oppressive atmosphere most extremely when the AKP government's foreign policy on Syria led to rising domestic tensions, especially in Hatay, a border province between Turkey and Syria with a significant Alevi population. As well as hosting Syrian refugees, the city became almost a base for Sunni militias fighting against Assad's Alevi dominated regime. Rising daily tensions led to a rapid increase in discomfort and unease among Hatay's Alevis. The situation became particularly serious in Reyhanlı, a district of Hatay province, when 53 people were killed in a bomb attack on 11 May 2013. Since the dead were all Sunnis, the AKP did not hesitate to utilise this deadly event to sharpen its aggressive policy towards the Syrian regime. Soon after, despite the intense polarisation due to the Reyhanlı attack, the AKP went ahead with its decision to name the much-debated third bridge over the Bosphorus after one of the Ottoman sultans, Yavuz Sultan Selim, who was associated with massacring Alevis during his reign. Thus, the AKP's foreign and domestic policy preferences both strengthened existing perceptions that the AKP was following a divisive, Sunni-centred line of policy.

The Nature of the Revolt and the Revolters

While the root of the revolt that started in Gezi Park concerns more than just a few trees, it is equally true that the increasing number of activities and protests about ecology and urban transformation paved the way for the wider revolt. There seems to have been an accumulation of silent dissent from a range of social movements ranging from struggles against nuclear, hydroelectric and thermal power plants to struggles against urban transformation and infrastructure projects related to mineral exploration and the construction of highways that destroy valued seaside locations. When capital aimed to destroy the Gezi Park, located at the centre of İstanbul, it released a critical mass of political energy beyond the sphere of influence of separate movements based on ecology and urban dissidence. As the company undertaking the Taksim Pedestrianisation Project began to demolish the park, activists from the ecology and urban movements bravely stood in front of the bulldozers, remaining in the park for days in spite of attacks and other harassment by the police. This resolute resistance led many different groups of people to pour into the Gezi Park, from feminists to LGBT people and dissident students, all of whom have experienced the steady enclosure and commodification of public spaces.

However, the factor that channelled the masses into frantic street fights between 31 May and 1 June was, without doubt, the police's own violence against the relatively small number of people who had pitched tents in order to guard the whole park. Their stubborn resistance through 31 May in the face of the violence committed by the police infuriated many people, instantly turning this occurrence into an 'event' *à la Badiou*. A mass of young people, who have grown up under the AKP government, presumably identifying all the authoritarian practices they face in their daily lives with the figure of Erdoğan, hit the streets, grasping within three to four hours most of the specifics of street warfare as could be seen in their rapid construction of barricades without precedent in the history of İstanbul. This insurrection confounded the police, and constituted a heterogeneous body that cannot be contained within the category of 'middle class'. It appears that the widening demands of the Gezi Park movement, from urban concerns to anti-authoritarianism and demands for freedom and democracy, encouraged the determined and militant cooperation and solidarity of many social sectors. These included people who would not otherwise have ever taken to the streets for political reasons, politically minded people who had long since abandoned their hopes in politically active groups. As mentioned earlier, the AKP's authoritarianism seems to have reached such a suffocating point in practice that even some of the children of İstanbul's bourgeoisie saw no harm in standing together at the same barricades with militants from leftist organisations whose names they could not even properly pronounce.

Despite this remarkable diversity, those participating in the revolt were mostly categorised by the mainstream media as 'middle class', and certainly various observations and surveys hastily conducted during the events made it easy to select such a description. However, the problem lay not in these raw observations, but in the veiling function of the category itself. In particular, 'open-minded' liberal analysts appearing in the mainstream media labelled the revolters 'Generation Y', immediately highlighting the new individualist philosophy and lifestyle habits of this generation that supposedly made them opposed to all kinds of authoritarianism. However, it is very difficult to reduce the revolt to the immediate economic position or demands of any social class or group. The motivation of the protesters was not primarily economic, unlike the protests in the USA, Spain, Israel and Greece. Whilst it can be said that a significant portion of those taking to the streets were young professionals, or those trying to make a step into that world, one should also add that these people also felt the specific troubles of this mode of life and work. That is, young people and their concerns are once again becoming prominent within the new sociological conditions of neoliberalism. In Europe and the USA, it was unemployed youth, lacking much hope in the future, who first hit the streets in the wake of the crisis of global capitalism. We also saw that this mass, whose lives oscillate between being a student and being an unemployed and/or a flexible/freelance worker, were a key force in the revolt in Turkey. As precariousness passes from being a legal status denoting a specific mode of employment to an intense description of the social modes of life of the masses, social unease also increases. As happened in the Gezi revolt, this situation can blur the classical distinction between political and economic demands, increasing the permeability between them. It would be well-advised now to keep an eye on Turkey without forgetting this transitivity. The evolution of the political consciousness of this generation, constantly facing state violence, and the possible attainment of a political answer is an open and critical question.

Among these masses, even those fortunate enough to have found white-collar jobs cannot escape being crushed and exposed to erosion of their character under Turkey's new, increasingly severe working regime. We know that late neoliberalism does not promise these groups the opportunities to 'slip through the net' formerly presented by early neoliberalism. Instead, this social sector is now being dominated by a condition in which opportunities for employment in the office and service sectors are undergoing a growing proletarianisation. While these developments could have been enough to provoke street protests, it is also likely that another specific factor underlay the actions of this sector. That is, the AKP has pursued a strategy of placing its own cadres within public offices since coming to power in 2002, which has had a critical effect on the daily lives of civil servants working in state schools, hospitals and other state offices. Therefore, the Gezi Park revolt raised critical questions for people who, day after day, have to deal and struggle with these 'mini Erdoğans'. Consequently, their feeling was one of 'If we lose, they will eliminate us'. Moreover, this 'threat/risk perception' is not just limited to the public sector. For example, there is evidence that the rapidly increasing market share of Islamist-conservative enterprises among private hospitals and education institutions has reached a level where secularly inclined workers in these sectors feel a sense of professional risk.

During the revolt, professionals from these sectors did not abandon their normal working hours, as could be seen from the way those that were able to participate in daytime clashes continuously looked at their watches, waiting for this period to end and the after-work participation of these professionals. It would not be an exaggeration to say that, after their harsh, stultifying and unsatisfying daytime work experiences, these professionals experienced the street protests and other 'subversive' practices as moments of emancipation. Their avoidance of radicalisation, such as missing working time, on the one hand, and their articulation into street radicalism after work ('Clark Kent in the morning, Superman in the evening' as they say), revealed, so to speak, the class formation of these sections. The working class, classically defined as blue-collar workers, did not come to the forefront in the course of the revolt. M. Görkem Doğan and Serkan Öngel's articles in this book contain fundamental insights explaining this situation. This revolt had repercussions in various localities in İstanbul. However, apart from the Gazi and Nurtepe neighbourhoods, which are largely populated by Alevis and politically dominated by certain leftist organisations, it either had no following or just made a minimal appearance in those neighbourhoods predominantly populated by poor labourers. That is, the power of the revolt was insufficient to dislocate the Islamic-conservative structure prevailing in such places. With regard to the revolt and the new political conditions, this situation represents the rigid side of reality.

The Political and Organisational Structure of the Revolt

When the Gezi resistance spontaneously broke out, the organised labour movement and the left were in a 30-year long period of defeat and isolation that has become more evident under the AKP government. As pointed out in the various chapters in this book, the trade union movement was far from grasping and organising new labour struggles; instead, just trying to protect its narrowed membership base. Except for the Freedom and Solidarity Party's (ÖDP) experience of attempting to construct a unified leftist party in the mid-1990s, the socialist left has lacked the political ability and organisational flexibility to embrace both the important struggles of the last ten years with their highly fragmented structure, such as ecological and urban movements, and the social dynamic produced by the anti-authoritarian indignation that has built up among the youth.

Taksim square has symbolic importance for Turkey's labour movement because many militants were killed there by the gladio organisation during the May 1 celebrations of 1977. Thus, the square is not only the main commercial, cultural and touristic centre of İstanbul, it is also the most important political centre for social opposition. Nevertheless, trade unions have failed to intervene over urban transformation projects recently carried out in Taksim. While they have insisted on celebrating May 1 celebrations in Taksim square because it is profoundly important in the history of social struggles in Turkey, they have neither opposed the urban transformation projects that would destroy the square as a public space and gentrify neighbouring Tarlabaşı, densely populated by Kurds and Romany, nor even got involved in the struggles against the Emek movie theatre's replacement by a shopping mall. They also failed to recognise the dynamic created by the crowds beginning to pour into the park in the face of harsh police violence from the first days of the Gezi resistance. Furthermore, organisationally speaking, trade unions were again absent when hundreds of thousands of people ignored the police and began to pitch tents in the park on June 1; they only managed to set up their own tents and booths after some days had passed. Only KESK, the most militant trade union confederation for public workers, called a strike, on June 4–5. Public workers, whose wages have been reduced during the AKP government and who were already uneasy at the government's aggressive strategy to insert its own cadres into public offices, already supported the resistance individually. However, KESK includes only 10 per cent of public workers, so its strike was not able to seriously hinder the functioning of state institutions. Nevertheless, thirty thousand public workers marched in Taksim. The greater meaning of the strike was the fact that it was the first politically motivated strike since 12 September 1980. Immediately after the evacuation of Gezi Park by the police, both KESK and DİSK called for a general strike on June 17. However, although this general strike increased public interest, the lack of strikers in the streets once again showed that trade unions are still not strong or ready enough to accommodate the social dynamics represented by the Gezi Park revolt.

Unlike trade unions, the organised left joined the Gezi revolt early. However, its long-standing fragmented structure and narrowed social base disrupted its ability to coordinate the movement and give it strategic vision. Faced by a leaderless young generation involved in politics for the first time in their life, the left could not generally know what to do with this revolt of the people. Some political organisations viewed the revolt as a transitory social upheaval and, in view of their own organisational interests, used it to get new members, as is usual on the Turkish left. Meanwhile, some other leftist organisations, realising that they did not have the capacity to lead the movement, virtually hid themselves, waiting for politics to return to its routine flow. Nevertheless, the youth, and leftist militants from all generations, played important roles during every stage of the protest, from clashing with the police through to providing logistics during the occupation of the park to preventing conflicts between groups. Overall, however, very few leftist organisations opened themselves to learn from the new grassroots movements or to interact with the energy of the people.

The most salient consequence of this handicap was the inability to develop flexible and democratic decision mechanisms that could have enlarged the social base of the movement once the park occupation started and rapidly generated tactics to fight the government's moves to taint the movement and decrease its legitimacy. Taksim Solidarity, a platform composed of professional chambers, trade unions and political organisations that led the movement from its beginning, did not open itself up to develop a more democratic and representative decision-making mechanism in the square or the park. The inability to give a more democratic form to Taksim Solidarity not only restricted its capacity for action but also amplified the disconnection between the institutions from which it was composed and 'independent' young people mobilised by the revolt, who were of course the original agents of the movement. At least (unlike as, for example, occasionally happened in the Brazilian revolt) protestors did not react against the left. Rather, with its slogans, flags and symbols, the socialist left was still the most visible political line in the field.

As Güven Gürkan Öztan shows in detail in his chapter, *ulusalcı* (the Kemalists' version of the term nationalist) political organisations reflecting the identity-based reaction of the republican-secular middle classes against the AKP government's threat to their own lifestyle collectively overcame their sense of intimidation and ineffectiveness arising from the Ergenekon and related trials. Such *ulusalcı* organisations that appeared at the protests included the Workers Party (İP), whose leading members had mostly been arrested during the Ergenekon investigation, the Turkey Youth Union (TGB) associated with this party, the Turkish Left (Türk Solu) group, which does not even attempt to hide its racism and anti-Kurdism, and various fascist groups. Within the context of the Gezi revolt, as is the case in all great and spontaneous rebellions, different political movements strove to give it a meaning appropriate to their own agenda. Especially outside the major cities, in Anatolian cities where the left's sphere of influence is very limited, *ulusalcı* groups succeeded in capturing the leadership of the movement, giving it an anti–government and nationalist rather than anti–authoritarian meaning. The clarity of the political messages of these groups also allowed them to influence secularly sensitive CHP voters. However, in major cities, such as İstanbul, where the revolt was much more widespread and the sociological base of the movement was more diverse, *ulusalcı* organisations could not respond to the flexible needs of the process. While they were more proficient early on in infusing their own slogans into the mouths of the masses, they withdrew in the later days of the revolt. Likewise, the CHP, the main opposition party, swiftly lost its previous relative visibility and could not overcome its proverbial inertia. Apart from some limited efforts by parliamentarians described within the party as the 'left wing' and the mobilisation of their own resources in support of the Gezi Park resistance by some CHP municipalities, the CHP was inert, merely hoping to benefit from the protests in upcoming elections.

Undoubtedly, the political group that was most confused by the Gezi revolt was the Kurdish movement. As a matter of fact, Kurds and especially young Kurds participated early on in the clashes against the police. They had been exposed to state violence for many years, coercively displaced by the state, and become the prime victims of urban transformation projects intensified by the AKP in western cities. However, BDP, the legal wing of the Kurdish movement, made a great effort to hide itself in the first days. One factor underpinning the hesitance of the Kurdish movement in the first days was the attempt by Turkish nationalists to dominate the revolt. This brought forth an understandable emotional resistance among the Kurdish movement's base against the revolt. However, the more important factor was that the Kurdish movement was worried about possible negative effects of the revolt on resolving the Kurdish question. The Gezi revolters directly opposed the AKP government, which was the sole addressee of the Kurdish movement during the on-going negotiations. However, following celebratory statements about the resistance from both Abdullah Öcalan and the KCK, the Kurdish movement mostly modified its view on the Gezi resistance, beginning to play an active role with flags and banners. Ironically, brutal police violence, the exclusionary language of the government, and its moves to divide the movement from within all created a much more unified sense of belonging among the masses, leading to an increase in communication between Kurds and other resisters. This intimacy, enabled by spending days and weeks in a common space, formed, perhaps for the first time, an environment that allowed Kurdish and Turkish youth to overcome their biases so as to discuss the conditions necessary for peaceful co-existence in the country.

Another crucial component of the Gezi resistance was football fans. In the neoliberal era opened up by the 12 September 1980 coup, not only political belonging but also all kinds of collectivisms underwent a process of rapid corrosion, with the whole society experiencing an all-encompassing atomisation. However, football fans sustained a strong sense of solidarity and common fate. In recent years, these groups have often experienced police violence both in stadiums and in the neighbourhoods of the teams they support. Therefore, in a climate where Turkey's traditionally close relationship between sports and politics had become much more intricate, they became quickly politicised. Recent tensions between the administration of Fenerbahçe, one of the biggest sports clubs in Turkey, and the Gülen community, one of the strongest supporters of the AKP government, initiated a process that led to the arrest and imprisonment of the club's president, Aziz Yıldırım. Subsequent violent street clashes between Fenerbahçe fans and police forces under the influence of the Gülen community were, so to say, a rehearsal for the Gezi revolt. On 1 May 2013, following the government's decision to ban football fans from using Taksim for celebrations, the Beşiktaş neighbourhood witnessed severe clashes between police and militants, with Çarşı, the fan group of Beşiktaş sports club, on the frontline. Çarşı supported the Gezi resistance from the very beginning, thereby gaining outstanding prestige, being perceived virtually as the 'guerillas' of the resistance. Other fan groups followed in their footsteps, not only in İstanbul, but also in other major cities like Ankara and İzmir, where the resistance found a vivid following, with football supporters' groups taking to the streets in an organised manner. Their support for the resistance was of paramount importance in significantly contributing to a country-wide legitimacy. From songs to graffiti and visual materials, they also played a decisive role in the protests' explosion of cultural creativity.

Finally, from the viewpoint of the AKP and its allies, the most infuriating group that took part in the Gezi resistance was undoubtedly the anti-capitalist Muslims. Though few in number, this group successfully destabilised the government's side with its discourse and actions 'from within'. In particular, the huge *iftars* (the meal eaten by Muslims after sunset during Ramadan to end the daily fasting) organised by this group on the pavement of İstiklal Street while blockaded the police barricades in opposition to the 'official *iftars*' organised by İstanbul's AKP municipality were one of the most emotionally moving events of the whole resistance.

The Situation on the AKP Side

How did the AKP, which has established such an expanded hegemony but which has also become intolerant of any kind of social or political dissidence at street level, react to these events, and how will this reaction affect itself? From the start, the government consistently resorted to the method that it knows best: suppression of resistance by the police, culminating in the killings of five young people. In addition, from the outset, it relied on the single-handed representation of the party under Erdoğan's figure, with his attempts to respond to the mass mobilisation by launching into personal scolding. Thus, during the revolt, Erdoğan's personal authoritarian qualities, expressed through his humiliating, arrogant and narcissistic leadership became clear to almost everyone, even to his supporters. One of the clearest example of these scornful qualities was a comment he made about both the 1 May 2013 protests and the Gezi Park revolt: 'When did the feet become the head?' Instead of limiting the protests, however, this response encouraged their growth. Even the terms used by Erdoğan to humiliate the revolters, such as *çapulcu* (marauders, looters), was reappropriated by the protestors and turned into a positive term of self-identification.

In accordance with the AKP's populist political strategy, this latest example of social dissidence was labelled as either the voice of the 'pro-tutelage bloc' or of 'marginal, terrorist, illegal organisations'. That is, the involvement of 'naive, well-intentioned citizens' was ignored and depoliticised. In short, the AKP asserted that the protests essentially represented the voice of the so-called *ulusalcı* or pro-coup 'power bloc', operating against the national will. However, in line with right-wing populist political language, 'national will' was equated with the will of the majority, which was taken to mean the will of the government, the AKP and, ultimately, its leader. The CHP, the main opposition party, was presented by the AKP as the political representative of the *ulusalcı*, pro-tutelage bloc, while the socialist left, the eternal foe of the Turkish establishment, became natural targets. In addition, the AKP blended typical nationalistic, statist arguments that 'external forces are concocting games to destabilise Turkey' with a key Islamist argument (one which, incidentally, the AKP had rarely resorted to until now) that national and international monopolistic capital ('the interest rate lobby') was directing the Gezi resistance from behind the scenes. Even the Brazilian uprising was soon linked to this international conspiracy, when the government claimed that it had 'deep suspicions' that the uprisings had occurred simultaneously in both countries, when they had recently broken off IMF negotiations. Soon after, the military coup in Egypt was added to this conspiracy scenario as well. The crucial field in which these tactics played out was the domestic media. At times this reached levels of absurdity, as when CNN International was delivering a live report from Taksim while its affiliate, CNN Türk, was broadcasting a documentary about penguins. This naturally became one of the revolters' many humorous catchphrases, with these domestic media institutions that intentionally ignored the revolt being referred to as the 'Penguin media'. In parallel with Erdoğan's inflexible attitude, the pro-AKP media, discussed extensively in Uraz Aydın's chapter, started a defamatory campaign that included targeting various prominent figures within the rebellion.

Unfortunately for the government, the sociological characteristics of the protesters, the nature of their demands and the style of their organisation and actions prevented the AKP's rightist populist language being fully effective. When this discourse failed to weaken the resistance, the government looked for other strategies, such as that put forward by various AKP figures. Thus, towards the end of the first week of protests, Erdoğan left the country to visit Tunisia and Egypt, allowing acting Prime Minister Bülent Arınç and President Abdullah Gül space to try and get the situation under control by adopting relatively moderate language. However, all their efforts came to naught when Erdoğan returned to continue and even intensify his ferocious rhetoric. While it seems that for now such intra-AKP tensions are being covered up, in order to suppress the revolt above everything else, given that several elections are scheduled to take place within the next two years, it seems highly probable that they will resurface.

It appears that the long-term effect of the country-wide protests on the AKP will be for it to abandon its hegemonic style of politics. Thus, we can see that the coming period will be characterised by a non-hegemonic style of politics oriented towards consolidating its own mass of voters. In fact, due to the recent developments, not only at the national level, but also at international and intra-party levels, the AKP's capacity for hegemony has certainly been reduced. For sure, one of the most crucial pillars of the AKP's hegemony has been the international field. However, criticisims, by the USA and the EU, of the AKP's response to the recent protests, and the AKP's fierce rejection of these criticisms suggest its sphere of influence at the international level may decrease. This has caused serious damage to the AKP's ambition, which is of great importance for its international hegemonic project, to play a sub-imperial role in the Middle East by demonstrating how to be a neoliberal, Islamic and democratic country. In this sense, the most tragicomic event was perhaps the warning issued by the Syrian government advising its citizens not to go to Turkey because of the deterioration in the security situation. Meanwhile, the recent military coup in Egypt following a huge mass mobilisation, has almost paralysed the AKP's regional policy, which was based on a projected alliance between Qatar and Turkey under AKP rule, Egypt under Muslim Brotherhood rule, and Syria under the expected rule of an Islamist coalition dominated by the Syrian Muslim Brotherhood. However, as of today, the process has become uncontrollable in Syria, the replacement of Qatar's Emir by his own son has increased uncertainty about Qatar's regional policy in the near future, and the military coup in Egypt against Muslim Brotherhood rule all suggest that the AKP should reconsider its regional policy. Moreover, neither the USA, the EU nor other Arab countries in the Middle East reacted negatively to the Egyptian military's intervention, leading Erdoğan to fiercely criticise especially those Western countries that hesitated even to describe the intervention as a military coup d'état. Even though the Turkish army, unlike its Egyptian equivalent, is no longer powerful enough to carry out a military coup, the AKP and its allies still use the threat of a possible military coup in Turkey to legitimise and consolidate their rule. This perhaps explains why the AKP and its allies took such offence at the Western world's silence about the Egyptian military coup.

At the same time, the AKP tried to utilise the case of Egypt to suggest that the Gezi revolt was an attempted coup d'état in civilian disguise. However, this time, this message failed to resonate beyond the 'natural boundaries' of the AKP's base because of the Gezi revolt effect. In fact, the AKP's mobilisation of its own base in the face of the protests against itself clearly signalled that its hegemonic style of politics was damaged or at least that it is starting to move away from this style. As soon as he returned to the country from Tunisia and Egypt, Erdoğan set about mobilising his '50 per cent' of the voters, whom he claimed he could hardly keep from coming onto the streets as well, through public meetings in various cities, especially İstanbul and Ankara. These meetings are sufficient proof that he has already started his election campaign for the local elections in the spring of 2014 and the later presidential election. One can clearly see that Erdoğan's political rhetoric at these meetings is nothing like the hegemonic language needed to win the hearts and minds of non-AKP voters, but is rather close to a language that declares all of them political enemies. Intra-party tensions, which find their symptomatic expression in Erdoğan's dominant personality, and which are founded on his control of political and economic resources, have started to become evident. However, the most pivotal tension is between the Gülen community and Erdoğan himself. We saw this tension during the Gezi protests in the community's openly expressed opposition to Erdoğan's presidential ambitions. The most striking example of this friction was Gülen's statements supporting more hegemonic and also, of course, authoritarian politics by criticising the use of physical force against the protesters in contrast to talking about winning over the hearts and minds of dissenters. Because both the party and the community viewed the rise of street politics and mass mobilisation as threatening, their tensions have had to be left unresolved for quite a while, but the struggle at those levels which constitute the real source of the conflict is still going on. The judiciary–police–media trinity, that forms the mainstay of the new authoritarian state apparatus constructed during the AKP era, is for the most part under the control of the Gülen community, which seriously concerns the AKP, particularly Erdoğan. The most critical point of tension, however, has an earlier origin, when the National Intelligence Organisation (MİT) Undersecretary, who had been appointed by the Prime Minister, was called to testify by the specially authorised prosecutor on charges of conducting terrorist activities because he was negotiating with the PKK. Taking into account recent reports that the AKP now wishes to remove Gülenist appointees from high-level bureaucratic positions, especially in the police and the judiciary, it seems that divisions will widen and continue as a sort of power struggle. This will unmistakably impair the hegemonic capacity of the party.

The AKP administration is now faced with a very difficult and delicate situation. Having already lost prestige both domestically and internationally due to its policy towards Syria and the outburst of the Gezi uprising, the government instantly withdrew to a defensive position. Erdoğan's inflexible attitude is an attempt at preserving his own electoral support and one should not assume that he will fail in this. While the government appeared confused in the first days of the Gezi revolt, it rapidly consolidated its stance through Erdoğan's unrelenting attitude. In the next two years, Turkey will have, in turn, local, presidential and general elections. In addition, the macro agenda will also be shaped by fundamental and inextricably interconnected issues, particularly the continued moves to resolve the Kurdish question, national and international tensions that are bound to appear because of the new Middle East policy based on Syria, and the ongoing process of drawing up a new constitution. Moreover, new policies announced by the US Federal Reserve seem to put at risk the hot money inflows necessary to sustain Turkey's economic growth. Here, the Gezi revolt has seriously transformed the nature of the wider political geography within which all these processes will take shape, making the current situation, which has already become very difficult for the AKP to control, thoroughly ambiguous and uncertain. In this regard, the next critical moment that we might anticipate is a possible AKP loss and CHP win in the İstanbul municipality elections. What makes this possible is the fact that a significant portion of the voters that the AKP has risked alienating by its actions during the Gezi revolt live in this city. Leaving aside the symbolic importance of losing İstanbul, the İstanbul municipality investments, whose budget exceeds that of some countries, have been and will be crucial for Islamist capital fractions, as discussed in Ahmet Bekmen's chapter. In the eyes of the AKP, therefore, İstanbul is not just a municipality but also a project for capital. Indeed, while Erdoğan's own political career first advanced through his İstanbul mayorship, perhaps this city can soon become the site of his inevitable political decline.

This Is Just the Beginning; the Struggle Continues . . .

This was the main slogan of the Gezi revolt. It is the best expression of the militant determination of the protesters. To reduce their resistance to a mere 'lifestyle defence' would be to miss the political transformation enabled by the revolt. In the 2002 elections that ended with the AKP's victory and particularly in the later 'Republic Demonstrations' held to protest the presidential candidacy of any pro-AKP figure, the prevailing political concern was related to political Islamism. Those who believed that the AKP was hypocritically hiding the fact that it was an Islamist party expressed their concerns with their slogan, 'Turkey is secular and will remain so'. In contrast, during the Gezi revolt, there were no reports of any slogans like this nor any emphasis on political Islam and hypocrisy. Instead, the main demand of the revolt was the following: 'Let's limit the king!' In other words, the masses directly opposed the authoritarianism epitomised in the figure of Erdoğan and all kinds of illegitimate practices of power, primarily police violence. For this reason, the Gezi revolt has had the transformative role of raising people's level of expectations in terms of the content of social and political dissidence in Turkey.

The immediate effect of this unexpected revolt is the way it has instantly cleared the stifling political atmosphere. Until the masses took the initiative, there was appeared to be no alternative to the AKP's conservative, authoritarian course of action from within the legal political field. However, the crucial aspect of the revolt is perhaps not in its content but in its form. That is, the Gezi revolt was a kind of mass mobilisation in which the form exceeded the content, and still does, because this revolt has left such an imprint on the way politics is done, on subjectivity and its mechanisms, that it is quite possible to say that the new situation cannot easily be reversed. First, it highlighted again the fact that politics is a matter of drawing boundaries and that these boundaries can only be drawn if one is positioned within a political struggle. In this sense, it made it abundantly clear that the real task of an effective social and political opposition is not, as Turkey's liberal and left-liberal circles have tended to do, to observe the country from a 'panoramic' point of view and to mentor political actors, especially the AKP, from a 'transcendent and objective' position. The Gezi revolt moved not within mainstream politics but within the actual political problematic – i.e., the problematic of authoritarianism – that badly needs to be overcome. It forced diverse groups to adopt a common attitude towards a particular issue, redraw the boundaries, concretise the adversary, and thus largely redesign 'the within'. While it did not solve the problem in terms of content, it remapped the geography in which social and political opposition will take form. Second, the material mechanisms of street politics have become valid again. In the centre of İstanbul, where barricades were constructed, we saw that the daily routine and the security shell that underlies it cracked, albeit partially and temporarily. For once, it became almost an ordinary experience to see people shouting slogans, appropriating streets, parks and squares, and whenever necessary, battling with the coercive apparatus of the state. Words like 'barricade' and 'resistance' became part of the vocabulary of people from whom one may have least expected to hear such words. All this produced the following dualisms: public space as an abstract field of discussion versus public space with its concrete places; the abstract notion of the citizen defined by written rights and obligations versus the street militant displaying the potency to break out of this framework of rights and obligations; and, perhaps most importantly, the continuum of mainstream politics and media holding sway over mechanisms of discussion, thinking and decision-making versus the possibility of concrete mechanisms constructed by people personally engaged in the struggle to produce a common intellect. For the time being, the ongoing forums being held in various parks are the most concrete examples of this possibility. It will take some time to see to what extent these organs will become permanent or evolve into more stable organisational forms. For now at least, it is not naive to expect that these new and autonomous forms of political thinking, discussion and decision-making will linger in the minds of many people. Therefore, the greatest gain of the revolt is that, as is the case in all grassroots revolts, it has shown how the masses gain self-confidence by themselves.

Notes on Contributors

İsmet Akça is Assistant Professor at Yıldız Technical University, Faculty of Economics and Administrative Sciences, Department of Political Science and International Relations.

İrfan Aktan is a journalist, and correspondent of the *Express* journal.

Uraz Aydın (Dr) is a Research Assistant at Marmara University, Faculty of Communication, Department of Journalism.

Ahmet Bekmen is Assistant Professor at İstanbul University, Faculty of Political Sciences, Department of International Relations.

Mehmet Sinan Birdal is Assistant Professor at Işık University, Faculty of Economics and Administrative Sciences, Department of International Relations.

Erbatur Çavuşoğlu is Assistant Professor at Mimar Sinan Fine Arts University, Faculty of Architecture, Department of City and Regional Planning.

A. Ekber Doğan is Assistant Professor at Mersin University, Faculty of Economics and Administrative Sciences, Department of Public Administration.

M. Görkem Doğan (Dr) is a Research Assistant at İstanbul University, Faculty of Political Sciences, Department of Public Administration.

Yasin Durak is a Research Assistant at Ankara University, Faculty of Humanities, Department of Sociology.

F. Serkan Öngel (Dr) is Director of the Research Institute at DİSK (Confederation of Progressive Trade Unions of Turkey).

Barış Alp Özden (Dr) is a Research Assistant at Yıldız Technical University, Faculty of Economics and Administrative Sciences, Department of Political Science and International Relations.

Ece Öztan (Dr) is a Research Assistant at Yıldız Technical University, Faculty of Economics and Administrative Sciences, Department of Political Science and International Relations.

Güven Gürkan Öztan is Assistant Professor at İstanbul University, Faculty of Political Sciences, Department of International Relations.

Julia Strutz is FWO-Aspirant at University of KU Leuven.

Erdem Yörük is Assistant Professor at Koç University, Department of Sociology.

References

Adaklı, G. (2010) '2002–2008 Türk Medyasında AKP Etkisi', in İ. Uzgel and B. Duru (eds.), *AKP Kitabı: Bir Dönüşümün Bilançosu* (Ankara: Phoenix).

—— (2006) *Türkiye'de Medya Endüstrisi. Neoliberal Çağda Mülkiyet ve Kontrol İlişkileri* (Ankara: Ütopya Yayınevi).

—— (2001) 'Yayıncılık Alanında Mülkiyet ve Kontrol', in D.B. Kejanlıoğlu, S. Çelenk and G. Adaklı (eds.), *Medya Politikaları* (Ankara: İmge Kitabevi).

Adaman, F. and Keyder, Ç. (2006) 'Poverty and Social Exclusion in the Slum Areas of Large Cities in Turkey', Report Prepared for the European Commission and the Ministry of Labour and Social Security of Turkey.

Adaman, F., Buğra, A. and İnsel, A. (2009) 'Societal Context of Labor Union Strategy: The Case of Turkey', *Labor Studies Journal*, Vol. 34, No. 2.

Adıgüzel, R. (2012) 'Bir Sendika (GMİS) ve İlginç Bir Örgütlenme Hikayesi!', http://haber.sol.org.tr/yazarlar/recep-adiguzel/bir-sendika-gmis-ve-ilginc-bir-orgutlenme-hikayesi-53846 (accessed 7 May 2012).

ADNKS Address Based Population Registration System Results (2012), http://www.tuik.gov.tr/VeriBilgi.do?alt_id=39 (accessed 20 January 2013).

Agamben, G. (1998) *Homo Sacer. Sovereign Power and Bare Life* (Stanford, CA: Stanford University Press).

Ağartan, T.I. (2012) 'Marketization and Universalism: Crafting the Right Balance in the Turkish Healthcare System', *Current Sociology*, Vol. 60, No. 4.

—— (2007) 'Turkish Health Policy in a Globalizing World: The Case of "Transformation of Health" Program', Paper presented at the 19th Annual Meeting of the Research Committee of the International Sociological Association.

Akan, T. (2011) 'Responsible Pragmatism in Turkish Social Policy Making in the Face of Islamic Egalitarianism and Neoliberal Austerity', *International Journal of Social Welfare*, Vol. 20, No. 4.

Akay, H. (2009) *Security Sector in Turkey: Questions, Problems, and Solutions* (İstanbul: TESEV Publications).

Akça, İ. (2011) '1980'lerden Bugüne Türkiye'de Siyaset ve Hegemonya: Bir Çerçeve Denemesi', *İktisat Dergisi* No. 515–516.

—— (2010a) 'Ordu, Devlet ve Sınıflar: 27 Mayıs 1960 Darbesi Örneği Üzerinden Alternatif Bir Okuma Denemesi', in E. Balta Paker and İ. Akça (eds.), *Türkiye'de Ordu, Devlet ve Güvenlik Siyaseti* (İstanbul: İstanbul Bilgi Üniversitesi Yayınları).

—— (2010b) *Military-Economic Structure in Turkey: Present Situation, Problems, and Solutions* (İstanbul: TESEV Publications).

—— (2010c) 'AKP, Anayasa Değişikliği Referandumu ve Sol: 'Yetmez Ama Evet'in Açmazları', *Mesele*, No. 45.

—— (2009) 'The Articulation(s) and Disarticulation(s) between Militarism and Capitalism in the Age of Neoliberalism: The Case of Turkey in the Post-1980 Period', Paper presented to the Conference on 'Militarism: Political Economy, Security, Theory', Centre for Global Political Economy, University of Sussex, Brighton, England, 14 – 15 May 2009.

—— (2006) 'Militarism, Capitalism and the State: Putting the Military in Its Place in Turkey' (Unpublished PhD Dissertation: Boğaziçi Üniversitesi).

Akça, İ. and Balta Paker, E. (2013) 'Beyond Military Tutelage? Turkish Military Politics and the AKP Government,' in E. Canan Sokullu (ed.), *Debating Security in Turkey: Challenges and Changes in the Twenty-First Century* (London: Lexington Books).

Akçay, Ü. (2009) *Para, Banka, Devlet. Merkez Bankası Bağımsızlaşmasının Ekonomi Politiği* (İstanbul: Sosyal Araştırmalar Vakfı).

Akdoğan, Y. (2006) 'The Meaning of Conservative Democratic Political Identity', in M. Hakan Yavuz (ed.), *The Emergence of a New Turkey: Democracy and the AK Parti* (Salt Lake City: The University of Utah Press).

—— (2003) 'Muhafazakar Demokrasi', *Türkiye Bülteni*, No. 3.

Akın, A., Özvarış, Ş. B., Çelik, K., Hodoğlugil, N. Ş., Coşuk, A., Üner, S. and Erdost, T. (2006) *Türkiye'de Toplumsal Cinsiyet Perspektifinin Sağlık Politikalarına Entegre Edilmesi: Bir Vaka Çalışması* (Ankara: Hüksam).

AK Parti (2012) The Political Vision of Ak Parti 2023 Politics, Society and the World, http://www.akparti.org.tr/upload/documents/akparti2023siyasivizyonuingilizce.pdf (accessed 25 October 2012).

AKP Programı, http://www.akparti.org.tr/site/akparti/parti-programi#bolum_ (accessed 20 October 2012).

Aksoy, Ş. (1995) 'Yeni Sağ ve Kamu Yönetimi', *Kamu Yönetimi Sempozyum Bildirileri*, Vol. 2 (Ankara: TODAİE).

Akşit, N. (2007) 'Educational Reform in Turkey', *International Journal of Educational Development*, Vol. 27, No. 2.

Aktan, İ. (2010) 'Makul ve Makbul Kürtler', *Birikim*, No. 260.

—— (2006) *Zehir Ve Panzehir Kürt Sorunu: Faşizmin Şartı Kaç?* (Ankara: Dipnot).

Aktay, Y. (2004) 'İslamcılığın Mümkün ve Meşru dili: Muhafazakârlık', *Karizma Dergisi*, No. 17.

—— (2000) *Türk Dininin Sosyolojik İmkânı* (İstanbul: İletişim Yayınları).

Akyüz, Y. and Boratav, K. (2003) 'The Making of the Turkish Financial Crisis', *World Development*, Vol. 31, No. 9.

Albo, G. (2009) 'The Crisis of Neoliberalism and the Impasse of the Union Movement', *Relay: A Socialist Project Review*, No. 26.

Alkan, T. A. (1991) 'Türkiye'de Sol'un Zihni Donanım Problemleri Üzerine Bir Deneme ve Bir Teklif', *Türkiye Günlüğü*, No. 15.

Alper, C. E. and Öniş, Z. (2003) 'Financial Globalization, the Democratic Deficit, and Recurrent Crises in Emerging Markets: The Turkish Experience in the Aftermath of Capital Account Liberalization', *Emerging Markets Finance and Trade*, Vol. 39, No. 3.

Altaylı, F. (2009) 'Erol Yarar'ın Sözleri', http://www.fatihaltayli.com.tr/content.cfm?content_id=5479 (accessed 1 August .2009).

Altınal, B.E. (2011) 'The Psychologization of the Islamic Discourse on Homosexuality', *Regional Network Against Homophobia*, 56–58. http://www.tacso.org/doc/Homophobia-1.pdf (accessed 3 November 2012).

Altınok, M. and Üçer A. R. (2009) Sağlıkta Dönüşüm Sürecinde Sağlık Harcamaları, http://www.tipkurumu.org/files/SaglıktaDonusumSurecindeSaglikHarcamalari-son.doc (accessed 13 April 2013).

Anderson, B. (1991) *Imagined Communities: Reflections on the Origin and Spread of Nationalism* (London: Verso).

Anderson, P. (2011) 'Lula's Brazil', *London Review of Books*, Vol. 33, No. 7.

Arat, Z. F. K. (2009) 'Gender Approach and Women's Rights in Political Party Programs: The Case of Turkey', Paper Presented at World Congress of the International Political Science Association.

Arıkan, B. E. (2008) *Türk Sağının Türk Sorunu: Milliyetçi Hareket Partisi* (İstanbul: Agora Kitaplığı).

Arın, T. (2002) 'The Poverty of Social Security: The Welfare Regime in Turkey', in N. Balkan and S. Savran (eds.), *The Ravages of Neoliberalism: Economy, Society and Gender in Turkey* (New York: Nova Science).

Arıkan, N. (2011) *28 Şubat Sürecinde Medya* (İstanbul: Okur Kitaplığı).

Arrighi, G. (2009) Uzun Yirminci Yüzyıl: Para, Güç ve Çağımızın Kökenleri (Ankara: İmge Yayınları).

Arsan, E. (2011) 'Gazeteci Gözüyle Sansür ve Otosansür', *Cogito,* No. 67.

ASKON (2009, 2012) *ASKON Üyeler,* www.askon.org.tr (accessed 21 January 2010 and 17 July 2012).

ASPB (Family and Social Policies Ministry) (2012) Kimsenin Kaybolmasına İzin Vermeyiz, Çünkü Biz Büyük Bir Aileyiz, http://www.youtube.com/watch?v=mxa 9T4oWplM (accessed 17 October 2012).

Ataay, F. (2006) *12 Mart'tan 12 Eylül'e Kriz Kıskacındaki Türk Siyaseti ve 1978–1979 CHP Hükümeti* (Ankara: De Ki).

——— (2002) 'Türkiye'de Neoliberalizm ve Parlamenter Siyasetin Krizi', *Praksis,* no. 5.

Ataay F. and Kalfa C. (2009) 'Neoliberalizmin Krizi ve AKP'ninYükselişi', in N. Mütevellioğlu and S. Sönmez (eds.), *Küreselleşme, Kriz ve Türkiye'de Neoliberal Dönüşüm* (İstanbul: İstanbul BilgiÜniversitesiYayınları).

Atabay, M. (2005) *İkinci Dünya Savaşı Sırasında Türkiye'de Milliyetçilik Akımları* (İstanbul: Kaynak Yayınları).

Atacan, F. (2005) 'Explaining Religious Politics at the Crossroad: AKP – SP', *Turkish Studies,* Vol. 6, No. 2.

Ataman, Ü. (2003) *4857 Sayılı İş Yasası'nın Değerlendirmesi* (Istanbul: Lastik-İş Sendikası Araştırma Yayınları).

ATHGM (General Directorate of Family and Community Services) (2012) Evlilik Öncesi Eğitim Programı, http://www.athgm.gov.tr/tr/html/18577/Evlilik-Oncesi-Egitim-Programi ; http://www.athgm.gov.tr/tr/html/18567/Aile-Egitim-Yayinlari (accessed 12 November 2012).

Atılgan, S. (2000) 'Eskiden Beri Gizlice, Yeni Sağ'la Açıkça: Kadınlar Evine', in Fulya Atacan (ed.), *Mübeccel Kıray için Yazılar* (İstanbul: Bağlam Yayınları).

Atikcan, E. Ö. and Öge, K. (2012) 'Referendum Campaigns in Polarized Societies: The Case of Turkey', *Turkish Studies,* Vol. 13, No. 3.

Atiyas, İ. (2012) 'Economic Institutions and Institutional Change in Turkey during the Neoliberal Era', *New Perspective on Turkey,* No. 47.

Atlas, İ. (1999) 'Yeni Mekanlar: Medya Fabrikalarına Bir Yenisi – Medya Plaza', in K. Alemdar (ed.), *Medya Gücü ve Demokratik Kurumlar* (İstanbul: Afa).

Avcı, G. (2009) *Ergenekon'un Medya ile Dansı* (İstanbul: Nesil Yayınları).

Avcı, Ö. (2012) *İki Dünya Arasında. İstanbul'da Dindar Üniversite Gençliği* (İstanbul: İletişim Yayınları).

Ayata B. and Yükseker, D. (2005) 'A Belated Awakening: National and International Responses to the Internal Displacement of Kurds in Turkey', *New Perspectives on Turkey,* No. 32.

Ayata, S. (2000) *Kapitalizm ve Küçük Üreticilik* (Ankara: Gündoğan Yayınları).

Ayaz, B. (1997) *Türkiye'de İnsan Hakları ve Kürt Sorunu Örneğinde Türk Basını* (İstanbul: Belge Yayınları).

Aybar, S. and Lapavitsas, C. (2001) 'The Recent Turkish Crisis: Another Step Toward Free Market Authoritarianism' *Historical Materialism,* Vol. 8.

Aydın, K. (2012) *Her Şeyin Başı Sağlık! Sağlığımız İçin Mücadeleye* (İstanbul: Birgün Kitap).

Aydın, M. (2008) *Sosyal Politika ve Yerel Yonetimler* (İstanbul: İz Yayıncılık).

—— (2001) 'Kafkasya ve Orta Asya'yla İlişkiler', in Baskın Oran (ed.), *Türk Dış Politikası: Kurtuluş Savaşından Bugüne Olgular, Belgeler, Yorumlar, Vol. 2: 1980–2001* (İstanbul: İletişim Yayınları).

Aydın, U. (2009) 'Gauches, Libéralisme et Démocratie. Les Mutations des Intellectuels Turcs (1980–2008)' (Unpublished PhD Dissertation: INALCO/Marmara University).

Aydınkaya, F. (2011) 'Yeni Kürt Milliyetçiliğinin İnşası ve Yeni Kürt Orta Sınıfının "Pasif Devrim Ütopyası"', *Dipnot*, No. 5.

Aydınlar Ocağı (1973) *Aydınlar Ocağı'nın Görüşü: Türkiye'nin Bugünkü Meseleleri* (İstanbul: Garanti Matbaası).

Aydınoğlu, E. (2007) *Türkiye Solu (1960–1980)* (İstanbul: Versus Kitap).

Bağımsız Sosyal Bilimciler (2009) *Türkiye'de ve Dünyada Ekonomik Bunalım, 2008–2009* (İstanbul: Yordam).

—— (2008) *2008 Kavşağında Türkiye* (İstanbul: Yordam).

—— (2007) *IMF Gözetiminde On Uzun Yıl 1998–2008: Farklı Hükümetler Tek Siyaset* (İstanbul: Yordam).

Bali, R. (2002) *Tarz-ı Hayattan Life Style'a* (İstanbul: İletişim Yayınları).

Balkan, E. and Yeldan, E. (1998) 'Financial Liberalization in Developing Countries: The Turkish Experience', in R. Medhara and J. Fanelli (eds.), *Financial Liberalization in Developing Countries* (London: Macmillan).

Balta Paker, E. (2010) 'Dış Tehditten İç Tehdide: Türkiye'de Doksanlarda Ulusal Güvenliğin Yeniden İnşası', in E. Balta Paker and İ. Akça (eds.), *Türkiye'de Ordu, Devlet ve Güvenlik Siyaseti* (İstanbul: İstanbul Bilgi Üniversitesi Yayınları).

Balta Paker, E. and Akça, İ. (2013) 'Askerler, Köylüler ve Paramiliter Güçler: Türkiye'de Köy Koruculuğu Sistemi', *Toplum ve Bilim*, No. 126.

Barkey, H. J. (1990) *The State and the Industrialization Crisis in Turkey* (Boulder, CO: Westview Press).

Batur, M. H. (1998) 'From Rational Reformism to Neoliberal Centralism: Institutional Politics of Economic Bureaucracy in Turkey 1960–1984' (unpublished PhD Dissertation: Boğaziçi University).

Bayramoğlu, A. (2001) *28 Şubat Bir Müdahalenin Güncesi* (İstanbul: Birey Yayıncılık).

—— (2004) 'Asker ve Siyaset', in A. İnsel and A. Bayramoğlu (eds.), *Bir Zümre, Bir Parti. Türkiye'de Ordu* (İstanbul: Birikim Yayınları).

Bekaroğlu, M. (2007) *Adil Düzen'den Dünya Gerçeklerine: Siyasetin Sonu* (Ankara: Elips Kitap).

Bekmen, A. (2003) 'Reinstitutionalizing Turkey: The New Right Experience' (unpublished MA Thesis: Boğaziçi University), http://www.academia.edu/863538/Reinstitutionalizing_Turkey_The_New_Right_Experience (accessed 12 April 2013).

Benli, F. (2008) 'A Statistical Examination of the Condition of Women in Turkey', AKDER (Women's Rights Organization against Discrimination), http://www.osce.org/odihr/39070 (accessed 7 November 2012).

Berksoy, B. (2012) 'Güvenlik Devleti'nin Ortaya Çıkışı, "Güvenlik" Eksenli Yönetim Tekniğinin Polis Teşkilatındaki Tezhürleri ve Süreklileşen "Olağanüstü Hal": AKP'nin Polis Politikaları', *Birikim*, No. 276.

—— (2010) 'The Re-structuring of the Police Organization in Turkey in the post-1980 Period and the Re-construction of the Social Formation', in L. Khalili and J. Schwedler (eds.), *Policing and Prisons in the Middle East: Formations of Coercion* (New York: Columbia University Press).

BIANET (2010) 'Demokratik Özerk Kürdistan Modeli Taslağı', http://www.bianet.org/files/doc_files/000/000/179/original/demokratik%C3%B6zerklik.htm (last accessed 24 December 2012).

BIANET (2007) 'TTB: Torba Yasa Kadrolaşmaya Yol Açacak', http://bianet.org/bianet/emek/91256-ttb-torba-yasa-kadrolasmaya-yol-acacak (accessed 29 November 2012).

Birdal, M.S. (2013) 'Queering Conservative Democracy,' *Turkish Policy Quarterly*, Vol. 11, No. 4.

Birleşik Metal-İş (2006) Metal İşçisinin Gerçeği, http://www.birlesikmetal.org/kitap/kitap_06/mig2006.pdf (accessed 20 August 2012).

Birleşik Metal-İş Gazetesi, December 2004.

Bloch, E. (2007) *Umut İlkesi* (İstanbul: İletişim Yayınları).

Boissevain, J. (1974) *Friends of Friends: Networks, Manipulators and Coalitions* (Oxford: Basil Blackwell).

Bonefeld, W. (2006) 'Democracy and Dictatorship: Means and Ends of the State', *Critique*, Vol. 34, No.3.

Bora, T. (2008) *Türkiye'nin Linç Rejimi* (İstanbul: Birikim Yayınları).

—— (2005) 'Turgut Özal', in Murat Yılmaz (ed.), *Modern Türkiye'de Siyasi Düşünce Cilt 7 Liberalizm* (İstanbul: İletişim Yayınları).

—— (1999) 'İstanbul of the Conqueror: The "Alternative Global City" Dreams of Political Islam', in Çağlar Keyder (ed.), *Between the Global and the Local* (Lanham, MD: Rowman & Littlefield Publishers).

—— (1995) *Milliyetçiliğin Kara Baharı* (İstanbul: Birikim Yayınları).

Bora, T. and Can K. (2004) *Devlet ve Kuzgun: 1990'lardan 2000'lere MHP* (İstanbul: İletişim).

Boratav, K. (1987, 2011) *Türkiye İktisat Tarihi 1908–1985* (İstanbul: Gerçek Yayınevi).

—— (1995) *1980'li Yıllarda Türkiye'de Sosyal Sınıflar ve Bölüşüm* (İstanbul: Gerçek Yayınevi).

Boratav, K., Türel, O. and Yeldan, E. (1994) 'Distributional Dynamics in Turkey under Structural Adjustment of the 1980s', *New Perspectives on Turkey*, No. 11.

Boratav, K., Yeldan, E. and Köse, A.H. (2000) Globalization, Distribution and Social Policy: Turkey, 1980–1998, *CEPA and The New School for Social Research, Working Paper Series*, No. 20.

Bourdieu, P. (1996) *Sur la télévision* (Paris: Raisons d'Agir Éditions).

Bozarslan, H. (2011) 'La crise comme instrument politique en Turquie', *Esprit*, No. 271.

—— (2001) 'Political Crisis and the Kurdish Issue in Turkey: 1984–1999', *Human Rights Review*, Vol. 3, No. 1.

Bozdoğan, S. (2001) *Modernism and Nation Building: Turkish Architectural Culture in the Early Republic* (Seattle/London: University of Washington Press).

Brodie, J. (2002) 'Citizenship and Solidarity: Reflections on the Canadian Way', *Citizenship Studies*, Vol. 6, No. 4.

Brown, W. (2003) 'Neo-liberalism and the End of Liberal Democracy', *Theory and Event*, Vol. 7, No. 1.

Buci-Glucksmann, C. (1980) *Gramsci and the State* (London: Lawrence and Wishart).

Buğra, A. (2008) *Kapitalizm, Yoksulluk ve Türkiye'de Sosyal Politika* (İstanbul: İletişim Yayınları).

—— (2007) 'AKP Döneminde Sosyal Politika ve Vatandaşlık', *Toplum ve Bilim*, No. 108.

—— (2006) 'The Turkish Welfare Regime in Transformation', *Journal of European Social Policy*, Vol. 16, No. 3.

—— (2004) 'Dini Kimlik ve Sınıf: Bir MÜSİAD ve Hak-İş Karşılaştırması', in N. Balkan and S. Savran (eds.), *Sürekli Kriz Politikaları* (İstanbul: Metis Yayınları).

—— (1998) 'Class, Culture, and the State: An Analysis of Interest Representation by Two Turkish Business Associations', *International Journal of Middle East Studies*, No. 30.

—— (1994a) *State and Business in Modern Turkey: A Comparative Study* (Albany, NY: State University of New York Press).

—— (1994b),'Political and Institutional Context of Business Activity in Turkey', in Ayşe Öncü, Çağlar Keyder and Saad Eddin Ibrahim (eds.), *Developmentalism and Beyond: Society and Politics in Egypt and Turkey* (Cairo: American University in Cairo Press).

Buğra, A. and Adar, S. (2008) 'Social Policy Change in Countries without Mature Welfare State: The Case of Turkey', *New Perspectives on Turkey,* No. 38.

Buğra, A. and Candaş, A. (2011) 'Change and Continuity under an Eclectic Social Security Regime: The Case of Turkey', *Middle Eastern Studies,* Vol. 47, No. 3.

Buğra, A. and Keyder, Ç. (2007) *Social Assistance in Turkey: For a Policy of Minimum Income Support Conditional on Socially Beneficial Activity* (Ankara: UNDP).

—— (2006) 'The Turkish Welfare Regime in Transformation', *Journal of European Social Policy,* Vol. 16, No. 3.

—— (2003) *New Poverty and the Changing Welfare Regime of Turkey* (Ankara: UNDP).

Buğra, A. and Savaşkan, O. (2012) 'Politics and Class: The Turkish Business Environment in the Neoliberal Age', *New Perspectives on Turkey,* No. 46.

Buğra, A. and Yakut-Çakar, B. (2010) 'Structural Change, the Social Policy Environment and Female Employment in Turkey', *Development and Change,* Vol. 41, No. 3.

Bulut, F. (1997) *Tarikat Sermayesinin Yükselişi; İslam Ekonomisinin Eleştirisi* (Ankara: Doruk Yayınları).

Burnham, P. (2000) 'Globalization, Depoliticization and "Modern" Economic Management', in Werner Bonefield and Kosmas Psychopedus (eds.), *Politics of Change* (New York: Palgrave Macmillan).

Buzan, B., Wæver, O. and de Wilde, J. (1998) *Security: A New Framework of Analysis* (Boulder, CO: Lynne Rienner Publishers).

Cam, S. (2002) 'Neo-liberalism and Labour within the Context of an "Emerging Market" Economy – Turkey', *Capital & Class,* Vol. 26, No. 2.

Cammack, P. (1989) 'Review Article: Bringing the State Back In?', *British Journal of Political Science,* Vol. 19, No. 2.

Cammack, P. (1998) 'Globalization and the Death of Liberal Democracy', *European Review,* Vol. 6, No. 2.

Can, K. (2002) 'Ülkücü Hareketin İdeolojisi', in Tanıl Bora (ed.), *Modern Türkiye'de Siyasi Düşünce: Milliyetçilik* (İstanbul: İletişim).

Cem, İ (2009) *Türkiye, Avrupa, Avrasya, Birinci Cilt: Strateji, Yunanistan, Kıbrıs* (İstanbul: İş Bankası Kültür Yayınları).

Cemal, H. (2003) *Kürtler* (İstanbul: Doğan Kitap).

Chase, R., Hill, E. and Kennedy, P. (1996) 'Pivotal States and U.S. Strategy,' *Foreign Affairs,* Vol. 75, No. 1.

Chatterjee, P. (1999) *The Partha Chatterjee Omnibus: Nationalist Thought and the Colonial World* (New Delhi: Oxford University Press).

Chodor, T. (2010) 'Lula's Passive Revolution and the Consolidation of Neoliberalism in Brazil', Paper Presented to the Oceanic Conference on International Studies, Auckland, 30 June–2 July 2010.

Cizre, Ü. (ed.) (2008a) *Secular and Islamic Politics in Turkey: The Making of the Justice and Development Party* (London and New York: Routledge).

—— (2008b) 'The Justice and Development Party and the Military. Recreating the Past After Reforming It?' in Ü. Cizre (ed.) *Secular and Islamic Politics in Turkey: The Making of the Justice and Development Party* (London and New York: Routledge).

Cizre, Ü. and Çınar, M. (2003) 'Turkey 2002: Kemalism, Islamism, and Politics in the Light of the February 28 Process', *The South Atlantic Quarterly,* Vol. 102, No. 2/3.

Cizre-Sakallıoğlu, Ü. (1997) 'The Anatomy of the Turkish Military's Political Autonomy', *Comparative Politics,* Vol. 29, No.2.

—— (1993) *AP-Ordu İlişkileri. Bir İkilemin Anatomisi* (İstanbul: İletişim Yayınları).

—— (1992) 'Labour and State in Turkey: 1960–1980', *Middle Eastern Studies*,Vol. 28, No. 4.

Cizre-Sakallıoğlu, Ü. and Yeldan, E. (2000) 'Politics, Society and Financial Liberalization: Turkey in the 1990s', *Development and Change*,Vol. 31, No. 2.

Clarke, J. and Newman, J. (1997) *The Managerial State: Power, Politics and Ideology in the Remaking of Social Welfare* (London: Sage Publications Limited).

Clarke, S. (1992) 'The Global Accumulation of Capital and the Periodisation of the Capitalist State Form', in W. Bonefeld, R. Gunn and K. Psychopedis (eds.), *Open Marxism Vol. 1* (London: Pluto Press).

Cleminson, R. (2012) 'The Emotions of the Market', *Revista Teknokultura*,Vol. 9, No. 1.

Coşar, S. and Yeğenoğlu, M. (2011) 'New Grounds for Patriarchy in Turkey? Gender Policy in the Age of AKP', *South European Society and Politics*,Vol. 16, No. 4.

Cox, R. (1996 [1989]) 'Middlepowermanship, Japan and Future World Order,' *Approaches to World Order* (Cambridge: Cambridge University Press).

Crozier, M., Huntington, S. P. and Watanuki, J. (1975) *The Crises of Democracy* (New York: New York University Press).

Cumhuriyet (1986), 6 December 1986.

Cumhuriyet (2000), 'Darbenin Bilancosu', 12 September 2000.

Çalık, M. (1992) 'Miras Davası'nda Yol Ayrımı: Hangi Türkiye?', *Türkiye Günlüğü*, No. 19.

Çandar, C. (2009) 'The Kurdish Question: The Reason and Fortunes of the "opening"', *Insight Turkey*,Vol. 11, No. 4.

—— (1992) '21.Yüzyıl'a Doğru Türkiye: Tarih ve Jeopolitiğin İntikamı', *Türkiye Günlüğü*, No. 19.

Çavuşoğlu, E. (2011) 'İslamcı Neo-Liberalizmde İnşaat Fetişi ve Mülkiyet Üzerindeki Simgesel Hâle', *Birikim Dergisi*, No. 270, pp. 40–51.

Çelik, A. (2010) *Vesayetten Siyasete Türkiye'de Sendikacılık (1946–1967)* (İstanbul: İletişim Yayınları).

Çelik, S. (2008) *Osmanlı'dan Günümüze Devlet ve Asker. Askeri Bürokrasinin Sistem İçindeki Yeri* (İstanbul: Salyangoz Yayınları).

Çınar, A. (2001) 'National History as a Contested Site: The Conquest of Istanbul and Islamist Negotiations of the Nation', *Society for Comparative Study of Society and History*, Vol. 43, No. 2.

Çınar, M. (2008) 'The Justice and Development Party and the Kemalist Establishment', in Ü. Cizre (ed.), *Secular and Islamic Politics in Turkey: The Making of the Justice and Development Party* (London and New York: Routledge).

—— (2005) *Siyasal Bir Sorun Olarak İslamcılık* (Ankara: Dipnot Yayınları).

Çolak,Y. (2006) '1990"lı Yıllar Türkiye'sinde Yeni Osmanlıcılık ve Kültürel Çoğulculuk Tartışmaları', *Doğu Batı*, No. 38.

Dalla Zuanna, G. (2001) 'The banquet of Aeolus: A familistic interpretation of Italy's lowest low fertility', *Demographic Research*,Vol. 4, No. 5, 133–162.

Dağtaş, E. (2006) *Türkiye'de Magazin Basını* (Ankara: Ütopya Yayınevi).

Davutoğlu, A. (2008) *Stratejik Derinlik: Türkiye'nin Uluslararası Konumu* (İstanbul: Küre Yayınları).

de Oliveira, F. (2006) 'Lula in the Labyrinth', *New Left Review*, No. 42.

Dean, M. (1999) *Governmentality: Power and Rule in Modern Society* (London: Sage).

Dedeoğlu, S. (2012) 'Equality, Protection or Discrimination: Gender Equality Policies in Turkey', *Social Politics: International Studies in Gender, State & Society*,Vol. 19, No. 2.

Delibaş, K. (2001) 'Political Islam and Grassroots Activisim in Turkey A Study of Pro-Islamist Virtue Party's Grassroots Activists and Their Affects on the Electoral Outcomes' (Unpublished PhD Thesis: The University of Kent).

Demir, Ö. (2005) 'Anadolu Sermayesi ya da İslamcı Sermaye', in *Modern Türkiye'de Siyasi Düşünce Cilt: 6* (İstanbul: İletişim Yayınları).

Demirel, T. (2004) *Adalet Partisi. İdeoloji ve Politika* (İstanbul: İletişim Yayınları).

Demirpolat, A. (2002) 'The Rise of Islamic Economic Ethic, Rationality and Capitalism in Modern Turkey: The Case of Konya' (Unpublished PhD Thesis: METU).

Deniz Feneri, (2012) *Yaşasın İyilik: 2012 Faaliyet Raporu*, http://www.denizfeneri.org.tr/e-dergi/fr2012/Default.html, (accessed 20 August 2013).

Dinçşahin, Ş. (2012) 'A Symptomatic Analysis of the Justice and Development Party's Populism in Turkey, 2007–2010', *Government and Opposition*, Vol. 47, No. 4.

Dinler, D. (2003) 'Türkiye'de Güçlü Devlet Geleneği Tezinin Eleştirisi', *Praksis*, 9.

DİSK Araştırma Enstitüsü. (2012) 'Sendikalar ve Yetki Sorunu Raporu-2' Report No. 9.

Doğan, A.E. (2011/12) '1994'ten Bugüne Neoliberal İslamcı Belediyecilikte Süreklilik ve Değişimler,' *Praksis*, Vol. 26.

—— (2010a), 'AKP'li Hegemonya Projesi ve Neoliberalizmin Yeniden Dirilişi', *Praksis*, No. 23.

—— (2010b) 'İslami Sermayenin Gelişme Dinamikleri ve 28 Şubat Süreci', in İ. Uzgel and B. Duru (eds.), *AKP Kitabı. Bir Dönüşümün Bilançosu* (Ankara: Phoenix).

—— (2007) *Eğreti Kamusallık: Kayseri Örneğinde İslamcı Belediyecilik* (İstanbul: İletişim Yayınları).

Doğan, E. (2005) 'The Historical and Discursive Roots of the Justice and Development Party's EU Stance', *Turkish Studies*, Vol. 6, No. 3.

Doğan, F. (2002) 'Üçüncü Meşrutiyet Nasıl İlân Edildi?', *İleri*, No. 12.

Doğan, M. G. (2005) 'Darbe Sonrası Yeni Birikim Rejimine Geçişte Örgütlü İşçi Hareketinin Geriletilmesinin İşlevselliği', *Eğitim Toplum Bilim*, Vol. 3, No. 12.

—— (2010) 'When Neoliberalism Confronts the Moral Economy of Workers: The Final Spring of Turkish Labor Unions', *European Journal of Turkish Studies* [Online], 11, Online since 21 October 2010.

Doğruel, F., Doğruel, A. S. and Yeldan, E. (2003) 'Macroeconomics of Turkey's Agricultural Reforms: An Intertemporal Computable General Equilibrium Analysis', *Journal of Policy Modeling*, Vol. 25, No. 6.

Durak, Y. (2011) *Emeğin Tevekkülü: Konya'da İşçi-İşveren İlişkileri ve Dindarlık* (Istanbul: İletişim Yayınları).

Duran, R. (2000) *Medyamorfoz* (İstanbul: Avesta).

—— (1996) *Apoletli Medya* (İstanbul: Patika).

Dursun, Ç. (2001) *TV Haberlerinde İdeoloji* (Ankara: İmge Kitabevi).

—— (1999) 'Türk Basınında Dağıtım Tarihçesi ve Yapısı', in K. Alemdar (ed.), *Medya Gücü ve Demokratik Kurumlar* (İstanbul: Afa).

Düzel, N. (2010) 'Dinç Bilgin ile Mülakat', *Taraf*, 8–9 March 2010.

Ecevit, Y. (2012) 'Türkiye'de Sosyal Politika Çalışmalarının Toplumsal Cinsiyet Bakış Açısıyla Gelişimi', in S. Dedeoğlu and A. Y. Elveren (eds.), *Türkiye'de Refah Devleti ve Kadın* (İstanbul: İletişim Yayınları).

Eder, M. (2010) 'Retreating State? Political Economy of Welfare Regime Change in Turkey', *Middle East Law and Governance*, Vol. 2, No. 2.

Eğilmez, D. B. (2012) 'Governing or Repressing Dissent via the Politics of Toleration: The Justice and Development Party versus the Working Class', *Turkish Studies*, Vol. 13, No. 3.

Eken, S. and Schadler, S. (2012) *Turkey 2000–2010: A Decade of Transition Discussions among Experts* (İstanbul: DEIK).

Ekzen, N. (1999) 'Medya ve Ekonomi: Türk Basın Endüstrisinde Yoğunlaşma-Toplulaşma-Tekelleşme Yapısı (1965–1995)', in K. Alemdar (ed.), *Medya Gücü ve Demokratik Kurumlar* (İstanbul: Afa).

Eley, G. (2007) 'What Produces Democracy? Revolutionary Crises, Popular Politics and Democratic Gains in Twentieth-Century Europe', in M. Haynes and J. Wolfreys (eds.), *History and Revolution. Refuting Revisionism* (London and New York: Verso).

Eley, G. and Nield, K. (1980) 'Why Does Social History Ignore Politics?' *Social History*, Vol. 5, No. 2.

Ercan, F. (2009) 'Sermayeyi Haritalandırmaya Yönelik Kavramsal Düzenekler', *Praksis*, No. 19.

—— (2003) 'The Contradictory Continuity of the Turkish Capital Accumulation Process: A Critical Perspective on the Internationalization of the Turkish Economy', in S. Savran and N. Balkan (eds.), *The Ravages of Neo-liberalism: Economy, Society and Gender in Turkey* (New York: Nova Publisher).

Ercan, M. R. and Öniş Z. (2001) 'Turkish Privatization: Institutions and Dilemmas', *Turkish Studies*, Vol. 2, No. 1.

Erder, S. (1999) 'Where Do You Hail from?' in Çağlar Keyder (ed.), *Istanbul: Between the Global and the Local* (Lanham, MD: Rowman & Littlefield Publishers).

Ergil, D. (1975) 'Class Conflict and Turkish Transformation (1950–1975),' *Studia Islamica*, Vol. 41.

Ergül, H. (2000) *Televizyonda Haberin Magazinelleşmesi* (İstanbul: İletişim Yayınları).

Eriksen, T. H. (1993) 'Formal and Informal Nationalism', *Ethnic and Racial Studies*, Vol. 16, No. 1.

Ertekin, O. G. (2012) 'Kırmızı Başlıklı Kızın Maceraları', *Express*, No. 126.

—— (2011) *Yargı Meselesi Hallolundu* (Ankara: Epos Yayınları).

Esping-Anderson, G. (1999) *Social Foundations of Postindustrial Economies* (New York: Oxford University Press).

—— (1990) *The Three Worlds of Welfare Capitalism* (Princeton, NJ: Princeton University Press).

European Union Twinning Project for Turkey (2006) *Towards Improving the Investment Climate in Turkey: Comments on the YOIKK Reform Process*, http://www.yoikk.gov.tr/upload/yoikk/ingilizce_rapor.pdf (accessed 12 April 2013).

EUROSTAT (2009) *Eurostat Pocket Books: Labour Market Statistics 2009* (Luxembourg: Publications Office of the European Union).

Evans, P. B., Rueschemeyer, D., Skocpol, T. (eds.) (1985), *Bringing the State Back In* (Cambridge and New York: Cambridge University Press).

Ferge, Z. (1997) 'The Changed Welfare Paradigm: The Individualisation of the Social', *Social Policy and Administration*, Vol. 31, No. 1.

Ferguson, J. (2007) 'Formalities of Poverty: Thinking about Social Assistance in Neoliberal South Africa', *African Studies Review*, Vol. 50, No. 2.

—— (1994) *The Anti-Politics Machine: 'Development', Depoliticization, and Bureaucratic Power in Lesotho* (Minneapolis: University of Minnesota Press).

Fernandez, A. E. and Mommen, A. (eds.), (1996) *Liberalization in the Developing World: Institutional and Economic Changes in Latin America, Africa and Asia* (London and New York: Routledge).

Fırat, G. (2002a) 'Türk Ulusundan Ayrı Bir Kürt Kimliği Var Mı?', *İleri*, No. 12.

—— (2002b) 'Sömürgeciliğe Karşı Milliyetçilik', *İleri*, No. 11.

Foucault, M. (1990) *The History of Sexuality, Volume I: An Introduction* (New York: Vintage Books).

Fröbel, F. (1983) *Dünya Ekonomisinin Günümüzdeki Gelişmesi Üzerine, Dünya Ekonomisi, Bunalım ve Siyasal Yapılar* (İstanbul: Belge Yayınları).

Fröbel, F. et al. (1982) *Uluslararası Yeni İş Bölümü ve Serbest Bölgeler* (İstanbul: Belge Yayınları).

Gambetti, Z. (2007) 'Linç Girişimleri, Neo-liberalizm ve Güvenlik Devleti', *Toplum ve Bilim*, No. 109.

Gamble, A. (1994) *The Free Economy and the Strong State: The Politics of Thatcherism* (London: Macmillan).

Gazete Vatan (20 July 2010) 'Kadınla Erkek Eşit Olamaz!' (Woman and man cannot be equal!), http://haber.gazetevatan.com/kadinla-erkek-esit-olamaz/318006/9/Haber (accessed 7 October 2012).

General Secretariat of the National Security Council (1982) *12 September in Turkey Before and After* (Ankara).

Geray, C. (2010) 'AKP ve Konut: Toplumsal Konut Yöneltisi Açısından TOKİ Uygulamaları', in İlhan Uzgel (ed.), *AKP Kitabı* (Ankara: Phoenix Yayınları).

Gill, S. (2011) *Who Elected the Bankers?*, http://stephengill.com/news/category/critical-perspectives-on-global-governance (accessed 12 April 2013).

—— (2000) 'The Constitution of Global Capitalism', Paper presented to the Capitalist World, Past and Present at the International Studies Association Annual Convention, http://www.theglobalsite.ac.uk/press/010gill.pdf (accessed 12 April 2013).

Goddard, V. A. (1996) *Gender, Family, and Work in Naples* (Oxford: Berg Publications).

Goonewardena, K. (2005) 'The Urban Sensorium: Space, Ideology and the Aestheticization of Politics', *Antipode*: 46–71.

Gough, J. (2002). 'Neoliberalism and Socialisation in the Contemporary City: Opposites, Complements and Instabilities', *Antipode*, Vol. 34, No. 3.

GÖÇ-DER (Migrants' Association for Social Cooperation and Culture) (1999–2001) *Zorla Yerinden Göç Edilenler İçin Ekonomik, Sosyal ve Kültürel Haklar Araştırma Raporu*. www.akdenizgocder.org/raporlar/992001MBarutraporu.doc (last accesed 10 April 2013).

Göker, E. (2012) 'Betonarme Demokrasi Kalıbında Kürtler', *Express*, No. 127.

—— (2009) 'Barizin Alimleri: Kanaat Teknisyenleri', http://istifhanem.com/2010/04/03/barizinalimleri/ (last accessed 27 December 2012).

—— (2004) *Why Class Struggle Matters: Rethinking Critical Institutionalism through the Political Economy of Capitalist Development in Turkey*, http://istifhane.files.wordpress.com/2010/04/rethinkingci1.pdf (accessed 12 April 2013).

Göktaş, K. (2012) 'Yeni Yargı: Kurumsallaşma ve Pratik', *Birikim*, No. 275.

Göle, N. (1993) Engineers: 'Technocratic Democracy', in Ayşe Öncü, Metin Heper, Heinz Kramer (eds.), *Turkey and the West: Changing Political and Cultural Identities* (London: I.B. Tauris).

Gönen, Z. (2012) 'Suçla Mücadele ve Neo-liberal Türkiye'de Yoksulluğun Zaptiyesi', *Birikim*, No. 273.

Görgülü, G. (1991) *Basında Ekonomik Bağımlılık ve Tekelleşme: 1970'lerden 1990'lara* (İstanbul: Türkiye Gazeteciler Cemiyeti Yayınları).

Gramsci, A. (1999) *Selections from the Prison Notebooks*, Quintin Hoare and G. Novel Smith (eds.) (New York: International Publisher).

Greif, A. (2006) *Institutions and the Path to the Modern Economy: Lessons from Medieval Trade* (Cambridge: Cambridge University Press).

Grüjten, D. (2008) 'The Turkish Welfare Regime: An Example of the Southern European Model?', *Turkish Policy Quarterly*, Vol. 7, No. 1.

Gülalp, H. (2003) *Kimlikler Siyaseti. Türkiye'de Siyasal İslamın Temelleri* (İstanbul: Metis).

—— (2001) 'Globalization and Political Islam: The Social Bases of Turkey's Welfare Party', *International Journal of Middle East Studies*, No. 33.

—— (1999a) 'Political Islam in Turkey: The Rise and Fall of the Refah Party', *The Muslim World*, 89: 1.

—— (1999b) 'The Poverty of Democracy in Turkey: The Refah Party Episode', *New Perspectives on Turkey*, No. 21.

Gülten-Karakaş, D. (2009) 'Sermayenin Uluslararasılaşması Sürecinde Türkiye Banka Reformu ve Finans Kapital-içi Yeniden Yapılanma', *Praksis*, No. 19.

—— (2008) *Global Integration of Turkish Finance Capital: State, Capital and Banking Reform in Turkey* (Saarbrücken: VDM Verlag).

Gündüz-Hoşgör, A. and Smits, J. (2008) 'Variation in Labor Market Participation of Married Women in Turkey', *Women's Studies International Forum*, Vol. 31, No. 2.

Günel, G. and Aytülün, O. (2006) 'The Impact of Microcredit on the Poor', in *International Conference on Human and Economic Resources Proceedings Book* (İzmir: İzmir University of Economics and SUNY Cortland).

Gürbilek, N. (1992) *Vitrinde Yaşamak. 1980'lerin Kültürel İklimi* (İstanbul: Metis).

Gürek, H. (2008) *AKP'nin Müteahhitleri* (İstanbul: Güncel Yayıncılık).

Gürses, D. (2009) 'Microfinance and Poverty Reduction in Turkey', *Perspectives on Global Development and Technology*, Vol. 8, No. 1.

Hale, W. and Özbudun, E. (2010) *Islamism, Democracy and Liberalism in Turkey* (London and New York: Routledge).

Halimi, S. (2004) 'Road Map for Privatisation: The Great Leap Backwards' *Le Monde Diplomatique*, English edition http://mondediplo.com/2004/06/08privatisationroad map (accessed 7 May 2012).

Hall, A. (2006) 'From Fome Zero to Bolsa Familia: Social Policies and Poverty Alleviation under Lula', *Journal of Latin American Studies*, Vol. 38, No. 4.

Hall, S. (1985) 'Authoritarian Populism: A reply to Jessop et al.', *New Left Review*, No. 151.

—— (1980) 'Popular-Democratic vs Authoritarian Populism: Two Ways of "Taking Democracy Seriously"', in A. Hunt (ed.), *Marxism and Democracy* (London: Lawrence and Wishart).

—— (1979) 'Culture, the Media and the "Ideological Effect"', in J. Curran, M. Gurevitch and J. Woollacott (eds.), *Mass Communication and Society* (London: Edward Arnold).

Harvey, D. (2006) 'Space as a Keyword', in *Spaces of Global Capitalism* (London/New York: Verso).

Heller, P. L. (1970) 'Familism Scale: A Measure of Family Solidarity', *Journal of Marriage and the Family*, Vol. 32, No. 1, 73–80.

Heper, M. (1992) 'The Strong State as a Problem for the Consolidation of Democracy: Turkey and Germany Compared', *Comparative Political Studies*, Vol. 25, No. 2.

—— (1985) *The State Tradition in Turkey* (Huntingdon: The Eothen Press).

Heper, H. and Evin, A. (eds.), (1988) *State, Democracy and the Military: Turkey in the 1980s* (Berlin and New York: Walter de Gruyter).

Hobsbawm, Eric J. (1994) *The Age of Extremes* (New York: Pantheon Books).

Hopf, T. (2002) *Social Construction of International Politics: Identities and Foreign Policies, Moscow, 1955 and 1999* (Ithaca, NY: Cornell University Press).

HUIPS (Hacettepe University Institute of Population Studies) (2006) *Türkiye Göç ve Yerinden Olmuş Nüfus Araştırması*. http://www.hips.hacettepe.edu.tr/eng/dokumanlar/ TGYONA%20_Ana_Rapor.pdf (last accesed 10 April 2013).

Human Rights Watch (2002) *Displaced and Disregarded: Turkey's Failing Village Return Program* (Washington, DC: Human Rights Watch).

Hürriyet Daily News (21 January 2013), 'Turkish PM Ups the Ante in Call for More Children', http://www.hurriyetdailynews.com/turkish-pm-ups-the-ante-in-call-for-more-children.aspx?pageID=549&nID=39513&NewsCatID=338 (accessed 7 January 2013).

Hürriyet (7 March 2010) 'Eşcinsellik Hastalık Tedavi Edilmeli' ('Homosexuality is a disease and should be treated') http://www.hurriyet.com.tr/pazar/14031207.asp (accessed 7 January 2013).

IFPRI (2007) *Impact Evaluation of the Conditional Cash Transfer Program in Turkey: Final Report* (Washington, DC: International Food Policy Research Institute).

Ilcan, S. & Basok, T. (2004) 'Community Government: Voluntary Agencies, Social Justice, and the Responsibilization of Citizens', *Citizenship Studies*, Vol. 8, No. 2.

Işık, O. and Pınarcıoğlu, M. (2001) *Nöbetleşe Yoksulluk* (İstanbul: İletişim Yayınları).

İİB (1963) *Pre-Plan for Eastern Marmara* (Ankara: Ministry of Development and Housing).

İnal, A. (2010) 'Tabloid Habercilik', in B. Çaplı and H. Tuncel (eds.), *Televizyon Haberciliğinde Etik*. http://ilef.ankara.edu.tr/etik (last accessed 04 January 2013).

İnanıcı, H. (2012) 'Türkiye'de Polis, İktidar ve İnsan Hakları', *Birikim*, No. 273.

—— (2011) *Parçalanmış Adalet. Türkiye'de Özel Ceza Yargısı* (İstanbul: İletişim Yayınları).

İnsel, A. (2003) 'The AKP and Normalizing Democracy in Turkey', *The South Atlantic Quarterly*, Vol. 102, No. 2/3.

—— (1996), *Düzen ve Kalkınma Kıskacında Türkiye: Kalkınma Sürecinde Devletin Rolü*, (İstanbul: Ayrıntı Yayınları).

İnsel, A. and Aktar C. (1985–87) 'Devletin Bekâsı İçin Yürütülen Çağdaşlaşma Sürecinin Toplumsal Sorunları', *Toplum ve Bilim*, 31/39.

İŞKUR (2011) 'Turkish Employment Institution Unemployment Insurance Services', http://statik.iskur.gov.tr/tr/sikca_sorulan_sorular/sss_issizlik_sigortasi_.htm (accessed 20 August 2010).

İTO (İstanbul Ticaret Odası) (1999) *Türk Sosyal Güvenlik Sisteminde Arayışlar: Özelleştirme ve Yeniden Yapılanma* (İstanbul).

Jacoby, T. (2005) 'Semi-Authoritarian Incorporation and Autocratic Militarism in Turkey', *Development and Change*, Vol. 36, No. 4.

Jayasuriya, K. (2005) *Reconstituting the Liberal Global Order* (London and New York: Routledge).

—— (2001a) 'Globalization and the Changing Architecture of the State: The Regulatory State and the Politics of Negative Coordination'', *Journal of European Public Policy*, Vol. 8, No. 1.

—— (2001b) 'Globalization, Sovereignty and Rule of Law: From Political to Economic Constitutionalism', *Constellations*, Vol. 8, No. 4.

Jayasuriya, K. and Hewison, K. (2004) 'The Antipolitics of Good Governance', *Critical Asian Studies*, Vol. 36, No. 4.

Jessop, B. (2008) *State Power: A Strategic-Relational Approach* (Cambridge: Polity Press).

—— (2005) 'Gramsci as a Spatial Theorist', *Critical Review of International Social and Political Philosophy*, Vol. 8, No. 4.

—— (2002) *The Future of the Capitalist State* (Cambridge: Polity Press).

—— (2001) 'Bringing the State Back in (Yet Again): Reviews, Revisions, Rejections, and Redirections', http://www.comp.lancs.ac.uk/sociology/soc070rj.html (accessed 12 April 2013).

—— (1990a) *State Theory: Putting the Capitalist State in its Place* (Cambridge: Polity Press).

—— (1990b) 'Accumulation Strategies, State Forms and Hegemonic Projects', in *State Theory: Putting the Capitalist State in its Place* (Cambridge: Polity Press).

—— (1979) 'Corporatism, Parliamentarism and Social Democracy', in G. Lehmbruch and P. Schmitter (eds.), *Trends towards Corporatist Intermediation* (Beverly Hills and London: Sage Publications).

Kandemir, O. and Aktaş, Y. (2011) 'Importance of Aid on Fight Against Poverty in Turkey', *International Journal of Economics and Finance Studies*, Vol. 3, No. 2.

Karadeniz, O. (2012) Asisp Annual Report 2012 Turkey: Pensions, Health Care and Long-term Care, http://www.socialprotection.eu/files_db/1298/asisp_ANR12_TURKEY.pdf (accessed 12 April 2013).

Karaömerlioğlu, A. (1998) 'The People's Houses and the Cult of the Peasant in Turkey', *Middle Eastern Studies*, Vol. 34, No. 4.

Karpat, K. (1976) *The Gecekondu: Rural Migration and Urbanization* (New York: Cambridge University Press).

Kavas, S. and A. Gündüz-Hoşgör (2010) 'Divorce and Family Change Revisited: Professional Women's Divorce Experience in Turkey', *Demográfia*, Vol. 53, No. 5.

Kaya, A. R. (2009) *İktidar Yumağı: Medya-Sermaye-Devlet* (Ankara: İmge Kitabevi).

Kaya, Y. (2011) '"Turkey's Turn to the East" and the Intra-Class Contradictions in Turkey', *Global Discourse [Online]*, 2: II, http://global-discourse.com/contents (accessed 12 April 2013).

Kazancıgil, A. (1981) 'The Ottoman-Turkish State and Kemalism', in Ali Kazancıgil and Ergun Özbudun (eds.), *Atatürk: Founder of a Modern State* (London: C. Hurst).

Keane, J. (1988) *Civil Society and the State: New European Perspectives* (London and New York: Verso).

KEIG (The Women's Labor and Employment Initiative Platform) (2012) 'Press Release, 10 May 2012', http://www.keig.org/eng/bilmekIstediklerimiz.aspx?id=16 (accessed 10 January 2013).

Keyder, Ç. (2004) 'The Turkish Bell Jar', *New Left Review*, No. 28.

—— (1987) *State and Class in Turkey: A Study in Capitalist Development* (London and New York: Verso).

Keyder, Ç. and Yenal, Z. (2011) 'Agrarian Change under Globalization: Markets and Insecurity in Turkish Agriculture', *Journal of Agrarian Change*, Vol. 11, No. 1.

Keyman, F. and Koyuncu Lorasdağı, B.K. (2010) *Kentler: Anadolu'nun Dönüşümü, Türkiye'nin Geleceği* (İstanbul: Doğan Kitap).

Kılıç, A. (2008) 'The Gender Dimension of Social Policy Reform in Turkey: Towards Equal Citizenship?', *Social Policy & Administration*, Vol. 42, No. 5.

Kılıç, E. (2010) *JİTEM (Türkiye'nin Faili Meçhul Tarihi)* (İstanbul: Timaş Yayınları).

Kışanak, G. (2013) 'Kürt Hareketinin Rosa'sı', *Express*, No. 132.

Kışlalı, M. A. (1996) *Güneydoğu: Düşük Yoğunluklu Çatışma* (Ankara: Ümit Yayıncılık).

Kipfer, S. (2002) 'Urbanization, Everyday Life and the Survival of Capitalism: Lefebvre, Gramsci and the Problematic of Hegemony', *Capitalism Nature Socialism*, Vol. 13, No. 2.

Kipfer, S. and Keil, R. (2002) 'Toronto Inc? Planning the Competitive City in the New Toronto', *Antipode*, Vol. 34, No. 2.

Kirişçi, K. (2005) 'Turkey: Political Dimension of Migration', in P. Fargues (ed.), *Mediterranean Migration Report 2005* (Florence: CARIM, European University Institute, Robert Schuman Centre for Advanced Studies).

Kissinger, H. (2001) *Does America Need a Foreign Policy? Toward a Diplomacy for the 21st Century* (New York: Simon & Schuster).

Knaus, G. (2005) 'Islamic Calvinists: Change and Conservatism in Middle Anatolia,' *European Stability Initiative Report*, 19 September.

Koç, Y. (1994) '*Hak İş* Konfederasyonu (1976–1980)', *Mülkiyeliler Birliği Dergisi*, Vol. 18, No. 171.

Koloğlu, O. (2006) *Osmanlı'dan 21: Yüzyıla Basın Tarihi* (İstanbul: Pozitif Yayınları).

KONDA (2011) Data-set acquired directly from KONDA on basis of mutual agreement.

—— (2007) *Political Tendencies Survey Summary Report: 2007 General Elections Tendencies Survey* (İstanbul: KONDA).

Konyar, H. (2001) 'Magazin Basınındaki Popüler Milliyetçi Söylemlerin İşlevleri', *Birikim*, No. 144.

Korkut, U. and Eslen-Ziya, H. (2011) 'The Impact of Conservative Discourses in Family Policies, Population Politics, and Gender Rights in Poland and Turkey', *Social Politics: International Studies in Gender, State & Society*, Vol. 18, No. 3.

Kozanoğlu, C. (2004) *Cilalı İmaj Devri. 1980'lerden 90'lara Türkiye ve Starları* (İstanbul: İletişim Yayınları).

Kozanoğlu, C (1995) *Pop Çağı Ateşi* (İstanbul: İletişim Yayınları).

Köse A.H. and Bahçe, S. (2009) 'Hayırsever Devletin Yükselişi: AKP Yönetiminde Gelir Dağılımı ve Yoksulluk', in B. Duru and İ. Uzgel (eds.), *AKP Kitabı: Bir Dönüşümün Bilançosu* (İstanbul: Phoenix Yayınları).

Köse, A. H. and Öncü, A. (2000) 'İşgücü Piyasaları ve Uluslararası İşbölümünde Uzmanlaşmanın Mekânsal Boyutları: 1980 Sonrası Dönemde Türkiye İmalat Sanayii', *Toplum ve Bilim*, No. 86.

Köymen, O. (2007) *Sermaye Birikirken Osmanlı, Türkiye, Dünya* (İstanbul: Yordam Kitap).

—— (1999) '*Cumhuriyet Döneminde Tarımsal Yapı ve Tarım Politikaları*', in *75 Yılda Köylerden Şehirlere* (İstanbul: Tarih Vakfı Yayınları).

Krishna, S. (1999) *Postcolonial Insecurities: India, Sri Lanka, and the Question of Nationhood* (Minneapolis: University of Minnesota Press).

Kudat, A. (2006) 'Evaluating the Conditional Cash Transfer Program in Turkey: A Qualitative Assessment', *Final report submitted to the General Directorate of Social Assistance and Solidarity, Prime Ministry, Republic of Turkey* (Washington, DC: International Food Policy Research Institute).

Kumbaracıbaşı, A. (2009) *Turkish Politics and the Rise of the AKP: Dilemmas of Institutionalization and Leadership Strategy* (New York: Routledge).

Kurtoğlu, A. (1998) 'Local Politics and Social Networks in Urban Turkey: The Case of Hemşehrilik in The Keçiören' (Unpublished PhD Thesis: METU).

Kurzman, C. (2002) 'Introduction: The Modernist Islamic Movement', *Modernist Islam 1840–1940: A Sourcebook* (Oxford: Oxford University Press).

Kuyucu, T. and Ünsal, O. (2010) '"Urban Transformation" as State-led Property Transfer: An Analysis of Two Cases of Urban Renewal in İstanbul', *Urban Studies*, Vol. 47, No. 7.

Küçükömer, İ. (2009) *Batılılaşma ve Düzenin Yabancılaşması* (İstanbul: Profil Yayıncılık).

Laclau, E. (2007) *On Populist Reason* (London and New York: Verso).

—— (2005a) *On Populist Reason* (London and New York: Verso).

—— (2005b) 'Populism: What's in a Name?', in Francisco Panizza (ed.), *Populism and the Mirror of Democracy* (London and New York: Verso).

—— (1977) *Politics and Ideology in Marxist Theory. Capitalism-Fascism-Populism* (London: NLB).

Laçiner, S. (2011) *Dışımızdaki PKK İçimizdeki İsrail* (İstanbul: Hayykitap).

—— (1999) 'Apo Krizi ve Medya', *Birikim*, No. 117.

Landau M. J. (1995), *Pan-Turkism: From Irredentism to Cooperation* (Indianapolis: Indiana University Press).

Lears, T. and Jackson J. (1985) 'The Concept of Cultural Hegemony: Problems and Possibilities', *The American Historical Review*, Vol. 90, No. 3.

Lee, S. and McBride, S. (2007) *Neoliberalism, State Power and Global Governance* (Dordrecht: Springer).

Lefebvre, H. (2007) *The Production of Space* (Oxford: Blackwell Publishing).

Lewis, L. (2001) 'The Decline of the Male Breadwinner Model: Implications for Work and Care', *Social Politics*, Vol. 8, No. 2.

Loopmans, M. and Decker, P. (2010) 'Social Mix and Passive Revolution: A Neo-Gramscian Analysis of the Social Mix Rhetoric in Flanders, Belgium', *Housing Studies* 2.

Luccisano, L. (2008) 'Mexico's Progresa Program (1997–2000): An Example of Neo-Liberal Poverty Alleviation Programs Concerned with Gender, Human Capital Development, Responsibility and Choice', *Journal of Poverty*, Vol. 8, No. 4.

Makal, A. (2002) *Türkiye'de Çok Partili Dönemde Çalışma İlişkileri: 1946–1963* (Ankara: İmge Yayınevi).

Mann, M. (1993) *The Sources of Social Power, Vol. II: The Rise of Classes and Nation-States 1760–1914* (Cambridge and New York: Cambridge University Press).

Mardin, Ş. (1992) 'Türk Toplumunu İnceleme Aracı Olarak "Sivil Toplum"', in Mümtaz'er Türköne-Tuncay Önder (eds.), *Şerif Mardin, Makaleler 1: Türkiye'de Toplum ve Siyaset* (İstanbul: İletişim Yayınları).

—— (1974) 'Super-Westernization in Urban Life in the Ottoman Empire in the Last Quarter of the Nineteenth Century', in P. Benedict, E. Tümertekin and F. Mansur (eds.), *Turkey: Geographic and Social Perspectives* (Leiden: E.J. Brill).

—— (1973) 'Center-Periphery Relations: A Key to Turkish Politics?', *Daedalus*, Winter.

—— (1969) 'Power, Civil Society and Culture in the Ottoman Empire', *Comparative Studies in Society and History*, Vol. 11, No. 3.

MARKA (2010) 'TR 42 Regional Plan for Eastern Marmara', www.marka.org.tr (accessed 1 August 2011).

Marois, T. (2012) *Interpreting Emerging Finance Capitalism in Turkey*, http://eprints.soas. ac.uk/13614/1/Interpreting_Emerging_Finance_Capitalism_in_Turkey_Thomas-Marois_ResearchTurkey_.pdf (accessed 12 April 2013).

—— (2011) 'Emerging Market Bank Rescues in an Era of Finance-led Neoliberalism: A Comparison of Mexico and Turkey', *Review of International Political Economy*, Vol. 18, No. 2.

Mavioğlu, E. (2012) *Cenderedeki Medya, Tenceredeki Gazeteci* (İstanbul: İthaki).

—— (2004) *Asılmayıp Beslenenler Bir 12 Eylül Hesaplaşması* (İstanbul: Babil Yayınları).

Mayer, T. (2000) 'Gender Ironies of Nationalism', in T. Mayer (ed.), *Gender Ironies of Nationalism: Sexing the Nation* (London: Routledge).

McSweeney, B. (1999) *Security, Identity and Interests: A Sociology of International Relations* (Cambridge: Cambridge University Press).

Memiş, E., Öneş, U. and Kızılırmak, B. (2012) 'Kadınların Ev-Kadınlaştırılması: Ücretli ve Karşılıksız Emeğin Toplumsal Cinsiyet Temelli Bir Analizi', in S. Dedeoğlu and A.Y. Elveren (eds.), *Türkiye'de Refah Devleti ve Kadın* (İstanbul: İletişim Yayınları).

Mert, N. (2007) *Merkez Sağın Kısa Tarihi* (İstanbul: Selis).

Migdal, J. S. (1988) *Strong Societies and Weak States: State-Society Relations and State Capabilities in the Third World* (Princeton, NJ: Princeton University Press).

Miller, R. A. (2007) 'Rights, Reproduction, Sexuality, and Citizenship in the Ottoman Empire and Turkey', *Signs*, Vol. 32, No. 2.

Milliyet (20 January, 2013) 'Başbakan Erdoğan: Bu ülkede kısırlaştırma hareketi yaptılar' (PM Erdoğan: They conducted a movement of sterilization in this country) http://siyaset.milliyet.com.tr/basbakan-erdogan-bu-ulkede-kisirlastirma-hareketi-yaptilar/siyaset/siyasetdetay/20.01.2013/1658093/default.htm, (accessed 28 January 2013).

Milliyet (2012) 'İlk Etapta 6 milyon konut Yıkılacak', 18 May 2012, http://ekonomi. milliyet.com.tr/ilk-etapta-6-milyon-konut-yikilacak/ekonomi/ekonomidetay/ 18.05.2012/1541939/default.htm (accessed 28 June 2012).

Milliyet (2007) 'İstanbul'da yaşamanın bir bedeli olmalı', 2 December 2007, http://www. milliyet.com.tr/2007/12/02/son/sonsiy10.asp (accessed 4 July 2012).

Ministry of Industry and Trade (2010) *Turkish Industrial Strategy Document 2011–2014*, http://www.sanayi.gov.tr/Files/Documents/TurkiyeSanayiStratejisiIngilizce.pdf (accessed 12 April 2013).

Mitchell, T. (1991) 'The Limits of the State: Beyond Statist Approaches and Their Critics', *The American Political Science Review*, Vol. 85, No. 1.

Moran, B. (2009) *Türk Romanına Eleştirel Bir Bakış* (İstanbul: İletişim Yayınları).

Morton, A. D. (2012) 'Sosyolojik Marksizmin Sınırları', *Praksis*, No. 27.

Mouffe, C. (2005) 'The "End of Politics" and the Challenge of Right-Wing Populism', in Francisco Panizza (ed.), *Populism and the Mirror of Democracy* (London and New York: Verso).

Mufti, M. (2009) *Daring and Caution in Turkish Strategic Culture: A Republic at Sea* (London: Palgrave Macmillan).

Munck, R. (2005) 'Neoliberalism and Politics, and the Politics of Neoliberalism', in A. Saad-Filho and D. Johnston (eds.), *Neoliberalism A Critical Reader* (London: Pluto Press).

—— (1997), 'A Thin Democracy', *Latin America Perspectives*, No. 97.

Musluk, C. (2010), 'Kürt Sorununa Liberal-Muhafazakâr "Çözüm" Denemesi', in Ç. Sümer and F. Yaşlı (eds.), *Hegemonyadan Diktatoryaya AKP ve Liberal Muhafazakâr İttifak* (Ankara: Tan Yayınları).

MÜSİAD (2013) 'MÜSİAD'la Tanışın', http://www.musiad.org.tr/syf.asp?kat=musiad (accessed 22 January 2013).

Mütevellioğlu, N. and Işık S. (2009) 'Türkiye Emek Piyasasında Neoliberal Dönüşüm', in Nergis Mütevellioğlu, Sinan Sönmez (eds.), *Küreselleşme, Kriz ve Türkiye'de Neoliberal Dönüşüm* (İstanbul: Bilgi Üniversitesi Yayınları).

Mütevellioğlu, N. and Sönmez, S. (eds.) (2009) *Küreselleşme, Kriz ve Türkiye'de Neoliberal Dönüşüm* (İstanbul: Bilgi Üniversitesi Yayınları).

Nasr, V. (2009) *Forces of Fortune: The Rise of the New Muslim Middle Class and What It Will Mean for Our World* (New York: Free Press).

Nauck, B. and D. Klaus (2008) 'Family Change in Turkey: Peasant Society, Islam, and the Revolution from Above', in R. Jayakody, A. Thornton and W. Axinn (eds.), *International Family Change: Ideational Perspectives* (New York: Erlbaum).

Nebiler, H. (1995) *Medyanın Ekonomi Politiği* (İstanbul: Sarmal Yayınevi).

Neocleous, M. (2008) *Critique of Security* (Edinburgh: Edinburgh University Press).

—— (1996) *Administering Civil Society: Towards a Theory of State Power* (London: Macmillan Press).

Ntvmsnbc (2012) 'Şimdi gideceğiz, evleri yıkacağız' 2 April 2012. http://www.ntvmsnbc.com/id/25335977/ (accessed 27 June 2012).

OECD (2008) *OECD Territorial Reviews: İstanbul, Turkey*, http://www.oecd.org/data oecd/1/62/40317916.pdf (accessed 15 July .2012).

OECD (2006) *Economic Surveys: Turkey*, http://www.oecd-ilibrary.org/economics/oecd-economic-surveys-turkey-2006_eco_surveys-tur-2006-en (accessed 25 December 2012).

Offe, C. (1984) 'Ungovernability: The Renaissance of the Conservative Theories of Crisis', *Contradictions of the Welfare State* (London, Sydney: Hutchinson).

Oğuz, H. (1995) *1980 Sonrası İşçi Hareketinde Durum* (İstanbul: Scala Yayıncılık).

Oğuz, Ş. (2009) 'The Response of the Turkish State to the 2008 Crisis: A Further Step towards Neoliberal Authoritarian Statism', Presentation at Third IIPPE International Research Workshop, http://www.iippe.org/wiki/images/a/ac/Oguz_IIPPE_Ankara.pdf (accessed 12 April 2013).

Ollman, B. (1993) *Dialectical Investigations* (New York and London: Routledge).

Onaran, Ö. (2002) 'Adjusting the Economy through Labor Market: The Myth of Rigidity', in N. Balkan and S. Savran (eds.), *Ravages of Neoliberalism: Economy, Society, and Gender in Turkey* (New York: Nova Scientific).

Oran, B. (2001a) 'Giriş: Türk Dış Politikasının (TDP) Teori ve Pratiği', in Baskın Oran (ed.), *Türk Dış Politikası: Kurtuluş Savaşından Bugüne Olgular, Belgeler, Yorumlar, Cilt 1: 1919–1980* (İstanbul: İletişim Yayınları).

—— (2001b) 'Dönemin Bilançosu', in Baskın Oran (ed.), *Türk Dış Politikası: Kurtuluş Savaşından Bugüne Olgular, Belgeler, Yorumlar, Cilt 2: 1980–2001* (İstanbul: İletişim Yayınları).

OSD (2012) 'General and Statistical Information Bulletin of Automotive Manufacturers 2012 – I, http://www.osd.org.tr/cata2012.pdf (accessed 20 August 2012).

Oyan, O. and Aydın A. R. (1987) *İstikrar Programından Fon Ekonomisine* (Ankara: Teori Yayınları).

Ozan, E. D. (2012) *Gülme Sırası Bizde 12 Eylül'e Giderken Sermaye Sınıfı, Kriz ve Devlet* (İstanbul: Metis Yayınları).

Öngel, F. S. (2011) Global Value Chains and Their Spatial Effects: The Gebze Example (unpublished PhD thesis: Mimar Sinan Fine Arts University).

Öngen, T. (2002) 'Political Crisis and Strategies for Management: From "Low Intensity Conflict" to "Low Intensity Instability"', in N. Balkan and S. Savran (eds.), *The Politics of Permanent Crisis: Class, Ideology and State in Turkey* (New York: Nova Science Publishers Inc.).

Öngider, S. (2005) *Son Klasik Darbe 12 Eylül Söyleşileri* (İstanbul: Aykırı Yayıncılık).

Öniş, Z. (2012) 'The Triumph of Conservative Globalism: The Political Economy of the AKP Era', *Turkish Studies*, Vol. 13, No. 2.

—— (2009) 'Beyond the 2001 Financial Crisis: The Political Economy of the New Phase of Neo-liberal Restructuring in Turkey', *Review of International Political Economy*, Vol. 16, No. 3.

—— (2007) 'Conservative Globalism versus Defensive Nationalism: Political Parties and Paradoxes of Europeanization in Turkey', *Journal of Southern Europe and the Balkans*, Vol. 9, No. 3.

—— (2006a) 'The Political Economy of Turkey's Justice and Development Party', in M. Hakan Yavuz (ed.), *The Emergence of a New Turkey: Democracy and the AK Parti* (Salt Lake City: The University of Utah Press).

—— (2006b) 'Globalization and Party Transformation: Turkey's Justice and Development Party in Perspective', in Peter Burnell (ed.), *Globalizing Democracy: Party Politics in Emerging Democracies* (London: Routledge).

—— (2006c) 'The Political Economy of Islam and Democracy in Turkey: From the Welfare Party to the AKP', in Dietrich Jung (ed.), *Democracy and Development: New Political Strategies for the Middle East* (New York: Palgrave).

—— (2003) 'Domestic Politics versus Global Dynamics: Towards a Political Economy of the 2000 and 2001 Financial Crises in Turkey', in Z. Öniş and B. Rubin (eds.), *Turkish Economy in Crisis* (London: Frank Cass).

—— (1998) *State and Market: The Political Economy of Turkey in Comparative Perspective* (İstanbul: Boğaziçi Üniversitesi Yayınları).

—— (1997) 'The Political Economy of Islamic Resurgence in Turkey: The Rise of the Welfare Party in Perspective', *Third World Quarterly*, Vol. 18. No. 4.

Öniş, Z. And Türem, U. (2001) 'Business, Globalization and Democracy: A Comparative Analysis of Turkish Business Associations', *Turkish Studies*, Vol. 2, No. 2.

Özal, T. (1992) "Türkiye'nin Önüne Hâcet Kapıları Açılmıştır (Mülâkat)" *Türkiye Günlüğü*, No. 19.

Özar, Ş. and Çakar, B. Y. (2012) 'Devlet, Aile ve Piyasa Kıskacında 'Erkeksiz Kadınlar', Paper presented at the conference Turkey Debates its Social Policies, İstanbul, 15–16 June 2012.

Özbay, F. (1995) 'Women's Labor in Rural and Urban Settings', *Boğaziçi Journal: Review of Social, Economic and Administrative Studies*, Vol. 8, No. 1–2.

Özbilgin, M. and Healy, G. (2004) 'The Gendered Nature of Career Development of University Professors: The Case of Turkey', *Journal of Vocational Behavior*, Vol. 64, No. 2.

Özcan, G. (2006) 'Türkiye'de Siyasal Rejim ve Güvenlikleştirme Sorunsalı', in B. Ülman and İ. Akça (eds.), *İktisat, Siyaset, Devlet Üzerine Yazılar. Prof. Dr. Kemâli Saybaşılı'ya Armağan* (İstanbul: Bağlam Yayıncılık).

—— (ed.) (1998) *Onbir Aylık Saltanat: Siyaset, Ekonomi ve Dış Politikada Refahyol Dönemi: Bir Koalisyonun Anatomisi* (İstanbul: Boyut Yayınları).

Özdağ, Ü. (2007) *Türk Ordusunun PKK Operasyonları (1984–2007)* (İstanbul: Pegasus Yayınları).

Özdek,Y. (2011) *Şirket Egemenliği Çağı* (İstanbul: Notabene).

Özdemir, A.M. and Yücesan-Özdemir, G. (2008) 'Opening Pandora's Box: Social Security Reform in Turkey in the Time of the AKP', *SEER-South-East Europe Review for Labour and Social Affairs*, No. 4.

Özdemir, Ş. (2006) *MÜSİAD: Anadolu Sermayesinin Dönüşümü ve Türk Modernleşmesinin Derinleşmesi* (Ankara: Vadi Yayınları).

Özden,Y. G. (2002) 'Üçüncü Meşrutiyet', *İleri*, No. 12.

Özel, I. (2012) 'The Politics of De-delegation: Regulatory (in)dependence in Turkey', *Regulation and Governance*, No. 6.

Özgen, T. (2002) 'Political Crisis and Strategies for Crisis Management: From "Low Intensity Conflict" to "Low Intensity Instability"', in N. Balkan and S. Savran (eds.), *The Politics of Permanent Crisis: Class, Ideology and State in Turkey* (New York: Nova Science Publishers).

Özkan, F. (2009) 'Gerçek Burjuva Sınıfı Biziz', http://www.haber7.com/haber/ 20090720/Erol-Yarar-Gercek-burjuva-sinifi-biziz.php (accessed 20 July .2009).

Özkan, U. R. (2009) 'The Translation of Competing Ideas to the Turkish Welfare-Production Regime', Paper Presented at the Annual Conference of the International Sociological Association's (ISA) Research Committee on Poverty, Social Welfare and Social Policy (RC19) entitled 'Social Policies: Local Experiments, Travelling Ideas'.

Özkazanç, A. (2007) *Siyaset Sosyolojisi Yazıları. Yeni Sağ ve Sonrası.* (Ankara: Dipnot Yayınları).

—— (1996) 'Türkiye'de Yeni Sağ', *Cumhuriyet Dönemi Türkiye Ansiklopedisi*, Vol. 15, (İstanbul: İletişim Yayınları).

Özkırımlı, U. (2002) 'Türkiye'de Gayrıresmi ve Popüler Milliyetçilik', *Modern Türkiye'de Siyasi Düşünce: Milliyetçilik* (İstanbul: İletişim).

Özler, I. and Sarkissian, A. (2009) 'Negotiating Islam, Civil Society, and Secularism: The Justice and Development Party in Turkey' (APSA 2009 Toronto Meeting Paper).

Özsu, F. and Ertekin, O. G. (2013) *Türkleşmek İslamlaşmak Memurlaşmak (AK Parti, Cemaat ve Yargının Hikayesi)* (Ankara: Nika Yayınevi).

Öztaş, K. A. (2002) 'Mazlum Ulusların Devrim ve Kalkınma İdeolojisi: Kemalist Milli Devrim', *İleri*, No. 9.

Öztürk, M. and Ercan, F. (2009) '1979 Krizinden 2001 Krizine Türkiye'de Sermaye Birikimi Süreci ve Yaşanan Dönüşümler', *Praksis*, No. 19.

Öztürk, Ö.(2009) 'Sendikal Mücadele, Sermaye Birikimi, MESS ve Koç Holding', *Praksis*, No 19.

Özuğurlu, M. (2009) 'Türkiye'de Muhalefet Krizi, Ulusalcılık, Örgütlü Emek Hareketi ve Sol', in N. Mütevellioğlu and S. Sönmez (eds.), *Küreselleşme, Kriz ve Türkiye'de Neoliberal Dönüşüm* (İstanbul: Bilgi Üniversitesi Yayınları).

Özyürek, E. (2008) *Modernlik Nostaljisi: Kemalizm, Laiklik ve Gündelik Hayatta Siyaset* (İstanbul: Boğaziçi Üniv. Yayınları).

Paker E. B. and Akça İ. (eds.) (2010) *Türkiye'de Ordu, Devlet ve Güvenlik Siyaseti* (İstanbul: İstanbul Bilgi Üniversitesi Yayınları).

Panitch, L. (1996) 'Rethinking the Role of the State', in James Mittelman (ed.), *Globalization: Critical Reflections* (Boulder, CO: Lynn Rienner).

—— (1994) 'Globalization and the State', *Socialist Register 1994* (London: Merlin Press).

Panizza, F. (2005) 'Populism and the Mirror of Democracy', in Francisco Panizza (ed.), *Populism and the Mirror of Democracy* (London and New York: Verso).

Panizza, F. (ed.) (2005) *Populism and the Mirror of Democracy* (London: Verso).

Park, B. (2008) 'Turkey's Deep State,' *The RUSI Journal* 153, no. 5.

Parla, A. (2001) 'The "Honor" of the State: Virginity Examinations in Turkey', *Feminist Studies*, Vol. 27, No. 1.

Parla, T. (1995) *Türkiye'nin Siyasal Rejimi 1980–1989* (İstanbul: İletişim Yayınları).

—— (1993) *Türkiye'de Anayasalar* (İstanbul: İletişim Yayınları).

Parla, T. and Davison, A. (2004) *Corporatist Ideology in Kemalist Turkey: Progress or Order?* (Syracuse NY: Syracuse University Press).

Patton, Marcie J. (2008) 'The Distributive Politics of the Soft-Islamist Government in Turkey' Paper Presented at the Annual Meeting of the ISA's 49th Annual Convention, Bridging Multiple Divides, http://citation.allacademic.com/meta/p253514_index.html (accessed 20 February 2013).

Peck, Jamie and Tickell, Adam (2002) 'Neoliberalizing State', *Antipode*, Vol. 34, No. 3.

Pedwell, C. (2012) 'Economies of Empathy: Obama, Neoliberalism and Social Justice', *Environment and Planning D: Society and Space*, Vol. 30, No. 2.

Petras, J. and Vieux, S. (1994) 'The Transition to Authoritarian Electoral Regimes in Latin America', *Latin America Perspectives*, No. 83.

Phongpaichit, P. and Baker, C. (2008) 'Thaksin's Populism', *Journal of Contemporary Asia*, Vol. 38, No. 1.

Pollitt, C. and Bouckaert, G. (2000) *Public Management Reform: A Comparative Analysis – New Public Management, Governance, and the Neo-Weberian State* (Oxford: Oxford University Press).

Porter, D. and Craig, D. (2004) 'The Third Way and the Third World: Poverty Reduction and Social Inclusion in the Rise of "Inclusive" Liberalism', *Review of International Political Economy*, Vol. 11, No. 2.

Portes, A. and Hoffman, K. (2003) 'Latin American Class Structures: Their Composition and Change during the Neoliberal Era', *Latin American Research Review*, Vol. 38, No. 1.

Poulantzas, N. (2000) *State, Power, Socialism* (London and New York: Verso).

—— (1978) *Political Power and Social Classes* (London: Verso).

Raco, M. (2003) 'Governmentality, Subject-Building, and the Discourses and Practices of Devolution in the UK', *Transactions of the Institute of British Geographers New Series*, Vol. 28, No. 1.

Radikal (8 March 2008) 'Kadınlar Günü öğüdü: En az üç çocuk yapın' (Women's Day Advice: Give at least three births), http://www.radikal.com.tr/haber.php?haberno=249531 (accessed 20 January 2013).

Roberts, A. (2010) *The Logic of Discipline: Global Capitalism and the Architecture of Government* (Oxford: Oxford University Press).

Roberts, K. M. (1995) 'Neoliberalism and the Transformation of Populism in Latin America. The Peruvian Case', *World Politics*, No. 48.

Rose, N. (2001) 'The Politics of Life Itself', *Theory, Culture & Society*, Vol. 18, No. 6.

Ruckert, A. (2010) 'The Forgotten Dimension of Social Reproduction: The World Bank and the Poverty Reduction Strategy Paradigm', *Review of International Political Economy*, Vol. 17, No. 5.

Said, E. (1995) *Orientalism: Western Conceptions of the Orient* (London: Penguin).

Salah, M. (1984) 'The Turkish Left in Perspective', *Khamsin*, no. 11.

Sarıkaya, E. and Özcan Z.Y. (2005) *Aile Sağlık Rehberi* (Family Health Guide). Ankara.

Sassen, S. (1991) *The Global City: New York, London, Tokyo* (Princeton, NJ: Princeton University Press).

Savran, S. (2010) *Türkiye'de Sınıf Mücadeleleri, Cilt 1: 1908–1980* (İstanbul: Yordam Kitap).

Saybaşılı K. (1995) *DYP-SHP Koalisyonunun Üç Yılı* (İstanbul: Bağlam Yayınları).

Sayer, D. (1987) *The Violence of Abstraction: The Analytic Foundations of Historical Materialism* (Oxford: Basil Blackwell).

Sazak F. (ed.) (2006) *Türkiye'de Sendikal Kriz ve Sendikal Arayışlar* (Ankara: EPOS).

Schamis, H. (1991) 'Reconceptualizing Latin American Authoritarianism in the 1970s: From Bureaucratic-Authoritarianism to Neoconservatism', *Comparative Politics*, Vol. 23, No. 2.

Scheurman, W. E. (2008) *Frankfurt School Perspectives on Globalization, Democracy, and the Law* (New York: Routledge).

Scott, J. C. (1998) *Seeing Like a State: How Certain Schemes to Improve the Human Condition Have Failed* (New Haven, CT: Yale University Press).

Seçkin, G. (1999a) '1990'lı Yılların Basın Kavgalarının Ekonomi Politiği ve Bir Örnek Olay: Doğan, Sabah ve Akşam Gruplarının (Ekim-Aralık 1995) Kavgası', in K. Alemdar (ed.), *Medya Gücü ve Demokratik Kurumlar* (İstanbul: Afa).

—— (1999b) 'Basında Ekonomik Gazeteler Dönemi: Muhabirsiz Gazeteler', in K. Alemdar (ed.), *Medya Gücü ve Demokratik Kurumlar* (İstanbul: Afa).

SGK (2008) 2008 Statistics Almanac, http://www.sgk.gov.tr/wps/portal/tr/kurumsal/istatistikler (accessed 20 August 2011).

Silver, B. (2003) *Forces of Labor: Workers' Movement and Globalization Since 1870* (Cambridge: Cambridge University Press).

Smart, B. (1989) *Foucault, Marxism and Critique* (London: Routledge).

Soja, E. W. (1989) *Postmodern Geographies: The Reassertion of Space in Critical Social Theory* (London: Verso).

Song, J. (2009) *South Koreans in the Debt Crisis: The Creation of a Neoliberal Welfare Society*, (Durham, NC: Duke University Press).

Sönmez, M. (2012) 'Rehine TÜSİAD, Rehine Medya', *Cumhuriyet*, 8–9 June 2012.

—— (2011) *Paran Kadar Sağlık: Türkiye'de Sağlığın Ticarilesmesi* (İstanbul: Yordam Kitap).

—— (2010a) *Teğet'in Yıkımı* (İstanbul: Yordam).

—— (2010b) *Türkiye'de İş Dünyasının Örgütleri ve Yönelimleri* (İstanbul: Friedrich Ebert Stiftung).

—— (2009) '2000'ler Türkiye'sinde AKP Hakim Sınıflar ve İç Çelişkileri', in İ. Uzgel and B. Duru (eds.), *AKP Kitabı Bir Dönüşümün Bilançosu* (Ankara: Phoenix Yayınevi).

—— (2007) *Doğu-Güneydoğu'nun Artan Yoksulluğu ve Çözümü: Barış*, http://eski.bianet.org/static/dogu2.pdf (last accesed 10 April 2013).

—— (2004) *Filler ve Çimenler: Medya ve Finans Sektöründe Doğan/Anti-Doğan Savaşı* (İstanbul: İletişim Yayınları).

—— (1992) *Kırk Haramiler* (Ankara: Arkadaş Yayınevi).

—— (1984) *Türkiye Ekonomisinde Bunalım 1980 Sonbaharından 1982'ye* (İstanbul: Belge Yayınları).

—— (1980) *Türkiye Ekonomisinde Bunalım 24 Ocak Kararları ve Sonrası* (İstanbul: Belge Yayınları).

Sönmez, S. (2009) 'Türkiye Ekonomisinde Neoliberal Dönüşüm Politikaları ve Etkileri', in N. Mütevellioğlu and S. Sönmez (eds.), *Küreselleşme, Kriz ve Türkiye'de Neoliberal Dönüşüm* (İstanbul: Bilgi Üniversitesi Yayınları).

Sönmez, Ü. (2011a) 'The Political Economy of Market and Regulatory Reforms in Turkey: The Logic and Unintended Consequences of Ad-hoc Strategies', *New Political Economy*, Vol. 16, No. 1.

—— (2011b) *Piyasanın İdaresi: Neoliberalizm ve Bağımsız Düzenleyici Kurumların Anatomisi* (İstanbul: İletişim Yayınları).

State Planning Organization and World Bank (2009) 'Social and Economic Benefits of More and Better Job Opportunities for Women in Turkey', http://siteresources.worldbank.org/ECAEXT/Resources/Turkey_FemaleReport_3_pager_final_final.pdf (accessed 28 January 2013).

Stavrakakis, Y. (2005) 'Religion and Populism in Contemporary Greece', in F. Panizza (ed.), *Populism and Mirror of Democracy* (London: Verso).

Stepan, A. (1988) *Rethinking Military Politics: Brazil and Southern Cone* (Princeton, NJ: Princeton University Press).

Sturgeon, T. J. (2006) 'Conceptualizing Integrative Trade: The Global Value Chains Framework', in D. Ciuriak (ed.), *Trade Policy Research 2006* (Ottawa: Department of Foreign Affairs and International Trade).

Sunar, İ. (2004) 'Populism and Patronage:The Demokrat Party and Its Legacy in Turkey', in *State, Society and Democracy in Turkey* (İstanbul: Bahçeşehir University Publication).

—— (1974) *State and Society in the Politics of Turkey's Development* (Ankara: Ankara Üniversitesi Siyasal Bilgiler Fakültesi Yayınları).

Sümer, Ç. and Yaşlı, F. (eds.), (2010) *Hegemonyadan Diktatoryaya AKP ve Liberal Muhafazakâr İttifak* (Ankara:Tan Yayınları).

Sütlaş, M. (2012) 'Hastaneleri' Yönetenler Değisti, Biliyor musunuz?', BIANET, http://www.bianet.org/bianet/ekonomi/141910-hastaneleri-yonetenler-degisti-biliyor-musunuz (accessed 12 April 2013).

Şafak, C. (2004) '4857 Sayılı İş Kanunu Çerçevesinde Taşeron (Alt İşveren) Meselesi', *Türkiye Barolar Birliği Dergisi*, No. 51.

Şen, M. (2010) 'Transformation of Turkish Islamism and the Rise of the Justice and Development Party', *Turkish Studies*, Vol. 11, No. 1.

Şen, M., Aksular, A. D. and Samur, Z. O. (2009) 'FBOs and Social Exclusion in Turkey', in D. Dierckx, J. Vranken and V. Kerstens (eds.), *Faith-Based Organisations and Social Exclusion in European Cities* (Leuven: Acco).

Şen, S. (1995) *Refah Partisi'nin Teori ve Pratiği: Refah Partisi, Adil Düzen ve Kapitalizm* (İstanbul: Sarmal Yayınevi).

Şener, M.Y. (2010) 'The World Bank's Risk Management Approach to Poverty as a Form of Neoliberal Governmentality? The Case of "the Social Risk Mitigation Project" in Turkey' (unpublished PhD Dissertation: University of Illinois at Urbana-Champaign).

Şenses, F. and Koyuncu, M. (2007) 'Socioeconomic Effects of Economic Crises: A Comparative Analysis of the Experiences of Argentina, Indonesia and Turkey', in A.H. Köse, F. Şenses and E.Yeldan (eds.), *Globalization as New Imperialism: Reconstruction of the Periphery* (New York: Nova Science Publishers).

Şenyapılı,T. (1996) *1980 Sonrasında Ruhsatsız Konut Yapımı* (Ankara:TKİB).

Şık, A. (2012) *Pusu (Devletin Yeni Sahipleri)* (İstanbul: Postacı Yeyınevi)

—— (2011) *000 Kitap Dokunan Yanar* (İstanbul: Postacı Yeyınevi).

Taggart, P. (2000) *Populism* (Buckingham and Philadelphia: Open University Press).

Tanör, B. (2010) *Anayasal Gelişme Tezleri* (İstanbul:YKY).

—— (2002) 'Siyasal Tarih (1980–1995)', in B. Tanör, K. Boratav and S. Akşin, *Bugünkü Türkiye 1980–1995* (İstanbul: Cem Yayınevi).

Taş, H. and Lightfoot, D. R. (2005) 'Gecekondu Settlements in Turkey: Rural-Urban Migration in the Developing European Periphery', *Journal of Geography*, Vol. 104, No. 36.

Taşkın, Y. (2008) 'AKP's Move to "Conquer" the Center-Right: Its Prospects and Possible Impacts on the Democratization Process', *Turkish Studies*, Vol. 9, No. 1.

—— (2006) 'Türkiye Sağı'nı Anlamak: Soğuk Savaş ve Sonrası İçin Bir İzah Denemesi', in B. Ülman and İ. Akça (eds.), *İktisat, Siyaset ve Devlet Üzerine Yazılar. Prof. Dr. Kemâli Saybaşılı'ya Armağan* (İstanbul: Bağlam Yayıncılık).

Taşpınar, Ö. (2008) 'Turkey's Middle East Policies: Between Neo-Ottomanism and Kemalism,' *Carnegie Papers 10* (Washington, DC: Carnegie Middle East Center, Carnegie Endowment for International Peace).

Taştan, Ö. Z. (2005) 'A Critique of the Poverty Alleviation as Social Policy: The World Bank's Social Risk Mitigation Project in Turkey' (unpublished MA Thesis: Middle East Technical University).

Taymaz, E. and Özler, S. (2004) 'Labor Market Policies and EU Accession: Problems and Prospects for Turkey', *Middle East Technical University Economic Research Center Working Paper*, No. 5.

Tayyar, Ş. (2011) *Kürt Ergenekonu. Derin PKK'nın Gizli Kodları* (İstanbul: Timaş).

TBMM, (10/254) Report of the General Assembly Investigation Commission with Application Number (10/254,258), Term 22, Legislation Year 5, Sequence Number: 1273.

Teichman, J. (1997) 'Mexico and Argentina, Economic Reform and Technocratic Decision Making', *Studies in Comparative International Development*, Vol. 32, No. 1.

TGMP (2012) *Turkish Grameen Microfinance Program in Numbers*, http://tinyurl.com/c2vneq3 (accessed 12 April 2013).

Thompson, E. P. (1991) *Customs in Common* (London: Penguin Books).

—— (1963) *The Making of the English Working Class* (New York: Vintage Books).

Tilly, C. (1990) *Coercion, Capital and European States, AD 990–1990* (Oxford: Basil Blackwell).

Topçu, T. (2001) 'Avrupa Çıkmazı ve Türkiye Avrupa Birliği İlişkileri', *İleri*, No: 4.

Torumtay, N. (1996) *Değişen Stratejilerin Odağında Türkiye* (İstanbul: Milliyet Yayınları).

TOSB (2009) 'TOSB Hakkında', www.tosb.org.tr, (accessed 25 February 2009).

TTB (Turkish Medical Association) (2012) '15 Sağlık Meslek Orgütü KHB'ye Karşı Ortak Deklarasyon Yayımladı', http://www.ttb.org.tr/index.php/Haberler/khb-3414.html (accessed 24 December 2012).

—— (2009) *Hekimlerin Değerlendirmesi ile Performansa Dayalı Ödeme* (Ankara: TTB).

Tuğal, C. (2012) 'Pasif Devrimlerde Toplum, Siyaset ve Bloklar' *Praksis*, Vol. 27.

—— (2009) *Passive Revolution: Absorbing the Islamic Challenge to Capitalism* (Stanford, CA: Stanford University Press).

—— (2007a) 'NATO'nun İslamcıları', *New Left Review Turkey Edition*.

—— (2007b) 'NATO's Islamists: Hegemony and Americanization in Turkey,' *New Left Review*, Vol. 44.

TURKSTAT (2011a) *Income and Life Conditions Survey, 2006–2009* (Ankara: Turkish Statistical Institute).

—— (2011b) *Women in Statistics 2011* (Ankara: Turkish Statistical Institute).

—— (2011c) *Marriage and Divorce Statistics 2011* (Ankara: Turkish Statistical Institute).

—— (2010) *The Summary of Agricultural Statistics* (Ankara: Turkish Statistical Institute).

—— (2006) *Family Structure Survey 2006* (Ankara: Turkish Statistical Institute).

TUSKON (2009, 2012) *TUSKON Hakkında*, http://www.tuskon.org/hakkimizda/?id=tuskon (accessed 20 January 2010 & 17 July 2012).

Tuzla Tersaneler Bölgesi İzleme ve İnceleme Komisyonu (2008) Tuzla Tersaneler Bölgesi'ndeki Çalışma Koşulları ve Önlenebilir Seri İş Kazaları Hakkında Rapor, İstanbul, http://www.ikkistanbul.org/site/downloads/tersaneler.pdf (accessed 07 May 2012).

TÜİK (2012) Gayri Safi Yurtiçi Hasıla, http://www.tuik.gov.tr/VeriBilgi.do?alt_id=55, (accessed 2 August 2012).

Tümertekin, E. (1997) *İstanbul, İnsan ve Mekan* (İstanbul: Tarih Vakfı Yurt Yayınları).

Tünay, M. (1993) 'The Turkish New Right's Attempt at Hegemony', in A. Eralp, M. Tünay and B. Yeşilada (eds.), *The Political and Socioeconomic Transformation of Turkey* (Westport, CT: Praeger).

Türk, H. B. (2012) 'AKP ve Kanaat Teknisyenleri', *Birikim*, No. 276.

Türkiye Denizciler Sendikası (1987) *Türkiye'de Yapılan Grevlerin Nicel ve Nitel Değerlendirmesi (1963–1980)* (İstanbul: Sema Matbaacılık).

Türkmen N. (2012) *Eylemden Öğrenmek: TEKEL Direnişi ve Sınıf Bilinci* (İstanbul: İletişim Yayınları).

Türköne, M. (2011) *Mankurtlar: Küçük Türkiye Milliyetçiliği* (İstanbul: Etkileşim Yayınları).

—— (1991) 'Seçkin Kültürü Olarak Türk Sosyalizmi', *Türkiye Günlüğü*, No. 15.

TÜSİAD (Turkish Industry and Business Association) (1997) *Türk Sosyal Güvenlik Sisteminde Yeniden Yapılanma* (İstanbul).

Uğur, A. and Alkan, H. (2000) 'Türkiye'de İşadamı-Devlet İlişkileri Perspektifinden MÜSİAD', *Toplum ve Bilim*, No. 85.

Usul, A. R. (2008) 'The Justice and Development Party and the European Union: From Euro-Skepticisim to Euro-Enthusiasm and Euro-Fatigue', in Ümit Cizre (ed.), *Secular and Islamic Politics in Turkey: The Making of the Justice and Development Party* (London and New York: Routledge).

Uysal, A. (2012) 'Bir Psikolog Olarak Polis: Polisin Toplumsal Olaylar Eğitimi ya da 'Kalabalık Yönetimi'', *Birikim*, No. 273.

Uzgel, İ. and Duru, B. (eds.) (2009) *AKP Kitabı Bir Dönüşümün Bilançosu* (Ankara: Phoenix Yayınevi).

Ünüvar, K. (2010) 'Siyasetin Üzerindeki Hayalet: Orta Sınıflar', *Birikim*, No. 260, December.

Üskül, Z. (2003) *Olağanüstü Hal Üzerine Yazılar* (İstanbul: Büke Yayıncılık).

—— (1997) *Siyaset ve Asker. Cumhuriyet Döneminde Sıkıyönetim Uygulamaları* (Ankara: İmge Kitabevi).

Van Velzen, L. (1978) *Kayseri'de Çevresel Üretim* (İstanbul: Ajans Türk Matbaacılık).

Waterbury, J. (1992) 'Export-Led Growth and the Center-Right Coalition in Turkey', *Comparative Politics*, Vol. 24, No. 2.

WEF (World Economic Forum) (2012) *Global Gender Gap Report 2012*, http://www.weforum.org/reports/global-gender-gap-report-2012 (accessed 7 January 2013).

Weyland, K. (2003) 'Neopopulism and Neoliberalism in Latin America: How Much Affinity?', *Third World Quarterly*, Vol. 24, No. 6.

—— (2001) 'Clarifying a Contested Concept: Populism in the Study of Latin American Politics', *Comparative Politics*, Vol. 34, No. 1.

—— (1996) 'Neopopulism and Neoliberalism in Latin America; Unexpected Affinities', *Studies in Comparative International Development*, Vol. 31 No. 3.

WHO (2012) *Turkey Health System Performance Assessment 2011* (Copenhagen: WHO Regional Office for Europe).

Williams, M. E. (2002) 'Market Reforms, Technocrats and Institutional Innovations', *World Development*, Vol. 30, No. 3.

World Bank (2011) *Strengthening the Effectiveness of the Social Safety Net Project* (Washington, DC: The World Bank).

—— (2009) *Informality in Turkey: Size, Trends, Determinants and Consequences*, http://site resources.worldbank.org/TURKEYEXTN/Resources/361711–1277211666558/bpg_SizeTrendsDeterminantsAndConsequences.pdf (accessed 19 December 2012).

—— (2003) *Turkey: Poverty and Coping after the Crisis: Main Report* (Washington, DC: World Bank).

—— (1994) *Averting the Old Age Crisis* (Washington, DC: World Bank).

Wright, E. O. (2000) 'Working-Class Power, Capitalist-Class Interests and Class Compromise', *American Journal of Sociology*, Vol. 105, No. 4.

Yalçınkaya, A. (2009) 'Alevilik Hendeğinde AKP'nin Devesi: "Alevi Açılımı" Neyi "Açıyor", in İ. Uzgel and B. Duru (eds.), *AKP Kitabı: Bir Dönüşümün Bilançosu* (Ankara: Phoenix Yayınevi).

Yalman, G. (2011) 'Discourse and Practice of Poverty Reduction Strategies: Reflections on the Turkish Case in the 2000s', in İpek Eren Vural (ed.), *Converging Europe: Transformation of Social Policy in the Enlarged European Union and in Turkey* (Farnham: Ashgate).

—— (2009) *Transition to Neoliberalism: The Case of Turkey in the 1980s* (İstanbul: Bilgi Üniversitesi Yayınları).

—— (2002) 'The Turkish State and Bourgeoisie in Historical Perspective: A Relativist Paradigm or a Panoply of Hegemonic Strategies', in N. Balkan and S. Savran (eds.),

The Politics of Permanent Crisis. Class, Ideology and State in Turkey (New York: Nova Science Publishers).

Yang, O. (2006) *Family and New Governance* (Seoul Korea: Ewha Women's University Press).

Yankaya, D. (2012) '28 Şubat, İslami Burjuvazinin İktidarı Yolunda Bir Milat', *Birikim*, No. 278–279.

Yaşlı, F. (2006) 'Kızılelmacılık ve Komplocu Zihniyet', *Birikim*, No. 204, April.

Yavuz, H. (2010) 'Giriş: Türkiye'de İslami Hareketin Dönüşümünde Yeni Burjuvazinin Rolü', *AK Parti: Toplumsal Değişimin Yeni Aktörleri* (İstanbul: Kitap Yayınevi).

—— (2009) *Secularism and Muslim Democracy in Turkey* (Cambridge: Cambridge University Press).

—— (2005) *Modernleşen Müslümanlar* (İstanbul: Kitap Yayınevi).

Yavuz, M. H. (2009) *Secularism and Muslim Democracy in Turkey* (Cambridge: Cambridge University Press).

—— (2004) 'Milli Görüş Hareketi: Muhalif ve Modernist Gelenek', in Y. Aktay (ed.), *Modern Türkiye'de Siyasi Düşünce: İslamcılık Cilt 6* (İstanbul: İletişim Yayınları).

Yavuz, M. H. and Özcan, N. A. (2006) 'The Kurdish Question and Turkey's Justice and Development Party', *Middle East Policy*, Vol. 13, No. 1.

Yazıcı, B. (2012) 'The Return to the Family: Welfare, State, and Politics of the Family in Turkey', *Anthropological Quarterly*, Vol. 85, No. 1.

—— (2008) 'Social Work and Social Exclusion in Turkey: An Overview', *New Perspectives on Turkey*, No. 38.

Yazıcı, E. (1993) *Yeni Bir Dünyanın Eşiğinde Türk-İş ve Değişim* (Ankara: Sistem Yayınları).

Yeğen, M. (2006) *Müstakbel Türk'ten Sözde Vatandaşa: Cumhuriyet ve Kürtler* (İstanbul: İletişim Yayınları).

Yeldan, E (2010) 'Global Crises and Turkey: A Macroeconomic Assessment of the Effects of Fiscal Stimulus Measures on Employment and Labour Markets', in *Crises and Turkey: Impact Analysis of Crisis, Response Measures* (Ankara: Ankara Office of International Labour Organization).

—— (2006) 'Neoliberal Global Remedies: From Speculative-Led Growth to IMF-Led Crisis in Turkey', *Review of Radical Political Economics*, Vol. 38, No. 2.

—— (2001a) *Küreselleşme Sürecinde Türkiye Ekonomisi: Bölüşüm, Birikim ve Büyüme* (İstanbul: İletişim Yayınları).

—— (2001b) 'On the IMF-Directed Disinflation Program in Turkey: A Program for Stabilization and Austerity or a Recipe for Impoverishment and Financial Chaos?', http://papers.ssrn.com/sol3/papers.cfm?abstract_id=290539 (accessed 12 April 2013).

Yentürk, N. (1999) 'Short-term Capital Inflows and Their Impact on Macroeconomic Structure: Turkey in the 1990s', *The Developing Economies*, Vol. 37, No. 1.

Yeşilyurt, N & Akdevelioğlu, A. (2009) 'Turkey's Middle East Policy under the JDP Rule', *The Turkish Yearbook of International Relations*, Vol. 40.

Yıldırım, D. (2009) 'AKP ve Neoliberal Popülizm', in İ. Uzgel and B. Duru (eds.), *AKP Kitabı Bir Dönüşümün Bilançosu* (Ankara: Phoenix Yayınevi).

Yıldız, A. (2008) 'Problematizing the Intellectual and Political Vestiges: From "Welfare" to "Justice and Development"', in Ü. Cizre (ed.), *Secular and Islamic Politics in Turkey: The Making of the Justice and Development Party* (London and New York: Routledge).

—— (2001) *Ne Mutlu Türküm Diyebilene: Türk Ulusal Kimliğinin Etno-seküler Sınırları (1919–1938)* (İstanbul: İletişim).

Yılmaz, B. (2012) 'Şartlı Nakit Transferi Kadını Güçlendirmede Nerede Duruyor? Mersin, Adana, Antep, Mardin ve Diyarbakır'dan Bir Saha Çalışmasının İlk Bulguları', Paper presented at the conference Turkey Debates its Social Policies, İstanbul, 15–16 June 2012.

Yılmaz, H. (1998) 'Kamu, Kamu Otoritesi ve Devlet: Habermas'ın Işığında Türkiye'yi Düşünmek', *Cogito*, No. 15.

Yoltar, Ç. (2009) 'When the Poor Need Health Care: Ethnography of State and Citizenship in Turkey', *Middle Eastern Studies*, Vol. 45, No. 5.

Yörük, E. (2012) 'Welfare Provision as Political Containment: The Politics of Social Assistance and the Kurdish Conflict in Turkey', *Politics & Society*, Vol. 40, No. 4.

—— (2010) 'Labor Discipline in the Informal Economy: The Semi-Formal Professional Code of Istanbul's Urban Apparel Factory', *Berkeley Journal of Sociology*, No. 53.

Yurt Ansiklopedisi Cilt 5 (Encyclopedia of Country Volume 5) (1983) (İstanbul: Anadolu Yayıncılık).

Yuval-Davis, N. (1997) *Gender and Nation* (London and New York: Sage Publications).

Yükseker, D. and Kurban, D. (2009) *Permanent Solution to Internal Displacement? An Assessment of the Van Action Plan for IDPs* (İstanbul: TESEV Publications).

Yüksel, E. (2004) *Medya Güvenlik Kurulu. 28 Şubat Sürecinde Medya, MGK ve Siyaset Bağlantısı* (Eskişehir: TC Anadolu Üniversitesi Yayınları).

Zabcı, F. (2006) 'A Poverty Alleviation Programme in Turkey: The Social Risk Mitigation Project', *South-East Europe Review for Labour and Social Affairs*, Vol. 1, No. 1.

Zedner, L. (2007) 'Pre-Crime and Post-Criminology?', *Theoretical Criminology*, Vol. 11, No. 2.

Zeybek, O. (2007) '(Re)Producing the Turk: Demography and Territory in Asia Minor, 1916–1960', http://www.uninvitedguest.net/index.php/2007/08/03/reproducing-the-turkdemography-and-territory-in-asia-minor-1916–1960/ (accessed 28 January 2013).

Index

www.ingramcontent.com/pod-product-compliance
Lightning Source LLC
Chambersburg PA
CBHW032117020426
42334CB00016B/985